Residential Broadband,
Second Edition

George Abe

CISCO SYSTEMS
CISCO PRESS®

Cisco Press
201 West 103rd Street
Indianapolis, IN 46290 USA

Residential Broadband, Second Edition

George Abe

Copyright © 2000 Cisco Press

Cisco Press logo is a trademark of Cisco Systems, Inc.

Published by:
Cisco Press
201 West 103rd Street
Indianapolis, IN 46290 USA

Printed in the United States of America   2 3 4 5 6 7 8 9 0

Library of Congress Cataloging-in-Publication Number: 99-64088

ISBN: 1-57870-177-5

Warning and Disclaimer

This book is designed to provide information about residential broadband. Every effort has been made to make this book as complete and as accurate as possible, but no warranty or fitness is implied.

The information is provided on an "as is" basis. The author, Cisco Press, and Cisco Systems, Inc., shall have neither liability nor responsibility to any person or entity with respect to any loss or damages arising from the information contained in this book or from the use of the discs or programs that may accompany it.

The opinions expressed in this book belong to the author and are not necessarily those of Cisco Systems, Inc.

Trademark Acknowledgments

All terms mentioned in this book that are known to be trademarks or service marks have been appropriately capitalized. Cisco Press or Cisco Systems, Inc. cannot attest to the accuracy of this information. Use of a term in this book should not be regarded as affecting the validity of any trademark or service mark.

Feedback Information

At Cisco Press, our goal is to create in-depth technical books of the highest quality and value. Each book is crafted with care and precision, undergoing rigorous development that involves the unique expertise of members from the professional technical community.

Readers' feedback is a natural continuation of this process. If you have any comments regarding how we could improve the quality of this book, or otherwise alter it to better suit your needs, you can contact us through e-mail at ciscopress@mcp.com. Please make sure to include the book title and ISBN in your message.

We greatly appreciate your assistance.

Publisher	J. Carter Shanklin
Executive Editor	Alicia Buckely
Cisco Systems Program Manager	Jim LeValley
Managing Editor	Patrick Kanouse
Project Editor	Jennifer Nuckles
Team Coordinator	Amy Lewis
Book Designer	Regina Rexrode
Cover Designer	Louisa Klucznik
Compositor	Argosy
Indexer	Kevin Fulcher

CISCO SYSTEMS

CISCO PRESS

Corporate Headquarters
Cisco Systems, Inc.
170 West Tasman Drive
San Jose, CA 95134-1706
USA
http://www.cisco.com
Tel: 408 526-4000
      800 553-NETS (6387)
Fax: 408 526-4100

European Headquarters
Cisco Systems Europe s.a.r.l.
Parc Evolic, Batiment L1/L2
16 Avenue du Quebec
Villebon, BP 706
91961 Courtaboeuf Cedex
France
http://www-europe.cisco.com
Tel: 33 1 69 18 61 00
Fax: 33 1 69 28 83 26

American Headquarters
Cisco Systems, Inc.
170 West Tasman Drive
San Jose, CA 95134-1706
USA
http://www.cisco.com
Tel: 408 526-7660
Fax: 408 527-0883

Asia Headquarters
Nihon Cisco Systems K.K.
Fuji Building, 9th Floor
3-2-3 Marunouchi
Chiyoda-ku, Tokyo 100
Japan
http://www.cisco.com
Tel: 81 3 5219 6250
Fax: 81 3 5219 6001

Cisco Systems has more than 200 offices in the following countries. Addresses, phone numbers, and fax numbers are listed on the Cisco Connection Online Web site at http://www.cisco.com/offices.

Argentina • Australia • Austria • Belgium • Brazil • Canada • Chile • China • Colombia • Costa Rica • Croatia • Czech Republic • Denmark • Dubai, UAE Finland • France • Germany • Greece • Hong Kong • Hungary • India • Indonesia • Ireland • Israel • Italy • Japan • Korea • Luxembourg • Malaysia • Mexico • The Netherlands • New Zealand • Norway • Peru • Philippines • Poland • Portugal • Puerto Rico • Romania • Russia • Saudi Arabia • Singapore • Slovakia • Slovenia • South Africa • Spain • Sweden • Switzerland • Taiwan • Thailand • Turkey • Ukraine • United Kingdom • United States • Venezuela

About the Author

George Abe is currently a venture partner at Palomar Ventures, investing in high technology and digital media start up companies. Previously, he spent five years as the Manager of Business Development and Consulting Engineer at Cisco Systems. His specialization was residential broadband access networks, consumer uses of the Internet, and digital media content development. He provided support for Cisco's entry into the cable modem market and was involved in consumer electronics business development. George has 17 years of experience in computer science including engineering, sales, quality testing, and marketing and is now on the Board of Directors of Switchcore AB, a publicly traded Swedish designer of semiconductor components for networking systems. With a BA and MS from UCLA, he is a member of the Board of Advisors of UCLA Anderson School of Management Venture Development Program that mentors MBA students starting high tech ventures.

In Memoriam

Jon Postel

    Protocol designer extraordinaire and friend

    Author or co-author of the following titles:

        RFCs 764 and 854, Telnet

        RFC 791, Internet Protocol (IP)

        RFC 792, Internet Control Message Protocol (ICMP)

        RFC 793, Transmission Control Protocol (TCP)

        RFC 768, User Datagram Protocol (UDP)

        RFC 821, Simple Mail Transfer Protocol (SMTP)

        RFC 937, POP Mail Protocol (POP)

        RFCs 765 and 959, File Transfer Protocol (FTP)

        . . . and hundreds of other Internet specifications

Dedication

To Rosie and Jimmy, who will be surfing a different Internet and watching a different television than their parents.

Acknowledgments

Thanks go to Mark Laubach, independent consultant; Michael Adams, of Time Warner Cable; and George Eisler, independent consultant for their comments and encouragement. Professionals all.

Finally, I must thank Cisco Systems; Palomar Ventures; my wife, Helen; and my children, Rosie and Jimmy, who patiently allowed me the self-indulgence to get this done.

Contents at a Glance

Table of Contents

Introduction

On July 11, 1997, a startup company with the catchy name of @Home went public on Wall Street. @Home was a system integrator providing data services over cable networks. Stock was offered at $10.50 per share and rose to $25 during its first day of trading. By the end of the first few weeks, its market capitalization was established at more than $2 billion. That's not bad for a two-year-old company that at the time had cumulative losses of $50 million and fewer than 10,000 customers.

Soon after, in January 1999, @Home merged with Excite, an Internet portal service, to form Excite@Home. In turn, Excite@Home is now substantially owned by AT&T, through AT&T's acquisition of TCI. Such is the current interest—perhaps frenzy—of product development, investments, and merger activity surrounding a new product area called residential broadband.

What's going on here? Who, besides the backers of @Home and Excite, are cashing in—and who is missing out? What are the issues? Residential broadband is a tremendously diverse subject, embracing high technology, government regulation in the public interest, and entertainment production values.

Residential broadband is the meeting ground for consumer electronics, the Internet, telecommunications, cable TV, satellites, politics, and Hollywood. How could there not be huge public and professional interest?

Purpose of This Book

A basic definition is needed before this book proceeds. *Residential broadband* (RBB) networks are fast networks to the home; in particular, they are fast enough to provide some video service. This generally requires speeds of at least 2 Mbps.

Networks capable of such speeds are familiar to businesses, and a lot is known about business networking. All large businesses seem to be wired today, and many smaller ones are as well. Many texts have been published on local-area networks, metropolitan-area networks, telecommunications (for example, telephony), and the like. But as a much newer phenomenon, RBB networks have not yet received equal press. This book aims to provide a comprehensive, accessible introduction to residential broadband. More specifically, this book has several goals:

- To describe new and existing entertainment and data services, and to evaluate how demand for them will drive the development of RBB
- To define basic technology requirements for implementing RBB, and to assess their state of readiness
- To overview business conditions and regulatory practices that affect rollout and viability of RBB networks

Although this book contains some technical discussions, it is not a comprehensive engineering reference. The concern here is broader and includes business and regulatory issues as well as technical ones. This also is not a business networking book. RBB networking differs from business networking in several respects:

- **RBB emphasizes entertainment**—Unlike business users, residential users require the delivery of entertainment.
- **RBB demands ease of use**—Residential users will have less access to professional support than business users.
- **RBB's scale is potentially huge in comparison to business networking**—There are many more homes than businesses (100 million households in the United States, compared to about 10 million businesses and offices). Systems catering to residences must have superior scaling properties compared to business-oriented systems.

These characteristics of RBB are actually design goals and will come up repeatedly in this book. They are the ends that must be satisfied by technological, business, and regulatory means if RBB is to thrive.

This book is a survey of the most current thinking about RBB. It is not a crystal ball. My goal is to provide a broad-based synthesis of available information—technical documents, journals, popular press, direct involvement with product development, and standards work—so that readers can make their own informed predictions about the future of RBB services. The scope of coverage here places some limits on depth, especially depth of technical detail, so another goal is to provide readers with sufficient direction and resources for further exploration of the subject.

In stating both positive and negative issues affecting RBB, it is not my intention to promote or criticize any industry. In preparing this book, I have come to know and admire representatives of many companies and organizations involved in aspects of RBB. Throughout, I have been very impressed with the effort, brainpower, and public spiritedness of these professionals in business and government, who will no doubt change the way we all receive and respond to information in our homes.

Audience

This book is aimed at anyone seeking a broad-based familiarity with the issues of residential broadband, including product developers, engineers, network designers, business people, persons in legal and regulatory positions, and industry analysts. Courses on residential broadband are beginning to be offered, and this book may also be appropriate for students in an issues-based class. Finally, I hope that consumers—the people who will be buying and using RBB services—will find the book to be an interesting peek into what the future holds for them.

Because of its breadth, some information in this book may be familiar to some readers already. But few readers are likely to be familiar with all the technical, business, and regulatory issues brought together here. The complexity and relative youth of RBB are such that anyone wishing to understand or guide its evolution should have some understanding of the full mix of influences on it.

In terms of background that readers should have in order to get the most out of the book, I've chosen to err on the side of giving plentiful background information instead of too little. Many engineering professionals in particular may find Chapter 2, "Technical Foundations of Residential Broadband," to give very familiar information that they prefer to skip or only skim. This is included for the benefit of nontechnical readers who need basic vocabulary as a foundation for the rest of the book. Throughout, chapter topics are clearly identified by section and subsection titles so that readers can opt out of reading any material with which they are already well acquainted.

Organization and Topical Coverage

Chapter 1, "Market Drivers," overviews services that are driving the market for RBB, emphasizing digital broadcast television, Internet access, and the convergence of these two.

Chapter 2, "Technical Foundations of Residential Broadband," surveys technical issues—both challenges and solutions—that are shaping the evolution of RBB. It's especially intended to help nontechnical readers get an overview of the technical issues without overwhelming them with details. This chapter presents a reference model on which specific network architectures in later chapters are based. The purpose of this is to help readers recognize both the consistent and the distinct components and challenges from network to network.

Chapters 3, "Cable TV Networks"; 4, "xDSL Access Networks"; 5, "FTTx Access Networks"; and 6, "Wireless Access Networks," present overviews of different types of access networks, those services provided by telephone companies, cable network operators, satellite operators, and newcomers.

Chapter 7, "Home Networks," focuses on the residential portion of residential broadband—the technologies and challenges associated with the home network. Topics include inside wiring and new consumer electronics devices needed to deliver services provided by Access Networks to the den, the kitchen, the entertainment center, or wherever in the home.

Chapter 8, "Evolving to RBB: Systems Issues, Approaches, and Prognoses," covers the crossroads where Access Networks meet Home Networks. Software and systems issues to be resolved in bringing these networks together are formidable.

The appendixes provide a list of equipment vendors, service providers, and industry groups, such as standards organizations, including their Web universal resource locators (URLs) and stock ticker symbols, where applicable. The URLs point to what these organizations say about themselves. The stock tickers point to what Wall Street says about them.

Timeliness

During the course of preparing this book, numerous changes were required to reflect the most recent product rollouts, Supreme Court decisions, standards decisions, and technical innovations. In this rapidly evolving field, more changes will no doubt have occurred by the time this book reaches readers. Throughout, I've tried to use appropriate language to indicate topics that were subject to change by the time of publication.

Since the publication of the first edition of *Residential Broadband* in late 1997, we have witnessed:

- The biggest phone company in the United States (AT&T) become the biggest cable operator.
- Sprint and MCI Worldcom, competitors of AT&T who needed to obtain their own broadband story, acquire wireless local loop operators.
- Broadcasters launch free, over-the-air digital TV service.
- Cable agree to data and digital video specifications called DOCSIS and OpenCable. This enabled rapid introduction of high-speed data services and established cable as the leader in broadband.
- Competitive and incumbent local exchange carriers launch their own high-speed data services over copper loops, after being given a wake-up call by cable services.
- Wireless technologies, taking note of issues of cable and copper loop technologies, prepare for launch of high-speed wireless services.
- Home networking equipment vendors specify standards and architectures to carry high-speed signals within the home over wireless and wired infrastructures.
- Media companies such as Disney investigate content development using the combination of digital TV and the Internet.
- Initial public offerings (IPOs) in the cable, xDSL, wireless services, and content development create billions of dollars of new market capital.
- Regulation rule on unforeseen matters of equal access and privacy.
- Above all, residential broadband networking become real.

But the more important solution to addressing the volatility of residential broadband has been to focus this book on important concepts that are not subject to rapid change. The interelatedness of technological, regulatory, and business issues and the potential evolution of existing networks into residential broadband networks are at the core of this book.

Finally, this edition also corrects some technical and format errors of the first edition. Perhaps we've introduced some new errors, but at least we tried to fix old ones. In that vein, I include my email address and ask that readers send comments and corrections to george.abe@ieee.org.

This chapter covers the following topics:

- Analog TV
- Digital TV
- Interactive TV
- Video on Demand
- Near Video on Demand
- World Wide Web
- Convergence of Digital TV and the Internet
- Datacasting
- Games
- Funding Models

CHAPTER 1

Market Drivers

Consumers receive a variety of services over multiple networks to the home today. They receive voice and data services over telephone networks, and they receive broadcast television services through cable TV networks and over the air. As technologies for the computer, entertainment, and communications industries converge to digital infrastructures, leaders in government and industry are contemplating the development of residential broadband (RBB) networks that will deliver these same services—and new services—to the home.

Although these RBB networks will offer great benefits to the consumer, they will be expensive to deploy. Service providers (telephone companies, broadcasters, cable operators, public utilities, municipalities, and Internet service providers) and their equipment vendors are poised to make multibillion-dollar bets that consumer demand for broadband networks and the content they deliver will be high.

What will compel the consumer to purchase the new RBB networks? Consumers won't pay for RBB services just to have access to a fast network. Existing telephone and broadcast television services by themselves don't justify the rollout of high-speed residential networks; they already work reliably, are reasonably priced, and provide a comfort level for consumers. Finally, it's difficult for people to imagine a service or an experience that they've never had exposure to before. Thus, it's a tougher to sell the consumer up to the next level.

To justify the rollout of RBB networks, new services (or *market drivers*) must be available to the consumer over the new networks. Although it is true that direct broadcast satellite (DBS) service has come down in price to meet cable pricing, for years this service was quite expensive. But consumers purchased millions of DBS units at a premium for digital television reception. Digital television offers better pictures and a wider program selection than over-the-air broadcasters or cable operators can offer over analog networks.

In addition, the Internet offers a tremendous variety of information and entertainment for the home. Digital television and the Internet, offered separately or in combination, are creating new forms of entertainment and information services to the home and are among the market drivers for RBB networking.

This chapter examines several possible market drivers for RBB, including these:

- Analog TV
- Digital TV
- Interactive TV

- Video on demand (VoD)
- Near video on demand (nVoD)
- World Wide Web
- Convergence of digital TV and the Internet
- Datacasting
- Games
- Funding models

Throughout this chapter, the goal is to define aspects of these services, which are either facilitators of or challenges to the deployment of RBB.

Analog Television

Digital broadcast television is viewed as a key market driver for RBB networking. Before considering digital television in more detail, though, it will be useful to review some important characteristics of analog television.

It's possible to argue that analog television is the most prevalent communications medium in the world. More televisions exist in the world than telephones, and the 1995 U.S. census reported that more homes had televisions than toilets.

The Three Standards

Three standards currently exist to encode and transmit analog TV worldwide: the National Television Standard Committee (NTSC), (sometimes referred to as Never Twice the Same Color), Phase Alternation Line (PAL), and Sequentiel Couleur Avec Memoire (Sequential Color with Memory, or SECAM). Table 1-1 shows some major characteristics of each standard.

Table 1-1   *Characteristics of Analog Broadcast Standards*

	NTSC	SECAM	PAL
Total lines/screen	525	625	625
Active lines/screen	480	575	575
Pixels/line	640	580	580
Bandwidth/channel	6 MHz	8 MHz	8 MHz
Picture rate/second	29.97	25	25
Megabits/second (Mbps) (uncompressed)	221.2	400.2	400.2
Countries	USA Japan Canada Rest of Europe	France French colonies Russia	Germany UK Australia

In the United States, TV channels are transmitted in increments of 6 MHz of bandwidth per channel. Channel 2 starts at 54 MHz, and Channel 6 ends at 88 MHz. (Between Channel 4 and Channel 5, 4 MHz of bandwidth is used for radio astronomy and radio navigation purposes). From 88 MHz to 108 MHz, FM radio is transmitted. Above the FM band, TV channels resume at 174 MHz with Channel 7 and continue upward in 6 MHz increments to Channel 13, ending at 216 MHz. Channels 2 through 13 are the very high frequency (VHF) stations. In addition, viewers can receive ultra high frequency (UHF) stations. UHF stations begin at 470 MHz for Channel 14 and continue upward in 6 MHz increments to Channel 69, ending at 806 MHz.

Table 1-2 shows spectrum allocation in the United States for frequencies covering broadcast television. Note that the broadcast TV frequencies are interspersed with other frequencies used mainly for governmental research, satellite communication, public safety, and amateur radio purposes.

Table 1-2 *Spectrum Allocations for Broadcast Television Frequencies*

Frequency Range (MHz)	Services
54 to 72	Channels 2, 3, and 4
72 to 76	Radioastronomy, aeronautical radionavigation, and fixed mobile
76 to 88	Channels 5 and 6
88 to 108	FM radio
108 to 174	Amateur radio, radioastronomy, aeronautical radionavigation space research (downlink), maritime, and fixed mobile
174 to 216	Channels 7 through 13
216 to 470	Amateur radio, satellite, mobile, public safety, radiolocation, and meteorology.
470 to 608	Channels 14 through 36
608 to 614	Radioastronomy
614 to 746	Channels 37 through 59
746 to 806	Channels 60 through 69
	These frequencies are little used for broadcast TV. The FCC has recommended reallocating this spectrum for public safety.

Channelization rules are different elsewhere. In Europe, channel spacing is 8 MHz rather than 6 MHz, in either PAL or SECAM. Australia uses 7 MHz PAL encoding; more bandwidth per channel means clearer audio and video quality than with NTSC. On the other hand, for a given amount of aggregate bandwidth, fewer channels are available to the viewer.

Analog Screens Versus Computer Monitors

One of the assumptions on which residential broadband relies is that content can be received on computer monitors as well as television screens. This assumption poses some difficulties because the entrenched standard, analog television, differs from computer monitors in two important aspects: display format and color coding.

Display Format

In all analog television, *interlacing* is used as the display format. Interlacing means that horizontal lines of pixels are illuminated in an alternating pattern rather than sequentially. Figure 1-1 illustrates interlacing display. The television picture tube is a rectangular array of colored pixels that must be illuminated to present a picture. The solid lines show the first illumination pass of the screen. Illumination starts in the upper-left corner and proceeds to the right side at a slight angle downward. Then a line is skipped and the following line (the third line) is illuminated, the fourth is skipped, then the fifth is illuminated, and so on until the bottom of the monitor is reached. The entire vertical scan (called a *frame*) is performed 59.94 times per second, per NTSC.

Figure 1-1   *Interlacing Display for Analog Television*

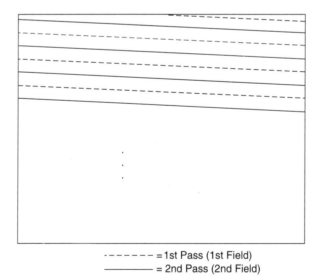

------- = 1st Pass (1st Field)
————— = 2nd Pass (2nd Field)

The process starts again at the top of the screen with the other lines being illuminated. These are shown as dotted lines in Figure 1-1. The total effect is to refresh the entire picture 29.97 times per second. The fact that lines are skipped does not affect the visual experience. The time spans and vertical spaces between the lines are too small for the human brain and eyes to notice.

In the worlds of 3D animation and motion graphics, when an object moves left to right very quickly, an effect known as *tearing* is the result. The motion happens so quickly that the movement that occurs during the time it takes to scan one field leaves a ragged edge when the two fields are viewed together.

In *progressive scanning* (or *proscan*, used in computer monitors), each line is illuminated sequentially, without skipping lines. This is a simpler approach than interlacing, and computer software (such as graphics and fonts) has been optimized for proscan. For computer monitors to display television signals, video cards need to perform *scan conversion*, which renders interlacing on progressive computer monitors.

Proponents of interlacing—namely the broadcasters and television manufacturers—maintain that it is superior to proscan for two reasons. First, interlacing is a form of bandwidth compression. Only half the image is broadcast at an instant, therefore allowing the full picture to be sent in half the bandwidth. Secondly, proponents assert that interlacing offers better, softer pictures, especially for outdoor, natural scenes. The human brain fills in the skipped lines, whereas progressive scanning tells too much and is too harsh because of its high resolution. Supporters of interlacing assert that proscan is viewed as upsetting to the psycho-visual experience over long-term viewing.

Color Coding

Computer monitors differ from TV in color coding as well. Whereas computer monitors use a red-green-blue (RGB) vector for each pixel to display color, television uses a luminance, hue, and intensity vector, called Y'UV coding for composite video and Y'CrCb coding for component video coding.

Television's system of color coding is an artifact of the transition from black-and-white to color. When television was only black-and-white, each individual pixel displayed only *luminance*, or brightness. To make color television backward-compatible with black-and-white TV, it was necessary to encode all colors using a luminance vector. That is, instead of coding colors using varying amounts of red, green, and blue, it was necessary to code colors in varying amounts of luminance and two other new vectors, called hue and intensity.

Additionally, the higher refresh rate for computer monitors is required due to higher contrast and luminance of display.

PC monitors were optimized for viewing static images (mostly printed fonts) from a distance of 2 feet. TV monitors are optimized for viewing objects in motion, thus offering lower resolution from a longer distance than PC range.

Table 1-3 summarizes the differences between televisions and computer monitors.

Table 1-3   *Color TV Versus Computer Monitors*

	Color TV Monitors	**PC Monitors**
Scanning	Interlaced	Progressive
Color coding	Luminance, hue, intensity (Y'UV)	Red, green, blue (RGB)
Pixels	640 x 480 (NTSC)	800 x 600 (SVGA)
		1024 x 768 for larger monitors
Picture resolution	Relatively low	Relatively high
Frames/second	29.97	72, for high resolution
Viewing distance	More than 7 feet	2 feet
Viewing angle	Comparatively wide	For straight-on viewing
Monitor size	Now up to 66 inches	Normally less than 25 inches
Image motion	Optimized for motion	Optimized for static images

Because of these functional differences, it is difficult to merge the two monitor types into a single form factor. Even if performed, one wonders if the cost is worthwhile.

Business Environment

Individual television stations are generally one of three types: 1. network-owned and operated, 2. affiliate, and 3. independent. The network-owned and operated stations (O&Os) are owned directly by the big national networks, specifically ABC, NBC, CBS, and Fox. Legislation exists to prevent concentration of media power in too few hands. Until the Telecommunications Act of 1996 (Telecom 96), networks could own at most 12 stations, which were permitted to reach no more than 25 percent of the national television audience. As of Telecom 96, no limits govern the number of stations, but each network's stations are permitted to reach no more than 35 percent of the U.S. population.

About 200 network affiliates exist for each national network. The national networks pay their affiliates to retransmit network programming, normally consisting of prime-time programming, national news, weekend sports, and soap operas. The compensation paid to the affiliates is a function of market size and competitive over-the-air stations. The network sells advertising during the national programs. Affiliates can obtain their own programming, schedule permitting, and make much of their independently derived money on local news.

Finally, there are the independent stations, which have no network affiliation. They purchase programming from the networks, syndicators, and independent producers, or they develop it themselves.

In total, there are more than 1500 broadcasters in the United States. A trade association called the National Association of Broadcasters (NAB) (www.nab.org) functions as the industry's lobbying arm.

Local content and advertising insertion are important services for affiliates and especially small independent stations, which do not have a guaranteed flow of network programming. Local content is also important for the national networks because consumers like to watch local events, traffic, weather, and advertising. Local content and ad insertion raises new technical problems as stations transition to digital transmission. New techniques to merge national content with local content will be required and will require new investment.

The point of this discussion is that the transition from analog to digital transmission will be costly, and the majority of stations in the United States—namely the independents and some affiliates—will face financial hardship during the transition.

Regulation

In the United States, as elsewhere, the broadcast television industry is regulated by national authorities: The U.S. Federal Communications Commission (FCC) regulates many aspects of broadcast television. Among these aspects are ownership rules of stations, media control, spectrum allocation, and technical specifications

In the past, the FCC and Congress have required backward-compatibility for TV innovations. For example, the FCC mandated that color television sets be capable of receiving and displaying black-and-white signals when color television was just becoming available in the 1950s. In the 1960s, a congressional mandate stated that TV sets must be capable of receiving UHF as well as VHF stations, over the objections of the TV industry. Requiring the combined reception of UHF and VHF was viewed as excessive government meddling, but it created new channel capacity and opportunities for programmers.

Regulations in the public interest also exist with regard to Must Carry rules imposed on cable operators (cable companies must carry local broadcast stations), foreign ownership of U.S. television stations (foreigners can't own majority shares of a broadcaster), and closed captioning (required by Telecom 96). There is every reason to believe that similar regulations will carry over to digital television.

In Canada, the Canadian Radio and Television Commission (CRTC) performs regulation. The jurisdictions of the FCC and CRTC are comparable, with the CRTC having greater oversight of the cable industry than the FCC. In the United States, municipalities have a strong regulatory role in cable, particularly with respect to franchise renewals, requirements for upgraded facilities, and the granting of bandwidth for public affairs and educational and governmental (PEG) uses.

Key Pressures on Analog TV

A convergence of interest is taking place among broadcasters, cable operators, TV manufacturers, and the government to change the existing analog television regime. Their various concerns can be summarized as follows:

- **Channel lineup and scarcity**—The Must Carry rule highlights a fundamental problem of analog TV, both over-the-air and cable. There is insufficient channel capacity for all the networks that broadcasters and cable operators want or need to get on the air.

- **Conditional Access (CA)**—Conditional access is the capability to preclude viewers from stealing programming. Cable operators experience significant pirating of signals, and analog scrambling has not been effective in stopping it.

- **Picture quality**—Picture and audio quality could stand some improvement. Screens are getting larger, and the proliferation of channels is stimulating increased production of made-for-TV film production. These should be presented more attractively.

- **Slow TV sales**—Even though roughly 110 million television sets are sold annually around the world, profit margins on TV sales are poor. There have been relatively few innovations in recent years to motivate sales; consumers tend to keep TV sets for a decade or longer. The TV industry needs a shot in the arm.

- **Spectrum auctions**—From the government's point of view, analog TV is wasteful of spectrum. The government would like to see other, more efficient uses of spectrum emerge. Then analog TV spectrum could be returned to the government and auctioned to feed the government's coffers in a relatively painless way.

- **Desire for new revenue streams**—Analog television provides little opportunity for new programming options and revenue streams, such as interactive service and e-commerce.

For more complete discussions of analog TV, see [Jack] and [Watkinson].

Digital TV

Originally, U.S. development of digital TV was motivated by a desire to reclaim the television manufacturing industry from Japan and Korea. By providing better pictures—a new video experience called high-definition television (HDTV)—U.S. manufacturers hoped to re-establish their former market leadership in television production and sales. During the 10-year process of defining HDTV, the technology metamorphosed into a method to deliver other media to the consumer. It now can deliver data service and multiple channels, where one existed before. Therefore, digital television is an obvious market driver for RBB. Digital television also resolves many of the key challenges facing analog TV.

This section focuses on the distribution of digital TV over-the-air, as defined by the FCC decision announced in December 1996 and approved by the FCC in April 1997. Other ways to distribute digital TV, such as cable, telephone networks, and direct broadcast satellite (DBS), will be discussed in Chapters 3 through 6.

The Origins of Digital TV

By the middle of the 1980s, the United States had pretty much lost the television manufacturing market to Japan. But even with their competitive edge, Japanese manufacturers recognized the need to improve standard television to generate new products and extend their market lead. One way to do this was to display better pictures, especially for large-screen television and large outdoor displays, such as those at baseball parks. Early in the 1980s, the government-operated Japanese national TV network, NHK, and their equipment suppliers embarked on a project to create high-definition television.

The Japanese system, called MUSE (multiple subnyquist sampling encoding), was an analog system that used more than 6 MHz per channel. Thus, it was incompatible with existing television and did nothing to alleviate the channel scarcity problem. Still, it had very nice pictures, to say the least.

In February 1987, the FCC formed the Advisory Committee on Advanced Television Systems (ACATS) to provide input to the commission, via a competitive process, on technology regarding advanced television. In the development process, HDTV changed from the Japanese analog model to a U.S. digital model, primarily due to pioneering work by Zenith Electronics, General Instruments, and the Massachusetts Institute of Technology.

The key facilitator to going digital was the development of digital compression techniques. Table 1-1 shows that standard NTSC TVs would need more than 220 Mbps of bandwidth to deliver pictures with existing pixel density and color. PAL and SECAM would need more than 400 Mbps. High-definition television, comparable with the MUSE system, would require more than a billion bits per second. These bit rates could not fit in a 6 MHz channel, so compression techniques were needed.

The solution was found using Moving Pictures Experts Group (MPEG) compression. MPEG compression enabled high-definition television to fit in 19.39 Mbps, a reduction in bit rate of more than 50 to 1, which could fit into a 6 MHz channel. This was a tremendous technical accomplishment, thought by many experts at the time to be undoable.

MPEG compression makes it possible to offer NTSC-quality pictures in less bandwidth than 6 MHz. Digital television with NTSC pixel resolution is known as *standard-definition television (SDTV)*. SDTV looks a little better than analog because of less ghosting and fewer vertical hold problems, yet it uses only a quarter or a third of the bandwidth of NTSC. By using less bandwidth, the broadcasters and cable operators could offer multiple channels of SDTV—or perhaps new services, such as Internet access—on the 6 MHz they would use for a single analog TV channel or a single HDTV channel. The capability of offering multiple program streams on a single 6 MHz channel is called *multicasting* or *channel multiplexing*. (This is a rather unfortunate coincidence because the IP community also uses the term *multicasting* to refer to a specific software feature described in Chapter 2, "Technical Foundations of Residential Broadband." To differentiate the two, we will use the terms *channel multiplex* and *IP multicast*.)

In November 1995, a partnership called the HDTV Grand Alliance presented its recommendation to the FCC. The members of the partnership include AT&T, General

Instruments Corporation, Massachusetts Institute of Technology, Philips Consumer Electronics, David Sarnoff Research Center, Thomson Consumer Electronics, and Zenith Electronics Corporation. The Grand Alliance recommended a modulation technique, video compression (both of which are discussed in Chapter 2), and display formats for high-definition TV. It was a digital technology that fit in 6 MHz. (Curiously, Japan steadfastly refused to go digital for advanced television until well after the Grand Alliance agreement.)

On April 3, 1997, the FCC announced rules by which the United States' over-the-air broadcast television system would transition to digital TV. This ruling ended a process that had begun more than a decade earlier with the formation of ACATS.

The Computer Industry Responds

As noted previously, television screens and computer monitors differed with respect to display format and color coding. After the Grand Alliance presented its proposal to the FCC in November 1995, the computer industry—represented by the Computer Industry Coalition on Advanced Television Service (CICATS) (comprised of Apple, Compaq, Cray, Dell, Hewlett Packard, Intel, Microsoft, Novell, Oracle, Silicon Graphics, and Tandem)—weighed in with comments. These manufacturers wanted greater accommodation for progressive display and removal of the requirement that the new digital monitors display HDTV. CICATS argued that a computer monitor (or, more specifically, the computer video circuitry dedicated to the video signal) should be capable of receiving a high-definition feed, but that its display—whether progressive or interlaced, high-definition or standard-definition—be left to the designer and manufacturer's discretion. The FCC concurred and, in December 1996, after nearly 10 years of discussion, development and trials, the FCC announced the final accord acceptable to broadcasters, consumer electronics vendors, computer manufacturers, and Hollywood.

Accounts of the entire evolution of HDTV are given in [Brinkley] and [Wiley].

The Agreement

The agreement among broadcasters, consumer electronics vendors, the computer industry, and Hollywood essentially provides that the 1995 Grand Alliance proposal be accepted, but without specifying a display format. The accepted Grand Alliance components are shown on the Advanced Television Systems Committee Web page (www.atsc.org) and are summarized here:

- **Video compression** is to be MPEG-2, with various compression options accepted. Multiple compression options permit service providers to exercise considerable control over bandwidth utilization and picture fidelity. (More on MPEG-2 in Chapter 2.)

- **Audio compression** is to be Dolby AC-3. This choice is somewhat odd; MPEG has an audio specification, but it was ignored.

- **Transport format** is MPEG-2 Transport Streams. This is the fixed packet length option of 188 bytes, which is suitable for wide-area networking in which data loss is possible.
- **Modulation scheme** is 8-VSB. Using this technique, a 6 MHz terrestrial broadcasting channel can support a bit rate of 19.39 Mbps, which is suitable for HDTV.
- **Video scanning formats** can be any of 18 accepted formats. The formats are summarized in Tables 1-4a and 1-4b.

Table 1-4a   *Progressive Video Scanning Formats for Digital TV*

Vertical Lines	Horizontal Pixels	Aspect Ratio	Frame Rate per second
1080	1920	16:9	24, 30
720	1280	16:9	24, 30, 60
480	704	16:9	24, 30, 60
480	704	4:3	24, 30, 60
480	640	4:3	24, 30, 60

The 480 by 640 display format achieves a 4:3 aspect ratio when the individual pixels are square.

Table 1-4b   *Interlaced Video Scanning Formats for Digital TV*

Vertical Lines	Horizontal Pixels	Aspect Ratio	Frame Rate per second
1080	1920	16:9	30
480	704	16:9	30
480	704	4:3	30
480	640	4:3	30

A broadcaster can transmit in any of the 18 authorized video scanning formats. The monitor receives all 18 formats but may display only a subset of them, depending on its design specifications. No monitor is required to display any particular format, including HDTV. So, for example, a digital TV can receive an HDTV feed but might display only SVGA format. In this particular example, the monitor must perform scan conversion and conversions on pixel density and aspect ratio. The digital TV is therefore a multisync monitor. A receiving monitor can be used for both television reception and computer display.

However, of the 18 formats, 3 formats are emerging as leaders. These are 720 lines of progressive, called 720p; and 1080 lines of interlaced, called 1080i, and 480 lines of progressive, called 480p. 1080i and 720p are used for HDTV, and 480p is used for SDTV.

Because many computer monitors have 1280 by 1024 displays already, they have the pixel density to display HDTV, whereas today's TV monitors cannot. Therefore, some computer advocates say that the first viewers of HDTV could use computer monitors, not television sets as the viewing device. For example, the 1280 by 720 Grand Alliance format can fit on a 1280 by 1024 computer monitor with room left over for picture-in-picture (PIP) enhancements or out-of-band text annotations.

The CICATS/Grand Alliance accord will likely benefit cable operators as well as over-the-air broadcasters. Many of the components of a digital set top box are common between over-the-air and cable. A digital set top box is a device that accepts digitally encoded television broadcasts and converts them to display on an analog TV. This process is called MPEG decoding, which is discussed in Chapter 2. The radio frequency (RF) components would be the same, thereby reducing costs. The main differences between cable and over-the-air are conditional access and modulation scheme. The exact configuration of a digital TV capable of over-the-air and cable reception is a work in process.

Figure 1-2 depicts the prototype of an HDTV broadcast studio.

At the heart of the studio is a data switch. It has the central role of moving bits around the studio. Bits are acquired over a satellite link or from local sources, such as a transcoder. Such transcoders accept NTSC perhaps from a cameraman with a live shot but who does not have a digital camera. Other sources of bits are nonlinear editors that are used to edit local content and are then spliced into the program stream. Local advertising insertion is also an important source of bits.

Bits are output to the viewer through a transmitter and VSB modulator. However, bits also can be sent through a network interface device to an external network for interactivity and management control. A need also exists for local station management to view the HDTV picture monitor and browse Web-based contact. Finally, programs need to be archived, and a two-way connection with a local disk store exists for that purpose. Part of the archival and retrieval process is the development of a query capability for speech recognition and face detection so as to automate the search process for film and video footage. This is part of the function of the resource manager as well.

The modern TV studio will be a very different setting than the current analog studio, and many old hands at TV broadcasting are going through a very steep learning curve.

The new components of digital TV systems are digital production equipment at the production end and decoders at the consumer end. At both ends there is substantial investment, perhaps millions of dollars for the broadcaster and the affiliate and a few hundred dollars at the consumer end. However, the benefits of digital are expected to outweigh the costs.

Figure 1-2   *Prototype HDTV Broadcast Studio*

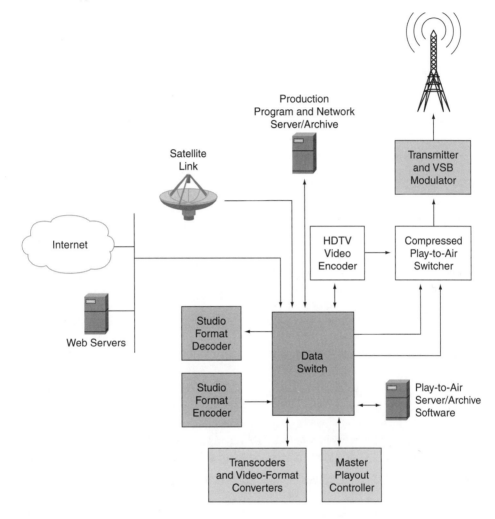

Benefits of Digital TV

Although the cost of digital conversion is not yet settled, the benefits of digital TV are clear. The next sections examine these benefits in more detail.

Increased Channel Capacity

NTSC analog TV occupies 6 MHz of bandwidth. Standard-definition digital TV channels (480 lines of progressive or 480p) can occupy as little as 1.5 MHz for equivalent viewing. A broadcaster can have three to five programs where it had one before. A cable operator or wireless cable operator with hundreds of megahertz of bandwidth can offer hundreds of programs. In addition to providing more room for programming, increased channel capacity provides for increased advertising space and revenues and new services such as Internet access.

Increased Programming Options

A corollary to increased channel capacity is new programming opportunities. For example, it will be possible to transmit multiple versions of an athletic event simultaneously. Multiple camera shots can be used by the broadcaster, and the viewer will select the particular camera angle she prefers at the moment. American football frequently uses more than a dozen cameras to televise a game. The director's job is to select a particular camera angle (blimp, huddle, wide angle, tight shot). With digital TV, it would be possible for the consumer to make the selection. This may be especially useful with picture-in-picture (PIP) televisions. Whether there will be a charge for this enhancement or whether consumers will come to expect it for free remains to be seen.

Of greater interest perhaps is Internet integration. The Internet has also proven to be popular with residential users. If the Web can be linked with digital TV on a single monitor, there are many possibilities for new forms of entertainment and information that emphasize the use of video. These new forms would increase viewership of digital television and help capture the legions of potential young viewers who are surfing the Net.

Another form of content involves the time shifting of advertising. As viewers are watching TV, they may see an advertisement they would like to keep and refer to later. In this case, they can bookmark the commercial, similarly to how they bookmark Web pages on a browser. Later, data can be transmitted from the browser to the content provider to activate the commercial and possibly add some other features, such as initiating a purchase order. The whole universe of order processing is a subject of great interest to advertisers and programmers.

Another form of digital programming is the virtual channel. A real TV channel occupies a certain amount of bandwidth and is transmitted to the consumer. A virtual TV channel can be assembled at the customer premises. A broadcaster can transmit computer commands that instruct a PC or digital set top to create pictures. One can imagine a cartoon channel that transmits the equivalent of PostScript or Java commands to the consumer. A consumer device accepts the computer commands and renders images and sounds; the actual images and sounds are not transmitted, they are rendered in the home. This form of programming is useful for channels such as the Cartoon Network. In this form, the virtual channel would occupy a fraction of the bandwidth required of a real TV channel.

Legions of creative talent in programming and advertising are experimenting with ways in which the Web and TV can be combined. An interesting place to view this convergence is at the headquarters of Creative Artists Agency (CAA), a major talent agency in Hollywood. This agency has assembled a multimedia laboratory specifically designed to show clients (writers, directors, and actors) the creative possibilities of the convergence.

Picture Quality

For most content, picture quality improves with digital compared with analog transmission, even with standard-definition digital. This is because there are fewer problems with ghosting or vertical hold. Broadcasters, both over-the-air and cable, can encode with MPEG-2 at speeds from 3 to 9 Mbps for SDTV. With this amount of control, broadcasters have a means to improve picture quality incrementally as picture and audio content dictate. Chapter 2 discusses MPEG-2 compression in greater detail.

Security

Digitally encoded programs can take advantage of computer techniques, such as Digital Encryption Standard (DES) encryption, to scramble programming, thereby preventing unauthorized persons (people who don't pay) from receiving premium service. The problem is large for both cable and over-the-air satellite services: Industry estimates put revenue loss due to piracy at more than $500 million annually. For example, a theft of service sting operation for the Mike Tyson-Bruce Seldon heavyweight championship fight in 1996 revealed an 18 percent piracy rate. Piracy rates such as this are particularly troublesome because boxing matches featuring Mike Tyson accounted for 50 percent of all pay-per-view revenues enjoyed by cable operators in 1996.

Improved TV Sales

With digital TV, consumer electronics manufacturers have the shot in the arm they need to rev up TV sales. There are 280 million analog TV sets in American households. With better pictures and new features, digital TV provides an incentive for viewers to replace their analog sets. In addition, digital TVs will be capable of connecting to personal computers, thereby expanding the TV market by competing with computer monitor vendors.

Spectrum Auctions and Local Government Use

Finally, in the United States, analog spectrum currently occupied by broadcasters is valued for its auction potential. Portions of the 402 MHz of prime real estate (the VHF and UHF frequencies) will be auctioned, with proceeds going to federal coffers. Other portions of the analog spectrum will be provided to local authorities for police and fire use. The sooner the analog frequencies are made available by the emergence of digital TV, the sooner the federal budget improves and local governments get more bandwidth. This has Congress particularly anxious to get on with the conversion to digital.

Transition to Digital Over-the-Air Television

The announcement made by the FCC on April 3, 1997, was truly historic for American television. It set a specific timetable for the transition of all TV to digital and laid out regulations for spectrum usage. This section overviews these transition issues and includes an example of how they will play out in one market.

Timetable

The major dates for the transition from analog to digital television are listed here:

- By Christmas 1998, the top 10 television markets will have digital broadcasts from the major networks. Viewers in these markets will have at least three digital channels to choose from. This deadline was met, and the broadcast industry got some brownie points from regulators who liked the good faith effort put forth by the industry.

- By 2001, all commercial networks will broadcast in digital.

- By 2002, all public broadcasting networks will broadcast in digital.

- By 2006, analog spectrum will be returned to the FCC for auction.

New digital television sets appeared on the market in late 1998. In 2006, analog TV goes blank. Consumers who have analog TVs at that time will need to buy set top converters, as they do for cable today.

Figure 1-3 summarizes key dates and events in the history of analog and digital television.

Despite the language of the Telecom Act of 1996, the date of 2006 to terminate analog transmission will certainly be flexible. More than 280 million analog sets are in place now, and 10 million digital sets a year are purchased. At that pace, less than a third of all sets will be digital-enabled by 2006. If such a small fraction of the American viewing public has a digital TV or set top converter, there will be legislative pressure to extend the date a year or two. Depending on the rate at which consumers purchase digital TVs, it could take many years beyond the appointed date before analog transmission can cease. Programming incentives are needed for viewers to buy digital to keep the process on schedule. This is why many observers feel that HDTV is necessary: It may be the best incentive to persuade consumers to get a new TV set.

Figure 1-3   *Time Lines for Analog and Digital Television*

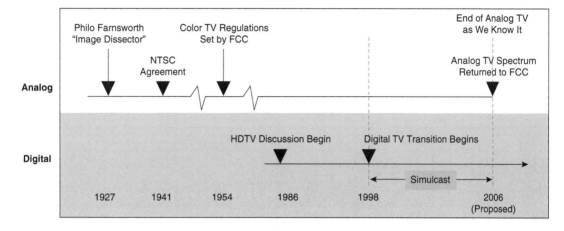

Spectrum Usage and Fees

The Telecommunications Act of 1996 stipulates that broadcasters will not pay for the digital spectrum—it will be distributed free, not auctioned. In return, broadcasters must provide free, over-the-air, advertiser-supported service. It is Congress' intent that there be free, over-the-air digital TV, and free digital spectrum is an expression of that intent.

Also, in return for free spectrum, new public service requirements will arise, such as provisions to provide free political campaign advertising on the digital channel as part of a campaign reform package. Details of this are to be determined in legislative proceedings in Congress on political campaign reform.

The broadcasters are free to use the digital spectrum in any manner they choose, which is to say SDTV that is permissible, thereby providing the broadcasters a channel multiplex capability. Some of the SDTV channels may be premium for fee channels. Because the spectrum was granted freely by the government, there should be a charge for the airwaves. The FCC has decided that the if the broadcasters charge a premium for any of their channels, then they pay 5 percent of collected revenue to the federal government, which is the same percentage paid by cable operators to municipalities for their cable franchise fee. This is a better deal for the broadcasters than going to auction.

Until the year 2006, when the analog spectrum is returned to the government, all the U.S. broadcasters will simulcast their content in analog and digital formats beginning whenever they can get digital transmission equipment installed. They will continue to broadcast in today's analog to keep consumers with analog sets viewing, and they will simulcast in digital for those with digital sets. HDTV and program multiplexes, which are market drivers for RBB, will be available only in digital form.

At Issue: Free Versus Pay TV

What content and applications will be provided over free, over-the-air, advertiser-supported service? A key question is whether new broadcast digital services such as HDTV, multichannel SDTV, Internet access, and chat siphon revenues from cable and satellite.

Thirty or more channels of free television with some support for data services may be a strong competitor to pay television. Free television may also have options for picture-in-picture and other advanced services. It remains to be seen what programming will be available and how popular it will be with consumers and advertisers.

Transition to Digital in Los Angeles

Table 1-5 shows the channel assignments for digital television in the Los Angeles area, as listed in the FCC's Order—Advanced Television Systems and Their Impact upon the Existing Television Broadcast Service, Mass Media Docket No. 87-268, released April 21, 1997 (FCC 97-115) and located at www.fcc.gov/oet/dtv.

Table 1-5   *Digital Channels for Los Angeles*

Analog Station	Digital Station	Power Area (kW) (sq km)	Population (thousands)	Coverage (%)
2	60	828. 39943	13460	81.1
4	36	680. 41063	13830	84.3
5	68	1000. 38228	13519	80.8
7	8	10. 34851	13722	95.5
9	43	342. 23622	12774	94.6
11	65	659. 32990	13278	94.1
13	66	650. 32263	13186	95.0
22	42	16516523	11629	92.1
28	59	182. 25452	12719	99.6
34	35	70. 22216	12586	99.7
58	41	55. 21665	12534	100.0

For example, KCBS Channel 2 is the CBS station in Los Angeles. It is now on Channel 2 and will be simulcast on Channel 60 for digital reception. Channel 60 will transmit at 828 kW. Because of the leap in frequency utilization from Channel 2 (54 MHz) to Channel 60 (752

MHz), Channel 60 will transmit at roughly 25 times the power of Channel 2 to achieve comparable geographic coverage. This significantly increases the station's electric bill. Even so, only 81.1 percent of existing Channel 2 viewers will expect to receive comparable reception of Channel 60.

Of course, CBS management will make certain modifications to ensure no loss of coverage (antenna shaping, retransmission from other CBS affiliates, cable, and microwave). But this example illustrates the technical and cost issues facing broadcasters when they simulcast analog and digital. Significant costs will be paid by the station without any incremental increase in audience. *The Wall Street Journal* reported (June 1998) that the Public Broadcasting Corporation (PBS) will pay an aggregate $1.7 billion for its 349 stations nationwide, for an average of $4.9 million per station. No doubt this will make pledge drives more urgent for some.

Key Challenges for Digital Television

From the perspective of broadcasters, manufacturers, and content creators, there are both challenges to overcome and benefits to reap in developing digital TV. Until the interested parties determine how to optimize their cost/benefit scenarios, the form and timing of digital TV remains unclear.

There are more than 1500 broadcasters in the United States, and the majority of these are not affiliated with the major networks. Without the financial resources of a major network behind them, many of the smaller broadcasters will be greatly challenged to deal with the financial realities of conversion.

The first investment is a new tower and transmitter. Then digital TV production equipment—such as encoders, cameras, monitors, editing equipment, transmitters, and the like—could cost up to $5 million per station. As noted earlier, the electric bill for many stations will increase substantially. The process of beginning simulcasts is likely to be quite staggered for financial reasons.

In some cases, the cost of going digital exceeds the book value of the station. In other words, some broadcasters will find it financially infeasible to go digital. Their broadcast licenses may well be sold to entities not currently associated with broadcasting, such as special interest (religious or political) groups or corporations (the real Microsoft Network).

Digital TV sets will be more costly than analog models for the foreseeable future. How to get consumers to pay a $500 or greater premium for a digital multisync TV? Either high-definition or new programming options would seem to be necessary. Furthermore, there is a lack of digitally encoded content. Much work needs to be done to get the world's film library recorded to digital form.

Much work remains to have interoperability of digital television. Decoders for DBS, cable, and over-the-air will use incompatible modulation techniques and security arrangements. It remains to be seen what this does to cost and customer satisfaction.

A final issue is antennas. Field trials performed by the staff at WGN in Chicago [McKinnon et al.] showed that indoor reception is possible, but care must be taken with regard to the placement and directionality of indoor antennas, the familiar "rabbit ears." The study concluded that new generations of antennas are needed. Companies are now selling advanced outdoor antennas for digital reception as well, and these all point to possible costs for the consumer.

On the other hand, we should point out that the studies also showed that, despite the concrete canyons of downtown Chicago, digital TV transmitted from the top of the John Hancock building (1200 feet high) provided 93 percent coverage, and areas as far as 55 miles from the transmitter reported successful DTV reception. Interestingly, the 7 percent that failed were close to the transmitter and were blocked by other tall buildings. DTV can handle multipath up to a point, but in extreme cases of multipath, DTV fails.

There is no avoiding the fact that much of the push for digital TV does not come from consumers: It comes from television manufacturers who want to market a new generation of consumer electronics, from governments who want to derive revenues from spectrum auctions, and from programmers who seek new distribution for their shows.

The process of going digital is not new. The cable industry, which has a big incentive to go digital to compete with DBS, has found the transition painful. Product development, deployment of customer units, costs to the consumer, content conversion to digital, security standards, and coexistence with analog service have all been nettlesome problems, which the broadcasters have noted as well.

Interactive TV

Interactive TV (ITV) has been a hitherto elusive dream of RBB proponents, but in 1998 things started to roll. This year exited with roughly 400,000 ITV users, with expectations for continued growth. Ever since it became clear that TV was becoming digital, it is considered a small marketing leap to offer a service in which viewers could talk back to the TV. At the heart of the marketing problem of ITV thus far has been the idea that TV would replace the PC in the home.

However, as various trials came and went, it became clear that the TV should not try to compete with the PC directly for Web surfing, email, and the like, but it should augment the broadcast TV viewing experience. Thus, ITV would address a different market than the strict PC user. The possibilities of viewers selecting, storing, and otherwise interacting with broadcast programming could present new creative opportunities and advertising outlets. ITV also allows ordering movies and interactive gaming using the TV monitor rather than a PC monitor. With this marketing realization, ITV has begun to obtain traction.

But interactivity implies two-way transmission, and TV is inherently one-way. So how is interactivity to be achieved? Currently, telephone modems are put in set-top boxes to retrieve pay per view billing information. New RBB networks create the possibility of putting faster links on the return path to create real-time interactivity with the broadcaster.

However, the notion of real-time interactivity with the broadcaster creates a basic scaling problem. How is a broadcaster to accept user commands from possibly millions of viewers, arbitrate among them, and return a specific program stream to the viewer requesting some command? Real-time ITV could possibly require interaction with live content. Furthermore, from the creative standpoint, what exactly does it mean to interact with *60 Minutes* or a situation comedy?

Another approach to interactivity is simply to give the look and feel of interactivity without actually sending commands back to the broadcaster. This involves the live selection of multiple program streams associated with a single program. Digital TV enables multiple streams per program. An example is the use of multiple cameras for sporting events and having the viewer select viewing angle. In addition to multiple camera angles, separate program streams can carry data associated with the program, such as athletic statistics. OpenTV (www.openTV.com) offers a leading example of how content can be tailored for this approach. The business model of OpenTV requires an agreement with a broadcaster to add program streams, mainly for advertising and data enhancement. Stream selection limits the viewer to the content streams offered by the broadcaster, but it offers some of the look and feel of interactivity.

Another form of interactivity would involve the viewer selecting from multiple programs on multiple networks to create her own virtual channel on a time-shifted basis. This is done by caching the content and having the viewer interact with the cache—this is what a VCR is. But instead of using tape, it is possible to cache the programs onto disk. For example, you can create your own virtual sports channel by caching sports programs from all broadcasters, not just, say, ESPN. It would be possible to store Web pages as well as program streams. In this environment, ITV means interacting with a local disk, which would also have an electronic program guide and perhaps even some customer advertising from the disk/set top supplier. Companies involved with developing set top boxes with disk drives include ReplayTV (www.replayTV.com) and TiVo (www.tivo.com).

The basic question of ITV is whether interactivity means to have a two-way communication across a network or interaction with content, which may be locally stored.

Lots of different notions of ITV are being tried, with little success to date. But lots of creative talent is being spent on the proposition that TV will be more than just a one-way experience. Time will tell.

Interactive TV Applications

Interactive TV applications come in two broad classes: those that are program-related and those that aren't. *Program-related* means that the data is associated with the viewed TV program, such as a Web page of football statistics associated with the game being showed. Normally, program-related data is composed by the content provider, then tagged and synchronized with the TV program. Nonprogram-related data is not created by the content provider of the TV program. Hence, the tagging and synchronization is unimportant.

Program-Related Applications

Program-related applications augment the one-way TV experience with Web pages and other data services. The content creator, therefore, must be adept at both TV production and Web production.

- **Navigation services** help users find desired programming among the myriad of broadcast and Web offerings, originally provided in advanced analog set-top boxes.

- **Informational services** provide streaming news or information such as stock quotes and weather updates.

- **Electronic Commerce (e-commerce)** provides home shopping and home banking.

- **Television enhancement** enhances an existing TV program with a related interactive service, such as play-along game shows, live opinion polls, and selection of sports statistics.

- **Customized commercials** are advertisements customized to viewer demographics or to the individual viewer herself. For example, a broadcaster can earmark a 30-second spot for car commercials for GM. Because pickup trucks with gun racks sell better in Nashville than New York, a different ad can be shown in those cities during the same spot, depending on demographic information or user input. Your neighbor may be watching a different commercial than you during the same spot; the advertiser can split time and get a more targeted response. TV advertising can be enhanced by the inclusion of URLs that viewers can click for further information or ordering. OpenTV and other early DTV service entrants offer such services. Similarly, movies can be ordered using Web GUIs and can be received as JavaScript.

- **Virtual channels** are TV channels which consist of low-bandwidth programs rendered at the viewer's premises rather than having the pixels transmitted from the broadcaster. TV channels are normally pictures sent from the broadcaster. For the right content, the broadcaster can send sprites or scripts with which the set-top box can render the entire program. This works for cartoon channels and some news and weather channels.

- **E-coupons and e-rebates** allow users with a printer to request coupons and rebates. The amount of the coupon can vary according to marketing factors. Alternatively, the coupon can be sent directly to the retailer upon online purchase.

Nonprogram-Related Applications

Nonprogram-related applications are data applications transmitted over television facilities which are not related to any TV show. Thus, the TV airwaves are simply a physical conduit for Web pages and other data, just as wires are. Since the bandwidth available over the air is limited, these applications are low bit rate when compared with, for example, fiber optic networks. The following are telephone or Internet applications on a PC, which a TV monitor could display.

- Web surfing using the TV monitor in lieu of the PC monitor
- E-mail

- Chat services

- Videoconferencing

- Networked games in which the user plays against other user over the network.

This list is not exhaustive: Broadcasters and ad agencies are inventing new applications. But these are some of the early proposed uses of ITV.

Video on Demand

Digital television has been discussed in a fair amount of detail because it is one of the most talked-about, most significant market drivers for residential broadband. However, several other emerging services may also prove to be important in fostering a market for RBB. One of these is *video on demand (VoD)*.

Service Description

VoD can be viewed as a special case of ITV. VoD enables consumers to order movies over a network rather than going to a video rental store. The sale and rental of video cassette copies of old and new motion pictures, called home video, is a $16.2 billion per year market in the United States, much greater than the $5.5 billion per year for domestic box office. Already, home video produces about 12 to 15 percent of the total revenue of a given Hollywood release. The scale of this market lures broadcasters and cable operators to consider VoD as a substitute for home video.

VoD service is a *pull-mode service*, which refers to the delivery method in which the subscriber demands and receives data from the provider. The consumer decides what to watch and when from a range of alternatives and then retrieves the selection. This is much like pulling information from a database.

VoD includes VCR controls, sometimes called *trick mode*, such as rewind, pause, and fast forward. Options also exist for jumping to selected scenes, choosing languages and subtitles, and captioning. It is widely believed that for VoD to be successful, features beyond simple VCR controls are necessary.

VoD's pull-mode delivery stands in contrast to *pay per view (PPV)* which operates in *push mode*. Push mode refers to the data delivery method in which the service provider transmits data to the subscriber on a fixed, predetermined schedule, or in response to some event such as the updating of data in the provider's database. The consumer simply decides whether or not to partake. Figure 1-4 depicts the conceptual differences between pull mode and push mode.

In push mode, no VCR-type controls are available. Given the service characteristics of push mode, it is especially appropriate for live, one-time events such as boxing and wrestling matches, which are the two most popular forms of PPV in the United States.

Figure 1-4 *Pull Mode Versus Push Mode*

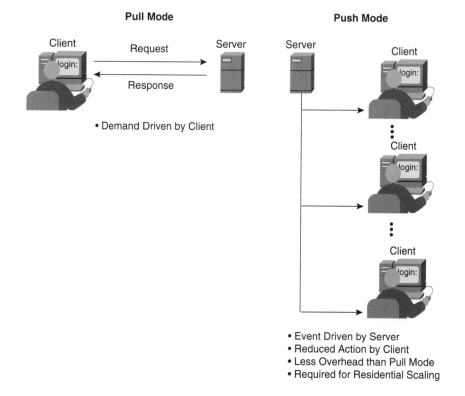

In a pull-mode environment, no two subscribers are likely to be watching the same movie or using the same trick modes at any given moment. Therefore, separate data flows are established, one for each viewer. Each data flow consumes bandwidth dedicated to a single consumer.

VoD was made feasible by the development of digital compression. Without compression, a single color movie would consume perhaps as much as 100 GB of storage and could not be transmitted, even over a T3/E3 link to the home. With MPEG, a movie can be stored in 3 GB (providing broadcast TV quality) and played out at 3 Mbps. These are still large numbers, but they are doable over proposed networks.

The measure of the success of a VoD offering is the *take rate*, which is the number of movies rented per month divided by the subscriber base. If there is a subscriber base of 1000 consumers and 2000 movies were rented in a month, the take rate is 200 percent. Take rates of 200 percent or more are necessary to make VoD financially viable.

Key Benefits of VoD

Video on demand is a convenient and highly customized way to view stored content such as movies, documentaries, and other educational fare. This gives the viewer access to larger libraries than are available at a single retailer. VoD also is convenient because it uses search mechanisms to locate what you want. Furthermore, the technology is highly customized because the viewer chooses what and when to watch instead of having the service provider decide.

Storage prices are dropping, and access is improving. The costs of the technology also are improving, whereas costs for video rental and sale are unlikely to drop further.

Finally, the content of VoD service is not speculative or risky, based on the proven success of the market for video rentals and sales.

Key Challenges to VoD

Royalty payments for content comprise roughly half the costs associated with VoD; the other half is engineering costs. Providers must have terabytes of stored data to have a marketable library, and the network must have good bandwidth reservation characteristics. The essential characteristic of pull-mode delivery is that every viewer has his own connection to the service, not one that is shared with any other viewer. Therefore, each viewer has his own network connection and bandwidth. If one person is watching a movie, the network must support, say 3 Mbps. If ten people are watching, 30 Mbps is required. Each connection is expensive because the lack of sharing creates relatively few economies of scale for the carrier.

A robust conditional access system is needed to prevent unauthorized viewers from watching programs they didn't pay for. But there has been a cottage industry for years of people breaking cable security systems. More resilient procedures are needed as the economic stakes of VoD grow.

Viewer preferences pose another challenge to VoD. Viewers like watching a rented movie more than once, or want to watch only part of a movie—these preferences cannot be accommodated economically by VoD. One partial solution is to permit the viewing of a single movie over an extended period of time. For example, a two-hour movie may be viewed over a 3-hour time period. This provides enough time for the viewer to have frequent rewinds.

Like other digital distribution methods, VoD is hampered at the moment by a lack of available content. Existing VoD libraries are not extensive enough. Hollywood has 16,000 movies in its film vaults, only a small fraction of which have been digitally encoded. Encoding pictures is a time-consuming and expensive process.

Experience from hotel movie rentals and various consumer trials indicates that, given a sufficiently large library of content to choose from, VoD can be a popular consumer service. However, it is expensive to deliver, and high costs have service providers looking for alternatives.

Near Video on Demand

An alternative to VoD is *near video on demand (nVoD)*, also known as advanced/enhanced pay-per-view or *staggercast*. Near video on demand provides widespread availability of movies without the need for a dedicated point-to-point connection between the viewer and the video server. This reduces server and network resources when compared with VoD, but at a loss of consumer flexibility. Given experience with pay per view, consumers appear to be willing to accept these limitations. With nVoD, the viewer is offered the same content continuously, whereas for DBS or PPV, the content is offered once. nVoD is an experimental service undergoing consumer research.

Service Description

With nVoD, the service provider elects to offer a particular movie beginning at certain intervals, say every 15 minutes, on a small number of channels, say four. The interval is called the stagger time, hence the term *staggercast*.

The network provider decides when to initiate the movie and on which channels. The subscriber tunes to one of the four channels. If the viewer simply watches the movie from beginning to end, this viewing experience is exactly the same as tuning to a movie on any broadcast channel.

However, if she wants the equivalent of rewind, she can switch to another channel that started 15 minutes later. If she wants only 5 minutes of rewind, she's out of luck. For fast forward, she can tune to another channel that started 15 minutes ahead of the program stream she first started watching. It's not precise rewind or fast forward, but the objective is to reduce cost by reducing the number of dedicated user connections, each of which consumes identical bandwidth. Four channels can service an entire viewing area using nVoD because each of the four channels operates in broadcast mode. This is in contrast to VoD, where four channels service exactly four viewers.

Stagger time can be reduced to 5 or 10 minutes, but this increases the number of channels allocated per movie.

Figure 1-5 depicts the operation of nVoD. In this example, *Gone with the Wind (GWTW)* is offered with 15-minute staggers over four channels.

Near video on demand fits the definition of push mode. The provider pushes the bit stream to the subscriber rather than the subscriber pulling bits from the server for exclusive use, as is the case for VoD. The royalty, compression, and set top costs are the same as those for VoD, but there are substantial server and network savings.

A typical stagger time between showings of a movie is 15 minutes. Because movies last about 2 hours in length, eight channels are needed for an even distribution of 15-minute staggers. The viewer has a limited amount of time to watch the complete movie, say, 6 hours. This permits lots of rewinds. Service providers typically offer three different nVoD movies at a time, thereby requiring 24 digital channels for the total nVoD service.

Figure 1-5   *Near Video on Demand*

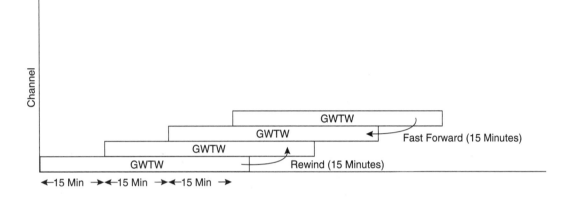

Key Benefits

Compared to VoD, nVoD offers substantial savings to the service provider by reducing server and network resources. Eight channels provide service to exactly eight viewers using VoD. But eight channels of nVoD can service a viewing population of thousands with 15-minute staggers. This is especially useful with recent releases, where there is a high probability that many viewers will be watching the same thing at roughly the same time.

Key Challenges to Near Video on Demand

Near video on demand still requires a large number of channels. In our example, 24 channels were needed to show only three movies. Cable and DBS operators will need to allocate channels to VoD or nVoD that would otherwise be used for standard broadcasting. Because many operators are strained for channel capacity, will they allocate enough broadcast channels to support an nVoD service? Or will they prefer to offer more network programming instead?

At the consumer end of the service, will consumers accept the loss of control to which they have grown accustomed with their channel-changers? Fifteen-minute staggers may not satisfy users who want finer granularity of rewind and fast-forward timing.

As with VoD, nVoD manufacturers must pay royalties and deal with a lack of digital video content.

The World Wide Web

In addition to video services, the second market driver for RBB networking is access to the World Wide Web.

According to Matrix Information and Directory Services (www.mids.org) and Network Wizards (www.nw.org), two authoritative sources of Internet statistics, the Internet consisted of 43,230,000 "advertised" connected computers (hosts) in 214 countries and territories as of January 1999. Because of the unknown numbers of multiuser computers and network or application gateways, it is not possible to correlate the number of hosts with the number of end users. However, market surveys estimate the number of active Internet users at well over 100,000,000 worldwide. (See the MIDS estimates at www.mids.org.) The current Internet annual host growth rate is 46 percent, which extrapolates to 100 million hosts by the second quarter of 2001.

Anecdotes abound, but an interesting set comes from the Olympic Games. IBM has been the official Web host for recent Olympic games. In 1996, the Olympic Web site for the Atlanta summer games registered 187 million hits. During the 1998 winter Olympic games in Japan, the Web site (www.nagano.olympic.org) registered 650 million hits over 16 days. More than 2 billion hits are expected for the 2000 summer games in Sydney, Australia.

Furthermore, electronic commerce (e-commerce) is firmly established as a viable retail alternative for mass-market consumers. Consumers are less fearful of security, which is, after all, no worse than giving your credit card to a waiter in a restaurant and having that person disappear with it for a few minutes. Also, the mere hint of a retailer selling goods and services over the Internet sends its stock price soaring. Major examples are Amazon.com (books, videos, and CDs), eBay (auctions), RightStart (infant merchandise), Ticketmaster (tickets), and dozens of others. Online services provide retailers other benefits, such as chat rooms, where people can discuss their purchases, pointers to background information, and comparison pricing. The Internet is completely revising retailing because of convenience, interactivity, and selection (and, in part, because of the exemption of online sales from sales tax).

As Web content becomes more tailored to fast networks—for example, by including more audio and video—we need to consider some practical obstacles to further scaling the Web to consumer market proportions (see Table 1-6).

Table 1-6   *Projected Internet Usage*

	U.S. Households (millions)	Computer Households	Internet Households
1997	99.9	42.0	25.1
1998	100.9	45.0	33.5
1999	102.0	48.0	40.7
2000	103.1	50.0	47.8

Source: Veronis, Suhler, and Associates

Key Issues of the Web

While millions of users browse the Internet, concerns exist as to its scalability to substantially larger audiences. Among the concerns are congested Web servers, long holding times, and high signaling rates. An approach to server congestion known as Web caching is discussed in Chapter 8, "Evolving to RBB: Systems Issues, Approaches, and Prognoses."

Holding Times

Holding time is the duration of a connection, during which resources (such as buffers), bandwidth, and control variables (such as indexes into databases) are held for the exclusive use of the client. Long holding times negatively impact the number of users that can be serviced simultaneously by the end-to-end system.

Web sessions tend to be longer in duration than voice sessions. This creates problems for telephone companies, which provide transit for data calls from modems or ISDN connections. These calls go through voice telephony switches. Call lengths have increased from about 3 minutes per voice call to more than 20 minutes per data call. Longer holding times through the voice switch increase the blocking probability per call (measured in probability of a busy signal) and eventually force the telephone company to buy additional voice switches to maintain grades of service mandated by their respective public utility commissions (PUC). Voice switches are much more expensive than data switches, so telephone companies have a strong incentive to offload the data calls from voice switches to data switches or routers.

The solution is to have a new class of access networks, such as cable TV (see Chapter 3, "Cable TV Networks") or the new generation of digital subscriber line technologies (see Chapter 4, "xDSL Access Networks"), which do not need the services of voice switches for data traffic.

Signaling Rates

Signaling refers to mechanisms by which one entity, such as a user application, communicates with another entity, such as a network, for control purposes. Examples of signaling are connection setup (such as picking up a phone to make a voice call), connection release (hanging up the phone in the voice scenario), or requests for some service characteristic, such as resource reservation.

Signaling is difficult and slow. Signaling rates, such as connection setups per second, are measured in dozens per second. For example, state-of-the-art ATM switches can do no more than a hundred or so call setups per second. These numbers compare unfavorably with a router, which has no call setup process for many applications and can move hundreds of thousands of packets per second.

Web access imposes strong signaling requirements on networking systems. Some experts predict a signaling crisis in networking systems because of the incapability of networks of all types to support signaling events calibrated in the hundreds or thousands per second, the scale required of RBB systems. Mechanisms must be found to reduce signaling rates for RBB to scale.

Convergence of Digital Television and the Internet

Computer issues may have been taken into account late in the process of the Grand Alliance's planning, but today they are omnipresent. In particular, the Internet's tremendous growth is already influencing digital TV.

From the point of view of viewer experience, current thinking on convergence of DTV and the Internet is to embed NTSC-quality or higher-quality video streams inside Web pages, much like JPEG images are part of Web pages. The controlling software for the viewer is the browser, just as it is for the Web today. The author of the Web page displays a motion picture at a specific pixel position on the screen of a certain size. A set of control protocols must be embedded in the Web page, which organizes the display of the video. Proprietary schemes exist to do this today, such as WebTV, recently purchased by Microsoft. But WebTV is a proprietary platform, and there are movements afoot to standardize the display video in Web content.

Issues of Convergence

Current digital boxes do not have the memory and programming capability to run Web browser software. The set top box in the home must be replaced in those home that have an analog descrambler. In homes in which there is no set top box (for example, homes with cable-ready televisions and homes that don't pay for premium channels), a new box must be obtained by the consumer. The commercial question arises as to whether the network operator provides the new set top box or whether the consumer buys it at retail.

Web site images transfer poorly to TV because TV is designed to display a relatively low resolution image. Conversely, computers display high resolution, so the crisp images one is accustomed to seeing on a PC monitor will seem fuzzy on a lower-resolution TV monitor.

The Internet is full of software bugs and viruses because applets are part and parcel of the Web experience. Internet service providers are not generally taken to task by the consumer if problems are caused in the home computer by a virus. But TV broadcasters and cable operators will probably not be as fortunate.

To addresses these problems, two camps are looking at the problem: ATSC (mentioned previously) and the Advanced TV Enhancement Forum (ATVEF; www.atvef.com). ATSC has three working groups:

- S13, focused on the packaging of data in the downstream path
- S16, focused on the reverse path
- S17, focused on content development and authoring tools

ATVEF is less ambitious and, some would say, more realistic. This group is focusing on content authoring and will use S13 and S16 work from ATSC for the networking.

ATSC Specifications

Before proceeding with discussions of these protocols, let's first describe system assumptions for the ATSC data broadcasting specification. The ATSC Data broadcast system diagram is shown in Figure 1-6.

Figure 1-6   *ATSC Data Broadcast System Diagram Head-End and Intermediate Diagram/Assumption*

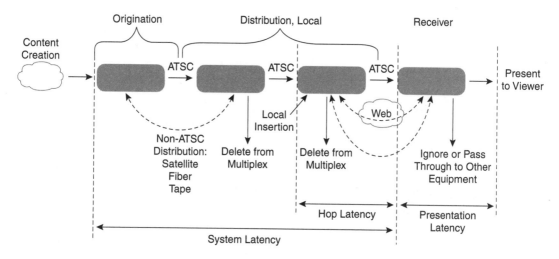

Head-end and intermediate entities need to (re)generate the channel multiplex. For example, a network may multiplex two shows and a stock ticker onto one channel, and local stations often will need to replace portions of the national feed with local material. This must be accomplished within the throughput latency and data rate limits of all components of the national broadcast passed through. End-to-end system latency is one of the key constraints of system design, especially when local content (emergency broadcasts, secondary audio such as language dubbing, and local advertising) are spliced in.

Receiver Diagram/Assumptions

Receivers are assumed to vary greatly in the number of services they are capable of presenting and their capability to store data or process it in some meaningful way. Some may decode and present several audio/video broadcasts along with multiple data services. Others may be designed to perform a single function (such as delivering a stock ticker) as inexpensively as possible. The buffering requirements in the residential gateway must accommodate both environments.

S13 Issues Addressed (Unidirectional Service)

S13 has defined four profiles for the delivery of data. These are summarized in Table 1-7. Opportunistic bit rate takes advantage of spare bandwidth left over from the variable bit rate MPEG streams, and therefore latency cannot be specified.

Table 1-7   *ATSC Datacast Service Profiles*

Profile Name	G1	G2	G3	A1
Maximum bit rate	384 Kbps	3.84 Mbps	19.39 Mbps	19.39 Mbps
Maximum latency	5 seconds	10 seconds	10 seconds	unspecified
Bit rate guarantee	yes	yes	yes	no

In addition to speed and latency, S13 defines a flow-control mechanism between the Broadcast System Provider and the Interactive System Provider, an encapsulation protocol, and a fragmentation protocol.

Synchronous and Synchronized Streaming Data

The ATSC supports synchronous and synchronized data. *Synchronous data streaming* enforces timing requirements within a single stream. Synchronous data streams are characterized by a periodic interval between consecutive packets so that both the maximum and minimum delay jitter between packets is bounded in a manner such that data is continuous. Synchronization is achieved by regenerating data and clock at the receiver. Synchronous data streams have no strong timing association with other data streams.

On the other hand, synchronized data streaming has the same intrastream timing requirements as does synchronous data streaming, with the additional requirement that the datastream be synchronized with the bits on a different stream.

Differences Between Streaming and File Transfer

Computer people tend to use the term *file transfer* when characterizing an application in which a file of information moves from one computer to another. In fact, the major protocol for doing so is called the File Transfer Protocol (FTP), first codified as RFC 765 (Jon Postel, 1980) and RFC 959 (Postel and Joyce Reynolds, 1985). This protocol goes back a ways, and the concept is well understood.

Digital media professionals use the term *streaming* when characterizing video feeds from a server or camera to a viewer. Both file transfer and streaming refer roughly to the same capability—the bulk transfer of bits from one hardware device to another—but key differences impact the networking tabulated in Table 1-8.

Table 1-8   *Comparison of File Transfers and Streams*

	File Transfers	Streams
One-way/two-way	Requires a bidirectional network; one direction is used to request the transfer.	Can be used over a unidirectional network. Streams can emanate from the source without client request.
Completeness	The receiver cannot jump into the middle of a file transfer and have anything useful. To use the file, the receiver must wait until the last bit is received and then use the data from the stored medium.	The receiver can jump into the middle of the stream. The receiver will miss the earlier content, but the remaining bits will make sense.
Real-time	Not required. A receiver can request a file now and begin receiving it later, and view or use the file at a later time.	Always in real-time. The stream is flowing now, and the receiver must receive it now. If not, the stream must be stored for later viewing, in which it looks much like file transfer.
Jitter tolerance	Relatively high. File transfer can experience variable delay because the file is stored before use.	Relatively low. Timing jitter will make the picture or audio quality degrade. If jitter is high, the stream must be stored for later viewing.
Synchronization	File transfers are autonomous entities, normally unrelated to other file transfers.	Often required. This means that a given stream must be synchronized with another, as in the case of a video stream synchronized with a corresponding audio stream (lip sync).

S16 Issues Addressed (Interactive Mode)

The problems for defining an effective standard for interactive service protocol can be highlighted by key questions as posed by S16's charter:

- How can broadcast receivers discover interactive services?
- For the forward channel, how will interactive services identify items of information, and how will information be organized?
- Given the likely range of lower-functioning receivers/set tops in the early years, what interactive services protocol is needed near term that can scale as higher-functioning receivers become available?
- For the return channel, what signaling protocols and what return path media will be used?
- How will hyperlinking work across multiple streams? What is the URL for a video stream? What is the URL for a TV program or a composite piece (for example, the video stream or the secondary audio stream) of the program?

Figure 1-7 *ATSC S16 Schematic*

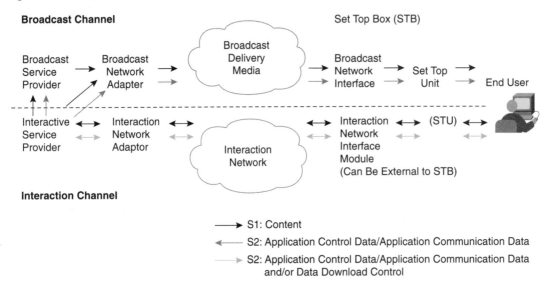

→ S1: Content

← S2: Application Control Data/Application Communication Data

⇢ S2: Application Control Data/Application Communication Data and/or Data Download Control

S17 Issues to Be Addressed (Authoring)

The controversial work of ATSC is done in S17, which addresses some of the previous issues, such as characterizing URLs for video streams. Authoring and software development environment is the locus of disagreement with ATVEF. The basic question is how to create TV images using Web tools. Can the author of DTV content use variations of HTML and expect the set top to render TV images in Java, JavaScript, Shockwave, Realmedia, and other plug-ins?

Two major approaches exist supported by two strong groups: the ATSC Digital Television Applications Software Environment (DASE; www.toocan.philabs.research.philips.com) and the Advanced TV Enhancement Forum (ATVEF; www.atvef.com). ATVEF is supported by Microsoft, Intel, and several content developers, such as Time Warner.

DASE

DASE is the S17 subcommittee of ATSC and was the first U.S. standards organization to look at DTV authoring.

The requirements addressed are listed here:

- Support for synchronous and synchronized streaming and file transfer.
- Identification of new typed objects for TV controls and video streams.
- Support for either triggered or self-timed objects. That is, without the intervention of the viewer, the source should send objects based on some event, such as a timer.

- Receiver that knows when to start decoding and when to present data.
- Content that can be prepackaged or locally inserted, or a combination.
- Concepts that can be reused over IP transport (authored content that can be reused on Web pages).
- End-to-end transfer of bits that exhibits deterministic behavior.
- Pixel accurate placement of objects on interlaced and proscan monitors.
- Images that provide the identical look as TV; this means alpha blending, or the capability to view dissolves and fades and exhibit translucency.
- Tight control of the stream by the sender. This means that when a stream containing links is initiated, the viewer is constrained as to the hyperlinks she can use. This is very different from the Internet. Advertisers and broadcasters want viewer control. Certainly, the viewer can tune to another channel, but when a viewer is on a channel, her latitude is restricted to the URL options made available by the broadcaster/service provider.

To fulfill these requirements, the DASE group specified an execution environment in the set top box. It assumes a Java Virtual Machine (JVM) exists in the set top and that the programmer will transmit Java commands for the set top to execute. This approach also enhances the Hypertext Markup Language (HTML), now used to author Web pages, to create a new markup language called Broadband HTML (BHTML) with specific hooks for TV. The features of would be these:

- Is based on HTML 4.0, but compatible with HTML 3.2
- Leverages use of Extended Markup Language (XML)
- Offers lots of new semantics for video
- Has tight integration with Java and operates as a plug-in
- Integrates with VRML and MPEG-4
- Uses a small footprint, less than 100 KB
- Renders pixel-accurate placement of images on interlaced and progressive scanned monitors
- Offers end-to-end timing controls

A BHTML author should be able to connect hyperlinks to TV functions such as channel selection (as well as connecting hyperlinks, such as crossover links, to browser functions). These and other TV functions are suggested. Accordingly, the HTML player runs on a set top TV or digital TV, not a PC.

The problem with the DASE approach is that it does not leverage the existing base of HTML documents and authoring tools. There will be a major retooling of the Web development environment to use BHTML.

ATVEF

The criticism of DASE is that it is overambitious and does not adequately leverage the current Web-authoring environment. In particular, Intel and Microsoft, along with content companies, worry that the DASE process has gone to far in specifying content authoring. Rather than having an execution environment in the set top box, they prefer to have only a presentation environment, namely HTML. They believe that all that is needed for standardization is a set of application program interfaces for standard tools. Therefore, a rival organization was established to use more off-the-shelf components rather than enhancing HTML.

ATVEF's proposal uses JavaScript, Cascade Style Sheet, and HTML in lieu of BHTML. Certain improvements for video will be accomplished with enhancements to HTML, called Dynamic HTML (DHTML), which is viewed as less disruptive than BHTML.

DASE proponents counter that ATVEF is deficient in a number of respects:

- ATVEF fails to offer pixel-accurate positioning on the monitor.

- ATVEF cannot validate content. Broken HTML links cannot be determined a priori.

- Worse yet, broadcasters purportedly require that viewers do not have carte blanche surfing capability. This is for two reasons: to prevent kids from watching pornography, and to make sure that viewers are watching Web pages linked to the TV broadcast. Viewer control is key.

- ATVEF does not provide for tight timing synchronization among video and text due to the absence of end-to-end timing markers, which can be decoded in the set top box.

The reason for the discussion of authoring and rendering in the DTV world is to provide an understanding of what will be perhaps the key software struggle of RBB. That is, what will the software environment be for the digital set top and the residential networking gateway? Microsoft has clearly won the desktop. The set top represents the next battle. It's Microsoft versus Japan versus U.S. cable set top manufacturers versus embedded systems in the struggle for consumer applications over TV. It makes for good theater, and to the winners will go tremendous market value.

Datacasting

A new market driver that combines aspects of digital TV and World Wide Web is gaining the attention of both the broadcasting and the Internet industries. The service, called *datacasting*, is the broadcast delivery of data over broadcast TV media, such as over-the-air terrestrial broadcast or cable TV.

Datacasting provides a means to reduce signaling problems evidenced by the Web. For many applications, going to push-mode form of delivery provides an opportunity for scaling to RBB proportions and providing important new revenue sources for the Web.

Datacasting is a bandwidth reduction and signaling reduction technique, which permits greater scaling of the servers and networks, which provide content. The tradeoff in both cases (push-mode data and nVoD) is reduced user control and flexibility. For many applications, such as stock quotes and news and software updates, the tradeoff for push mode makes sense.

The basic idea is that data content providers will distribute data over broadcast media (over the air, cable, and satellite) within DTV channels. This is an opportunity for a new type of ISP. Whereas most Internet folks view video being transported inside IP packets on the Internet, broadcasters have a different idea. They believe that IP packets can be transported like TV program signals. The user's digital set top merely tunes to the data channel, decodes the data, and diverts it to a data port on the set top. A set top box would have both an Ethernet and an ATM port for data and TV interface, such as an RGB cable.

Data distribution over TV is not new. For more than 20 years, text information has been transmitted over analog TV spectrum using spare analog bandwidth in each TV channel, called the *vertical blanking interval (VBI)*. The VBI was originally required as a guard band for receivers to solve vertical hold problems. As TV receivers got better, it became possible to use this bandwidth (up to 96 Kbps) for other purposes. In fact, in older or cheaper TV receivers, the VBI is still necessary for video, so data reception over the VBI may be impaired for these older TV sets.

Some companies such as Wavephore (Nasdaq:wavo) have attempted to make a business of data distribution over the VBI, but with little success so far. One would expect that this is mainly due to the limited amount of bandwidth available in VBI.

With the advent of DTV—specifically, channel multiplexing—much more bandwidth is available than what was formerly available over VBI. DTV offers 19.39 Mbps per 6 MHz channel, ostensibly to support full HDTV. However, it is technically possible to transmit NTSC-quality pictures and sound in 3 Mbps or even lower, depending on the screen size, the distance the viewer is from the screen, and the nature of the picture.

If the original picture can be transmitted in 3 Mbps, what is to become of the other 16.3 Mbps? Media conglomerates can transmit multiple TV programs. For example, Disney owns (completely or a majority of) ABC, ESPN, and the Disney Channel. It would be possible for Disney to simulcast all three channels in digital form in the 19.39 Mbps. Similarly Rupert Murdoch owns Fox, FX, Fox Sports, and Fox News; NBC can do the same with CNBC and MSNBC.

But this won't happen because the broadcasters collect fees from cable and satellite operators for the extra channels. Disney, for example, collects $1 per sub per month just for ESPN. This is more than $700 million a year, just for rights fees.

So ESPN will stay on cable/satellite. Channel multiplex exposes the lack of content at the broadcaster disposal. Distribution of popular Web pages or the contracted distribution of software updates, such as Windows 20xx, represents a way to use that extra bandwidth. Because there are more than 1500 broadcast affiliates in the United States, each with a potential of 16 Mbps of data capacity, several gigabits are available to the nation's broadcasters, representing significant new revenue streams. FCC Chairman William Kennard put it succinctly when he said that DTV is the broadcasters' access network to the home.

Of course, there are technical, marketing, and regulatory impediments to be discussed in due course. One interesting problem is how to preserve VBI text when a program converts to digital transmission without reauthoring the text. But the FCC removed an important regulatory hurdle when it ruled that broadcasters need only pay a minimal charge for money received for such services. That ruling relieved the broadcasters of the concern that if they charged a subscription fee for use of their free over-the-air spectrum, they would need to go to auction. The potential of the Internet (and the lack of programming to fill all those channel multiplexes) gives rise to the interest in pushing data over the airwaves.

Applications for Datacasting

Datacasting is particularly well suited for applications which require the distribution of common data to multiple users without the need for interactivity. These applications, therefore, differ from Internet applications in that Internet applications are typically interactive and point to point, whereas datacasting applications are not interactive and point to multipoint. Also, datacasting does not use the Internet for transport. There is the possibility that widespread success of datacasting could siphon substantial amounts of traffic off of the Internet. That, of course, would depend on the attractiveness of datacasting applications. Some of these are covered in the following sections.

Virtual Channels

TV channels are normally pictures sent from the broadcaster. For suitable content, the broadcaster can send sprites or scripts with which the set top box can render the entire program. This works for cartoon channels and some news and weather channels.

Software Distribution

One potential application of datacasting is software updates. Many popular software programs are retrieved from Web servers by millions of users. For example, to extract the latest version of Netscape browsers, the user goes to www.netscape.com and asks for the download. The user is then presented with a list of servers, from which he selects the source of the update. Because of the popularity of Netscape browsers, the company needs to have multiple servers distributed worldwide, and the user picks one that presumably is closest in proximity. The user chooses a site, hoping it is not too busy at that time. (This is a kind of user-initiated load balancing). Having done so, a connection is set up to that server, and the download is sent.

This process imposes a number of problems. First, hundreds of requesters may be converging on a single server at once. When you pick your server, you do not know the usage on that site. Perhaps a geographically more distant site has less congestion and can therefore offer better service.

More importantly, to retrieve your update, a connection is established with the server, and a dedicated bit stream is created between you and the server. If your colleague in the same building is retrieving the same update at the same time from the same server, you two will be duplicating use of server and network resources unnecessarily.

Eutelsat (Paris, France) is undergoing a trial of data distribution services over satellite. Other software can be downloaded, such as updates to set top boxes. Other home networking devices, such as residential gateways, can similarly be updated. Among the applications would be encryption key distribution fault management of the set top box and computers and software updates.

Datacasting bypasses the wired, terrestrial Internet and is a cheaper way to distribute software than pressing and mailing CDs.

Web Caching at Home

Users could have mass data storage at home that can be updated overnight. They can interact with a local data cache rather than going to the public Web.

Real-Time Data Services

Stock quotes, emergency broadcasts, and weather updates are well-known forms of live information update that can be distributed economically by datacasting.

This list is not exhaustive. Some broadcasters envision customized viewer profiles, which allow for a form of customized broadcast. But these give an idea of some of the potential of datacasting.

Problems Posed by Datacasting

Datacasting can be unidirectional or bidirectional (using a separate, non-broadcast return path, such as the Internet). In the downstream path, the bit rate can be constant or variable (opportunistic, in the parlance of the DTV world). In all these cases, content authoring problems also arise, due to the noninteractive nature of datacasting.

In the case of unidirectional transmission, there are the usual questions of framing, flow control, and error detection. The new question arises as to what hyperlinking means in a broadcast or channel multiplex setting. Even in the case of a slow return path, potentially hundreds of thousands of viewers may communicate with the broadcaster at any instant—what new approaches are required for congestion management and access control? And, in either case, there is a whole new class of HTML authoring required. From WebTV, it is apparent that just putting Web pages on a TV monitor doesn't cut it. Viewers want something that looks like TV on their TV. That means pixel-accurate placement, transparency, translucency, wipes, fades, and dissolves.

Another issue for datacasting is that HDTV may be the killer application its supporters hope it is. If that happens, the entire 19.39 Mbps would be used for HDTV. Datacasting would be pushed back until such time as HDTV could be transmitted on less than 19.39 Mbps so that some bandwidth can be freed up.

Games

For those who have children, the popularity of video games is unmistakable. Sony, Sega, and Nintendo are among the chief beneficiaries of holiday season gift-giving. With enhanced computing capability, games are being devised in which the computerized opponent learns the behavior of the player and changes its actions accordingly. The seriousness of games is reflected in the cost to produce them. Production costs regularly exceed $10 million, with some costing as much as $30 million, as reported for the forthcoming game Shenmue from Sega. The desire for ever-faster twitch games with more realistic visual images and sound are propelling a new generation of microprocessors. Among the more important of these are the Sega Dreamcast and the Sony PlayStation II.

Sega Dreamcast uses a 128-bit processor, called the Hitachi SH-4, which has already been introduced in Japan in the fourth quarter of 1998 and will be introduced in the United States in the fourth quarter of 1999. Not to be outdone, Sony and Toshiba announced a new generation of PlayStation processors, called PlayStation II, in February 1999. Shipments are planned for the fourth quarter of 2000. This is also a 128-bit processor, but with more memory than Dreamcast (32 MB), an embedded graphics chip, an embedded sound synthesizer, and a digital video disk (DVD). Sony's assertion is that the chip is capable of three times the number of floating-point operations than a Pentium III 500 MHz processor. Games will be sold in stores on a DVD because the current CD-ROM does not have enough storage. The console also has a high-speed serial interface called Firewire, a software MPEG-2 decoder, or software MPEG-4 decoder. MPEG-2 and MPEG-4 are discussed in Chapter 2 and Firewire is discussed in Chapter 7, "Home Networks".

With computing power such as this, the game console could add 3D graphics and interactive services and could become the centerpiece of the home entertainment server, offering some competition to the current Pentium-based platforms now found in the home.

Parallel with increased computing power, the next step for games is to become interactive so human players can play against each other instead of 2D robots. Slow networks can easily perform slow-motion games such as board games, like chess. But what adolescent wants that? For twitch games, in which reaction time is measured in split seconds, fast networks with reliable latency are required. Given the history of the success of chat rooms on the Internet, interactive games would appear to be a natural. In that vein, a number of games have online options. An additional feature of some games is the capability to chat with your adversary or partner, as the case may be, while the game is in process. So you can talk to your opponent just before shooting him.

A major issue with games is the revenue model. It's easy to see how Sega or Nintendo make money; it is less obvious to see how the service provider makes money. Interactive twitch games require a very fast, very predictable network. As we explore later in this book, these networks face a number of issues and thus are expensive. How will the service provider recoup costs?

Will there be a subscription charge for games, such as a premium TV channel? How can the service provider display advertising on the monitor? (There's no way my son will be looking at advertising just as he draws a bead on his opponent!) The revenue model probably will be transactional. Kids join a group, each pays an admission fee, and off they go into the game and do their thing. After the game, scores are tallied. Then a new group repeats the process. Can Mom and Dad monitor costs?

Despite these problems, the rollout of RBB networks is driven in part by the belief that interactive games leverage the interest in chat rooms and existing video games, and thus are a market driver for RBB networks.

A Word on Telephony

This book does not dwell on telephony because it is not viewed as a broadband service. The entire voice traffic in the peak hour in the United States can be accommodated on a single fiber bundle.

But the importance of voice lies in the degree to which RBB service providers will want to address the voice market to justify the cost of RBB rollout.

Voice in the United States is a $190 billion service business and nearly a $660 billion service business worldwide. These numbers dwarf all broadband communications revenues. So cable operators and wireless operators may want apiece of that revenue, and telephony companies will certainly want to protect that revenue.

Some network operators will want to offer full-service networking, which would include Internet service, broadcast video, and telephony. The justification for doing so may lie just in the voice.

Funding Models

Where will the money come from for residential broadband networking deployment? Billions of dollars will be required in central sites for the production and distribution of content, for networking infrastructure, and for consumer electronics devices.

Four classes of funding can be considered:

- Work-at-home subsidies
- Subscription
- Transaction
- Advertising

Work-at-Home Subsidies

Businesses (or the government, through tax deductions) often pay for some high-tech consumer products for business use. This was true of personal computers, fax machines, pagers, and ISDN, which were originally paid for by companies for use by their employees at home. In turn, the companies wrote these purchases off as business expenses, so the tax-payers ultimately picked up part of the tab. Using this method, high-tech devices in the home in effect are not paid for by the early adopter of the technology.

This funding model benefits product development by transferring the cost away from the consumer. Stimulated by work-at-home subsidies, a market may become large enough to drive manufacturing and sales volume to the point at which prices are reduced for purely consumer applications. The questions for residential broadband are whether it will be subsidized in this way initially, and whether its work-at-home applications eventually will be extensive enough to trigger reduced costs to consumers.

For example, while some hobbyist interest in the personal computer arose in the early 1980s, the personal computer market was largely a business phenomenon during its early years, spurred on largely by the development of word processors and spreadsheets. (Remember Wordstar and Visicalc?) The scale of the business market for PCs became large enough to reduce costs for major PC components so that PCs came into reach of work-at-home. Separately, Apple Computers realized that home computing was financially out of reach for a mass market and chose to address the educational market. By servicing markets as large as business and education, economies of scale could be achieved so that component costs were reduced. Vendors reduced prices even more to expand markets even further by trimming features from commercial offerings and adjusting their distribution and support services.

The analogous situation for RBB is that the work-at-home employee will use RBB services for business purposes and will have the company defray the expenses. After hours, the employee will use the same services for personal use.

Subscription Revenues

Subscription revenue refers to the periodic service charges paid by consumers in exchange for an ongoing service. Subscriptions for most consumer services, such as newspapers, magazines, cable TV service, and basic telephone, are in the relatively tight range of $10 to $30 per month. Consumers have a limited tolerance for regular charges, and marketers target the pricing for this range. Basic RBB services will fall into a similar range.

Transaction Fees from Electronic Commerce

In most media today, subscription revenues alone do not generate a profit. Whether it is newspapers, magazines, Internet access, or monthly cable charges, subscription revenues must be augmented with transaction or advertising revenue to make the business profitable. The same is likely to be true for RBB.

Transaction fees are charges paid per specific event or transaction, such as payments for VoD or PPV screening, fees paid to receive information off the Web, or surcharges paid for home shopping.

It is not an exaggeration to say that the Internet has completely changed retailing. Amazon, eBay, Autobytel, and dozens of others have made purchasing consumer goods and services on the Internet an easy and time-saving experience and have fueled enormous stock market gains. Electronic commerce (e-commerce) is generating the kind of capital that underwrites continued investment in the Internet.

Advertising

Along with e-commerce, advertising will be the second major funding source for the Internet. Television advertising is a $34 billion business in the United States alone. Total U.S. advertising (newspapers, magazines, and broadcast) was $173 billion in 1996 and is increasing at 5 percent per year, which exceeds the growth rate of the population and GNP. Even newspapers, thought by many to be outmoded in this electronic age, collect upwards of $37 billion in the United States for print advertising and classified ads.

When dividing TV advertising by households, U.S. advertisers spend about $340 per household per year to get their collective messages out. (The rest of the world is about $157 per year). This exceeds what most projections are for annual Internet subscription fees or annual basic cable TV fees. Advertising pays, especially for consumer markets, and it will continue to pay.

Web advertising can be sold in ways very similar to print and television advertising. For example, a Web site can charge based on the size of an ad (full page, quarter page, and so on) for a specific period of time (a week, a month), with rates varying by the expected number of visitors to that site. The ad buyer has no guarantee, of course, that anyone will read the ad, much less buy because they read it. So the ad buyer is accepting the risk, and the Web site is accepting the money.

The Internet permits a variety of advertising models beyond those available to print publishing or broadcast TV. Advertising rates are set by Nielsen and other agencies that make a business of counting how many times a Web site is visited. It is therefore very important for the advertiser to get an accurate count of how many times a site is seen. This poses problems when Web caches are used to display information. Web caches are discussed in Chapter 8.

Advertising has the potential to produce the greatest amount of funding in the shortest period of time. Entertainment is a key RBB market driver not only because it commands a significant audience, but also because it provides the venue for delivering advertising. Even with ratings of the national broadcasters sagging (down to 64 percent for the four major networks in spring 1997 sweeps from more than 75 percent in 1990), their ad rates continue to hold firm because they remain the only means to reach a mass audience quickly in an increasingly fragmented advertising market.

The acquisition by Yahoo! of Broadcast.com for $5.7 billion attests to the power of advertising and market share on the Internet.

Case Study

Most industry observers have long believed that residential broadband is largely a high-income, urban phenomenon. There is relatively little buildout of cable, xDSL, or even wireless local loop solutions for the inner cities or rural towns. This paucity has created discussions of the nature of universal service and whether it applies to broadband services as well as traditional voice services.

But despite the problems of rolling out service to rural America, there are exceptions. An interesting case in point is in Glasgow, Kentucky, population 14,000, located on the Kentucky-Tennessee border in the foothills of the Appalachian Mountains. The case of Glasgow offers lessons and presents an important policy question.

In 1985, the municipal power company, the Glasgow Electric Plant Board, decided to go into the cable TV business to give a little competition to the incumbent cable operator who was not enjoying high customer satisfaction at that time. Glasgow Electric decided to do this by overbuilding—that is, laying their own cable in parallel with the existing cable infrastructure. Their intent was to offer standard analog cable TV.

Despite litigation, predatory pricing, and continued competition from the incumbent, Glasgow Electric was capable of rolling out a municipally owned service and, to this day, maintains more than 60 percent of market share for cable TV. This despite the fact that their prices are higher than the incumbent's and that the staff still works on electricity distribution.

After the rollout of cable TV service, there was another opportunity in the early 1990s to expand service. Glasgow discovered the Internet, and before almost every other city in the United States, Glasgow Electric offered high-speed data service over its cable system. As of this writing, 15 percent of Glasgow Electric's cable subscribers purchase high-speed data service, probably the highest take rate of any system in the country.

Three lessons are learned: First, RBB is not necessarily a high-income urban phenomenon.

Second, a full set of services (electric utility, entertainment video, and Internet access) with lots of customer interaction can overcome a pricing disadvantage, even in small towns. Telephone companies and cable operators shudder at the thought of rolling a truck to the customer site; truck rolls can cost more than $50 each. But Glasgow views truck rolls as opportunities to provide high-touch customer contact, which people like and will pay for.

Finally, Glasgow emphasizes the importance of local content. Mass media content requires some element of local news, weather, and gossip. Popular shows in Glasgow are Little League games and, interestingly, small claims court—even showing tapes of small claims court works. Personalized content is why chat rooms work and why telephone service works.

The policy question raised by Glasgow is that systems like theirs are threatened by statutes enacted by states (Texas being the most prominent among them) that expressly forbid municipalities and related entities from offering telecommunications services. Excess government is the reasoning, but one would suspect a dose of big company lobbying as well.

However, users in small towns normally don't attract big company or even little company interest in providing advanced services. Those citizens may have no recourse but to do it themselves through their local municipal authorities. The matter has gone to court, and so far the states have been upheld and the FCC has elected not to intervene on the behalf of municipalities, on the theory that a dispute between a state and its municipalities is strictly a state matter.

Visit Glasgow at www.glasgow-ky.com.

Summary

Consumers worldwide have high utilization of telephone and television services over existing telephone, over-the-air, and cable networks. For the most part, the services are of acceptable quality with a reasonable price.

To justify the multibillion-dollar rollout of residential broadband services to the home, new services will be required to stimulate consumers or advertisers to underwrite the costs. Table 1-9 summarizes the market drivers that are fulfilling or may fulfill this role.

Residential broadband is interesting work, which is not the least of the reasons why it is evolving and attracting top-flight talent in entertainment and engineering. The next chapter overviews the engineering challenges and technical foundations of RBB, in various stages of solution. The remainder of this book frames the discussion on service evolution and delivery, exploring what pieces of the RBB network puzzle exist and what pieces are missing so that readers can evaluate who the winners and losers will be.

Table 1-9 *Summary of Market Drivers for RBB*

Service	Characteristics	Key Challenges and Disincentives	Key Benefits and Incentives
Digital TV	Offers highest-quality video using HDTV Uses multichannel SDTV free over the air	Involves cost of infrastructure overhaul from analog to digital; costs include cameras, towers, transmitters, and consumer electronics equipment Requires no incremental revenues to broadcasters	Offers more channels Delivers better picture Liberates prime analog TV spectrum for other uses and provides auction revenue for the federal government
Interactive TV	Provides real-time selection of video streams or interaction with video cache Uses point-to-point technology	Offers content development Has a poor track record to date Requires return path	Opens a new venue for advertising Opens a new creative outlet
Video on Demand	Offers real-time selection of streaming content Supports trick modes Uses point-to-point technology	Involves cost of royalties, networking, and storage Has high bandwidth requirements Offers content availability Provides channel availability from cable and DBS	Has a potential scale of market that is the same as home video (sales and rentals) Affords high consumer control Builds on consumer interest in videocassette rentals
Near Video on Demand	Is an enhancement to impulse PPV Uses point-to-multipoint technology	Relies on questionable consumer interest, so no tricks modes are available Provides channel availability from cable and DBS	Saves resources compared with VoD Builds on consumer interest in PPV
Web	Uses point-to-point technology, unless IP multicast is supported by Internet service providers	Provides scaling issues for the Internet Competes with broadcast TV for entertainment	Builds on consumer interest in the Web Facilitates transactional revenues and online shopping

Table 1-9   *Summary of Market Drivers for RBB (Continued)*

Service	Characteristics	Key Challenges and Disincentives	Key Benefits and Incentives
Convergence of DTV and the Internet	Augments Web pages with NTSC- or higher-quality video Uses both point-to-multipoint and point-to-point technology	Has not settled standardization of authoring environment Requires new set top boxes in the home (Who pays?) Exposes TV monitors and set top boxes to computer bugs and viruses	Opens a new venue for advertising Offers a new outlet for the creative process Would enable standard Web functions such as e-mail or Web surfing on the TV in a standardized manner
Datacasting	Is a specific case of converged DTV and Internet Uses point-to-multipoint technology	Relies on questionable consumer interest due to embryonic content development and applications Has bandwidth availability that may be preempted by HDTV	Offers an alternative to the Web for data distribution Builds on broadcaster interest in software and data distribution
Games	Offers real-time competitive interaction with other humans on the Internet Uses multipoint-to-multipoint technology	Has no clear revenue model Requires very high performance networks and customer premises equipment	Represents a new generation of games coming to market Has a proven consumer market

References

Books

Brinkley, Joel. *Defining Vision: The Battle for the Future of Television.* Orlando, FL: Harcourt Brace, 1997.

Jack, Keith. *Video Demystified: A Handbook for the Digital Engineer.* Eagle Rock, VA: LLH Technology Publishing, 1993.

Poynton, Charles. *A Technical Introduction to Digital Video,* Second Edition. New York: John Wiley, 1996.

Vogel, Harold. *Entertainment Industry Economics.* New York: Cambridge University Press, 1995

Watkinson, John. *Television Fundamentals.* Oxford, UK: Elsevier Press, 1996.

Articles

Comerford, Richard. "Consumer Electronics." *IEEE Spectrum*: January 1997.

"Digital TV: Cost Risk for Pure Play Broadcasters." *The Wall Street Journal*: 2 January 1997.

ETSI ETS 300 468. "Digital Broadcasting Systems for Television, Sound and Data Services; Specification for Service Information (SI) in Digital Video Broadcasting (DVB) Systems."

Juhn, Li-Shen, and Li-Ming Tsent. "Fast Data Broadcasting and Receiving Scheme for Popular Video Service," IEEE Transactions on Broadcasting: March 1998.

McKinnon, Michael, Marc Drazin, and Gary Sgrignoli. "Tribune/WGN DTV Field Test." *IEEE Transactions on Broadcasting*: September 1998.

Petajan, Eric. "The HDTV Grand Alliance System." *IEEE Communications*: June 1996.

Pugh, William, and Gerald Boyer. "Broadband Access: Comparing Alternatives." *IEEE Communications*: August 1995.

Wiley, Richard. "Digital Television: The End of the Beginning." *IEEE Communications*: December 1995.

Web Sites

www.dvb.org

Primarily European DTV and datacasting specifications

www.smpte.org

Society of Motion Picture and Television Engineers

www.sbe.org

Society of Broadcast Engineers

www.scte.org

Society of Cable TV Engineers

www.toocan.philabs.research.philips.com

The Web home of DASE

www.atvef.com

The word on datacasting, from Wintel and some content providers

www.atsc.org

The Web home of Advanced Television Systems Committee (ATSC), which summarizes the digital TV agreement

www.cs.cmu.edu/afs/cs.cmu.edu/user/bam/www/numbers.html

Computer and Internet numbers compiled by Brad Myers, at Carnegie Mellon University

www.fcc.gov/oet/dtv

FCC DTV channel allotments as of April 1999

www.nab.org

National Association of Broadcasters' Web site, with lots of technical information about television

law.house.gov/cfrhelp.htm

The U.S. House of Representative Internet Law Library

www.openmarket.com/intindex/index.cfm

Fun Internet numbers, with thanks to Harper's Magazine

www.whitehouse.gov/fsbr/ssbr.html

The White House Social Statistics Briefing Room, with up-to-the minute social statistics from the White House and the Census Bureau

www.nw.com/

Network Wizards, a source of Internet statistics

www.mids.org

Matrix Information and Directory Services, Inc, a source of Internet statistics

This chapter covers the following topics:

- DAVIC Reference Architecture
- Modulation Techniques
- Noise Mitigation Techniques
- Metallic Transmission
- Fiber Optic Transmission
- Wireless Transmission
- Network Performance
- Signaling
- IP Multicast
- The Limits of Audio/Visual Perception
- MPEG-2 Compression and Systems
- MPEG-4 Scene Description

CHAPTER 2

Technical Foundations of Residential Broadband

A Reference Model for RBB

This section develops a generic RBB network—that is, a reference model that incorporates the key features of RBB networks. A reference model is useful in establishing vocabulary and pointing out parallel features among various technical approaches. In addition, a reference model can help identify points of congestion in end-to-end service delivery.

Our purpose is to identify the functions of three logical elements of an end-to-end RBB network: 1. Core Network, 2. the Access Network, and 3. the Home Network. The Core Network is covered in this chapter. The Access Network is covered in Chapter 3, "Cable TV Networks"; Chapter 4, "xDSL Access Networks"; Chapter 5, "FTTx Access Networks"; and Chapter 6 "Wireless Access Networks." The Home Network is dealt with in Chapter 7, "Home Networks."

Useful reference models for RBB networks have been developed by the Digital Audio Visual Council (DAVIC; www.davic.org) and ATM Forum Residential Broadband Working Group (ATMF RBB, www.atmforum.com). The DAVIC Reference model was originally written in DAVIC 1.0 Specification Part 02, System Reference Models and Scenarios, September 1995. The ATM Forum Reference model is presented in the organization's document (BTD-RBB-01.01, "Residential Broadband Baseline Document Draft," February 1997).

Figure 2-1 depicts the end-to-end schematic for the reference model. The Core Network, Access Network and Home Network domains are segmented in this way to emphasize boundaries of control.

Figure 2-1 *Reference Model for RBB Network*

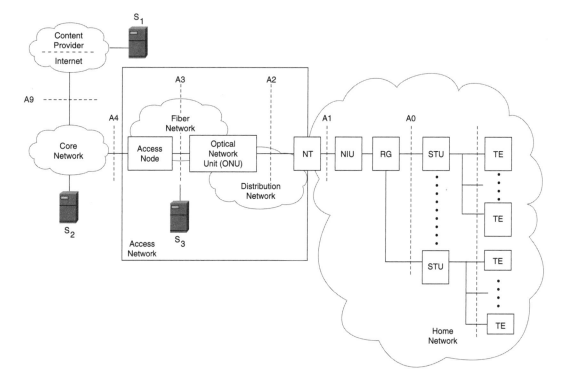

Core Network

The *Core Network* provides high-performance bit pumps to move bits between the content provider and the Access Network. It is the repository for network management and application servers, such as Web servers and video servers. Speed and manageability are critical in the Core Network. The principle functions of the Core Network are listed here:

- Switching, routing, and transmission
- Handling concentration of traffic to the content provider
- Handling service registration for multiple content providers
- Multiplexing and switching for multiple Access Networks
- Providing navigation aids and directory services
- Enforcing Quality of Service (QoS)
- Performing load balancing
- Caching servers on behalf of the content providers.

The Access Network may also perform some of these functions. For example, it is logical to place caching servers in the Access Network as well as the Core Network.

The protocol options to consider in the Core Network are IP or MPEG over Asynchronous Transfer Mode (ATM), packet mode over SONET (POS), and IP over Dense Wavelength Division Multiplexing (DWDM).

Figure 2-2 illustrates protocol stacking for the ATM approach, which has the (possible) current advantage of being conventional wisdom.

Figure 2-2   *ATM Core Network Protocol Stack*

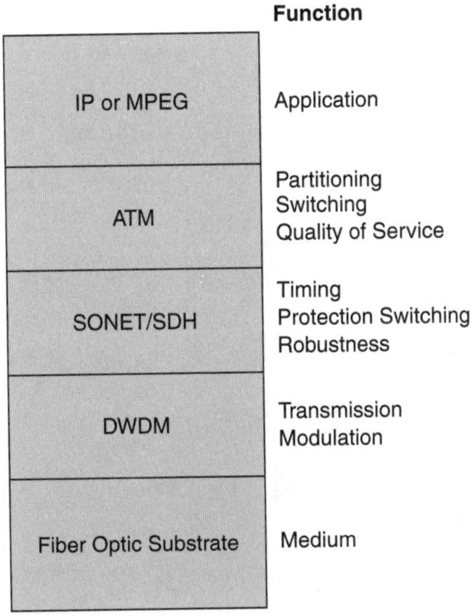

	Function
IP or MPEG	Application
ATM	Partitioning Switching Quality of Service
SONET/SDH	Timing Protection Switching Robustness
DWDM	Transmission Modulation
Fiber Optic Substrate	Medium

In this approach to Core Network design, IP and MPEG packets from the application are segmented into ATM cells at the edge of the Core. ATM virtual circuits (VC) guide the packets through the Core to the intended destinations. Key issues of ATM point mainly to signaling overhead and the complexity of mapping IP addresses to ATM addresses. Call setup rates for ATM are still in the low hundreds per second, which puts ATM at a disadvantage with respect to pure IP networks. However, ATM does provide a partitioning capability so that multiple users share the same Core (unbeknownst to each other) with a high degree of QoS.

This figure also points out that ATM is layered on top of SONET/SDH networks, which in turn are layered on top of a fiber optic DWDM network.

POS advocates point out that the QoS and partitioning features of ATM can be replicated at the packet layer; therefore, there is no need for ATM at all.

However, some go further to say that SONET/SDH can be bypassed as well. SONET/SDH provides timing and error protection. But timing would be relatively less important for applications that can maintain strict timing control at the packet layer and that provide for a rerouting capability. Therefore, there is some discussion of an IP over DWDM architecture, which eliminates the cost of the ATM switches and the SONET/SDH add/drop multiplexers (ADMs) but potentially at some critical functionality loss.

These approaches are shown in Figure 2-3.

Figure 2-3   *Core Network Alternatives*

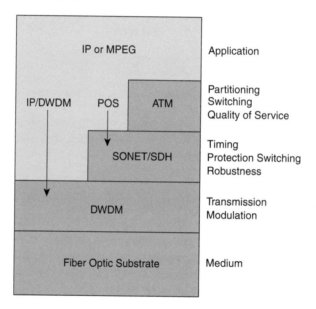

If sophisticated QoS schemes are implementable in packet mode (pure IP networks) cost-effectively, then the advocates of ATM and SONET/SDH will have some difficult questions to answer. Time will tell.

Access Network

The *Access Network* is the part of the carrier network that touches the customer's premises. The Access Network is also referred to as the local drop, local line, or last mile.

The principal functions of an Access Network are listed here:

- Transmitting, switching, routing, and multiplexing traffic from the consumer to the Core Network

- Classifying traffic from consumers by QoS; that is, the Access Network differentiates best-effort traffic from traffic with guaranteed bandwidth

- Enforcing QoS
- Providing navigation aids and directory services
- Caching servers on behalf of the content providers
- Performing tunneling or packet encapsulation
- Enforcing the MAC protocol
- Enforcing packet filtering
- Providing software updates to the Home Network
- Authenticating users
- Providing measurements used for invoicing

These functions are performed cooperatively with the Core Network and the Home Network, which means that there must be clear interfaces among these systems.

At Issue: Network Intelligence

An important system design question is how network intelligence is to be optimally distributed between the Core Network and the Access Network. *Intelligence* here refers to processing of user signaling (for example, call setup requests). [Quayle] argues that the Access Network should be relatively dumb and the Core Network relatively intelligent. Also, large databases for invoicing and resource management should be maintained in the Core Network. Because there are relatively few Core Network nodes and a large number of Access Network nodes, total system costs are optimized by concentrating the expensive (intelligent) pieces in the Core Network.

Others argue that because the Core Network must move bits as fast as possible, it must be simple, even dumb. Therefore, intelligence is pushed to the periphery, even to the customer premises. The case for dumb networks (overprovisioned, underengineered networks) and smart peripheral equipment (and people) is argued most publicly by David Isenberg (www.isen.com). ATM switches, for example, are relatively simple, with most of the hard software functions performed outside the switching fabric. However, because some Access Networks require a Media Access Control protocol, there is a requirement to interpret user signaling in the Access Network. Hence, for these networks, there is some requirement for some intelligence in the access. Whether or not both Core and Access Networks will be dumb remains to be seen.

Finally, on a commercial matter, it may be the case that the Access Network and the Core Network will be different companies. Each will assert that intelligence should be put into its network, which boosts added value.

Many types of Access Networks are discussed widely in the popular and trade press. Table 2-1 shows a list of the Access Networks in operation or in contemplation, with associated standards for telephony, video, and data. The acronyms will be discussed in due course; we only attempt to indicate here which Access Networks could support which broad class of service.

Table 2-1 *Access Networks and Standards*

Access Network	Telephony Standards	Video Standards	Data Standards
Broadcast DTV	—	Analog TV (NTSC, PAL, SECAM), digital TV using ATSC or DVB	ATSC/DASE ATVEF
Cable	PacketCable	OpenCable SCTE DVS	Data Over Cable Service Interface Specification (DOCSIS), DAVIC/DVB
ADSL/G.Lite	Analog	Switched Digital Video (TBD)	IP/PPP/ATM (ADSL Forum)
Other DSLs	Voice over ATM (VoATM) or Voice over IP (VoIP)	Switched Digital Video (TBD)	Various packet mode protocols such as the Point-to-Point Protocol Over Ethernet (PPPoE)
FTTx	VoATM/VoIP	Switched Digital Video (TBD)	FSAN and other initiatives
3G Wireless	IMT-2000	—	IMT-2000
Local Multipoint Distribution Service (LMDS)	VoIP/VoATM	TBD	TBD
Multichannel Multipoint Distribution Service (MMDS)	—	Analog TV, digital TV using 8-VSB	DOCSIS
High Altitude Long Operation (HALO) aircraft	TBD	—	TBD
Blimps	TBD	—	TBD
Powerline, use of electric power lines for data transmission	TBD	—	TBD

Though multiple types of Access Networks exist, there are three architectural elements, which they share. These are the access node, the Optical Network Unit, and the Network Termination (NT in Figure 2-1).

The major aforementioned Access Networks are covered in subsequent chapters. HALOs, blimps, and powerline are viewed as too experimental as of this writing. However, powerline transmission deserves some mention because of its potential.

Powerline is the use of electric utility wires to transmit data. Because computers and networking equipment need electricity, it makes sense to consider using the electrical outlet for a data connection as well. The issues with using powerlines have revolved around electrical emissions, noise on the lines and cost. Also, it is not possible to pass data through a transformer. However, changes in transformer design are giving rise to the possibility of this new Access Network. Principal developers include Northern Telecom (www.nortel.com), United Utilities of Great Britain, and Sydkraft of Sweden (in conjunction with the Swedish Internet Service provider, Tele2). Northern Telecom and United Utilities maintain a powerline Web site at www.nor.webdpl.com.

A typical U.S. power grid supports only four to eight homes per transformer, so powerline is viewed as expensive. But in Europe, each transformer supports 100 to 200 homes. A networking device at the transformer site is amortized over a larger number of homes, thereby making powerline more cost-effective. If noise and emission problems can be solved, this could represent an interesting alternative.

Access Node

The access node (AN) serves some or all of the following functions:

- Modulating forward data onto the Access Network
- Demodulating return path data
- Enforcing the Media Access Control (MAC) protocol to arbitrate access from multiple users onto the Access Network
- Multiplexing traffic from the Access Network to the Core Network
- Separating or classifying traffic prior to multiplexing onto the Core Network, such as differentiating traffic that is subject to QoS guarantees from traffic that receives best-effort support
- Enforcing signaling
- Performing passive operations, such as splitting and filtering

Enforcement of the MAC protocol is one of the more complicated functions of the AN. For some Access Networks, when multiple consumers vie for bandwidth connections simultaneously, arbitration rules are required to determine who gets to use the network at that moment. Without some controls, the Access and Core Networks would be obliged to provide an indefinite amount of bandwidth and connections. The MAC protocol arbitrates access to the

Access Network. It is enforced by the AN, which engages in a protocol exchange, or peers, with the NIU on the customer premises. Important MAC protocols are token-passing schemes, Slotted Aloha protocols, and Collision Sense Multiple Access protocols.

Examples of ANs are Cable Modem Terminal Server (CMTS) in the Multimedia Cable Network System (MCNS) architecture for cable data modems (discussed in Chapter 3), Digital Subscriber Line Access Multiplexer (DSLAM) for concentration (discussed in Chapter 4), and the ATM Digital Terminal (ADT), referenced in the ATM Forum RBB Baseline Document.

Optical Network Unit

The function of the Optical Network Unit (ONU) is to terminate fiber and convert the optical signal on fiber to electrical signals on wired networks. A major difference among Access Networks is the proximity of the ONU to the consumer. The closer the ONU is to the consumer, the higher the speed and usually the greater the service reliability. Carriers and consumers alike would like to have fiber as close as possible to the home—perhaps even inside the home—as service called Fiber to the Home (FTTH).

Network Termination

The Network Termination (NT) is a carrier-provided or customer-provided piece of equipment that is located on the side of the home. Some of its functions are listed here:

- Coupling home wiring and carrier wiring
- Grounding
- Handling RF filtering
- Handling splitting
- Performing media conversion
- Performing remodulation
- Handling security and interdiction
- Handling provisioning

The NT is the legal and commercial demarcation point between the Access Network and the consumer. This means that if something goes wrong on the network side of the NT, the carrier is obliged to fix it. The NT is situated on the customer premises, but many countries include it as a part of the Access Network.

In the United States, the NT is considered to be customer premises equipment because the customer purchases it. In Europe, it is considered carrier property. For purposes of this reference model, the NT is part of the carrier network because it usually is under carrier control, even though the customer purchases it. The fact that it can be purchased from a number of suppliers other than the Access carrier is not relevant architecturally.

NT functions differ widely among Access Networks, but the main functions are usually passive (coupling, splitting, grounding, RF filtering, and so on). In some cases, the NT can have an active function, such as signaling. For example, service activation might be enabled by signaling between the carrier and the NT. This becomes an important concept for Fiber to the Home (FTTH), which is discussed in Chapter 6.

Chapter 7 contains more discussion of various Home Network components.

Why Multiple Access Networks Exist

Proponents of specific Access Networks claim that one Access Network would fit all applications. While it is technically feasible that a single network could service all market drivers, there are reasons why multiple Access Networks exist:

- **Embedded base**—Telephone companies and cable operators have put billions of dollars into the ground. This represents investment that cannot be easily replaced. The sensible thing is to leverage it.

- **Different applications**—Broadcast television lends itself economically to shared media, such as air and cable. Retrofitting broadcast media to accommodate point-to-point applications involves software tricks. Similarly, retrofitting broadcast applications over point-to-point media also involves software tricks.

- **Different population densities**—Some technologies are more economically viable in urban areas than rural areas, and vice versa.

- **Different geography**—Vast expanses of oceans and rivers create a cost penalty for wired networks. On the other hand, obstacles such as hills, buildings, vegetation, and heavy rainfall reduce transmission quality for wireless networks.

- **Different business conditions**—In developing countries, which are characterized by a lack of mature wired infrastructure, broadcast technologies can create a fast infrastructure. Regulations such as those imposing limits on market dominance of a single carrier can foster or inhibit some technical options.

- **Entrepreneurship**—The availability of capital underwrites a lot of development of various technologies.

Because of these variations, subsequent chapters consider a variety of Access Networks to understand the strengths and weaknesses of each.

Home Networks

The Home Network consists of the following aspects:

- The Network Interface Unit (NIU), essentially a modem
- The Residential Gateway (RG), which adds network functionality
- The Set Top Unit (STU), which performs application-specific functions, such as decoding digital TV
- The Terminal Equipment (TE), a television, personal computer, or other device
- Consumer premises distribution, either wired or wireless

In the home, the personal computer and consumer electronics industries will wage a spirited battle for the consumer dollar. PCs, TV set-top boxes (STB), and game stations will blur as each acquires some of the functions of the others.

Modulation Techniques

With that brief overview of the architectural elements of an RBB network, we now discuss some of the basic technology to make it all happen. We begin with the most basic problem of transmission: that of modulation technique.

Modulation techniques (also called line-coding techniques) are permutations of various properties of a constant waveform, such as amplitude, frequency, and phase, to encode uniqueness, which is, after all, information. Digital transmission through any medium (metal, fiber, or air) requires the use of modulation schemes to infuse digital information onto the medium. Modulation schemes differ as to speed of service they provide, quality of the medium they require, noise immunity, and complexity, which are proxies for cost. Even after decades of development, modulation is still a hotly debated issue among experts. Many incompatible schemes have developed, and research is still in process.

Some important modulation schemes used in existing systems are listed here:

- On/Off Keying (OOK)
- 2B1Q
- Quadrature Phase Shift Keying (QPSK)
- Quadrature Amplitude Modulation (QAM)
- Discrete Multitone (DMT)

The following sections discuss these schemes in greater detail.

On/Off Keying

On/Off keying (OOK) is an intuitively simple modulation scheme used in fiber optic transmission. When a sender wants to transmit a binary 1, the laser goes on (light is transmitted). For a binary 0, the laser is off. To transmit an arbitrary binary sequence, the transmitter simply turns its laser transmitter on and off, obviously very quickly. The time duration that the laser is on or off is called the *symbol time* (see Figure 2-4). The number of symbols per unit time is called the *symbol rate*. When symbol rates are very fast—on the order of billions of symbols per second—the important engineering problem of *clock recovery* arises to keep the sender and receiver synchronized. However, for relatively low symbol rates—measured in thousands or even millions per second—the current state-of-the-art fiber and electronics clock recovery permits reliable transmission.

Figure 2-4   *On/Off Keying Example*

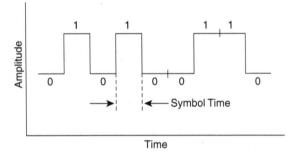

The bit stream in Figure 2-4 conveys the bits 010100110.

2B1Q

In On/Off keying, one logical bit was conveyed per symbol. However, it is possible to convey more bits per symbol with variations in the symbol. For example, 2B1Q (2 binary, 1 quaternary) has four levels of amplitude (voltage) to encode two bits. Because there are four voltage levels, each level translates to two bits per symbol.

Bits	Voltage Level (Amplitude)
00	+3
01	+1
10	−1
11	−3

Figure 2-5's example conveys the 12 bits 110110001101 in six symbol times. Thus, two bits are transmitted for each symbol time. It is therefore possible to increase the bit rate of a wire or of a wireless channel either by increasing the symbol rate of the transmission (to make things go faster) or by increasing the number of bits per symbol (to make things smarter). Modulation schemes can be compared according to their *spectral efficiency,* or the measure of how many bits can be transmitted for a given amount of bandwidth.

Figure 2-5   *A 2B1Q Example*

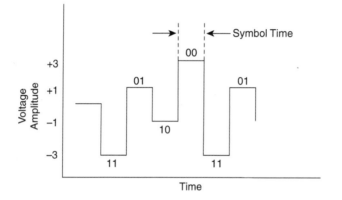

2B1Q is an amplitude modulation technique used for ISDN and high data rate digital subscriber line (HDSL) service in the United States. It is defined in the 1988 ANSI spec T1.601.

2B1Q modulation produces two bits per symbol and hence can transmit twice the data of another modulation scheme that transmits one logical bit per symbol. If you want more bits per symbol, more voltage levels are needed. For example, to encode three bits per symbol time, you need eight voltage levels. To encode k bits per symbol time, you need 2^k voltage levels. However, as speed requirements increase, it becomes increasingly difficult for the receiver to discriminate among many voltage levels with consistent precision.

The limits on spectral efficiency of 2B1Q preclude its use with very high bit rates, including RBB applications such as video or high-speed data retrieval. However, 2B1Q has the advantage of being a well-understood modulation scheme that is relatively inexpensive and robust against the kind of interference observed in a telephone plant, where its use is very appropriate.

Quadrature Phase Shift Keying

Another aspect of the waveform, specifically phase, can also be modulated to encode information. The simplest form of phase modulation, which does not use any amplitude modulation, is *phase shift keying (PSK)*. However, PSK is not commonly used because of its low spectral efficiency.

Quadrature phase shift keying (QPSK) transmits two waves with a common frequency, offset by 90°, each of which is amplitude-modulated. QPSK achieves a modest spectral efficiency of two bits per symbol time and can operate in the harsh environments of over-the-air transmission and cable TV return paths. Because it is well understood, robust, and relatively low-cost, QPSK is widely used in modern systems, such as for direct broadcast satellite. It is also recommended for use on the return path in cable modem systems (discussed later in Chapter 3).

Quadrature Amplitude Modulation

QPSK is a special case of a more general technique called *Quadrature Amplitude Modulation (QAM)*. Like QPSK transmission, two waves are involved: the I wave and the Q (or quadrature) wave. These are transmitted at the same frequency offset by 90°. As an example, one variant of QAM is QAM-64. With QAM-64, each of the waves is amplitude-modulated independently with eight levels of amplitude modulation, yielding 64 different amplitude levels jointly expressed by the two waves; hence the term QAM-64. The use of a quadrature wave and amplitude modulation give rise to the term quadrature amplitude modulation.

QAM can yield a higher spectral efficiency than 2B1Q. For example, with QAM-64, three bits are modulated on each carrier, thereby yielding six encoded bits per symbol. Cleaner lines (flat frequency response and high carrier/noise ratio) permit even more aggressive modulation. QAM-256 enables four bits to be encoded on each carrier, yielding eight bits per symbol. More aggressive modulation means more spectral efficiency (bits/symbol) and therefore more data per unit time on the medium.

Various flavors of QAM are referred to as QAM-nn, where *nn* is an integer indicating the number of states per symbol. The number of bits per symbol time is *k*, where 2^k=nn. For example, if four bits per symbol are encoded, the result is QAM-16; six bits per symbol produces QAM-64. (You may also see the notation as 64-QAM, but we will use the prior notation.)

QAM is a well-known technique that has been used for years in analog phone modems (V.32 and V.34), where it was necessary to get a lot of bits through a relatively narrow voice grade telephone line. QAM-16 is proposed as an optional modulation scheme for return path data traffic on cable plants. The Society of Cable Television Engineers (SCTE) has specified the QAM-64 and QAM-256 modulation for digital video transmission over cable TV plants.

Other important modulation techniques similar to QAM are Vestigial Sideband (VSB), used in digital terrestrial television in the United States, and Carrierless Amplitude Modulation/Phase Modulation (CAP), used in ADSL modems, which is discussed in Chapter 4.

Figure 2-6 illustrates the QAM process. For ease of display, the I and Q waves are shown offset by half the frequency, or 180°. In actuality, the offset for QPSK and QAM is 90°, but that is a little more difficult to diagram.

Figure 2-6   *QAM Modulation*

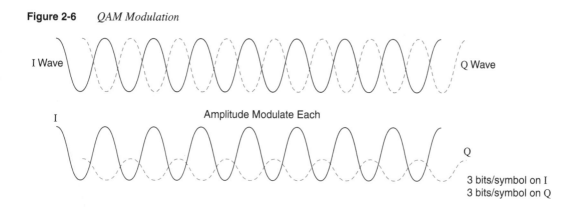

Discrete Multitone

QPSK, QAM, and CAP are examples of modulation techniques that permute a single carrier (or two copies of a single wave, slightly offset from each other). These are called *single-carrier techniques*. Frequency, amplitude, and phase of the carrier can be modulated to encode information. These are well-understood techniques with a lot of industrial and defense experience behind them.

But with the development of *digital signal processing (DSP),* multicarrier techniques are now possible. Multicarrier techniques use an aggregate amount of bandwidth and divide it into *subbands*, thereby yielding multiple, parallel, narrower channels. Each subband is encoded using a single-carrier technique (such as QAM), and bit streams from the subbands are bonded together at the receiver. Important examples of multicarrier techniques include orthogonal frequency division multiplexing (OFDM) and discrete multitone (DMT).

Consider Figure 2-7, which shows an example of multicarrier modulation using the current ANSI T1.413 standard for ADSL. Here, 1 MHz is segmented into 256 subbands of 4 kHz each. The transmitter modulates each subband using a single-carrier modulation technique. The receiver accepts the subband and bonds the 256 carriers together.

OFDM and DMT differ in that OFDM uses a common modulation scheme for each subband. That is, each subband transfers the same number of bits per second. OFDM is used in European over-the-air broadcast digital television. In the case of over-the-air broadcast, all subbands are presumed to have uniform noise characteristics, so a common modulation technique makes sense.

DMT enhances the OFDM model by allowing variable spectral efficiency among the subbands. Some subbands can use more aggressive modulation schemes than other subbands. DMT is used in wired media such as ADSL, where the noise characteristics of each subband may differ. Subbands, which have high noise problems, can be avoided.

Figure 2-7   *Multicarrier Modulation*

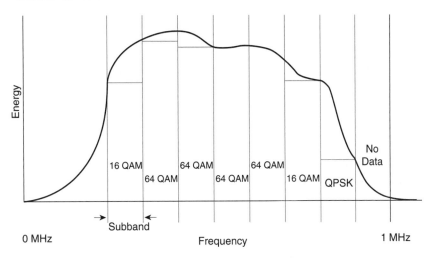

Multicarrier techniques have a latency penalty (time delay to transmit a digital bit) compared with single carrier. In the DMT case for ADSL, there are 256 subbands of 4 kHz each. So no bit can travel faster than allowed by 4 kHz, even if the line was perfectly clean.

One of the noisiest debates about modulation techniques is between proponents of DMT and proponents of CAP for use in ADSL. DMT for ADSL uses 256 subbands, whereas CAP uses a single carrier with amplitude modulation, very similar to QAM. At the time of this writing, CAP has an advantage over DMT in that it consumes less power (thereby generating less heat) and costs less because it is more mature (more units in the field, greater integration). It is easy to see how DMT scales and why DMT has been selected by ANSI T1E1.4 and the International Telecommunications Union (ITU). Furthermore, a number of U.S. telephone companies have selected DMT. Because of these factors (and because of commercial issues with respect to the licensing of CAP), it appears DMT is gaining the upper hand for ADSL.

Considerations in Selecting Modulation Techniques

Selection of modulation technique for each Access Network has been highly contentious, partly because there's a lot of money at stake. Standards organizations for cable TV, xDSL, and HDTV have spent years arguing the requirements of modulation, let alone the choice. While commercial self-interest, academic background, national pride, embedded base and personal ego play a role, there are engineering and cost tradeoffs to consider as well.

Some of the majors engineering considerations are listed here:

- **Scale**—Will the modulation support large systems and fast bit rates?

- **Noise immunity**—Can the modulation scheme operate reliably in with real-world impairments?

- **Packaging**—Can Application Specific Integrated Circuits (ASICs) be built? Can implementations be used in a variety of environments, such as different Access Networks? How large are the components, and how much power does the technique consume?

- **Performance**—What is the spectral efficiency? What is the latency?

- **Cost**—This is the dominant factor when dealing with consumer markets.

The modulation schemes described in this chapter are likely to be residential broadband alternatives. Table 2-2 lists services and their respective modulation schemes, current as of this writing.

Table 2-2   *Modulation Techniques for Current Services*

Service	Modulation Technique
ISDN (United States)	2B1Q
U.S. Direct Broadcast Satellite	QPSK
U.S. Digital Over-the-Air Broadcast	Vestigial Sideband (VSB)
U.S. Digital Cable Forward Channels	QAM-64, QAM-256
U.S. Digital Cable Return Channels	QPSK
European Digital Over-the-Air Broadcast	OFDM
High Bit Rate Digital Subscriber Line (HDSL)	2B1Q
Asymmetric Digital Subscriber Line (ADSL)	DMT, CAP

Viewpoint: Interoperability of Modulation Techniques

The proliferation of modulation techniques raises interoperability problems for most consumer electronics devices. For digital TV, for example, the likelihood now exists that a television built for over-the-air digital broadcasts will not be capable of receiving a cable TV digital transmission without a separate box.

The consumer could end up with three set tops: an analog NTSC descrambler for analog cable, a VSB MPEG decoder for digital over-the-air reception, and a QAM MPEG decoder for digital cable reception. Or there will be new generations of TV with input jacks for all three types of reception. Either way, the results are market confusion and additional costs.

Noise-Mitigation Techniques

The signal-carrying capabilities of wire will be stretched to the limit by high-speed services. Signal errors will be caused by noise on the line. Because broadband networks will be used to transmit video, errors cannot be tolerated—at least, not many of them—without severe picture degradation and even total loss of picture. Errors in data transmission generally are less severe than errors in video transmission because networking protocols can make adjustments. But in the extreme, errors in data transmission can lead to a loss of session.

Therefore, noise-mitigation techniques tailored to fast networking are to be used for RBB. The two most prominent are concatenated Reed Solomon forward error correction and spread spectrum. Forward error correction enables the receiver to detect and fix errors to data packets without the need for the transmitter to retransmit packets. Spread spectrum enables the successful transmission in very hostile transmission environments.

Forward Error Correction

Forward error correction (FEC) techniques such as Reed Solomon (RS) are vital for the system to maintain speed. Forward error correction enables the receiver to detect and fix errors to data packets without the need for the transmitter to retransmit packets. If retransmission techniques were used, a great deal of latency would be incurred by the round trip of negative acknowledgment of the original packet and retransmission of the second packet. Three trips would have to be made across the network.

FEC is accomplished by segmenting the data stream into fixed-size blocks and adding redundant bits (called Hamming codes) to each block. The addition of the Hamming codes enables the receiver to perform numeric calculations on the packet, to determine which bit is in error, and then to fix it. The technique works when erred bits are spread out. If too many errors are grouped together, the technique fails to identify the erred bit. (For a discussion of Hamming Codes, see [Claiborne].)

Interleaving

Within the context of error correction, *interleaving* is a process whereby bits are reordered so that errors due to impulse noise are spread over time. For example, the top of Figure 2-8 shows a transmission sequence of 24 bits, with a burst error affecting bits 7 through 10. In the interleave process, the bits are reordered into an interleave buffer, as shown. The erred bits are now spread out, and forward error correction is applied to the reordered bits in the interleave buffer. This illustration shows a very simple reordering in the interleave buffer. However, in practice, more sophisticated reordering schemes are used. For example, the reordering may differ from block to block. This creates robustness in the presence of noise characteristics, which are repetitive.

Figure 2-8 *Interleaving in Forward Error Correction*

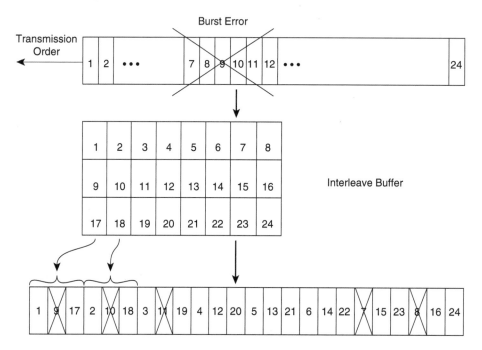

Apply FEC to Reorder Stream

By concatenating interleaving with Hamming code error correction, erred bits can be reduced by factors of up to 10,000. Results presented in the ATM Forum (ATM Forum 95-1154; Esaki, Guha) indicate an improvement in packet error rate of 10^5 for full-size AAL5 (65 KB) packets, and 10^2 for 9180-byte packets.

The price of interleaving is latency. The entire bit stream experiences delay because the bits must be taken in and out of the interleave buffer (serialization delay), and Reed Solomon calculations must be performed. The amount of latency increases with the number of bits interleaved. More burst protection means more latency. Experts have argued that it is possible that a transmitter can transmit at near the theoretical limits of a medium by simply extending the interleaving. But because there is a necessary tradeoff of signal quality and latency, compromises must be made.

DAVIC has settled on an interleaving latency that protects against burst impulse noise of 25 microseconds, yielding latency of 600 microseconds in duration.

However, American interests—particularly CableLabs—argued for a more flexible scheme than fixed interleaving. As a result, in the United States, the Data Over Cable Service Interface Specification (DOCSIS: www.cablemodem.com) has specified a variable-depth interleaver, which provides interleaving from 0 to 96 microseconds. The International Telecommunications Union (ITU) is in the process of specifying modulation and forward error control standards for digital TV. As part of the organization's deliberations, two options to interleaving are specified in Annexes A and B of the digital TV specification. These two options are described in Table 2-3.

Table 2-3   *Comparison of ITU Annex A and Annex B Interleaving*

	Annex A	**Annex B**
Latency	600 microseconds	0 to 3750 microseconds
Maximum Burst	25.6 microseconds	0 to 96.0 microseconds
Reed Solomon (see notation below)	(204,188)	(128,122)
Supporters	DVB	DOCSIS

Web references to each of these supporting organizations are presented in Appendix B, "Professional Organizations and Regulatory Agencies."

Notation

Typical Reed Solomon (RS) approaches to FEC involve interleaving and coding. The notation for Reed Solomon is characterized by (N, K) where N is the total number of bytes per block and K is the intended number of data bytes per block. The quantity (N–K)/2 is the number of erred bytes per block correctable by the coder.

For example RS(204,188) denotes the shorthand notation for RS encoding for MPEG packets. An MPEG packet is 188 bytes in length; 16 bytes are added for error correction, yielding a block size of 204 bytes. The burst error protection is 8 bytes per block (16 divided by 2).

Spread Spectrum/Code Division Multiple Access

The advent of increased computing capability is enabling the widespread proliferation of an old technique for transmission called spread spectrum. Like many technical innovations, spread spectrum was motivated by military reasons and was developed by government research. In World War II, military communications suffered from enemy jamming for open air transmission. Spread spectrum was designed to provide communication through intentional jamming. This property makes spread spectrum useful for transmission through hostile transmission environments, such as cable systems or urban wireless environments, environments so hostile that they seem to resemble jammed transmissions.

Two broad types of spread spectrum techniques exist: *frequency hopping spread spectrum (FHSS)* and *direct sequence spread spectrum (DSSS)*.

Frequency Hopping Spread Spectrum

Let's say that a transmitter wants to transmit on a certain frequency, but jamming frequencies or noise is interfering with the intended transmission over relatively few frequencies. The transmitter sends data to a receiver and later hops to a different frequency. After a short burst of transmission, it hops to a third frequency, and so forth. The transmitter cannot hop randomly because the receiver wouldn't know what frequency to tune to. So this technique requires that the transmitter and receiver agree in advance on the hop sequence. Because the transmitter and receiver don't know when jamming will occur, they will often hop without having encountered jamming. If jamming does occur, they have the mechanism to avoid it. Frequency hopping is a well-known technique used for wireless data transmission.

Frequency hopping can occur very quickly. In fact, it is possible to hop on every transmitted bit. A more advanced technique, called fast frequency hopping, involves multiple frequency hops per bit.

Figure 2-9   *Fast Frequency Hopping*

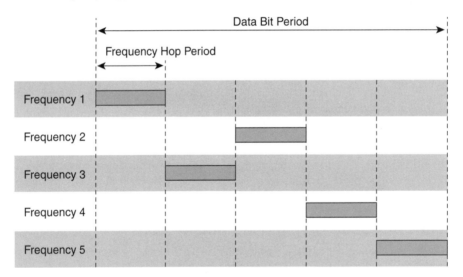

In the case of very high transmission rates, there may be performance limitations associated with frequency hopping. When the transmitter hops to a new frequency, the receiver takes some time to train to the new frequency. This training time limits performance.

The interesting sidebar to the development of frequency hopping spread spectrum is that one of the original patent holders was the Hollywood actress Hedy Lamarr. Originally an Austrian, Lamarr acquired notoriety as the first woman to appear nude in a feature film, the 1932 Czech production of *Ecstasy*, which was banned in the United States in 1935. Later, Lamarr married the Austrian arms dealer Fritz Mandl, who shared his thoughts on weapons systems with her, not really suspecting that she would understand him. Upon learning that Mandl was selling arms to the Nazis, Lamarr left him, came to the United States, and patented the idea of FHSS in 1942 with musical composer George Antheil for use in guiding radio controlled torpedoes. The original innovation used 88 frequencies, the number of keys on a piano. Not surprisingly, the innovation was not taken seriously by the military, and the patent lapsed, largely unused.

Direct Sequence Spread Spectrum

To improve performance, another technique was developed more recently, called direct sequence spread spectrum (DSSS).

When a transmitter wants to send binary digits, we normally conceive of a single electrical voltage level for a fixed, known period of time. For example, in our previous discussion of 2B1Q, a voltage of +3 indicated two binary 1s.

However, it is not necessary that binary digits use a *single* voltage level. In Figure 2-10, for example, the sender and receiver can agree beforehand that instead of a binary 1 being indicated by a +3 volts for, say, seven microseconds, they can agree that a binary one will be indicated by seven alternating voltage levels of +3, +3, +3, −3, +3, −3, −3, with each voltage level lasting one microsecond each. The total period of time to transmit a binary 1 is the same—seven microseconds—but the coding during that seven microseconds differs. Each of the subintervals of time is called a *chip*, and the number of chips per unit time is referred to as the *chipping rate*. With the development of modern microprocessors, chipping rates in the millions per second are achieved. This has enabled the widespread proliferation of spread spectrum.

Figure 2-10   *Direct Sequence Spread Spectrum*

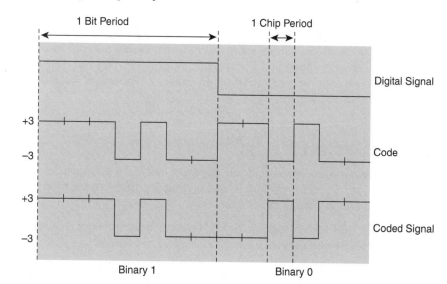

The sequence of chips is called a *spreading code*. The spreading code used by one connection differs from the spreading code used by another. In fact, it is important that connections use different spreading codes (said to be orthogonal codes). This is to say that different connections have different definitions of binary 0s and 1s. If two sessions use a common spreading code, then they would interfere with each other. If a receiver gets a binary 0 or 1 with a spreading code he is not using, that bit would appear as noise and the receiver would ignore it. On the other hand, if the receiver recognizes the bit because it has the right spreading code, but it is from the wrong source, interference happens.

When a pair of users establishes a spreading code between themselves, they are able to understand what a binary 0 and 1 look like. However, to all other users sharing the same spectrum, their session looks like noise because the others cannot decode the 0s and 1s of the communicating pair. As more users join the shared spectrum with their orthogonal spreading code, the background noise for everyone increases. Eventually, things get so noisy that communication is impaired. This results in reducing the distance that a wireless communication can work. As users drop off the network (for example, hang up their phone), the distance of effective communication can increase. This changing of distance causes what are called "breathing cells" when DSSS is used for cellular telephony.

Why would one transmit with such a complicated coding mechanism? The answers are security and robustness. Back to our problem of the enemy intruder. If the intruder does not know that a binary 1 is represented in such a complicated way, it can't decode the message.

Regarding robustness, if transmission is corrupted due to intentional jamming or too poor media characteristics (such as rain-attenuated wireless transmission), the receiver may get only six of the ten chips correctly. However, it can conclude that the sender intended to send a binary 1 because a majority of the received chips comply with the spreading code.

The criticism of spread spectrum has been its complexity and loss of spectral efficiency. Modern DSP and VLSI techniques mitigate the complexity problem, although the process is still relatively complex. Spectral efficiency is a problem if there is only one transmitter because that user uses more spectrum. But if multiple transmitters exist, they can share the spectrum using code division multiple access (CDMA) so that there is no loss of spectral efficiency system-wide.

Metallic Transmission Media

This section presents some physical characteristics of metallic wiring familiar to consumers, specifically phone wire and coaxial cable used in cable TV. Fiber transmission and wireless media will be discussed later in this chapter.

Copper wiring is a ubiquitous, well-understood medium. It comes in two broad classes, for this discussion: phone wire and coaxial cable. Both classes have variants, but each has been standardized on a few options. Phone wire consists of two thin copper wires, which are twisted in a helical pattern around each other. The twisted pair is wrapped in an insulating cover of plastic, rubber, or lacquer. At its limit, phone wire can transmit 1 MHz for a distance of roughly 3 miles, or 30 MHz for a distance of 200 yards. The distance that electricity passes through phone wire is resistance (measured in ohms), which in turn is partly a function of the wire's thickness, or *gauge*. Table 2-4 lists various wiring gauges with their diameters and electrical resistance.

Table 2-4   *Wire Gauge*

Gauge	Diameter (inches)	Feet/Ohm
18	0.0403	156.5
20	0.0320	98.5
22	0.0253	62.0
24	0.0201	39.0
26	0.0159	24.5

Note that the higher the gauge number, the smaller the diameter and the shorter the distance traveled.

Coaxial cable consists of a single, thicker length of copper with stronger, metallic shielding. It can transmit up to 750 MHz for a distance of a mile or so.

Table 2-5 summarizes several important data services in terms of bandwidth and type of metal wire used.

Table 2-5   *Representative Services and Bandwidth for Metal Wire Transmission*

Service	Upper Limit Bandwidth	Type of Wire
Voice service	3.4 kHz	Phone
Alarm service	8 kHz	Phone
ISDN	80 kHz	Phone
T1 using 2B1Q	250 kHz	Phone
Cable TV	350–750 MHz	Coaxial cable

The distance and signal integrity obtainable from phone wire or coaxial cable is limited by certain local factors associated with general problems of high frequency on wires.

Problems Associated with High Frequency on Wires

The types of wire listed provide well-known, stable services for the indicated frequencies. But RBB intends to push frequency used on phone wire and on cable to their limits. This will be difficult due to impairments associated with high-frequency transmission on metal wire. Some of these impairments are listed here:

- More attenuation
- More crosstalk
- More resistance
- More phase error

Attenuation

Signal loss, or *attenuation*, is a function of frequency, distance, and temperature, As frequency increases, the distance the signal can travel decreases by the square root of the frequency. So a 40 MHz signal will travel half as far as a 10 MHz signal. Also, the velocity of signal through a wire is a function of frequency. The higher the frequency, the slower the signal. Signal strength also drops with distance. Finally, signal strength drops with temperature. The warmer the ambient temperature, the greater the signal loss. That's why in the case of extreme cold, superconductors work extremely efficiently in conducting electricity.

Because optical signals through glass fiber retain signal strength better than electronic signals through metallic wires, they provide improvements required for RBB services.

Crosstalk

When two adjacent wires are carrying signals, there is the possibility that signals from one wire will enter the other wire as a result of electromagnetic coupling. Crosstalk increases with increasing frequency. At low frequencies used by voice, crosstalk is not noticeable. However, at frequencies required by high-speed services, this can be a principle cause of signal degradation.

Resistance

As signals are transmitted through wires at very high frequencies, a phenomenon called the skin effect occurs. This is the behavior whereby electricity migrates to the outside wall of the wire, leaving little conductivity in the middle of the wire. In fact, in extreme cases, it is possible to replace the core of the wire with cheaper nonconductive material such as plastic or wood. As electricity migrates to the skin, resistance increases because less of the wire is used. Increased resistance weakens signals.

The skin effect explains why there are no services above 1 GHz over wired media, whereas over-the-air spectrum can be used for frequencies in the range of 20 to 30 GHz.

Phase Error

Higher frequency signals not only weaken more quickly when compared with lower frequencies, but they are also a little slower, which causes a phase error. For modulation techniques dependent on phase, this can introduce bit errors.

External Impairments

Apart from inherent problems associated with high frequencies, metallic networks encounter external impairments as well. Many of these impairments have to do with noise—that is, disturbances that reduce the clarity of the signal being sent. A challenge for RBB engineers is to characterize noise for specific networks so that proper encoding and noise-mitigation techniques can be used. Noise characterization involves determining whether impulse noise or narrowband noise is the major cause of imperfections, at what frequency the noise occurs, and what the cause of the noise is. Noise characterization of cable TV networks continues to be the subject of research by CableLabs, a research consortium for North American cable operators located in Louisville, Colorado. Telcordia Technologies (once known as Bellcore, then controlled by the major Bell Operating companies, and now owned by SAIC Corporation) does the same for telephone companies.

Leakage

Outdoor insulation and the conductive outer shield of coaxial cable suffer wear and tear. Eventually, lesions form in the insulation, allowing radiation from the conducting material to leak through the perforation to the outside. This is a source of signal loss. Moreover, the radiated signal that emanates from the wire can cause interference with wireless services, such as radio transmission. This is a reason why the FCC has rules limiting signal leakage.

Another reason for leakage is poorly fitted couplings at the customer site, such as F connectors for cable TV not tightly joined to the cable box. This presents a system management problem because such leakage is outside the control of the carrier.

Impulse Noise

Impulse noise (or burst noise) occurs when one wire picks up an unintended signal that lasts for a very short period of time (a few microseconds) but that interferes with a wide frequency range. Sources of impulse noise include other wires, motors, and electronic devices. This is often caused by imperfections in the wire, such as corrosion or malfunctioning amplifiers. Lightning or any other source of strong electric sparks also cause impulse noise.

Spread spectrum is useful for mitigating impulse noise because the intended signals are spread out over longer periods of time, long enough to persist through the impulse noise.

Narrowband Interference

Whereas impulse noise affects a wide range of frequencies for a short period of time, narrowband interference adversely affects a small number of frequencies over a long period of time. Amateur radio, or AM or FM radio interference, are types of narrowband interference. Consider AM transmission occurring at 1070 kHz. If there is a signal at the same frequency in a wire, and if there is a lesion in the wire or a loose fitting, then receivers at the end of the wire will pick up the signal at 1070 kHz.

One way to avoid the interference is to identify the frequency range of the noise in advance and simply not transmit on that frequency. This is a technique that is under consideration by some proponents of ADSL, which is discussed in Chapter 4. If you don't know the interfering frequency, you can use Frequency Hopping Spread Spectrum (FHSS), which was discussed earlier in this chapter.

Loading Coils

Loading coils are passive (unpowered) devices that lengthen the distance voice can travel over phone wire. The positive effect is better voice fidelity over longer distance. The negative effect is that higher frequencies needed for any digital service, such as ISDN, ADSL, or leased line T1 service, are filtered out. Loading coils were devised decades ago, before thoughts of high-speed services.

Loading coils are needed on the roughly 15 percent of loops of the United States that are longer than 18,000 feet. But the way provisioning works, if one line in a small binder (50 lines) requires loading, then all lines are loaded for ease of installation. The result is that no one knows how many loaded loops exist; still, it is on the order of 20 percent.

The problem of loading coils is a big one, but it is slowly resolving itself because the coils are removed one by one with the introduction of new services.

Thermal Noise

Differences in ambient temperatures change the resistive quality of a wire. Lowering temperatures lowers resistance, thereby increasing signal quality. Warm temperatures tend to lengthen wires, which affects timing, an important part of synchronization, as we shall see in Chapter 3. Time differences can be significant over a 3-mile radius for phone wire or a 50-mile radius for coaxial cable.

Bridged Taps

Telephone circuits in their cleanest form are a pair of copper wires, which connects your handset directly to the telephone company office.

Bridged taps are extra copper wires that tap into the original wire for possible connection to another device. These were originally installed for flexibility in field installations. If the phone company was stringing wire to your house and there was another house along the way that *may* need a line in the future, a wire was branched off.

This was good for field installation operations but it causes *echoes* (signals echo off the end of the branch into the mainstream network) and changes timing on the circuit. If lots of taps are present on the line, the echoes can become serious enough to impair high-speed transmission.

Additionally, some taps may be unterminated. Unterminated wires cause the additional problem of leakage, which causes a loss of signal strength.

Locating bridged taps to correct them can be difficult because network providers often have incomplete records of where they occur. Without the provider's knowledge, the consumer can instigate bridged taps with do-it-yourself phone wire installation. In both telco and cable networks, bridged taps must be addressed through some noise-mitigation technique.

At Issue: Legacy Wiring Challenges for Telcos

A continuing concern among telephone companies worldwide is how much of their existing local loop plant is actually usable for high-speed networking. Age, rust, corrosion, broken insulation, loading coils, bridged taps, and occasional poor record-keeping about all these problems jeopardize the potential to provide RBB services over legacy wiring. The amount of wiring that can be repurposed for RBB makes a big difference in the financial spreadsheets for new services at the telcos. The more wiring that must be installed, the longer it will take to deploy, the more it will cost, and the greater advantage goes to telco competitors, such as cable operators. The condition of wiring also could have an impact on regulatory deliberations, as the telcos may seek some rate relief to upgrade legacy systems. The process of loop qualification must be watched closely to calibrate the near-term rollout of RBB services.

Fiber Optic Transmission

Fiber optic technology is a major reason for the feasibility of residential broadband. More than metal wires, fiber has the carrying capacity to supply high-speed services to millions of homes. Fiber optic cables are made from very clear glass, much more transparent than window glass. Fiber technology uses lightwave signals to transmit data, whereas metal wire uses electromagnetic signals. The clarity of the glass permits the distribution of lightwave impulses for possibly hundreds of miles.

Coding uses simple On/Off keying. A transmitter indicates a binary 1 by turning on the light. If the light is off, it indicates a binary 0. Light is perceptible when the receptor senses photons. More complicated coding schemes, such as amplitude modulation, are possible, but simple OOK works with current technologies for digital transmission.

Description of Key Fiber Elements

This section examines three central aspects of the fiber system: the fiber itself, the light sources, and modulation techniques.

Fiber

Fibers are broadly categorized into two groups: single-mode fiber and multimode fiber. The term *mode* refers to the path a photon takes in going from one end of the fiber to another. In multimode, a photon careens off the fiber wall as it goes from one end to the other, thereby defining a path. Another photon (there are a lot of them) will probably take a different path. The number of possible paths is a function of the core diameter with the wider the diameter, the more the paths.

According to the recommendations in ANSI T1E1.2/93-020R3, the core of multimode fiber is 62.6 microns in diameter, and the cladding is 125 microns. This is compatible with the FDDI multimode fiber spec ISO/IEC 9314-3.

As each photon bounces off the fiber core, it loses some energy. This limits the distance over which multimode fiber is usable without amplification. A second effect is that because the paths of photons that make up a data bit are of different lengths, a given bit is spread in time. Figure 2-11 shows two photons following different paths in a multimode fiber; photon B will arrive at the destination before photon A. The time difference between the arrival of photon A and photon B is called the *delay spread*. Because photons A and B are part of the same symbol (binary bit), significant delay spread can cause interference between bits. This is called *intersymbol interference* (ISI) and is impairment for metallic and wireless communications as well.

For single-mode fiber, all photons take the same path down the center of the core. This is because the core of the fiber is very narrow. According to the recommendations in ANSI T1E1.2/93-020R3, the fiber has an 8.3-micron core with 125-micron cladding. Much less signal loss and less ISI occur. Therefore, single-mode fiber is capable of greater distances and higher bit rate. The fact that the diameter of the fiber optic core is narrower than that of multimode, however, means that other elements of the system, such as connectors, transmitters, and receivers, must operate with much smaller tolerances. This makes the other components more expensive and difficult to handle.

Figure 2-11   *Fiber Cross-Section*

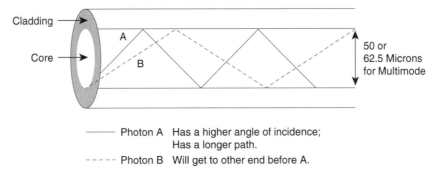

Modulation Techniques

Modulation Techniques

The fiber can be modulated using On/Off keying, frequency modulation, or amplitude modulation. Symbol times are very short, on the order of picoseconds. Computer folk tend to think of fiber as a digitally encoded medium, which it can be. But the cable folk required analog modulation.

When cable TV was implemented, it was intended to mimic over-the-air analog broadcast signals. This meant that cable signals were analog as well. If fibers were to be encoded digitally, then it would have been necessary to convert from analog to digital (for fiber transport) and back to analog (for display on analog TV sets). The cable industry wanted to avoid extra analog-to-digital (A/D) conversions, even though there would have been possible benefits of data compression and improved picture fidelity—it was just too costly. Amplitude-modulated fiber enables analog line coding, which was the key that propelled the cable industry to deploy fiber.

Benefits

As compared with metal, fiber has more bandwidth, can travel longer distances without amplification or regeneration, is safer to handle, weighs less, and has much lower material cost. Single-mode fiber can carry light for up to 70 km, whereas coaxial cable must be amplified every 0.5 km, and phone wire has a reach of maybe 5 km, or up to 18,000 feet.

Fiber does not rust, which means less outside plant maintenance and lower ongoing operational costs for local loop networks. Fiber also is impervious to electromagnetic interference and is secure. In addition, it is extremely difficult (though not impossible) to wiretap, which is either good or bad, depending on which side of the law you stand.

Fiber promotes high reliability. A service break caused by a fiber cut can be corrected by switching to a redundant network in approximately 50 milliseconds. This nearly instantaneous switch won't be noticed by consumers or most networking applications. Carriers are moving to ring and other redundant topologies to secure their fiber networks.

Impairments

Fiber is wonderful stuff, but it has its limitations. Like metal wire, it is subject to attenuation in certain circumstances. Plus, there are some impairments unique to fiber.

Attenuation

In fiber, attenuation refers to the loss of optical power as light travels through the fiber. Measured in decibels per kilometer (dB/km), attenuation ranges from more than 300 dB/km for plastic fibers to around 0.2 dB/km for 1550 nanometer (nm) single-mode fiber (a nanometer is a billionth of a meter). For 1310 nm fiber, loss is about 50 percent greater than for 1550 nm. Additionally, each fiber splice adds attenuation of about 1 dB per splice. Due to fiber age, chemical makeup, construction, installation care, and other factors, the fiber loss per kilometer may not be the same for every link.

Also, over time, cracks occur in the fibers. In freezing conditions, fiber optic cable can be damaged when moisture inside imperfect insulation turns to ice. As ice crystallizes, it can exert pressure on the fiber cable inside the conduit. That pressure can cause fissures in the fiber and thereby degrades the signal, or it can break the fiber and kill the signal altogether

Dispersion

Dispersion causes light to spread as it travels down a fiber and limits bandwidth. Some photons will travel straight down the middle of the fiber. Other photons will bounce off the walls of the fiber and go careening through the fiber. The photons going down the middle will arrive earlier than the bouncing photons. So the affect of dispersion is loss of temporal integrity. The bit rate through fiber must be low enough to ensure that pulses do not overlap.

The question arises whether attenuation or dispersion is the more significant limiting factor in fiber transmission. The answer depends on speed and attenuation and optical loss budget. Most cable operators will operate with a maximum optical budget of around 37 dB. Because 1310 single-mode fiber attenuates at roughly 0.5 dB/km (fiber attenuation, splices, bends, kinks, and a safety margin), a distance of 74 km can be supported. For OC12 over 1310 nm single-mode fiber, the dispersion distance is roughly 40 km. For OC3, which is slower but more forgiving than OC12, distance is about 160 km.

Handling Problems

Fiber is difficult to handle because electrons are more forgiving than photons. As an example, the core of single-mode fiber is 9 microns in diameter. This makes splicing, as well as the construction of connectors and sockets, very difficult. The splices must be scrupulously clean and absolutely flush. Furthermore, the ends of the splices must be perfectly aligned, whereas there are no alignment problems with electricity. Any little contact, and electrons move—not so with fiber. Handling problems will become particularly acute for fiber to the home. Great care and fine tools are needed to align the glass cores on the respective segments. New devices are available to do splice automatically, but you need to be a telephone company to afford them.

Cuts and Other Damage

Fibers can be cut more easily than copper—and when they are cut, the effects are large. One industry rule of thumb points toward one fiber cut per year per half mile of fiber. Alcatel says that typical fiber breaks require 6 to 12 hours to locate and repair. Separately, Fiber Optics News reports 390 fiber cuts in the United States in the year ending June 1996. Reported fiber outages not caused by cuts—including storms, fire, vandalism, and rodent damage—were 247. The catastrophic effect of cuts means that redundancy is a must, thereby greatly increasing the number of fiber miles of a system.

Bending

If you bend copper wire, electricity flows through the bend without loss. If you bend fiber excessively, light escapes the core and ultimately the fiber may break. The amount of tolerable bend is a function of the refractive index of the core and surrounding cladding. Fibers specify a minimum bend radius; any tighter bending than the specified radius and transmission can stop altogether. Most single-mode fiber can tolerate a bend radius no less than an inch.

Clipping

Fibers transmit signals within an allowable dynamic range, and there cannot be too much or too little laser power. When excessive power is input into an amplitude modulated laser, the laser may shut off briefly. This is known as laser *clipping*. Clipping can occur when several light sources are input simultaneously. This primarily affects wide-area transmission and is a potential problem for hybrid fiber/coaxial cable systems. Furthermore, in cable systems, the symptoms of clipping can look very much like impulse noise on the coaxial cable.

An Improvement to Fiber

Even with the continued purchase and installation of fiber, more capacity will be needed. Fiber is expensive to install: Underground fiber installation in urban areas can be as high as $70,000 per mile. So carriers are looking for ways to better utilize the fiber they have.

Dense wavelength division multiplexing (DWDM) is a new technology that provides in fiber the equivalent of frequency division multiplexing in metallic wire. The idea is that separate parallel channels are transmitted on a single fiber, with one wavelength (or color) for each channel. Current products from Ciena Corporation enable 16 channels of 2.5 Gb each for a total of 40 Gb per fiber for a half mile. DWDM can operate over existing single-mode fiber and therefore substantially reduces upgrade costs for large carriers.

A single fiber bundle of 36 fibers can carry 15 million phone calls at 64 Kbps per call, enough to accommodate the entire voice traffic of the United States at peak hour.

The growth of RBB and the growth of fiber are linked. Fiber alone has the carrying capacity to move data across Core Networks. It will be key to scaling some Access Networks and may even find its way into the home.

Table 2-6 show fiber deployment worldwide in millions of kilometers, according to KMI Corp, a research firm that tracks fiber.

Table 2-6 *Fiber Deployment in Millions of Kilometers*

Year	Fiber Deployment (millions km)
1997	35
1998	41
1999	47
2000	56
2001	66

Wireless Transmission

Most of the technical aspects of wireless transmission will be addressed in Chapter 6. However, we make a few points to compare basic wireless transmission with metallic or fiber media.

Broadcast TV and cellular telephony are familiar forms of wireless communication. Whereas broadcast TV is a high-speed, one-way service and cellular telephony is a low-speed, two-way service, innovations are under consideration to provide high-speed, two-way communication using wireless.

Consumers have shown a willingness to pay for the convenience of being untethered. Cellular telephony has lower-quality, normally fewer service options and definitely higher pricing than wired telephone service. Nonetheless, it has experienced explosive growth worldwide. More than 500 million cellular handsets are in the hands of consumers today, as opposed to perhaps 150 million Internet users. And the lead of cellular telephony seems to be lengthening over Internet users annually. In 1998, more than 125 million cellular handsets were sold worldwide.

The movement to residential wireless high-speed two-way service is spurred on by these factors:

- The observation that consumers will pay a premium for wireless service
- The availability of technology such as digital signal processing (DSP) advances, which make new coding and noise-mitigation possible
- The availability of spectrum as a result of recent government actions in the United States and abroad

The bit-carrying capability of a wireless channel is governed by these factors:

- The amount of spectrum available (more spectrum means more bits)
- The frequency of the channel (lower frequencies means more distance)
- The modulation technique, which governs spectral efficiency

Local Multipoint Distribution Service (LMDS) has the largest amount of contiguous bandwidth available, at 1.1 GHz. This certainly compares favorably with, say, broadcast TV, which has 6 MHz.

Secondly, just as with metal, the higher the frequency, the less distance the signal can travel. LMDS is offered at 28 GHz, whereas broadcast TV is offered starting at 54 MHz. Thus, LMDS can travel only a few miles, and broadcast TV signals can be received for dozens of miles.

Finally, more aggressive modulation can yield more bits per symbol. Satellite services use a robust modulation, such as QPSK, which provides two bits per symbol; because it uses lower frequencies, broadcast digital TV can use more aggressive modulation, such as VSB or OFDM (in Europe).

Impairments

Open-air transmission is subject to serious impairments, and cellular phone subscribers can attest to this. Most impairments are conceptually the same problems as those confronted in wired media, but some variations exist. Among the key impairments are line of sight, multipath, absorption, and interference problems.

Line of Sight

If the frequency used is low enough, then radio signals can penetrate walls and roofs, like TV or cell phones, both of which operate at below 1 GHz. Beyond that, however, line of sight will be required between the transmitter and the receiver. Interference from natural elements such as trees and manmade structures must be taken into effect when deploying antennas and telling customers where they can receive service.

Multipath

When an open-air signal is transmitted, the signal is not radiated on a straight line to the receiver but is subject to dispersion. Attempts are made to guide the radio energy to minimize dispersion, but dispersion happens nonetheless.

If a structure is adjacent to the line of sight, then dispersed signals will bounce off the structure before terminating at the receiver. Because the dispersed signal took a different and longer path than a signal that took line of sight, two signals will arrive at the destination by different paths, hence the term *multipath*. Moreover, because the reflected signal took a longer path, it will arrive at the destination later. The result is delay spread, similar to the case of multimode fiber. Delay spread causes confusion at the receiver, and certain mitigation techniques are required. Excessive delay spreads and an excessive number of paths can render the intended signal indecipherable.

Absorption

For signals of sufficiently high frequency, rain can absorb enough energy to make the intended signal too weak. The only antidote to this is to use lower frequencies (usually very hard) or to use shorter paths by deploying more transmitters (also very hard and expensive). Because of the effects of rain and foliage, certain wireless services are infeasible in tropical geographies.

Interference

Other transmitters that inadvertently use the same spectrum in the same geographical area can adversely affect transmission. This can happen due to faulty equipment. For example, frequency reuse is a useful tool to maximize spectrum use over a wide geographical area. With frequency reuse, two transmitters may be granted use of the same frequency, provided that they are widely separated so as not to interfere with each other. A familiar case is AM radio: A station in Los Angeles may use the same frequency as a station in New York, but they won't interfere.

However, if two transmitters are closely spaced and one of them has a transmitter that is using excessive power, then they may interfere. This is why the Federal Communications Commission has regulations on power.

Spectrum allocation and various wireless services are discussed in Chapter 6.

Transmission Media Summary

Table 2-7 summarizes the maximum bit rate and distance characteristics of various media. These are compared according to generally available engineering practice as of this writing. Innovations are happening that will increase the maximum bit rate and distance.

Table 2-7   *Transmission Media*

Medium	Modulation Technique	Bandwidth	Bit Rate	Distance
Coaxial cable in the downstream path	QAM-64/256	750 MHz, in downstream path	3.75 Gbps, in downstream path	Less than one mile, then add amplifiers
Coaxial cable in the upstream path	QPSK	Various, from 200 kHz to 3.2 MHz	Various, from 400 Kbps to 5 Mbps	Less than one mile, then add amplifiers

Table 2-7   *Transmission Media (Continued)*

Medium	Modulation Technique	Bandwidth	Bit Rate	Distance
Coaxial cable in upstream path	QAM-16	Various, from 200 kHz to 3.2 MHz	Various, from 800 Kbps to about 10 Mbps	Less than one mile, then add amplifiers
Phone wire	DMT, CAP	1 MHz in downstream path	6 Mbps, in downstream path	3 miles
Phone wire	QAM, DMT	30 MHz	51 Mbps	About 200 yards, service called VDSL
Single-mode fiber	OOK and DWDM	16 frequencies of 2.4 GBps each	40 Gbps	350 miles
Broadcast TV spectrum	8-VSB	6 MHz	19.39 Mbps	Greater than 50 miles
LMDS spectrum	QPSK	1.1 GHz	2 Gbps	Less than 3 miles

Many other wireless options depend on the amount of bandwidth and where it is located. Some options are discussed in Chapter 6.

Network Performance

The installation of thousands of route miles of fiber optic cable and the auctioning of many gigahertz of wireless spectrum has created an abundance of bandwidth. While it is unlikely that bandwidth will ever be free, as some pundits predict, it is certainly getting cheaper.

But abundant bandwidth would not be useful without corresponding improvements in the performance of switchers and routers. It is in the performance of hardware that improvements have been striking.

For the past decade, microprocessor innovation—particularly Intel microprocessor innovation—has obeyed Moore's Law, named after the former head of Intel. Moore's law asserts that a doubling of the price performance of microprocessors occurs every 18 months. This rapid improvement in microprocessors has brought the price performance of computers within reach of the consumer. Furthermore, these computers generate the bits that go onto the Internet.

However, a set of innovations exceeds Moore's law, and that is the pace of price/performance of networking equipment. If one measures network equipment performance as the product of number of ports times forwarding capacity, then networking equipment has been exceeding Moore's law by a factor of two since the early 1990s.

Further developments are forthcoming. Numerous startup companies are developing full custom silicon designs that are capable of many gigabits per second on a form factor of 200 square millimeters. Such custom semiconductors will facilitate the development of routers and switches capable of terabit throughput. One such vendor is Switchcore AB of Sweden (www.switchcore.com), which is developing a single-chip 16 Gbps forwarding engine. Other internal developments are taking place at the major switching companies, such as Cisco, and numerous startups around the world.

We therefore conclude that the pace of performance improvement in networking hardware can keep pace with the performance improvement in the underlying media.

Signaling

Media and router performance are increasing very rapidly, so one may conclude that the time of infinite throughput is at hand. However, such is not the case. Signaling could pose a serious impediment to full use of the bandwidth that media and routing/switching will make available.

Signaling refers to the process by which an end system notifies a network that it wants service. The network responds with resources (bandwidth, buffering, and entries in databases) that allow the connection to proceed, or it notifies the end system that resources are not available. At the end of a connection, signaling is used to release resources. During a session, signaling is used to change attributes, for example, adding bandwidth, a third-party, or capabilities such as access to services.

The most familiar example of signaling is picking up a telephone and dialing a phone number. A computer at the telephone company notices when you pick up the phone. Upon receiving the phone number, a route is established to your requested destination, and bandwidth is reserved. If you dial a 500-, 800-, 888-, or 900-number, there is a database lookup to find the "real" phone number that is hidden from the caller, and a route is established to the phone number found in the database. Recent innovations, such as the implementation of packet network in the telephone network, enable all this signaling to occur much more quickly than previously. Even so, the call setup process is time-consuming and expensive. Modern switches are capable of only a few hundred call setups per second.

Signaling requires a round trip from the origination point of the network to the destination to determine whether sufficient resources are available at that instant in time. A round trip goes through the Access Network and the Core Network, during which lots of things happen: Switches reserve resources such as memory, data bases are consulted, transmission links are checked for bandwidth availability, and end systems are validated for proper addressing.

As an alternative to the significant housekeeping chores of telephone signaling, connectionless networking emerged as a highly scalable networking architecture. The Internet is the paradigm of connectionless networking.

Connectionless protocols such as IP impose a minimal signaling burden on data communications equipment and end user devices because they do not have a call setup process. If resources are available, the packet arrives. If not, the packet is discarded. No call setup takes place. It's easier to ask for forgiveness than for permission.

Signaling protocols exist for all networks. In addition to the telephone example cited previously, examples of signaling protocols are Resource Reservation Protocol (RSVP), for IP networks such as the Internet; ATM Q.2931, which establishes call setups for ATM; and various flow setup protocols for packet switching.

Viewpoint: Signaling Rate as an RBB Bottleneck

When one hears of RBB networks, one generally thinks of the requirement for bandwidth and speed. However a strong argument can be made that the fundamental technical bottleneck for RBB is not bandwidth but signaling rate. To take an extreme example for illustration, if a telephone switch were capable of only one call setup per minute, then it wouldn't matter that the switch can transmit 1 Gbps of information. The throughput would never be realized because so few callers could use the switch (of course, no one can talk that fast anyway).

The same holds for data switching equipment. If routers and ATM switches cannot support sufficiently high signaling rates, then the bandwidth offered by fiber optic network cannot be realized.

Current measurements on the Internet, obtained from the North American Network Operators' Group (www.nanog.org), show that one can expect on average less than 20 packets per data flow and that traffic is highly bimodal in terms of packet length. That is, packets are either very short (64 bytes) or very long (1500 bytes, about the maximum length of an IP packet). A large fraction of Internet packets are acknowledgments, which are of minimal length.

The impact of short flow length is to increase the signaling required to sustain maximum throughput through the network. For example if an IP switch has 16 ports of OC48 (2.488 Gb) port speed each, aggregate speed of the switch is 40 Gb. If average packet size is 256 bytes, then the router must transmit 20 million packets per second. If there are 20 packets per flow, then the router must be capable of 1 million flow setups per second. This is far beyond the capability of any IP switch, ATM switch, or voice switch available today—or likely to be available in the near future. These statistics suggest that signaling rate will choke the switch long before packet forwarding is choked.

These calculations are not meant to suggest that a million flow setups per second are needed for RBB. In fact, we don't know what the required flow setup rate is because the applications are not built yet. The point is simply that the bottleneck through a network may not be bandwidth, but signaling. Therefore, applications and networks should be designed with signaling rate in mind.

IP Multicast

IP Multicast is what makes push mode data work over point-to-point networks. In particular, it reduces signaling. It also reduces data volume and tends to synchronize reception of common data flows to multiple receivers. These are useful—even necessary—characteristics for mass market network services.

In the hybrid fiber coax and wireless cases, broadcasting of data is a natural consequence of the physical medium. In the point-to-point wired case, multicast, a software technique that replicates packets efficiently, achieves broadcasting of data. Multicast is more difficult to implement than broadcast because it must track who will and who won't receive packets. Broadcast simply assumes that everyone within receiving range should receive the packet.

IP Multicast Description

Figure 2-12 depicts the unicast case in which there are three clients on a network. Rosie and Jimmy are supposed to receive packets for a particular application from the server, and Junior is not. In this case, the server replicates packets for Rosie and Jimmy, and the router R1 forwards both packets.

Figure 2-12   *Unicast Replication of Packets*

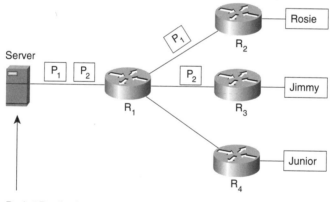

Packet Replication

Figure 2-13 depicts the multicast case for the same application. In this case, the server emits one packet, and the router R1 replicates the packet for Rosie and Jimmy. Work is distributed from the server, a single point, to the network, where many routers can replicate packets. The link between the server and R1 carries only one packet, versus two for the unicast case. Note that R1 is smart enough not to replicate a packet for Junior. Multicasting requires considerably more intelligence in the routers than either the unicast or broadcast models. One reason is the requirement to build packet-distribution trees, which list the nodes through which packets travel to reach all multicast receivers. In Figure 2-13, the distribution tree consists of the server (which serves as the root of the tree) and routers R1, R2, and R3, but not R4.

Figure 2-13   *Multicast Replication of Packets*

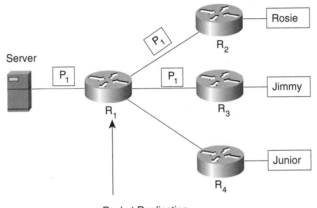

A primary goal of these packet-distribution trees is to identify locations where packet replication is performed and thereby minimize replication. That is, if there are multiple receivers on a given branch of the network, only one copy of the packet should be sent to that branch, where it can then be replicated by an appropriate router.

To take a more complicated scenario, the server can be providing broadcast video services to possibly hundreds of viewers. The server is connected to 10 routers, each of which is connected to 10 routers, which in turn are connected to 10 more, and so on. Figure 2-14 illustrates this example. Let's say there is a total population of 100,000 viewers of whom 1000 are viewing a program at a particular moment.

It would be infeasible for the server to create 1000 copies of every packet to go to each viewer. In this case, the server creates only five packets, and other routers downstream from the server replicate as needed so that all 1000 viewers get the bit stream. As long as there is only one server or source of video, then this is a system that can scale to ultimately serve perhaps millions of viewers.

Multicast is a crucial technology for scaling for RBB networks over wired, point-to-point networks. This technology enables a sender and the point-to-point network delivering the content to transmit the minimal amount of data to the consumer with a minimal amount of signaling.

Figure 2-14 *A More Complex Multicast*

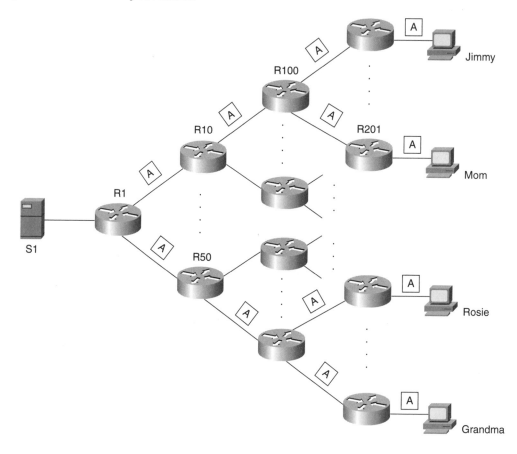

Benefits of IP Multicast

It is believed (we don't know for sure yet because no one has built a large consumer multicast network) that multicast flows tend to be longer in time duration and that packets will on balance be larger than flows and packets in a unicast model. Longer flows occur because user-initiated signaling does not interrupt them as frequently. Longer packets exist on average because the server can package data into larger packets, and there will likely be fewer acknowledgments, which are of minimal packet size. Longer flows and longer packets tend to increase bandwidth and decrease switch utilization.

Finally, there is conjecture that multicast is more compatible with an advertising model for data distribution than HTTP. In an advertising model, content is controlled at a central source for wide distribution with minimal consumer interaction. The advertiser is not relying on the client to click on an icon to receive a screen full of advertising; the advertising is simply sent.

Challenges of Multicast

Multicast can be quite CPU-intensive for large multicast groups in which receivers can come and go frequently, as with the viewing of TV. Another issue of IP multicast is that it uses the UDP rather than TCP at the IP transport layer. UDP improves performance but has the side effect of lacking some robustness.

Other concerns are conditional access (who has access to the multicast stream and how are users are authenticated), invoicing (whether advertising is the only revenue model suitable for multicast), and normal operational management and monitoring. Complex multicast schemes over wires require very careful thought.

Charging for participation in multicast groups will stimulate ISPs to provide more multicast services. The problem is how to charge for the service. Tariffing can be enforced by duration of the multicast, the speed at which the receiver can accept packets and membership fees. To apply tariffs, the service provider must know who is on the multicast at any time, when they leave, at what quality of service they connect, and total duration of the session. Because there is a single source with clients in multiple geographic areas, it is unlikely that multicast tariffing will have any distance sensitivity. Such measurements are works in progress as of this writing.

Content providers of multicasts may have restrictions on who can participate and whether traffic is encrypted. Along with the requirement to tariff the service, some form of directory service probably is required. Variations of security are listed here:

- Unrestricted (anybody can come and go as desired, and traffic is not encrypted)
- Restricted and not encrypted (a limited list of subscribers can come and go as desired, but the traffic is not secured via encryption)
- Restricted, encrypted

An encrypted multicast group will have a unique key that will be distributed securely to users while the multicast is in session.

Because of these concerns, there is relatively little deployment of IP multicast to date. In fact, some thought is being given to an alternative that uses TCP as the transport protocol, called TCPSAT. As its name implies, the original motivation comes from the transmission of IP over satellites. Because satellite is inherently a broadcast medium, observers are wondering out loud whether multicast over satellite (or cable, for that matter) is superior to IP multicast in its pure form.

The Limits of Audio/Visual Perception

While there are limits to what networks can deliver economically, there are also limits to what humans can perceive. Human perception is not infinitely sensitive, so some coarseness of data can be accepted, which tends to make life easier for the network developer.

For example, the limit of human auditory sensitivity is in the range of 20 Hz to 20 kHz per second. So there is no point in a network providing audio service above that pitch.

Television in the United States is shown at 30 frames per second. Generally, there is no need to show at higher rates because viewers can't tell the difference anyway. One exception where humans can tell a difference is for flashing lights. Flashing lights at 30 frames per second is noticeable. Human eyes are much more sensitive to brightness than to color.

Other important picture rates are listed here:

- Film, 24 frames per second (fps)
- European television, 25 fps
- Computer monitors, 72 fps

Human motor response for interactive games is less well calibrated. Some people are quicker than others. If human motor response is less than 1/75th of a second (about 15 milliseconds), then computer monitors will fail to deliver interactive experience for interactive games. If less than 1/30th of a second, then TVs will fail.

Latency for interactive games, therefore, must be less than 33 ms on an NTSC monitor, and less than 15 ms on a proscan monitor. The latency budget for the network is even more stringent because processor delay of the game player must be added.

The threshold of human voice response used by the phone industry is 100 ms. If voice takes longer than 100 ms round-trip, then the conversants can't differentiate a speaker's pause from network delays. This is also a useful number to use as an upper boundary for any latency that requires hand-eye coordination. If you subtract the time it takes the monitor to display an image, then network and computer processing delays are bounded by 67 ms (100 ms–33 ms) for TV sets and 85 ms (100 ms–15 ms) for PC monitors.

At Issue: Bandwidth Guarantees Versus Prioritized Packets

A corollary to the viewpoint that signaling may be the bottleneck in RBB networks is the view that it is preferable to prioritize packets rather than provide bandwidth guarantees in the network to provide reliable transport for video.

In software terms, this raises the question of whether it is worthwhile at all to support the Resource Reservation Protocol (RSVP) and ATM Switched Virtual Circuits or whether to abandon bandwidth guarantees and simply route individual packets based on a priority setting in the packet.

This is an important question because bandwidth guarantees require signaling, an end-to-end exchange of information among network elements as to the availability of resources (bandwidth, buffers) at the time the call request is made by the consumer. If resources are not available, the call is blocked, just as the phone system operates.

The end-to-end resource identification takes time and, as indicated previously, can be the bottleneck of network processing. So far, the industry is supporting bandwidth guarantees. At low levels of consumer acceptance, as during the rollout of new RBB services, end-to-end signaling may not be an issue. But if transport schemes such as packet or SONET develop, then the question will likely recur.

MPEG-2 Compression

MPEG-2 (Moving Picture Experts Group) refers to a family of protocols designed for encoding, compressing, storing, and transmitting audio and video in digital form. MPEG-2 is the protocol of choice for digital video of the HDTV Grand Alliance, but it supports both progressive and interlaced displays.

MPEG-2 is capable of handling standard-definition digital television (SDTV), HDTV, and motion picture films. MPEG-2 supports data transmission, which is used for sending control information to digital set-top boxes and can be used for transmitting user data, such as Web pages. It is backward-compatible with MPEG-1, which means that MPEG-2 decoders can display MPEG-1-encoded files, such as CD-ROMs. This compression technology also has full functionality for video on demand (VoD). MPEG-2 chips are on the market for real-time encoding, and there is a specification for MPEG-2 adaptation over ATM AAL5.

MPEG-2 is rapidly assuming a central role in broadband networking, and it is easy to see why. Without digital compression, RBB would not be possible. Uncompressed video consumes too much bandwidth (see Table 2-8).

Table 2-8   *Uncompressed Video Bandwidth Requirements*

Format	Pixels per Line	Lines per Frame	Pixels per Frame	Frames per Second	Millions of Pixels per Second	Bits per Pixel	Megabits per Second
SVGA	800	600	480,000	72	34.6	8	276.5
NTSC	640	480	307,200	30	9.2	24	221.2
PAL	580	575	333,500	50	16.7	24	400.2
SECAM	580	575	333,500	50	16.7	24	400.2

continues

Table 2-8 *Uncompressed Video Bandwidth Requirements (Continued)*

Format	Pixels per Line	Lines per Frame	Pixels per Frame	Frames per Second	Millions of Pixels per Second	Bits per Pixel	Megabits per Second
HDTV	1920	1080	2,073,600	30	62.2	24	1492.8
Film, various depending on content	2000	1700	3,400,000	24	81.6	32	2611.2

With numbers such as those in Table 2-8, compression is a must for storage and transmission. For digital broadcast video and film, MPEG-2 is the standard among broadcasters and cable operators.

This discussion of MPEG focuses on two technical characteristics: video compression and Systems Operations.

MPEG-2 Video Compression

The formal specification for MPEG-2 video is written in "Generic Coding of Moving Pictures and Associated Audio: Video," Recommendation H.222.0, ISO/IEC 13838-3, April 1995.

MPEG-2 achieves compression in two modes: spatial compression and temporal compression.

Spatial Compression

Spatial compression refers to bit reduction achieved in a single frame. This type of compression uses a combination of tiling the image into blocks of bits (8x8), discrete cosine transform, and Huffman run length encoding to achieve bit reduction. Spatial encoding is lossy—that is, some information is lost in the compression, but *knobs* (control parameters) exist to trade off image loss against compression and processing. Some of these knobs are user-controlled; others are automatically adjusted in the encoding process.

Temporal Compression

Of greater interest for network analysis is *temporal compression*. Unlike spatial compression, temporal compression achieves the majority of bit reduction. Temporal compression refers to bit reduction achieved by removing bits from successive frames by exploiting the fact that relatively few pixels change position in 1/30th of a second, the time period between adjacent frames. A picture can be coded using knowledge of a prior picture and applying motion prediction so that just the motion vectors of blocks or macroblocks are sent instead of coding a complete picture. This achieves superior compression than, say, motion JPEG, which uses the same spatial compression as MPEG-2 but has no provision for temporal compression.

In addition to compression, the quality of video presentation is affected other factors:

- Viewing distance
- Bit rate
- Picture content
- Size of display monitor

These factors must be considered when setting knobs for temporal compression. With respect to bit rate, focus group testing [Cermak] has shown that 3 Mb MPEG-2 video is comparable to normal cable TV and VHS over a wide range of content. However, increasing bit rates to 8.3 Mb does not improve viewing quality significantly: 8.3 Mb MPEG was viewed as comparable to the original uncompressed signal.

Frame Types

Frame types are central to temporal compression. To achieve temporal compression, three different kinds of frames are defined:

- *I-frames*, or intra-frames, which are complete (spatially compressed) frames
- *P-frames*, or predicted frames, which are predicted from I frames or other P frames using motion prediction
- *B-frames*, or bidirectional frames, which are interpolated between I and P frames

P-frames achieve a bit reduction on the order of 50 percent from their corresponding I-frame. B-frames achieve bit reduction on the order of 75 percent. These compression estimates are for 4 Mb MPEG-2 video with standard TV definition and not too much motion. Actual bit reduction differs according to picture content and the mix of I-, P-, and B-frames in the stream and various knob settings for spatial compression.

Frame Ordering and Buffering

Figure 2-15 shows a sequence of MPEG-2 frames in display order. This order is different from the order in which frames are decoded at the consumer set top.

The decoder receives an I-frame (Frame 1). The next frame received is Frame 4, which is a P-frame. Actually, this is a bit of a misnomer. A P-frame is not a picture sent by the encoder. Rather, it would be more precise to say that a P-frame is derived by the decoder from information (motion vectors) sent by the encoder. Frames 1 and 4 are buffered in the decoder and are used to compute B-frames 2 and 3 by interpolation

Figure 2-15   *MPEG Temporal Compression in Display Order*

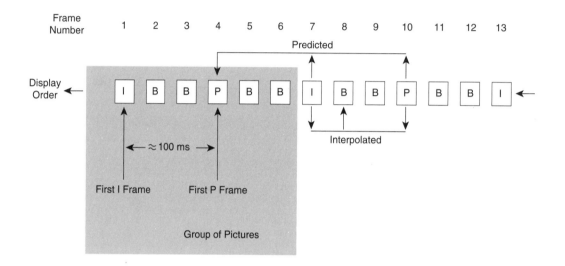

The use of B-frames means that the order in which frames are displayed by the receiver is not the order in which frames are decoded at the receiver. In Figure 2-15, the display order for the first four frames at the receiver is (I, B, B, P). But the order of decoding is (I, P, B, B). This is because the P-frame is computed first and is used with the I-frame to compute the two intervening B-frames.

An I-frame (Frame 7), is transmitted. The original I-frame (Frame 1) is discarded from the decoder buffer memory, and the first P-frame (Frame 4) is used with Frame 7 to interpolate for B-frames 5 and 6. With the receipt of the new I-frame, the process is repeated. If many I-frames exist, picture quality tends to be higher, but so does bandwidth use. Still, frequent use of I-frames is necessary when motion compensation fails to produce good pictures.

The use of B-frames is a controversial issue. They impose buffering requirements on the order of 1 to 2 MB and latency at the receiver. Some vendors, such as General Instruments, an expert and pioneer in the field of digital TV (and an original Grand Alliance participant), have resisted the use of B-frames, believing that the cost to the decoder does not justify bandwidth reduction on the network. Attitudes about B-frames are becoming more friendly as the costs of memory drop, but there are still important tradeoffs among buffer size, latency, bandwidth, set top memory cost, and picture quality.

Using Figure 2-15 again, some control parameters can be defined. First, the term *group of pictures* refers to the set of frames between I-frames, including the first I-frame. The group of pictures is shown in the shaded portion of Figure 2-15. The number of pictures in the group of pictures is called the *I-frame distance*; in this example, the I-frame distance is six. There also is a *P-frame distance*, which is the number of frames between a P-frame and the subsequent P- or

I-frame, including the first P-frame. In Figure 2-15, the P-frame distance is three. I-frame distance and P-frame distance are important knobs. For television, which presents 30 frames per second, I-frame distance is on the order of 15, which means that an I-frame is sent every half-second. P-frame distance is on the order of 0 to 3.

Networking Implications

Frame architecture has implications for networking. I-frames anchor picture quality because P- and B-frames are derived from them. Therefore, it is important that I-frames be transmitted with high reliability, higher than P- or B-frames. Thus, when transmitting MPEG frames over ATM or Frame Relay, it is advisable that I-frames be given priority.

MPEG-2 creates streams of compressed video with timestamps. This timestamp is provided inside an MPEG-2 packet so that the timing and ordering of the I-, B-, and P-frames is correct. Note that because the MPEG-2 layer itself has a timestamp (Program Clock Reference, or PCR), it does not depend on the network layer to provide a timestamp for it. That is one reason why the ATM Forum decided that AAL5 would be used for carrying MPEG-2 streams rather than AAL1, which has a synchronous residual timestamp (SRTS).

Encoder Operation

The job of the encoder is to compute compressed target frames from a perfect pixel-by-pixel image received by the camera. The image received by the camera is called the *original image*. Before any spatial compression is performed, the encoder caches the original image. As the encoder is calculating the motion-compensated frame, it compares work in process with the original frame. If the encoder decides that the original frame and the target frame are hopelessly out of sync (say, due to a scene change), then it can abort the process and immediately calculate a fresh I-frame. In addition to scene changes, other cases in which motion compensation breaks are when background figures are covered or uncovered by foreground figures or during extreme changes in luminosity.

MPEG-2 does not specify how an encoder works; it specifies only how the decoder works. The encoder's only explicit responsibility is to produce an MPEG-2-compliant bit stream; how it does so is up to the vendor.

The rocket science of encoders lies in determining as early as possible when the original and target frames are out of sync and taking proper corrective action, within bandwidth requirements. Encoders can vary widely in determining when motion compensation is no longer required and turning knobs other than simply recomputing I-frames.

Real-time encoding is made possible by the speed of modern processors. If one assumes that a processor capable of 200 million instructions per second, and if a frame must be displayed 30 times per second, that yields a little more than 6 million instructions per frame that can be used. It is expected that software encoders will be sufficient for most images, although for demanding scenes and environments, hardware assistance will be required.

MPEG-2 Systems Operation

Compressed video and audio streams are just the first step in defining a compression system. MPEG also defines an end-to-end software architecture for linking bit streams to programming and control information. This is defined in the MPEG-2 Systems specification, "Generic Coding of Moving Pictures and Associated Audio: Systems," Recommendation H.222.0, ISO/IEC 13838-1, April 1995. The following sections overview the important components of MPEG-2 systems operation.

MPEG-2 Transport Stream Packet Format

MPEG-2 Systems Standard defined two data stream formats: the *Transport Stream (TS),* which can multiplex several programs and is optimized for use in networks where data loss is likely; and the *Program Stream,* which is optimized for multimedia applications, for performing systems processing in software. The TS is used for video over fiber, satellite, cable, ISDN, ATM, and other networks, and also for storage on digital videotape and other devices. For purposes of RBB, attention has centered on the MPEG-2 TS as the format, so we will focus on it here.

The basic difference between the Transport Stream and the Program Stream is that the TS uses fixed-length packets and the Program Stream uses variable-length packets. The TS has a fixed length of 188 bytes, with a variable-length header of a minimum 32 bits. Table 2-9 displays field identifiers, field length, and function of the TS packet.

Table 2-9   *Transport Stream Packet Format*

Field	Length in Bits	Function
Synchronization	8	0x47
Transport error indicator	1	Unrecoverable bit error exists
Payload unit start indicator	1	Control information
Transport priority	1	Gives priority to this packet over other packets with the same PID
Program Identifier (PID)	13	Identifies content (such as control table) or audio, video, closed-captioned streams
Scrambling	2	00 means no scrambling; the three other values are user-defined
Adaptation control	2	00 Reserved
		01 No Adaptation field exists
		10 Adaptation field exists, but there is no payload
		11 Adaptation and payload exist
Adaptation field	256	See following fields
—Length	8	Length of Adaptation field

Table 2-9   *Transport Stream Packet Format (Continued)*

Field	Length in Bits	Function
—Program Clock Reference (PCR)	42	Timing information
—Lots of Other Flags	Variable	

The Adaptation field can be of length 0 to 256 bits. If it is greater than 0, bits are taken from the data portion of the packet, or *payload*, to yield a total packet length of 188 bytes.

The fields with network implications are the PID and transport priority. Certain PIDs and packets with high transport priority should be given preference by the network. All other fields are used primarily for image decoding.

Program Identifiers

As noted in Table 2-9, 13 bits of the header constitute the *Program Identifier (PID)*. The PID identifies the contents of a Transport Stream packet. Most Transport Stream packets will carry digital audio, video, or closed-captioned text data for a TV program. The PID identifies which program the data is for. In addition, four PIDs are used for control purposes, specifically 0, 1, n, and m. Table 2-10 summarizes these and other PIDs.

Table 2-10   *PIDs and Their Functions*

PID	Payload
0	Program Association Table (PAT), which points to the Program Map Table (PMT).
1	Conditional Access Table, which contains authentication information.
n	PMT, pointed to by PAT, which binds PIDs to particular programs.
m	Network Information Table (NIT), an optional field that identifies physical transport, such as cable channel frequency, satellite transponder, modulation scheme, and interleaving depth. Its use is private and is subject to the whims of the carrier.
0x0010 through 0x1FFE	User data and program content. These PIDs carry audio, video, and closed-caption data.
0x1FFF	Null packets, used for rate adaptation.

PIDs are of particular significance for channel selection. In the analog world, channel selection is performed when the receiver tunes to a single subband of a frequency multiplex broadband channel. In the digital world, channel selection is performed by joining a broadcast stream of digitally encoded packets. In the case of MPEG-2, tuning is PID selection.

A television program or movie consists of at least three streams: a video stream, an audio stream, and a text stream, containing closed-captioned text. Other streams may be associated with the program, such as foreign language audio. The PID identifies the streams.

Each program, therefore, consists of at least three PIDs. Programs are mapped to PIDs through the PMT. When a consumer wishes to view a channel, she consults an electronic program guide that displays what's available to watch, and then the user makes a selection; in turn, a remote tuner selects the PIDs for decoding.

Figure 2-16 illustrates the interactions of the Program Association Table, Program Map Table, and the Transport Stream.

Figure 2-16 *PID Usage*

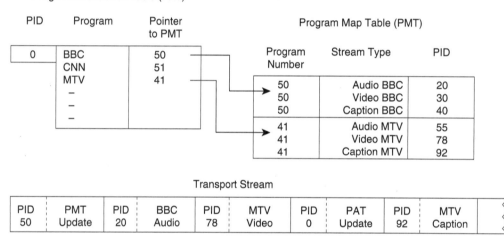

The figure shows a Transport Stream consisting of a multiplex of three TV channels: BBC, CNN, and MTV. The Program Association Table (PAT, PID=0) has an inventory of all channels available on the TS and a PID pointer to the PMT entry, which identifies the PIDs of the data streams for each channel. In this case, Transport Packets with PID=50 will have information about BBC, namely which other PIDs will carry audio, video, and caption data for BBC. Likewise, any TS packet with PID=41 will carry PMT information about MTV. Note that PID=0 updates will occur to refresh the PAT. As an example of standardization of control parameters, the Grand Alliance and the DVB Project have specifications on how frequently the PAT and PMTs are updated, in both cases at subsecond intervals.

Five transport stream packets are shown in Figure 2-16 and are described as follows:

Packet	PID Value	MPEG TS Payload
1	50	Contains update information for the BBC PMT. For example, it may be necessary to change the BBC video PID.
2	20	Contains BBC audio. The payload contains MPEG encoded audio for the BBC program. The set top decoder which is tuned to BBC would intercept this packet to render the audio feed.
3	78	Contains MTV Video. The payload contains MPEG encoded video for the MTV program. The set-top decoder, which is tuned to MTV, would intercept this packet and render it for viewing.
4	0	Is the PAT Update. Periodically, the PAT must be updated so that there is an accurate set of PIDs.
5	92	Contains MTV caption. The payload contains text information, which is displayed for closed captioning.

When a viewer wants to watch BBC, he won't know that PIDs 20, 30, and 40 carry BBC packets. But the decoder knows from the PAT and PMTs what PIDs to select.

Another use of PMT entries is to identify pure data streams, such as Internet service. For example, the PAT can point to a PMT that identifies, say, stock quote push mode data, which can be distributed inside IP packets inside MPEG frames. Users who desire stock quotes can select the corresponding PIDs, just as they would select a TV program.

The example of Figure 2-16 also demonstrates that the stream of PIDs on a channel represents a multiplex of, in this case, two TV programs: MTV and BBC. Recall that a single 6 MHz channel can carry 27 Mbps. With MPEG-2, a program can use as little as 3 to 5 Mbps. It is through the use of PMTs and PIDs that programs can be multiplexed on a single channel.

Another important notion is timing. Frames for a particular program must be displayed at the proper time, and the associated audio must be rendered concurrently. For example, in Figure 2-16, frames 3 and 5 (MTV video and captioning) must be displayed currently. Because the audio, video, and closed-captioned packets occur at various places in the multiplex, presentation timing must be coordinated. Frames 3 and 5 will have a presentation time stamp (PTS) that indicates to the decoder when to display.

The presentation time stamp is an offset of the Program Clock Reference (PCR) in Table 2-9. Formally, an MPEG television program is a set of packets having a common PCR. For example, in the multiplex of packets in Figure 2-16, MTV will have a different PCR from BBC. That is, all MTV packets will be relative to the MTV PCR, and all BBC packets will be relative to the BBC PCR.

Electronic Program Guides

A key application and illustrative use of MPEG systems tables is the *electronic program guide* (EPG).

The EPG is the key piece of video real estate to be seen by the consumer. Its importance is roughly equivalent to the first page of a Web site portal. Its most common form is the onscreen program guide, which simultaneously permits single-key VCR advanced recording. This is intellectual property patented by (and aggressively enforced by) Gemstar (Pasadena, California; Nasdaq GMST). In addition to broadcast fare, these also contain information on pay-per-view events, such as pricing, parental guidance ratings and language.

Data for EPGs is stored in a hierarchical set of tables collectively known as the Service Information Protocol (SI), which are downloaded inside MPEG TS packets to the consumer set-top box. Well-known PIDs are used in the U.S. standard (ATSC, www.atsc.org) to signal the set-top box to decode and store the SI tables. In the European DVB standard (www.dvb.org), the SI PIDs are not statically assigned but rather are pointed to by another table, allowing for an additional level of indirection and, hence, flexibility, should PID definitions change over time. The view in the United States is that static PIDs offer a faster program-acquisition time.

The protocol used to create the EPG is the service information (SI) protocol. The SI provides information on available services, where the services are located, and how the services are categorized. For example, the SI indicates that the UCLA-USC football game is on channel xx, which is on transponder number tt on satellite zz, where xx, tt, and zz are numbers stored in the SI tables. Furthermore, the game may be aggregated with other similar athletic events or other PPV events into groups of programs. In Europe, groups of programs are called bouquets; in the United States, they are called virtual channels.

The organization of the tables is discussed using the DVB specification because it is a little more general than the American table organization. Otherwise, the American specification is nearly identical. There are four SI tables:

- Network Information (NIT);
- Bouquet Association (BAT);
- Service Description (SDT);
- Event Information (EIT);

The NIT (PID 16) contains information on the Access Network carrying the program. It indicates the medium (cable, satellite, MMDS, terrestrial DTV) and, given that context, identifies static information.

For example, for every satellite the NIT identifies satellite name (such as Galaxy V), polarization, position, and transponder number. For cable systems, it identifies the frequency used, modulation scheme, FEC, and interleave depth.

The BAT identifies groups of programs. Any program can be a member of multiple bouquets. For example a UCLA football game can be a member of a UCLA bouquet, or a football bouquet, or both. In addition to bouquet name and a set of programs, the BAT also has conditional access (security) information, language, bouquet descriptor, and country availability information. This latter feature is important in Europe, where the national boundaries are close, which means that licensing must be enforced on a smaller geographical basis. The bouquet descriptor is used by the set-top box to key into a table of icons for display on the monitor.

The SDT identifies characteristics of the MPEG TS, such as which bouquet it is a member of, what events it contains, country availability, running status (for VoD or nVoD events), and a service descriptor, again used to key into a table of icons. A feature of the SDT is that it permits a matrix of information on multiple services to be displayed on the TV monitor. The cells of the matrix could be still pictures, MPEG clips, or text. The EIT contains information specific to an event. It contains start time, duration, parental guidance, language, event name, content descriptor, running status, security information, and other information. It contains information on one or more events following the current event, or preview information on programs on other transport streams.

SI tables must be stored, refreshed frequently, and displayed from the consumer set-top box. This means that the set-top box must have a sophisticated file management and operating system, like any other computer. Naturally, Microsoft thinks it owns this space, and acquisitions such as WebTV indicate their interest in operating systems for consumer entertainment environments. But there are others contenders as well, including PowerTV, used in Scientific Atlanta (NYSE:SFA) digital set tops, OS9 by Microware, and others. The operating system environment for set tops is to be one of the most contentious commercial battles in the residential broadband business.

The DVB specification predates ATSC. When ATSC analyzed the DVB work, it apparently decided that improvements could be made to speed channel-acquisition time. DVB generally uses more redundant information in tables, whereas ATSC uses more static information and is judged to be more complex. It remains to be seen how much of a performance advantage, if any, the ATSC specification has.

MPEG-2 Challenges

While MPEG-2 compression has succeeded in producing very high compression ratios (upwards of 50:1), some caveats remain.

Picture Quality

Both spatial and temporal compression produce signal loss. How well two different scenes will compress is not always obvious.

For example, a cable operator testing digital video control parameters used an auto race and a fishing scene as viewing samples. The auto race showed cars on a racetrack speeding by billboards. The fishing scene showed sunlight glistening off the water and leaves flapping in a breeze. Intuition suggests that the fast-motion racing scene would be more difficult to compress than the slow-moving fishing scene.

The fishing scene was very pretty in analog. But in MPEG-2, the motion compensation broke down. MPEG-2 had problems with the leaves and the water because luminosity changed rapidly in a lot of places on the image. The result was a poor picture, even at relatively high bit rates. In the same test, auto racing looked quite good at a lower bit rate. MPEG-2 temporal compression accounts well for the movement of objects from frame to frame through the use of motion vectors, but there is no explicit temporal compression for quick and numerous luminosity changes from frame to frame.

Scenarios that represent video compression problems for MPEG-2 are listed here:

- Quick changes in luminosity at multiple places in the image, as demonstrated in the fishing scene; flashbulbs also present problems
- Circular motion because motion compensation assumes objects move in a straight line
- Sharp, high-contrast edges, as for fonts and graphics
- Multiple motions, where a single image splits into two or more, which confuses motion compensation
- Alternating wavy lines, a variation on problems posed by circular motion

Decoder Costs

B-frames impose a memory and processing requirement on the decoder. Most new MPEG decoders with B-frames require more than 2 MB of memory. As higher-resolution video becomes popular, bandwidth restrictions may become even more important, which will tend to increase the use of B-frames and thus the cost of decoders.

Datacasting

Data services such as Web access and text annotation of broadcasts will be accommodated within MPEG streams. The adaptation of IP within MPEG is under investigation by the ATSC, as discussed in Chapter 1, "Market Drivers," in the "Datacasting" section.

Low Latency Modes

B-frames also impose latency. Latency is not a big issue for broadcast, VoD, or nVoD. But it is a problem for real-time video, such as videoconferencing. Low latency forms of MPEG are needed to reduce or eliminate B-frames. MPEG has a low latency mode in which buffers are allowed to underflow for extended periods of time. When this occurs, the decoder may lose timing information until the underflow situation is corrected. Further work is in progress on low latency MPEG.

Tighter Integration with Networking

A mechanism is needed by which the networking layer and MPEG transport can help each other. A relatively straightforward case would be one in which the network gives priority to I-frames and significant PIDs. The network should be made aware of the existence of I-frames and should give them preferential queuing. Preferential treatment should also be given to PAT and PMT updates, packets with PCRs, and frames explicitly marked for high priority.

MPEG-2 is a major architectural element of digital TV. It specifies audio and video compression, but, more importantly, it defines a framework or system specification to organize the data elements.

MPEG-4

Even as Access Networks are becoming faster, advances in computing power on smaller platforms continues to spur development of new compression algorithms and standards. Just as MPEG-2 was being deployed, the MPEG committee embarked on a new approach to compression and controls with the development of MPEG-4. (By the way, MPEG-3 was originally intended as a specification for high definition. However, HDTV became embedded in MPEG-2, so the MPEG-3 dropped by the wayside).

MPEG-4 takes a novel approach to image processing. With MPEG-2, a visual scene is considered as a set of colored pixels. In MPEG-4, a scene is considered as a set of software objects, not unlike the composition of Web pages. Each object could have its own compression scheme. A computing device on the viewer's premises would decode each software object—that is, make a picture or sound out of each object, and display it at the correct position on the viewer's screen at the correct time. By decomposing a scene into objects, greater compression can be obtained to achieve a comparable picture because some objects can be heavily compressed and others more lightly compressed

For example, consider a soccer game. A scene can be considered as a collection of audio and video software objects. One object may be the playing field; another object may be the sky. The playing field is relatively static and therefore can be treated with motion compensation vectors. But the ball can be displayed with MPEG-2 compression, and the players can be displayed with wavelet or a more advanced form. Similarly, the announcer's voice may be encoded using

Dolby AC-3 for good clarity, but the crowd noise can be encoded with a less-precise, more highly compressed technique.

More important perhaps than mere compression, software objects facilitate interactivity. Going back to the soccer game, another object could be a billboard in the distance or on the railing of the stadium. That billboard would be a software object, essentially a hyperlink, that can be customized according to the audience. There is already a variety of insertion techniques by which an MPEG stream is augmented with local content. The viewer may be able to click on that billboard to get further information. In fact, it would be possible in principle for the local affiliate to have its own set of billboards and thereby have its own advertising.

When a scene is decomposed into a set of software objects, there is the possibility for higher degrees of compression (because some objects can be highly compressed, unlike pixelization of MPEG-2 images), greater interactivity (because viewers can interact with specific objects rather than the entire scene), and a richer set of authoring tools (because the objects can be independently created).

A key element in the definition is the file format—that is, how bits are to be laid on in a stream for authoring and distribution. A number of options currently exist, such as Real Video (Real Networks) and Advanced Streaming Format (ASF, Microsoft). But the early lead is held by Quicktime (Apple Computer), originally defined in 1991, which was recently endorsed by the International Standards Organization (ISO) as a file format standard. The fact that Quicktime was developed nearly a decade ago has helped it become the most widely distributed media format on Web pages, now supporting nearly 100,000 multimedia Web sites. The decision to endorse Quicktime was approved by IBM, Sun, Silicon Graphics, and Netscape, no doubt largely with the motivation that it was not Microsoft.

The issue with MPEG-4 is the decoding cost. Because decoders will be in consumer appliances, it is important that they be inexpensive. But current estimates are that a decoder will require from 2 billion to 10 billion operations per second to yield NTSC-quality video. The encoders will need to be even more powerful. If MPEG-2 is a lesson, then the encoder will require more than 10 times the compute power of the decoder. But improvements in semiconductors and the lure of object-based rendering make the prospects for MPEG-4 positive.

In addition to MPEG-4, other techniques can be considered, such as enhancements to HTML, such as Extensible Markup Language (XML). The choice of MPEG tools or Web tools is a key battleground of how the software environment for RBB will evolve. That choice is in part dependent on one's view of how much interactivity users will demand and whether the center of gravity of RBB content will tilt toward digital TV or to Web browsing.

Summary

RBB investment and deployment will require familiarity with a wide range of technical subjects. New technology creates new businesses. Fiber optics, noise-mitigation techniques, MPEG, and advanced data networking techniques such as multicast have made residential broadband technically feasible. Table 2-11 summarizes the technical foundations of RBB covered in this chapter.

With the wide perspective on market drivers and technology established in the first two chapters of this book, the following chapters turn to a more in-depth consideration of particular kinds of networks and their implications for residential broadband. In each case, technical, financial, regulatory, and market obstacles and facilitators of the networks will be considered. Cable networks are covered in more detail in Chapter 3.

Table 2-11   *Summary of Technical Foundations of RBB*

Technology	Factors Supporting Use in RBB	Factors Challenging Use in RBB
Metal Wire Transmission	Is an entrenched, widely employed infrastructure.	Has high-frequency transmission on metal wire that is especially subject to impairments. Uses metal wire, which is prone to external impairments that cause noise.
Modulation Schemes	Is a required aspect of communications; a number of robust, well-established, well-understood techniques exist.	Uses multiple modulation schemes; relative lack of standardization limits interoperability and raises costs.
Noise-Mitigation Techniques	Combats the effects of ingress and burst noise, without incurring a round-trip delay. Is viewed as a required aspect of communications.	Creates delay. Requires compute power and buffering.
Fiber Optic Transmission	In comparison with metal wire transmission: increases bit rate; covers greater distance without amplification or regeneration of signal; lowers maintenance cost; requires less space; requires less weight; safer to handle. Is immune to eavesdropping.	Has unique impairments of its own: microfissures; difficulties in handling; incapability to be bent like wire; precise alignment of lasers required. Uses laser transceivers, which are more expensive than electrical counterparts. Is immune to eavesdropping.
Signaling	Is a required aspect of communications. Uses connectionless protocols, such as IP, which minimize signaling burdens and promote scalability. Works with packet networks in telephone systems, which enable faster signaling than previously possible.	Is time-consuming and imposes a processing burden on communications software. Can be the bottleneck that restricts bandwidth through networks.

continues

Table 2-11   *Summary of Technical Foundations of RBB (Continued)*

Technology	Factors Supporting Use in RBB	Factors Challenging Use in RBB
IP Multicast	Enables broadcast of data and video over wired networks. Is an important scaling technique for Internet because it reduces signaling and packet replication.	Uses complex software, requiring the cooperation of client systems. Uses complex accounting and security. Uses scaling that is difficult for multiple sources of multicasts. Is not widely deployed by Internet service providers.
MPEG-2 Compression	Achieves substantial reduction in storage and bandwidth requirements for audiovisual content; without it digital media would not be practical. Defines a framework for organizing program information.	Does not work well for all video content; tradeoffs in visual quality are required. Makes networking more complex; requires integration with networking. Imposes delays.
MPEG-4 Compression	Achieves substantial reduction in storage and bandwidth requirements for audiovisual content. Supports interactivity by allowing users to interact with objects rather than pixels. Leverages Quicktime file format. Would enable HDTV to coexist with other services on the same channel.	Requires substantial computer power in the receiver. Uses standards that are not completed.

References

Books

Claiborne, David. *Mathematical Preliminaries for Computer Networking.* New York: John Wiley and Sons, 1990.

Hewlett-Packard. *Testing Digital Video.* Cupertino, California: Hewlett-Packard, 1997.

Varaiya, Pravin, and Jean Walrand. *High-Performance Communication Networks.* San Francisco, CA: Morgan Kaufman Publishers, 1996.

Articles

Balabanian, Vahe, Liam Casey, Nancy Greene, and Chris Adams, "An Introduction to Digital Storage Media-Command and Control." *IEEE Communications* Vol.34, No. 11: November 1996.

Cermak, Gregory, Sandra Teare, James Stoddard, and Ernest Tweedy. "Consumer Acceptance of MPEG2 Video at 3.0 to 8.3 Mb/s," Proceedings of the International Society for Optical Engineering, Volume 2917: 19-22 November 1996

Chiariglione, Leonardo (Convenor), "Generic Coding of Moving Pictures and Associated Audio: Systems." *Recommendation H.222.0* ISO/IEC 13838-1: April 1995.

Ciena Corporation. "Form S-1 Registration Statement, Preparatory to the Initial Public Offering of Ciena Stock." 12 December 1996.

Dutton, Harry. "High Speed Networking Technology." *IBM International Technical Support Centers* GG24-3816-01: June 1993.

Hong, Peter, "A Starlet's Secret Life—As an Engineer." *Los Angeles Times*: 30 August 1997.

Koenen, Rob. "MPEG-4:Multimedia for our Time." *IEEE Spectrum* Vol 16, No. 2: February 1999.

Quayle, Alan, and BT Labs. "Telecommunications Operators Needs and Requirements of an Interface between the Core and Access of a Broadband Network." *ATM Forum/96-1045*: August 1996.

Internet Resources

www.atmforum.com

The ATM Forum, which has a residential broadband working group

www.cisco.com (search on whatever you need, such as "multicast")

Cisco's Web page has many good white papers. Use the search engine to find information on many topics.

www.lucent.com/ideas/perspectives/trends/index.html

Broad technical perspective from Bell Labs

www.davic.org

The home page of DAVIC

www.ietf.org

Internet Engineering Task Force Home Page

www.protocols.com

Pointers to network protocols

www.ntonc.org

National Transparent Optical Network Consortium

www.ipmulticast.com

Home of the IP Multicast Initiative

www.isi.edu

The complete set of Internet documents maintained by the University of Southern California Information Sciences Institute

www.oiforum.com

The home page of the Optical Internetworking Forum (OIF)

cas.et.tudelft.nl/~glas/ssc/technOld/

Spread spectrum overview written by Jack Glas of the University of Delft, Netherlands

sss-mag.com

Spread spectrum scene, with lots of spread spectrum, wireless, and RF info

www.cselt.it/mpeg

The home page for MPEG standards

www.mpeg.org

More information on MPEG-2 and MPEG-4

www.isen.com

Why stupid networks are a smart idea

www.fcc.gov/oet/faqs/freqchart.html

FCC FAQ on spectrum allocation

www.ntia.doc.gov/osmhome/allochrt.html

U.S. spectrum allocation chart according to the NTIA of the U.S. Department of Commerce; shows how to order a very nice wall chart

strategis.ic.gc.ca/SSG/sf01608e.html

Spectrum allocation in Canada, according to Industry Canada

www.mtnd.com

Mitsubishi Telecommunications Network Division

This chapter covers the following topics:

- History of Cable
- Business Rationale
- Architecture
- Hybrid Fiber Coaxial (HFC) Systems
- Upstream Transmission
- Digital Video Services
- Data Services
- Integration of Video and Data
- Business Obstacles
- Summary

CHAPTER 3

Cable TV Networks

AT&T, formerly Ma Bell, is the largest provider of cable TV service in the United States. This one simple observation encapsulates the breathtaking changes that have occurred in the cable industry just since 1997. In late 1997, it would have been totally unforeseen (except, perhaps, in the mind of Michael Armstrong, CEO of AT&T) that AT&T would be the kingpin of cable in 1999. But with the acquisitions of TCI and MediaOne for more than $100 billion, AT&T directly serves 25 million U.S. homes for TV and has agreements for access to another 30 million homes for telephone service through agreements with Time Warner Cable and Comcast. This is a complete sea change in the structure of the American communications industry.

Other companies have invested in cable as well. Microsoft has acquired a stake in Comcast, and European cable operators and Paul Allen's Vulcan Ventures have invested in Charter and Marcus cable. The recapitalization of the cable industry has alleviated a major concern of the cable industry, namely that cable would not have the financing to go toe to toe against the phone companies. That is not a problem any longer. In addition to recapitalization, cable has undertaken technical changes that have improved its speed and operations. Cable has embarked on industry standardization as it prepares to digitize its services. Before discussing these changes, we first take a look at the recent past and present of this very dynamic service industry.

Present cable TV networks are shared, wired networks used primarily for one-way television transmission. In this case, the term *shared* refers to the fact that multiple households connect to a common piece of copper wire. This topology minimizes the number of route miles of wiring and is a natural topology for broadcast. However, cable networks require demultiplexing of traffic from different households to enforce security, provide bandwidth guarantees, and problem isolation. These problems are being addressed with new software techniques; cable networks are being upgraded for two-way transit and higher-speed communications. In this revamped mode, plans exist to use cable networks for digital TV, telephony, and high-speed Internet access.

As a result, cable TV networks have the early lead over telephone companies and other service providers in offering broadband services in the home, particularly for Internet access. AtHome (www.home.net; Nasdaq: ATHM) reported 460,000 cable data subscribers in the company's first-quarter 1999 filing to the SEC. At that time, there were an estimated 800,000 cable data subscribers worldwide. One of the most impressive statistics is that Shaw Cable of Canada reported 100,000 cable data subscribers, nearly 7 percent of its entire subscriber base. Cable TV networks have speed, ubiquity, and experience in offering residential services, especially television. These advantages make it possible to offer digital television and high-speed Internet access to millions of consumers quickly over the existing network. Furthermore, cable TV is managed by executives with a history of entrepreneurial spirit who have overcome great odds to create the businesses they have, despite the recent infusion of fresh capital.

Such speed and multichannel potential raise the possibility that enhanced cable systems can be considered as platforms for innovative applications, such as video on demand (VoD), interactive television, and networked games. Time Warner Cable considers its new cable full-service networks as development platforms for such applications. The company is particularly interested in the use of software objects to enhance the viewer's experience. Treating the cable network as an application platform fosters a new sense of creative development.

However, despite their apparent advantages, cable operators are faced with commercial and technical challenges as they try to keep their lead in the race of supplying broadband to the home. This chapter covers the technical and business obstacles that face facilitators of cable television's transition to residential broadband. Primarily, it focuses on digital TV and data applications.

History of Cable

Community Antenna Television (CATV), commonly called cable TV, was invented to solve a dire consumer problem: poor TV reception. Rabbit ears and rooftop antennas don't suffice for people who live in valleys where nearby hills block good over-the-air reception, such as in the upper Appalachian mountains. In fact, according to the Pennsylvania Cable TV association (www.pcta.com/histcabl.html), cable TV began in Pennsylvania (although others contend that CATV was born in Oregon). The following message was posted on the mailing list of the Society of Cable Television Engineers:

```
SITE
OF THE FIRST COMMUNITY ANTENNA
TELEVISION INSTALLATION
IN THE UNITED STATES.
COMPLETED, FEBRUARY 1949
ASTORIA, OREGON

CABLE TELEVISION
WAS INVENTED AND
DEVELOPED BY
L. E. 'ED' PARSONS
ON THANKSGIVING DAY
1948. THE SYSTEM
CARRIED THE FIRST TV
TRANSMISSION BY
KRSC-TV CHANNEL 5
SEATTLE. THIS MARKED
THE BEGINNING OF
CABLE TV.
```

Whether Cable TV began on the East Coast or the West Coast, it was originally a small-town phenomenon. The culture of rural independence and opportunism continues to differentiate this industry from its competitors.

Despite their best efforts, cable TV operators were a struggling lot from their beginning until the mid-1970s. The business was very capital intensive, and the operator had to install thousands of miles of wires, erect buildings to house satellite and television transmission facilities, negotiate franchise agreements with municipalities, and conclude programming agreements before the first dollar was made. This was a risky investment proposition, especially because cable offered no distinctive programming at the time. It was funded primarily by subscription and local advertising, but there was no national advertising and little transactional revenue from pay-per-view.

Furthermore, cable had touchy relationships with the cities in which it operated. To offer service, cable required franchises from municipalities in which it provided service. Until the 1980s, local authorities exerted strong control over cable operators. Cities charged large franchise fees, could require carriage of local broadcast, and regulated prices to their citizens. These were costs that over-the-air broadcasters did not have, and they put cable at a competitive disadvantage. However, the difficulties in dealing with the cities were offset by the fact that the cable operator got an exclusive franchise to operate in the locality.

Even today, the subject of city-cable operator relationships continues to be sensitive. Franchise renewals are frequently challenged by consumers and cities asserting that the cable operator has offered poor service or has not fulfilled other provisions of the franchise agreement. Some franchise agreements included provision of public, educational, and government (PEG) access to channel capacity, increased bandwidth, and service-level agreements.

So, undercapitalized and lacking compelling content that could differentiate cable from NBC, ABC, and CBS, cable did not catch on in a big way until the mid-1970s. In 1974, a technological innovation occurred that was to launch the cable industry out of its funk and into two-thirds of American homes today. That innovation was the commercial satellite.

Until the mid-1970s, satellites had been used exclusively for government purposes, mostly defense or space exploration. With satellites, however, programs from multiple producers could be broadcast on a single transponder (aggregated) and could be rebroadcast to cable operators all over the country. This provided a means for producers to challenge the ironclad hold that the movie distributors had on the distribution of first-run movies. Originally, satellite distribution was not directed at the broadcasters, but rather at the film industry.

The first company to aggregate and rebroadcast for cable distribution was Time Inc., which founded Home Box Office (HBO) in 1974. Viewers who wanted to watch HBO paid a monthly fee to watch programs they could not watch on over-the-air television. HBO caught on, and cable was on its way because it had content (movies) the broadcasters did not have, at prices that were competitive with or cheaper than movie theater tickets and video rentals. HBO is still the largest premium cable network in the United States, with more than 20 million subscribers.

After the success of HBO, other programmers followed. A climate for more original programming was created, and new channels carried only on cable—such as MTV, ESPN, and CNN—became part of popular culture both in the United States and abroad.

Cable had the advantage of greater channel capacity compared with over-the-air broadcasts. Some over-the-air bandwidth is set aside for use by police, fire, military, air traffic control, radio astronomers, and other public uses. The need to share the airwaves with public services, coupled with certain engineering issues, limits the number of over-the-air channels for a given metropolitan area to roughly 10 to 12. However, it was possible for cable systems to offer at least 30 channels over 300 MHz of cable bandwidth. Updated systems using fiber-optic cables have up to 750 MHz of bandwidth and offer more than 100 channels.

Decisions regarding use of over-the-air spectrum is controlled by the Office of Spectrum Management of the Federal Communications Commission (FCC). For details of spectrum allocation in the United States, see the Web page for the U.S. Department of Commerce Office of Spectrum Management (OSM), at www.ntia.doc.gov/osmhome/osmhome.html.

Because of superior reception, innovative programming, and increased channel capacity, cable operators succeeded in developing a new industry beginning with its inception in the 1950s. Table 3-1 shows some key cable statistics as of 1997.

Table 3-1   *Number of Cable Subscribers per Region*

North America	73 million
Western Europe	43 million
Asia	19 million
Latin America	13 million
Eastern Europe	9 million
Worldwide cable subscribers	157 million

Cable's Business Rationale for Residential Broadband

Later sections in this chapter consider some of the business challenges and disincentives to cable's transition to RBB. The obstacles will be easier to understand after discussions regarding technical aspects of the upgraded system. Understanding the incentives, however, is pretty straightforward.

First, there is a defensive aspect to cable's motivation for transitioning to RBB. RBB service is a necessary defensive measure against the threat of direct broadcast satellite and new telco services. In particular, DBS has signed more than 9 million subscribers, threatening cable's customer base for premium pay channel service.

Defensive measures aside, extending the capabilities of cable TV networks from the current broadcast video business to high-speed Internet access seems natural. Cable has a large capital base to use as leverage for incremental applications. In addition to being the incumbent, cable has specific technical and business advantages with which it can succeed in providing a wide range of high-speed home services:

- Ubiquity
- Speed
- Reduced signaling
- Tariffing
- Port conservation
- Vertical integration

The next sections examine these advantages in greater detail.

Ubiquity

Cable service is available to nearly all residences in the United States and serves nearly 65 million homes. Worldwide, there are 157 million subscribers. Such widespread coverage helps attract advertising.

Speed

Chapter 2, "Technical Foundations of Residential Broadband," indicated that coaxial cable has more bandwidth than the twisted-pair copper wires used in current telephone access networks, and it has significantly more bandwidth than wireless networks. The speeds achieved by cable are so high that content providers delivering over cable are considering changing their content specifically to exploit the speed of cable, for example, by adding more audio and visual content to Web pages.

Reduced Signaling

Cable is always on, which means that a call setup process, such as ringing a telephone, is not needed. The subscriber does not have to request that the cable operator transmit specific content; it simply arrives in push mode. Reduced signaling is a prerequisite for widespread residential applications.

Tariffing

Because cable is always on, there is no time-dependent pricing. Pricing is subscription-based (monthly access fee) or transactional (pay-per-view). This is predictable and user-friendly pricing.

Port Conservation

Because cable is a shared medium, the cable operator needs only a single physical port at the carrier premises to support hundreds or thousands of users. This is in contrast to telephone companies that must allocate a port for each subscriber. [Gillett] reported in 1995 that nearly a 30:1 cost advantage exists for cable compared with ISDN when measuring cost per bit of peak bandwidth per subscriber. Port conservation is an important cost advantage for cable in relation to telephone service.

Vertical Integration

Finally, the top cable operators in the United States are important content providers. AT&T is closely aligned with Liberty Media (due to the prior relationship of TCI and Liberty Media) and has 25 percent of Time Warner Entertainment (through its acquisition of MediaOne). Time Warner owns the majority of Time Warner Entertainment, which includes Warner Brothers, Turner Broadcasting, and a host of magazines (*Time*, *Life*, *People*, *Sports Illustrated*, and *Fortune*). Microsoft has designs on becoming a content provider and owns a stake in Comcast. When content providers own cable properties, they have guarantees of a high-speed outlet for their visual content and plentiful content to occupy the many channels cable affords.

Architecture

Figure 3-1 shows a schematic of a cable system that is not upgraded with fiber. Video programming for cable systems is obtained by satellite or microwave at places called *head ends*. Head ends have facilities to do the following:

- Receive programming (for example, from NBC, CBS, and cable networks such as MTV and ESPN)

- Convert each channel to the channel frequency desired, scramble channels as needed (for the premium channels)

- Combine all the frequencies onto a single, broadband analog channel (frequency division multiplexing)

- Broadcast the combined analog stream downstream to subscribers

Downstream traffic is also referred to as *forward* traffic. As of December 1996, there were 11,660 cable head ends in the United States.

The combined downstream video traffic emanates from the head end and is injected into a *trunk cable*. To provide geographical coverage, *splitters* divide the traffic at branching points, and the replicated traffic goes into *feeder cables* that emanate from the trunk cables. Subscribers are connected to the feeder cables or trunk cables with the addition of a *drop cable* (300 feet of cable or less) and a connector between the drop cable and the feeder, called a *tap*.

Figure 3-1   *Cable System Schematic*

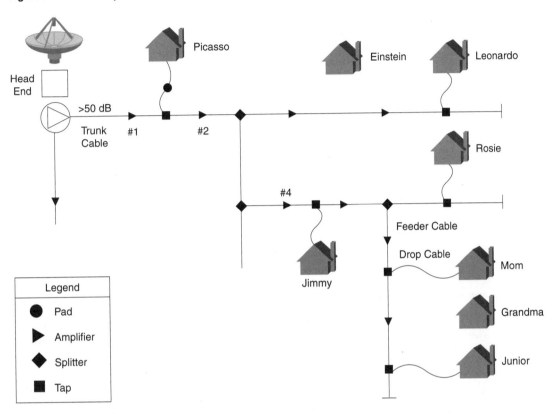

Another approach to connecting users is to use long drop runs of low-loss cables (more expensive than normal drop cables) to a central tap, thus eliminating some of the distribution system. This improves reliability and reduces theft of service.

In the home, there is the familiar *F-connector*, a cylindrical connector with a center pin sticking out, that is plugged in to a set-top box or cable-ready TV or VCR. An F-Connector is a low-cost male and female screw-on connector for RF coaxial cable, consisting of a straight bare center wire (male) or socket (female) conductor and a threaded cap (male) or post (female) for the coaxial cable shield. F-connectors for cable range in styles and costs from very inexpensive press-on connectors to more costly (and reliable) gold plated waterproof crimp-on connectors.

The head end and its connected coaxial cables and subscribers comprise a cable system. The operator of a cable system is a cable operator. Big companies, called multiple system operators (MSOs), are established and, as the name suggests, operate multiple systems. MSOs may own systems that are geographically contiguous or widely dispersed. Geographically contiguous systems offer a greater economic advantage than wide, dispersed systems. MSOs are aggregating their systems into large contiguous regions through mergers and acquisitions. The major MSOs in the United States are AT&T (through its acquisition of Tele-Communications Inc. [TCI] and MediaOne), Time Warner Cable (owned by Time Warner), Cox Cable, Comcast, Cablevision, and Adelphia. Important MSOs in other countries are Canal Plus (France); A2000 (Netherlands); Deutsche Telecom (Germany); and Rogers Cable, Cogeco, Videotron, and Shaw (all in Canada).

Signal strength attenuates by the square root of frequency as it moves through the cables (trunks, feeders, and drops). So, higher frequency signals lose strength faster than lower-frequency signals. This is one reason why programmers desire lower-numbered channels. Signal strength is also attenuated by splitters and taps.

To maintain signal strength, the signals are boosted in the forward path with amplifiers roughly every kilometer. Because higher channels attenuate faster and because the distances over which they must travel can be long, amplification for the higher frequencies might yield excessive power levels for low-frequency channels. So there is a need to equalize power across the transmitted frequency band at the end points to reduce distortion.

To cover a distant site, an amplifier might be turned up high, resulting in too much signal strength and distortion. So, nearby homes need a *pad*, a passive device that induces attenuation. For example, in Figure 3-1, amplifier 1 is cranked up to provide service to Leonardo, thereby requiring Picasso to have a pad on his drop cable.

The result is a tree and branch topology with the head end as the root and the subscribers as the leaves. It is possible that the farthest subscriber could be 50 to 70 miles from the head end. Splitters and taps are necessary to distribute television signals but have the side effect of weakening signal strength by introducing signal loss at each occurrence.

In Figure 3-1, eight homes are passed by cable, and six are actual subscribers. A *home passed* is a residence that can be a subscriber with the addition of a drop cable. About 95 percent of all homes in the United States are passed. Einstein and Grandma count as homes passed even though they are not subscribers. The *take rate* is the ratio of homes that pay for the service to homes passed. In this example, the take rate is 6/8, or 75 percent. As of December 1996, the take rate in the United States was 64.1 percent, according to Nielsen Media Research.

Hybrid Fiber Coaxial Systems

Coaxial cable systems provide great improvements in television reception in many parts of the country. Even in areas where reception was good, CATV was popular because of increased programming options. Many new channels were premium or pay-per-view channels, thereby affording broadcasters new sources of revenue and giving content creators new outlets for their work.

The Introduction of Fiber Trunks

Despite the success of coaxial cable networks, pure coaxial cable systems are insufficient in several ways for high-speed residential broadband service. First, channel capacity is still insufficient to compete with Direct Broadcast Satellite (DBS). Coaxial systems can provide roughly 40 channels, but DBS subscribers can receive more than twice as many channels, affording them more innovative programming options. DirecTV in particular has done well with enhanced sports packages. Cable networks require additional channel capacity to be competitive.

Second, coaxial systems lack robustness. If an amplifier malfunctions near the head end (for example, by losing power), all subscribers downstream from the bad amplifier lose service. Referring back to Figure 3-1, if amplifier 4 breaks, then Jimmy, Rosie, Mom, and Junior will lose service.

Third, signal quality is insufficient for large numbers of users. In Figure 3-1, Junior or Leonardo might be 40 to 50 miles from the head end. The number of amplifiers between the head end and the last subscriber is called the *cascade depth*. Junior is six amplifiers from the head end; that is, his cascade depth is 6. Cascade depths of 40 to 50 are possible in some systems in the United States. Amplifying a signal 40 times is like copying a tape 40 times: The last signal is never quite true to the original.

Finally, coaxial cable systems are *very* complicated to design and operate. Referring back to Figure 3-1, if many new subscribers living near Jimmy begin service, it is possible that their taps would cause enough attenuation to require a new amplifier for serving Mom's neighborhood. But even if there were no changes in subscribership, there are dozens of amplifiers, splitters, pads, taps, cables of various impedences, thermal changes (which lengthen or shorten cables as ambient temperature changes), and pirates (doing their dastardly deeds between the head end and subscribers) spread over a 40- to 50-mile radius. Keeping power equalized for all subscribers is a difficult problem.

Ongoing operational network design is also complicated by rusting components, leakage due to perforation of insulation, temperature gradients, loosened fittings, malice, and other annoying causes. These imperfections are difficult to find and, when found, typically require onsite maintenance. Each instance of onsite maintenance costs about $50 to $100 per incident for an onsite visit or *truck roll*, which compares unfavorably to the $20 to $40 monthly charges paid by subscribers. Software programs exist to assist technicians, but for the most part, they use manual processes as well as a lot of intuition and experience.

To combat these problems, cable operators came up with the idea to use fiber optic cable in place of coaxial cable trunks. The total system would have both fiber and coaxial cables, hence the term *hybrid fiber coaxial (HFC)* networks. With the invention of the linear light source and analog fiber systems, it became practical to introduce fiber into the trunks. The requirement for analog fiber systems was to maintain compatibility with the existing analog metallic plant. Also, the use of analog fiber was cheaper and more reliable than conversion to and from digital fiber.

By using fiber, the cascade depth can be reduced to a handful of amplifiers, perhaps four or five. Reliability and equalization problems associated with deep cascades are reduced. The systems offer more bandwidth and are easier to design. Figure 3-2 shows how the system in Figure 3-1 would evolve with the introduction of fiber.

The diagram shows that trunk coaxial cables have been replaced by multiple fiber cables. If a fiber link breaks, fewer homes lose service. The fiber cables are terminated at media translators called *fiber nodes* that convert optics into electronics. Therefore, the cable system is segmented into smaller *clusters*, each of which is defined by those homes served by a single fiber node. In this case, Picasso, Einstein, and Leonardo are passed by a single-fiber node and therefore are in the same cluster. It is the intent of MSOs to limit clusters to 500 to 2000 homes passed.

Figure 3-2   *Hybrid Fiber Coaxial (HFC) Schematic*

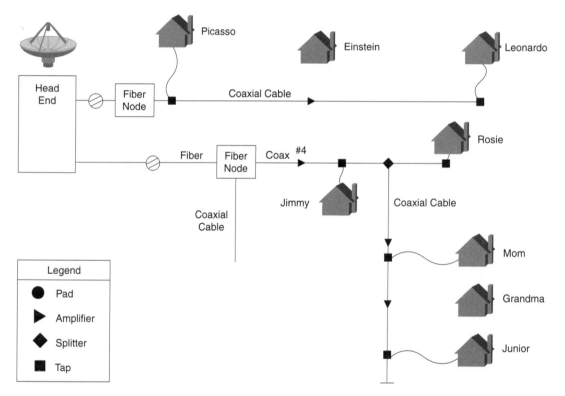

One to six coaxial cables are attached to the fiber node. In the forward direction, the fiber node splits the analog signal so that the same signal is sent on each coaxial cable. Traffic flowing in the opposite direction—that is, from the home to the head end—is referred to as *upstream, reverse,* or *return* path. In the return path, traffic is received from the coaxial cables and is multiplexed in the frequency domain onto the fiber. The definition and purposes of the return path are discussed in more detail in the section "Upstream Transmission" later in this chapter.

Between the fiber node and the subscriber, the assembly of coaxial cables, amplifiers, splitters, and taps is the same as the pure coaxial cable scenario. HFC systems reduce the number of amplifiers, thereby increasing available bandwidth and reducing maintenance.

A key innovation underpinning HFC deployment was the development of amplitude modulated fiber-optic transmission. Until the invention of the linear light source in the 1980s, it was not possible to have *amplitude modulated (AM)* fiber; without AM fiber, it was not possible to have analog transmission over fiber. Without analog transmission over fiber, cable would have had to perform analog-to-digital and digital-to-analog conversions (as discussed in Chapter 2) to use fiber, which is a costly proposition. AM fiber was central to the evolution of HFC cable systems. Figure 3-3 shows how a cable HFC network maps to the DAVIC reference model.

Figure 3-3   *Mapping to the DAVIC Reference Model*
Courtesy of Digital Audio Visual Council (www.davic.org)

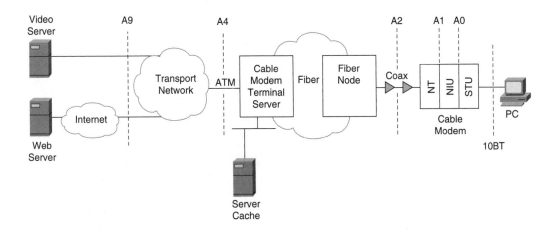

HFC Upgrade Costs

The cost of upgrading to fiber varies by geography, labor rates, and to some extent on what dollars are allocated to upgrade costs and what dollars are allocated to operational costs. Because metallic cables need periodic replacement anyway, it makes sense to replace metallic cables with fiber cables during normal maintenance. Coaxial cable can be reused to feed electric power to the fiber node, and thus find a second life.

The cost of upgrades includes the cost of optoelectronics (fiber and laser transmitters), changes to the cable plant (connectors, power supplies, passives, and occasionally new cable), and labor. An important cost factor is whether the new cable is overhead or buried (aerial or burial). Numbers to upgrade systems are typically proprietary. The S1 prospectus of Ciena Corporation (www.ciena.com; Nasdaq-CIEN) indicates a total cost of $70,000 per route mile.

Upstream Transmission

The introduction of fiber trunking is the first step in cable TV networks' evolution to full-service RBB networks. The second major step is to create an upstream transmission capability in the HFC plant so that subscribers can send data as well as receive it. The terms *upstream*, *reverse*, and *return path* are used interchangeably to describe traffic and paths that go from the consumer to the head end.

Existing Return Paths

Previously, many return path amplifiers were installed by cable operators to meet franchise requirements, such as video from the city council chambers, for management communications for intelligent amplifiers and to poll set-top units to collect *impulse pay-per-view (IPPV)* billing information. IPPV information is retained in the set top and is polled periodically by the MSO to obtain invoicing information. IPPV and monitoring are low bit rate uses of the return, so little return bandwidth is required. Today, with higher bit rate requirements for data, more return bandwidth and more aggressive modulation schemes are required than are necessary for simple invoicing data collection.

The vast majority of systems today assign upstream frequencies in the range of 5 to 42 MHz below the frequencies used for broadcast television. Systems that split the upstream from downstream frequencies at frequencies below 54 MHz are referred to as *low split*.

Mid-split systems separate the upstream from downstream frequencies above 100 MHz. Exactly where the return and forward paths split is decided by the operators. In a representative mid-split system, the return path is in the range of 5 to 108 MHz, and the forward path is 174 to 450 MHz, noted as 5-108/174-450. A *high-split* system of 5-150/174-750 provides the greatest amount of return path.

Mid- and high-split systems are useful for two-way communication, but they infringe on frequencies used for legacy broadcast television. By starting the forward at 174 MHz, channels 2 through 6 are lost. Three broadcasters in any given market would lose their natural channel assignments. Consequently, low-split systems are the focus for RBB rollout. Mid- and high-split systems are being considered for custom networks installed by operators, specifically for industrial or governmental uses.

To provide reverse path or upstream support, amplifiers are needed on the coaxial cable in the upstream direction, and laser transmitters are needed in the fiber node to transmit back to the head end. Because return path frequencies are low, there is less signal loss in the return path than in the forward path, so fewer return path amplifiers are needed. The capital cost of return amplifiers is low compared with that of forward path lasers. Furthermore, low-cost Fabry-Perot lasers are typically used in the fiber nodes to illuminate the return path. Because of these relatively low-cost components, the capital cost of upgrading to two-way is only about $10 per home passed.

In addition, labor costs must be considered. Estimates from some operators cost about $300 per mile to improve signal fidelity for return path. Improving signal fidelity means to clear away noise, tighten the cable plant against leakage, equalize frequency response, and perform other installation preparation. The cost per home passed is less than $10, which, like capital costs, is relatively low. However, the work is labor-intensive and requires skilled labor. Given the thousands of miles that need to be installed, labor availability is a restrictive factor in creating and maintaining the return path. The availability of labor can be a significant problem because telephone companies compete for labor within the same pool.

Telephone Return

Due to return path impairment problems, some cable operators are choosing to defer enabling the return path and opting for telephone return instead, at least for an interim period. By using telephone return rather than cable return, two-way services for data and video on demand can be offered by the introduction of HFC only. Telephone return technology is well understood, and two-way service can be initiated by the MSO quickly.

Telephone return means that the consumer, or the subscriber modem, makes a telephone call to a terminal server when the consumer requires return path service. The terminal server may be located at the head end, a super head end, a telco facility, or a facility operated by an Internet service provider (ISP).

Viability of Telephone Return

Many observers contend that telephone return is not a viable long-term strategy for cable operators—it might not even be a profitable short-term one. Consider the following:

- The customer might pay for message units. Telephone return is advocated in geographical areas that do not justify return path buildout. But these areas, primarily rural areas, are also likely to be farthest from the dial point of presence and therefore are charged for message units.

- The consumer loses use of the telephone while it is being used for return path needs and might need an additional phone line to compensate.

- Call setup is too long. Dialing takes a minute or so, which makes the TV viewing experience or Internet experience unsatisfying.

- For TCP traffic, the slow return path limits the forward speed. The return path contains the acknowledgments that keep forward traffic moving. A 28.8 Kbps return path will limit the forward speed to 500 Kbps or so. This is a lot, but not the 27 Mb advertised for cable.

- The cable operator must pay for the terminal server and access lines. If you count costs for rack space and management of multiple terminal servers, the cost differential between telephone return and enabling the cable return path narrows.

Because of the lack of satisfaction with telephone return and the relatively low cost of implementing two-way cable, systems using telephone return are expected to proliferate slowly. On the other hand, two-way cable systems are proliferating briskly, thereby obviating the need for telephone return.

Frequency Allocation

Cable operators will be distributing both analog and TV programs over HFC networks as long as analog TV is broadcast over the air. Analog distribution is required throughout the period of transition from analog to digital over-the-air broadcasting to protect the viability of the embedded base of analog/cable-ready TV sets. Channel capacity will be divided between the analog and digital channels according to the availability of digital programming and management preferences of the MSOs. The analog channels will be carried from 54 MHz up to roughly 350 to 400 MHz. Digital channels will start at this cut-off frequency and proceed to 550 or possibly 750 MHz. Table 3-2 shows a representative frequency allocation in the United States after fiber and return path upgrades are applied to a cable network.

Table 3-2   *Cable Frequency Allocation*

Frequency Range (MHz)	Direction	Primary Application	Comment
5 to 42	Upstream	Return path data, telephony, network management, pay-per-view billing	Low frequency; supports longer distances without amplification compared with forward traffic, but is subject to ingress noise.
54 to 350	Downstream	Analog TV	Upper bound will vary by operator. As over-the-air TV goes digital, this range will be reduced.
350 to 750	Downstream	Digital TV	Frequency range will vary by operator.
750 to 1000	Upstream	Additional return path	Need to augment the limited capacity of 5 to 42 MHz. High frequency is subject to greater attenuation. Requires new types of return path amplifier. Expensive and problematic.

Frequency use will vary in Europe because of 8 MHz channelization and analog TV stations that begin above 65 MHz.

The proliferation of fiber and return path systems are key elements in the improvement in the physical capability of cable systems. But a better cable plant alone is not sufficient to support RBB service. Another key factor has been the development of standards for digital TV, data service, and telephony over cable systems. Cable's practical, proactive approach to standardization has enabled equipment suppliers, semiconductor designers, and content developers to plan and execute on a known physical plant. The key standards in the U.S. are OpenCable™ for digital television, Data-over-Cable System Interface Specification (DOCSIS) for data service, and PacketCable, for cable telephony.

Digital Video Services over Cable

When John Malone, CEO of TCI, talked about the 500 channel service in 1994, we surmise that he was referring to MPEG-2-encoded digital TV over HFC. HFC systems would be built with 750 MHz of forward bandwidth, offering 110 or more passbands of 6 MHz each. Each 6 MHz passband would be MPEG-2-encoded to yield four to six digital channels. Here's how.

Take 6 MHz and remove 500 kHz from each side for guard band, yielding 5 MHz. Use QAM 64 modulation on the 5 MHz. QAM-64 is selected by American and European standards bodies as the modulation scheme of choice for cable systems. QAM-64 encodes 6 bits per Hertz, yielding just over 30 Mb of raw throughput. Use Reed-Solomon forward error correction, which consumes 10 percent of raw throughput for error detection and correction, yielding 27 Mb. Twenty-seven Mb can comfortably support four to six channels of MPEG-2 programming.

It is believed that 750 MHz, shared among 500 to 2000 households, would satisfy bandwidth requirements for legacy analog television, near video on demand (nVoD), video on demand (VoD), Internet access, and the dozens of new networks and local or public service programming networks. To achieve the full potential of this bandwidth, some standardization will be required to reduce costs to the operators.

Principles of Operation

At the MSO head end, programs are acquired from a variety of analog and digital means. Analog channels will be received from satellite or terrestrial over-the-air means, just as they are in a nonupgraded (fiberless) plant. Analog programs will be passed along transparently to the viewer, with scrambling applied as needed.

Digital channels could be handled in a variety of ways. Recall that the modulation schemes of over-the-air digital TV and cable TV differ. Over-the-air will be transmitted in 8-VSB modulation, and cable digital TV will be transmitted using QAM-64 or QAM-256.

The possible options for the retransmission over cable of digital over-the-air TV channels are listed here:

- Receive channels in 8-VSB at the cable head end and pass the digital programs transparently through to the consumer. At the consumer site will be a decoder, which will decode 8-VSB for the over-the-air channels and QAM-64 for the cable digital channels (ESPN, Discover, HBO, and so on). That is, the decoder must be aware of the format of the program and decode accordingly.

- Receive channels in 8-VSB at the cable head end and remodulate the programs to QAM-64 at the head end. All programs, whether originated from over-the-air or from cable, will be sent in QAM. The remodulation technology is available, and it relieves the set-top box from decoding different types of streams.

- Receive channels in pure MPEG baseband and modulate the channels onto QAM. This can happen, for example, if a cable head end is located near a network affiliate and arrangements can be made to drop fiber between the broadcaster site and the head end.

The analog channels and digital channels are combined, or frequency division mutiplexed, into the frequency range of 54 MHz up to perhaps 750 MHz, thereby forming a broad channel lineup of analog and digital channels.

To assist the consumer in navigating through the dozens or hundreds of channels, an electronic program guide (EPG) will be produced by the operator. In the case where the broadcasters offer their own EPG to inform the user of their channels, some conflict may arise between the MSO and the broadcaster over how the EPGs are presented. For example, if Disney offers a channel multiplex, how will the cable operator display the various Disney options?

New functions must be added at the head end to enable digital program insertions. For example, advertisements must be produced in MPEG format and spliced into program streams at the head end to localize advertising. Emergency broadcasts must also be spliced into or preempt MPEG programming, and new conditional access must also be applied. Conditional access for analog differs from digital.

In the end, the issues confronting cable head end operators are similar to the issues confronting broadcast stations when going to digital. There will be new equipment, new costs, and new skills required, but lots of new opportunities for the operator as well.

Digital Set-Top Box

At the consumer site, an MPEG-2 set-top decoder transforms the digital transport stream so that an analog TV set can present the image, a process called *decoding*. Analog programs will pass through the decoder directly to the analog TV.

The basic functions of the digital set-top box are listed here:

- Diplex filters to separate upstream from downstream traffic
- Handle demodulation of downstream traffic from the HFC

- Handle modulation of upstream traffic onto the HFC
- Create an electronic program guide that displays programming options, including virtual channels and access to chat rooms linked to programs
- Perform MPEG-2 PID selection
- Perform MPEG-2 decoding
- Manage analog interfaces (RGB and audio) outlets to analog TV sets
- Descramble analog TV broadcasts
- Manage infrared controls (for channel selection) and VCR controls
- Transmit return path signals
- De-encrypt downstream traffic
- Encrypt upstream traffic
- Authenticate
- Manage separate, or out of band (OOB), control channel
- Perform IP stack and IP address filtering

Optional components include the following:

- Interactive game interfaces, such as joysticks
- Data communications interfaces, such as Universal Serial Bus (USB) or Ethernet
- Web browser interfaces to support interactive data services
- Java engines, which enhance Web browsing and provide an application interface
- Smart cards for authentication
- Copy protection circuitry, to prevent unauthorized copying of digital content

Digital TV set tops will require use of the return path for user-control purposes, such as channel selection, trick modes, pay-per-view ordering, and fault monitoring. Applications such as WebTV, Wink, or OpenTV also will have user interaction with a data application. At the time of this writing, a rough estimate of the cost of elements of digital set tops were as follows:

Microprocessor, with 4 MB of memory and flash memory	$90
Transmission elements (tuner, equalizer, modulator, and FEC)	$50
MPEG chips, graphics, and audio processor	$50
Chassis, power supply, final assembly, PCB, and test	$50
Analog and infrared interfaces	$10
Software licenses (OS, encryption)	$10
Total cost	$260

This total is the cost to the manufacturer; consumers would pay more, probably around $400. As time passes, the cost will decrease.

Set-top boxes for analog cable delivery have been required for conditional access for premium viewers. Viewers who did not choose premium services did not have need for a set-top box (STB); they would simple purchase a cable-ready TV. Those who don't have premium channels outnumber those who do.

The MSOs that needed to enforce conditional access were required to go to the Big 2 (General Instruments and Scientific Atlanta) for analog set-top boxes. General Instruments and Scientific Atlanta have incompatible conditional access systems, so if one MSO chose one vendor at the head end, it could not choose the other for the customer premises. Also, the set-top boxes were provided by the MSO, which meant that the MSO carried the customer set-top box on their balance sheets, which had negative financial implications.

The development of digital TV meant an opportunity for the MSOs to open the design of the set-top box so that there would be more competition among vendors. This presumably would lower their costs, improve functionality, and get the set-top box into retail distribution and off their balance sheets. All these were perceived as wins for the MSOs. Hence, they embarked on a standardization effort called OpenCable. Although it is unclear at the time of this writing whether OpenCable will succeed in establishing an industry standard, it illustrates the issues associated with digital TV on cable.

OpenCable Initiative

The OpenCable Initiative (www.opencable.com) is an effort that began in September 1997 and is supported by CableLabs and the Society of Cable Television Engineers (SCTE; www.scte.org) to standardize key elements of a digital set top for digital television service over HFC systems. OpenCable does not address standardization issues for current and future generations of analog set tops. It concentrates on digital standards to create interoperable set-top boxes and to create new functionality for digital TVs, VCRs, DVD players, and personal computer NICs that process video. It is intended that OpenCable-compliant devices be available at retail and also be provided by the MSO. However, due to differences in service offerings of cable operators, there is no guarantee that an OpenCable device can be used if the consumer moves to another system.

The key elements subject to standardization are listed here:

- **Consistent services**—Two OpenCable boxes from different manufacturers must provide the same services when deployed on a common cable system. In particular, the cable operator would like to provide a common look and feel, whether the box were purchased retail or leased from the operator. This means that the user interface should be downloaded to what could be boxes of different manufacture.

- **Backward compatibility**—An OpenCable device should be capable of passing through analog programming and should be interoperable with existing head end services.

- **Portability**—The 1996 Telecom Act mandated the retail availability of DTV navigation devices. Any device available at retail carries with it the presumption that it is usable when the consumer moves from system to system. This is not guaranteed because different cable systems may offer different services, but is a design goal of OpenCable.

- **Conditional access**—The security system should be replaced in the case of a security breach or should be otherwise modified at the discretion of the MSO. This implies some form of modularity, which is introduced by way of a smart card that plugs into the set top, called the *Point of Deployment (PoD)* module.

- **Software development environment for navigation tools**—This primarily applies to electronic program guides and video services, such as interactive TV, VoD, electronic commerce, and tiered services. For example, tiered services allow MSOs to package groups of channels independently from the manner in which the channels are acquired from the content providers. HBO may broadcast multiple channels in digital format, but the operators can be free to reaggregate the various HBO streams to suit their particular marketing purposes.

- **Platform independence**—An OpenCable device should operate on any hardware platform, such as a personal computer, PowerPC, or videogame processor.

Over time, it is also expected that OpenCable will evolve to include data and voice capability. As of this writing, however, the intention is to develop a specification for video.

Security and the Point of Deployment Module

The first step in the development of OpenCable was agreement between General Instruments and Scientific Atlanta to harmonize their respective conditional access systems. Accordingly, an agreement on a common specification was reached, called Harmony.

The implementation of Harmony was to be on a smart card that plugs into the set-top box. The card, called the Point of Deployment (PoD) module, contains keys necessary to view premium programs. It is also the repository for billing information for electronic commerce transactions. The PoD module is interrogated by the head end to release billing information from time to time. Another requirement of this security module is that the set-top box can operate without it for basic programs—that is, programs not requiring conditional access. Furthermore, it is required that if a premium channel is being viewed with the PoD module, that emergency alerts preempt programming; that is, the PoD module can interfere with the premium programming but not with emergency alerts. It turns out that the engineering of the PoD module to satisfy these two requirements is tricky because the PoD module is provided by the carrier and is renewed periodically. Figure 3-3 shows a schematic of an OpenCable set-top box from [Adams].

Figure 3-4   *OpenCable Schematic*
Courtesy: Michael Adams, Time Warner Cable, SCTE DVS

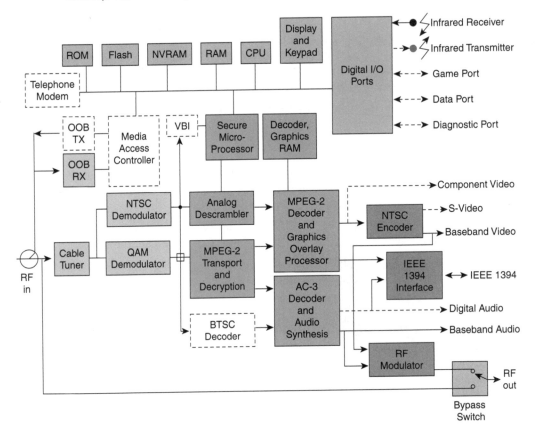

The boxes outlined with dashes are optional elements of OpenCable. The F-connector delivers cable programming over the RF in. There are two tuners: one to receive the video feed, either analog or video, and another to receive an out-of-band QPSK channel for control information, or data, marked OOB RX.

For legacy analog TV service, the tuner receives the analog signal and passes it to an NTSC demodulator and an optional VBI decoder. The VBI decoder is used to display text information at the bottom of the TV screen. Graphics may be introduced from a graphics processor and CPU, and the analog signal is sent to the TV monitor via a channel 3/4, an S-Video interface, or an optional component video interface

Digital TV programming is QAM demodulated and sent to an MPEG decoder for rendering and decryption. Graphics are also introduced, after which the video can pass through an analog or a digital interface to the TV monitor. If it sent out an analog interface, it uses the channel 3/4 or

S-Video interface. This would seem to be a terrible waste because so much work has gone into a fully digital program stream, but at the last few feet, the whole apparatus provides a legacy, analog TV image. Therefore, there is the provision for a digital interface using the IEEE 1394A interface. This interface is also known as Firewire and will be discussed further in Chapter 7, "Home Networks." For now, we only indicate that Firewire is the digital interface of choice for OpenCable.

In the return path, there is a provision for an out-of-band transmitter, denoted OOB TX, which transmits QPSK modulated data to the head end. This transmitter can be used for impulse pay-per-view accounting, data services, VoD selection and control, and interactive television. A telephone return path can also be used. In addition, computing components are required to support what is actually a full functioning computer. Among these elements are a CPU, read-only memory, Flash memory, RAM, and non-volatile RAM. These components are needed to support booting, remote management by the operator, software downloads, processing and display of electronic program guides, and above all, support for application development.

Conditional access information is received in the out-of-band channel (that is, independently of the programs) and is used to grant access to the MPEG stream through the CP or control program.

This box has all the costs of an analog set-top box, with MPEG decoding, a POD module, a QPSK tuner, a 1394 interface, and a lot of new software.

Walled Garden or Open Systems?

While standardization is intended to benefit the cable operator, it is not entirely clear that all cable operators see the benefits of an open standard. Some MSOs find comfort in their proprietary worlds ("walled gardens") in which they can control the user interface and maintain vertical integration. Standardization would threaten this, and some marketing staffers in the cable industry would prefer to pay the premium for a closed system and retain control of the user environment. Their case is emboldened because it is not clear how much money can be saved to going to a standard, open set top. Going retail almost certainly would entail loss of control of the user interface.

How does this tension play out in OpenCable? General Instruments is shipping a pre-OpenCable set top called the DCT5000 and has sold these to AT&T/TCI/MediaOne. If millions of DCT5000 set tops are installed, OpenCable becomes moot.

Even so, it is likely that all vendors will give lip service to OpenCable and say they are compliant. Therefore, it remains to be seen how diluted the compliance tests become if de facto standards emerge.

Challenges to Digital Video Service

Despite gains in two-way cable plant, fiber distribution, and standardization, challenges remain for TV service over cable.

Competition from Satellite

The DBS industry has acquired roughly 9 million subscribers in the United States as of June 1999. This is about 15 percent of the cable subscriber base. Overseas, DBS providers such as Sky are likewise enjoying strong subscriber growth in Europe and Asia. Furthermore, satellite operators have recently been permitted to offer local TV stations, a capability they were largely barred from providing on technical and regulatory grounds. Both the technology, solved by a technique called *spot beaming*, and the regulatory environment, which relaxes rules soon with the delivery of local channels, have provided the impetus to DirecTV (www.directv.com; NYSE-GMH) and Echostar (www.echostar.com; Nasdaq-DISH) to provide local channels in major metropolitan areas of the United States. Many satellite homes in the United States continue to keep cable services, mainly for local channels. With local access on satellite, it remains to be seen how many of these homes with both services will unplug one or the other.

Copy Protection

Digital interfaces, such as IEEE 1394, facilitate the pristine copies of content with the attachment of a CD or DVD burner. Hollywood studios, recording companies, and their representatives, such as the Motion Picture Artists Association (MPAA) and the Recording Industry Artists Association (RIAA), need assurances that their copyrights are enforceable. They are discussing copy protection alternatives with hardware developers.

Mechanisms are being discussed to provide digital watermarks, which will enable the tracing of stolen content. A proposal from consumer electronics manufacturers in Japan and Intel addresses ways to limit the number of copies that can be made from a single source. This technology, called 5C, would permit no copies, one copy, or an unlimited number of copies to be made from a single consumer-purchased item. The recent flap in the music industry regarding MP3 copies of music has put the recording industry into fast forward on the development of copy protection. Without an agreement on copy protection, the content providers will be reluctant to provide content in digital form.

Must Carry Rules for Digital TV

MSOs are fearful that current Must Carry rules will apply to digital TV distribution. Under current Must Carry rules, cable operators are required to carry the analog channels in the serving area. Without this carriage, small broadcasters are fearful they will not be carried on cable and will lose their advertising. This would put many of the smaller broadcasters, who wield power within the NAB, out of business.

When broadcasting goes digital, things get complicated. Several new questions present themselves:

- Will the cable operators be required to carry the digital simulcast of an analog channel when they already carry the analog channel? Haven't they satisfied the Must Carry rule by simply carrying the analog?

- If they are required to carry the digital form, or when the broadcaster only has digital formatting, will the cable operator be obligated to carry the programming in the original digital format? That is, if the broadcaster carries HDTV, will the cable operator be required to carry HDTV format, or can the cable operator downgrade to standard-definition TV, thereby saving some bandwidth on the cable system? Cable operators complain loudly that it is bad enough that they may be required to carry digital; they would be really annoyed if they would be required to carry high-definition TV.

- Finally, if the broadcaster elects to transmit a channel multiplex, is the cable operator required to carry all the streams in the multiplex? Or can it carry just the main channel, whatever that is? For example, broadcasters could elect to transmit data services. Would the MSOs be required to carry such data services? This would pose a competitive problem inasmuch as the MSOs have their own data services already, such as Roadrunner and @Home.

At the time of this writing, these issues are before the FCC. No matter how the FCC decides, it is likely that the matter will be litigated and taken to the highest courts in the land. The original Must Carry rule was taken to the U.S. Supreme Court, where it was upheld on a narrow 5 to 4 margin. Legislative action may ensue as well.

Viruses and Bugs

Advanced digital set-top boxes are basically computers connected to a broadband network. They have processors, memory, and operating systems, so they could also be subject to the problems of personal computers on the Internet. In particular, set-top boxes may be subject to computer hacks, computer viruses, and plain old software bugs that could impair TV viewing.

Data Services over Cable

The second major market for two-way cable is data, such as Internet access. The intent of data services over cable is to provide high-speed Internet access for computers with Ethernet or Universal Serial Bus (USB) ports. Personal computers, including recent models of Apple Computer, support both Ethernet and USB. Cable networks can provide high-speed, always connected services for relatively low costs. Cost advantages arise because cable provides a natural multiplexing function. That is, one cable port at the head end can connect hundreds of users simultaneously. Telephone networks, on the other hand, require a separate line card for each phone line. This cost advantage is discussed in [Gillett].

Accordingly, the idea of moving data over cable TV networks is an old one. Cable modems were merchandised as early as 1987 by companies such as Fairchild Electronics. The Fairchild M505 Broadband Modem was QPSK and QAM-modulated, yielding up to 10 Mb of full-duplex service. Many of its characteristics are surprisingly similar to the cable modems being developed today. The idea then was to use coaxial networks primarily for intranet use. So, the 1980s generation of modems lacked the scaling properties necessary for public carrier use.

With the growth of the Internet, cable operators have begun thinking of their HFC networks as a logical vehicle for improved data service. Internet access is an inherently asymmetric service, meaning that more data comes from the head end than to the head end, a characteristic that matches the bandwidth capabilities of low-split cable networks. Furthermore, cable networks have the ubiquity to quickly offer service to large segments of the population. Finally, the convergence of Internet access with digital TV made it necessary for cable operators to offer data service and to prevent cannibalization of their video service.

For these reasons, cable has significant leverage and motivation to deploy residential data service. Various research groups are predicting big things for broadband data service. The following are variables affecting the sales of cable modems:

- How many systems are upgraded to fiber
- How many systems are two-way-enabled
- How well operators can recruit and train field engineering talent and keep their plants clean enough to offer high-bit rate services
- How well Web servers can deliver significantly faster service to showcase the speed of cable networks when compared with their telco counterparts
- How popular competitive technologies will become, including ISDN and 56 Kbps modems and new phone company services called xDSL
- Pricing of high-speed services by Internet service providers

Data services are expected to generate roughly $500 per subscriber per year. This yields annual revenues on the order of $2 billion per year by 2001, by some projections. Though this is far less than U.S. cable's current revenue of $28 billion per year, it does represent a significant new revenue stream and has the added benefit of reducing customer churn for video services.

Fairchild long ago exited from the data/cable business, but the company was supplanted by a number of companies that developed proprietary technologies. Among these were Motorola and Applitek. Applitek became LanCity, which was acquired by Bay Networks, which was in turn acquired by Northern Telecom (www.nortel.com; NYSE: NT).

In 1995, the cable industry began exploring the possibility of standardized cable modems. By standardizing, a critical mass of equipment could be developed through common development to provide lower-cost modems. A group of cable operators in North America formed a partnership called the *Multimedia Cable Network System Partners Ltd. (MCNS)* partnership, whose objective was to develop a purchasing specification for its members so that a critical mass of buying commitment and development could lower costs and improve functionality. Accordingly, MCNS joined with CableLabs (www.cablelabs.com), the research and development group supported by the cable industry, to develop the Data-Over-Cable Service Interface Specification (DOCSIS). Motorola and other companies, such as Terayon (www.terayon.com; Nasdaq-TERN) continue to sell their proprietary systems, but the interest here is to explicate the DOCSIS specification.

The DOCSIS 1.0 specification has been adopted for standardization by the Society of Cable Television Engineers (SCTE), the American National Standards Institute (ANSI), and the International Telecommunications Union (ITU).

Principles of Operation

The components for a cable modem are shown in Figure 3-5. These are similar to the components of a digital set top, but without the MPEG elements. Because the cable does not include MPEG elements, it is cheaper than a digital set-top box.

Figure 3-5   *Cable Modem Schematic*

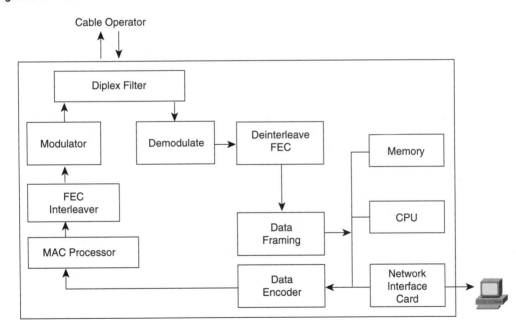

The operations of data services over HFC will be demonstrated by explicating the DOCSIS specification, version 1.1, which is the most current specification as of this writing. The discussion is segmented into three parts:

- **Channelization and modulation**—Spectrum allocation, modulation, and symbol rates
- **Startup**—What happens when a new modem is attached to the network?
- **Continuing operations**—How a modem sends and receives data after startup

Channelization and Modulation

For data services to operate, the cable plant must provide minimum levels of quality. Therefore, DOCSIS specifies requirements for noise characteristics. Some examples are carrier-to-noise ratio (not less than 35 dB) and burst noise (not longer than 25 microseconds). Cable plants failing to meet minimum quality requirements cannot be expected to support DOCSIS traffic.

Downstream traffic is modulated with QAM-64 or QAM-256, selectable by the cable operator over the U.S. standard of 6 MHz increments anywhere from 50 to 860 MHz. QAM-64 yields 5.057 million symbols per second, or 30.3 Mbps, and QAM-256 yields 5.361 million symbols per second, or 42.9 Mbps. To make data service as compatible as possible with digital TV service, DOCSIS specifies MPEG-2 Transport Frames as the framing protocol; that is, IP data packets are placed in the payload section of MPEG-2 frames. This allows data and video to be multiplexed on a common 6 MHz channel. Interleaving is applied to the forward channel. Depending on the amount of burst protection, latency of 0.22 to 4.0 milliseconds is induced.

While the forward path operates within 6 MHz channels, DOCSIS return paths vary according to the bandwidth. The bandwidths supported by DOCSIS are shown in Table 3-3. Return paths occur anywhere in the range of 5 MHz through 42 MHz. The center frequencies are located with 32 kHz precision. The upstream channel can have either QPSK or QAM-16 modulation over one of five bandwidth options. The gross bit rates available under DOCSIS upstream channels are a function of bandwidth and modulation scheme.

Table 3-3 *DOCSIS Return Path Bit Rate Options*

Bandwidth	Symbol Rate (ksymbols/ second)	Bit Rate Using QPSK	Bit Rate Using QAM-16
200 kHz	160	320 Kbps	640 Kbps
400 kHz	320	640 Kbps	1.28 Mbps
800 kHz	640	1.28 Mbps	2.56 Mbps
1.6 MHz	1280	2.56 Mbps	5.12 Mbps
3.2 MHz	2560	5.12 Mbps	10.24 Mbps

The bandwidth, placement, and modulation schemes are selected by the cable operator and are a function of line quality. Cleaner return paths can entertain higher symbol rates. As of this writing, the most common bandwidths are 800 kHz and 1.6 MHz with QPSK modulation. As cable plants improve noise characteristics, there will be greater use of QAM-16.

The use of the cable return path is shared among all active transmitters. Thus, the 10.24 Mb in the best case is shared among whomever is transmitting back to the head end at any given moment. Also, there is significant overhead that is to be subtracted from these bit rates. Therefore, a single individual user can experience much less than the stated bit rates but generally will have faster service than current telephone or ISDN-based services.

DOCSIS can be modified for Europe with the following changes to the U.S. specification:

- 8 MHz-wide channel instead of 6 MHz
- European standard Intermediate Frequency (37 MHz instead of 45 MHz)
- Return path capability up to 65 MHz instead of 42 MHz
- DVB Forward Error Correction (ITU J.83 Annex A instead of Annex B)

Startup

When a new cable modem is installed on a cable network, there must be a very user-friendly installation process. Basically, everything needs to happen automatically. The modem needs to know which frequencies to listen to and on which frequency to transmit for downstream and upstream data, respectively. It needs networking information as well, such as an IP address and packet filters.

The basic steps at startup are listed here:

- Obtain physical-layer information, such as which downstream to use, which upstream frequencies to use, modulation scheme, and symbol rate
- Obtain network-layer information, such as an IP address and access list filters
- Authenticate the cable modem and establish an encryption key

Obtain Physical-Layer Information

When a customer's cable modem is taken out of its cardboard box, it has no idea on which frequencies it will be receiving data from the head end, nor does it know which frequencies it will use to transmit to the head end. So, the first order of business is to learn these frequencies and obtain other physical-layer information.

The modem does so by scanning downstream frequencies for standard control packets. These packets contain messages, called *upstream channel descriptors*, that are broadcast downstream expressly for newly attached modems from the *Cable Modem Terminal Server (CMTS)*. Among other information, the upstream channel descriptor contains the following:

- Frequency on which the cable modem is to transmit on the return path
- Symbol rate used to transmit
- Maximum number of bytes that can be transmitted the next time permission to send is granted
- Modulation technique, either QPSK or QAM-16

The cable modem tunes to a relatively low frequency and ascertains whether that frequency is an analog TV channel or a digital TV channel. If analog, it tunes to the next higher frequency and continues to look for a digital channel.

Eventually, the modem will find a digital channel. Because digital channels are above 350 MHz, modems will normally begin scanning above that frequency. The cable modem then needs to discern whether the digital channel is used for TV or DOCSIS. To do so, it waits for a well-known PID of "1111111111110," which has the hexadecimal notation of "1FFE." This PID is specified by DOCSIS to contain control information. Naturally, that PID cannot be used by the operator to indicate TV program information.

Having found the well-known PID, the cable modem can decode the MPEG packets, recover the data, and obtain the upstream channel descriptor. Because the downstream can be anywhere from 50 to 860 MHz, there are potentially hundreds of channels for the cable modem to scan. Each must be scanned serially, and each channel may have multiple PIDs to decode. Therefore, the process of hunting for the upstream channel descriptor can take seconds or even minutes. This process can be especially time-consuming if there is a system-wide outage and all cable modems in a neighborhood must go through startup at roughly the same time.

Because the process can be lengthy, some cable modems start scanning from frequencies above 350 MHz because frequencies below 350 MHz are presumed to be analog. Also, if there has been a reset, most cable modems can remember startup parameters by retaining them in nonvolatile memory. That is, if a cable modem went through initialization at one point, parameters such as frequency and symbol rate are retained. When reinitialization is required, the cable modem will attempt to use these retained parameters first.

After the upstream channel descriptor is read, the cable modem waits for timing information (in a separate synchronization message) and an indication of when to transmit in a message called the *bandwidth allocation map*.

Control packets from the CMTS are not encrypted; it would be impossible for an uninitialized modem to sign on to the system without prior knowledge of the encryption keys.

After the modem knows which downstream and upstream frequencies it will use and has permission to transmit, it announces to the head end that it is here and begins *ranging*. Ranging is the process by which a cable modem learns its distance from the head end. This is required to synchronize the boundaries of the time slots on which to send. Ranging is accomplished by the cable modem sending a short message to the head end and measuring the response time interval. Ranging is a continual process because of thermal changes that cause the cable to expand and contract during the day.

During the ranging process, the CMTS also manages the transmit power of the cable modem. The problem is that if a single cable modem is transmitting with insufficient power, it cannot be heard reliably by the CMTS. On the other hand, if the cable modem transmits with excess power, it could drown out other cable modems on the same cable plant. During initialization, the cable modem transmits at low power. Often the CMTS will not hear the cable modem and a timer will expire. The cable modem will transmit at a higher level, and the process is repeated until the CMTS is happy with the power level it receives.

Obtain Network Information (IP Address Acquisition)

After the ranging process, the cable modem is ready to obtain an IP address and other network parameters. It would be customer-unfriendly and would create security problems if the customer were to configure his own IP address.

The modem obtains an address by using the *Dynamic Host Configuration Protocol (DHCP)*. DHCP is the standard Internet protocol for dynamic assignment of IP addresses. When a subscriber requires an address, the cable modem launches a particular type of broadcast packet, called a DHCP Discover, onto the return path. The CMTS router at the head end receives the DHCP Discover and authenticates the cable modem. It then returns the IP address of the server to the cable modem, and the cable modem sends a DHCP request to the DHCP server. The DHCP server returns an IP address to the router, which caches it and relays the information to the subscriber cable modem. The router will identify and store the MAC address of the modem. Thus, the router keeps a database of all necessary address bindings for a particular user.

In addition, the initialization process provides other information to the cable modem by use of a trivial file transfer (TFTP). The DHCP address server can be linked with a subscriber management database to provide bandwidth guarantee parameters (semantics to be determined), packet filters (semantics to be determined), graphical user interfaces (customized per user), and the time of the day from the head end. The time of day is needed to timestamp error messages.

Security

The controlling document on security is the Baseline Privacy Plus (BPI+) Interface Specification (BPIv1.1-IO1-990316), available at www.cablemodem.com.

Inasmuch as HFC is a shared medium, user data encryption is required for privacy. Without that, is possible for excessively clever customers who have proper network analysis equipment to snoop on the data traffic of their neighbors. Baseline privacy not only protects the customer from intrusion, but, perhaps more importantly from the MSO's point of view, it protects the cable company against unauthorized use.

The key elements of BPI+ are an encryption protocol and a key management protocol.

Encryption   User data is encrypted with the U.S. *Data Encryption Standard (DES)*, which has varying levels of strength. To make DOCSIS an exportable product, the encryption must go with it. However, due to national security concerns, the federal government places limits of the strength of encryption algorithms that can be used domestically or exported commercially. The DES used in DOCSIS provides relatively light encryption strength.

DES works simply by having the sender and receiver share a secret before data is transmitted. The shared secret, or key, is an integer that is used by the sender to scramble data and by the receiver to descramble data to render the original data, within the safe confines of the customer or carrier premises.

Key Management   Obviously, it is necessary that there be a key exchange protocol before data can be exchanged. Because the keys contain important information, their exchange is also encrypted. The encryption for key exchange uses a triple DES, a relatively strong form of encryption. The algorithm for exchanges uses public key exchange.

Authenticate the Cable Modem

For the service provider to be protected with proper conditional access, it is necessary to authenticate the user cable modem. Otherwise, it would be possible for an intruder to impersonate a legitimate cable modem and thereby obtain keys and access.

The method to authenticate the cable modem uses a relatively recent innovation in cryptography called *digital certificates*. When a cable modem is manufactured, the following information is installed into the cable modem permanently:

- A serial number
- A cryptographic public key
- An Ethernet MAC address
- The manufacturer's identification

The union of all these data elements is referred to as an *X.509 digital certificate*.

When a customer signs onto the network, his cable modem sends the embedded X.509 certificate information to the head end. The head end validates the certificate and then uses the customer's public key to encrypt subsequent data packets.

Special precautions are taken in the event that the cable modem is a member of a multicast group or has preferred quality of service. In both cases, the cable modem is assigned to a class of users. That class is determined by multicast group membership or membership in a group of cable modems enjoying higher quality of service. In these two cases, the key exchange is processed by the group.

These measures are in addition to any application-level end-to-end security. Security is the subject of discussions in various standards organizations and remains an open issue.

Security vulnerabilities are specific to user environments. For example, Windows 95 users on cable data systems have been advised to disable file sharing in the Networking menu of the Windows 95 Control Panel file. Otherwise, it is possible for others on the cable system to peer into the disk drives of the exposed user. However, turning off file sharing creates problems for users who have local-area networks. Additional software is needed to provide security on cable systems while enabling file and print sharing.

It should be observed that security measures for data are fundamentally different from security measures for digital video or analog scrambling. Security for data relies on unique descrambling or de-encryption per user session. Broadcast security cannot be done this way because all viewers receive a common program. Therefore, common descrambling or de-encryption is required. This means that data security is structurally different from broadcast security, and dual security mechanisms are required.

Continuing Operations

After determining upstream and downstream frequencies, ranging, acquiring an IP address, and obtaining security, the cable modem is finally ready to exchange data. Figure 3-6 shows a schematic of the path and process the data follows.

Figure 3-6   *Data and Cable Schematic*

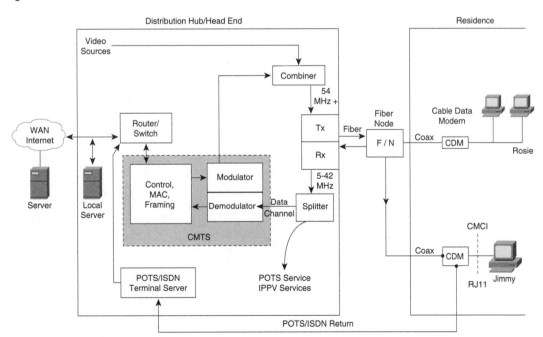

In the forward path, data is received at the Cable Modem Terminal Server (CMTS) from the Internet or private intranets. It is modulated, upconverted to the proper forward frequency, multiplexed with standard video traffic in the analog domain (in the combiner), and transmitted through the distribution plant.

In the return path, traffic is received at the head end. Some of the upstream traffic is split off for other purposes, such as pay-per-view, telephony, and monitoring. The splitting is performed in the analog domain using diplex filters. The remaining data traffic is sent to a QPSK or QAM-16 demodulator, which then sends bits to a terminal server, indicated as the CMTS in Figure 3-6. Traffic is then sent to a local router or switch for transmission to a local server, the Internet, or another cable subscriber. If the cable plant is not capable of two-way service, telephone return can be used. Jimmy's cable modem in Figure 3-6, for example, has an internal telephone modem and an RJ-11 jack for this purpose.

DOCSIS uses an entire 6 MHz channel for the forward path. This enables the MSO to use the same RF multiplexing equipment for data used for video. Six MHz of bandwidth on the forward allows 27 Mb of data per channel, using QAM-64 modulation and RS FEC (net of overhead). The 27 Mb is shared among all subscribers in a system. For example, if there are 27 subscribers online at any instant, each can expect to receive 1 Mb of forward path service, far exceeding the capability of telephone modem and ISDN service.

DOCSIS cable modems are required to operate in bridged mode and run the IEEE 802.1d spanning tree algorithm. Loops are not permitted on the customer premises local-area network.

There is also a provision for the cable modem to join a multicast group using standard Internet Group Management Protocol (IGMP) messages. Multicast is particularly well suited to the cable environment because cable is a natural broadcast medium. When cable modems join multicast groups, the replication problem is simplified and the cable modem is left with the work of retaining packets bound for the multicast group.

Return Path Bandwidth Arbitration

Because only a single source of data is in the forward path, data is transmitted in broadcast mode from the head end to one or more subscribers in the cluster. On the return path, multiple customers may request use of the return bandwidth simultaneously. Therefore, there needs to be a bandwidth arbitration mechanism on the return path. This mechanism is bandwidth arbitration or the Media Access Control (MAC) protocol. If Junior and Rosie decide to transmit at nearly the same time, their bits will collide, rendering both transmissions indecipherable when they reach the head end. There must be a way for them to decide which one goes first and for how long before relinquishing the upstream to the other, or to someone else.

The objectives of any MAC are to do the following:

- Support the maximum number of possible users per cluster
- Minimize latency on data transfer
- Provide fairness so that all users get some access
- Achieve maximum bandwidth utilization of the return path
- Support multiple classes of service

Well-known LAN schemes such as Ethernet and Token Ring were not considered in the cable environment, due in part to their distance limitations. If Rosie was 10 miles from the head end, a round trip would take 120 microseconds. At 10 Mbps, that would mean that 1200 bits would be in flight before a collision could be detected. A short message could be sent by another user in the interim. Instead, in Ethernet or Token Ring setups, Rosie and everyone else would have to wait for the packet to pass. Polling techniques, such as Token Ring, consume excessive amounts of time for the polling sequence, so polling has never been considered by data and cable vendors.

Instead of using standard Ethernet techniques, DOCSIS opted for a collision-avoidance or credit-allocation scheme built largely on the lines of the original LanCity cable modem system. In fact, substantial parts of the DOCSIS protocol were authored by LanCity (now Nortel) engineers.

With credit schemes, the CMTS sends credits to the subscriber modems, granting them access to the upstream for a specified period of time. The time interval at which cable modems are allowed to transmit is limited by their grants. After grants are exhausted, the cable modems must stop transmission. The CMTS controls the amount of data transmitted per request.

The key features of the DOCSIS return path arbitration mechanism are as follows:

- User data and requests to transmit user data are sent in fixed-length increments, or time slots.
- Variable-length packets may be sent by obtaining multiple time slots per request.
- Mechanisms exists to provide for quality of service.
- CRC checksums are used to detect errored packets, but there is no means to correct errors at the MAC layer.
- Requests to transmit occur in special packets or may be "piggybacked" inside user data packets, thereby reducing the need for special request packets and reducing bandwidth use.

Credit mechanisms must ensure that the CMTS can provide grants fast enough to keep bandwidth utilization high. If grants from the head end come to the subscribers too slowly, the subscriber modems stop transmitting. The result is that the return path is underutilized. Because the return path contains acknowledgments that permit forward path traffic, the forward path might become underutilized as well.

Normally, only one request may be outstanding from a single subscriber at a time. With a 4 ms interleaving delay on the forward path, a 1.6 ms round trip propagation delay, and processing time, it can take more than 6 ms from the time a request is made by the subscriber to the time the grant is received. Efficient MAC algorithms are required to ensure that grant requests are expedited.

When subscribers collide, they are unaware of the event unless informed by the head end. The head end detects the collision and informs the cable modem that the collision occurred. When informed of a collision, the cable modem performs a backoff and tries again.

MAC design on shared media with large propagation delays remains an interesting research topic and the subject of intense competition.

Apart from normal data exchange, continuing operations require a high level of management. Some of the key ongoing management functions are listed here:

- **Power management**—The head end continually monitors power levels of each cable modem and orders them to decrease or increase transmit levels as needed, in a process very similar to the original ranging process.

- **Changing upstream channels**—If there are significant levels of narrowband interference on the upstream, the head end will command the cable modems using that impaired return path to hop to another frequency. This information is sent in the upstream channel descriptor.

- **Changing upstream parameters**—On the other hand, if the return path is performing well, the head end may elect to increase the use of the existing return path. For example, the head end can command the cable modem to increase the symbol rate.

Alternative Approaches

This review of data services concentrated on the DOCSIS approach. It should be mentioned that other proprietary approaches from companies such as Terayon (www.terayon.com; Nasdaq: TERN) and Motorola (www.motorola.com; NYSE: MOT) have found market acceptance. Com21 (www.com21.com; Nasdaq: CMTO) has a DOCSIS product as well, but it also has an ATM-based alternative. However, these products have not been explored here because of the relative lack of available sources and because DOCSIS presents the design issues and concepts completely for explanatory purposes.

Table 3-4 summarizes DOCSIS channelization characteristics.

Table 3-4   *DOCSIS Return Path and Forward Path Characteristics*

Characteristic	Return Path	Forward Path
Also known as	Reverse path, upstream	Downstream
Channelization	200 kHz, 400 kHz, 800 kHz, 1600 kHz, 3200 kHz	6 MHz

Table 3-4   *DOCSIS Return Path and Forward Path Characteristics (Continued)*

Characteristic	Return Path	Forward Path
Modulation scheme	QPSK, QAM 16	QAM 64
Access	Via MAC protocol	Broadcast
Shared bandwidth	320 Kbps to 10 Mbps, depending on symbol rate and modulation	27 Mb

Challenges to Data over Cable

Widespread industry development of cable for data depends on resolving several technical challenges:

- Competition from xDSL and other services
- Return path noise problems
- Problem isolation
- Scaling techniques

The next sections explore these issues in greater detail.

Competition

The lucrative market for high-speed data services will attract service providers using other technologies. Among the key competitors will be the big telephone companies that will offer various forms of digital subscriber loop services (discussed in Chapter 4); new generation carriers, offering fiber access to multiple dwelling units (discussed in Chapter 5); and wireless carriers using various technologies (discussed in Chapter 6). Cable is particularly well suited to broadcast applications, such as TV distribution. But data services, especially for commercial purposes, often require a symmetric bandwidth capability—that is, as much bandwidth coming from the client as going to the client. Cable is not well suited to this profile.

Return Path Problems

The return path is enabled in the frequency range of 5 to 42 MHz. This is low frequency that has good attenuation properties. On the other hand, because there is heavy use of those frequencies by other services, ingress noise is a problem.

More importantly, the shared nature of the return path creates a funneling effect. Impairments are received by coaxial wires (which act as giant antennas) in the home and are sent upstream. These impairments are funneled together as the signals move upstream because of cable's tree and branch topology. This means that noise gets increasingly louder as you go upstream, rendering the signal potentially indecipherable. (For a summary of issues of return path problems, see [Prodan].)

Sources of Ingress

Ingress noise is picked up by the cable from outside sources, through leakage and bridged taps. Here's a partial list of problems that result in ingress noise:

- HAM radio and citizen's band (CB) radio. Both are allocated frequency by the FCC within the 5 to 42 MHz passband. Also, there is a business band radio service near the CB band.

- Poorly insulated equipment in the home, such as microwave ovens, televisions, radios, and electric motors (vacuum cleaners and so on). If these are operating near a loose F-connector, the noise will be picked up on the cable and sent upstream.

- Emissions from outside the home, such as lightning, neon lights, vehicle ignitions, and powerline interference.

- The output of digital signals from the home terminal. Sometimes the source of noise could be the cable modem or the digital set top itself.

- Tampering and malice.

- Loose or poor quality F-connectors and bad cable quality and installation in the home

- Corrosion. The design life of taps is 15 years, but in reality, street taps don't last longer than 5 years.

Despite the miles of cable owned by the operator, noise characterization studies have determined that most ingress noise on return path cable plants comes from inside consumer's homes, which is out of the control of the cable operator.

Scaling Techniques

Because cable is a shared medium, care must be taken to avoid congestion as the number of users grows and the usage of each user grows. In both cases, there needs to be a plan for how to manage scaling for video and ATM for data services and control functions.

Multiple Return Paths per Forward Channel

In the event that path traffic grows, collisions might increase without a corresponding increase in forward traffic. In this event, it might be necessary to add an additional return path to complement the forward channel. Now there are two return paths, each with its own port.

In Figure 3-2, for example, Jimmy and Rosie share a common fiber node on the return path. Because the return is used heavily, the cable operator could assign Jimmy and Rosie to different frequencies for the return path, even though they use the same forward channel. Control messages from the CMTS must instruct the respective modems to use their assigned frequencies. Management processes at the head end are responsible for load balancing across the return paths.

Having multiple return paths potentially complicates the MAC design process. Data received on two different ports at the same time is not a collision, but the MAC will still consider it a MAC collision unless proper care is taken.

Additional Forward Channels

A single forward channel provides a shared 27-Mb service to a neighborhood. When take rates and individual utilization permit, another forward channel can be allocated to data service. This means one less channel for analog data or multiple digital TV channels. The tradeoff of bandwidth between data and broadcast use is strictly an economic tradeoff.

Smaller Clusters

A final scaling technique is to extend fiber farther into the neighborhood. Initial rollouts of two-way services may be limited to clusters of 2000 homes passed. In response to congestion, it might be necessary to reduce clusters to 1000 or even 500 homes passed. Unlike using multiple return channels or additional forward channels, this step requires capital expenditures. So, for those MSOs that don't commit to small clusters early, this is likely to be the last resort.

Equal Access

In the current telephone regulation environment in the United States, local telephone companies are required to offer equal access to any long-distance telephone service provider. This is because telephone service has been referred to as a common carrier bearer service, much like railroads, highways, and other public infrastructures. At the time of this writing, MSOs have no similar regulatory requirement at the federal level; that is, MSOs offering data service are not required to offer equal access to ISPs. Thus, in the current environment, a cable operator such as AT&T can offer @Home service exclusively. While it is possible to connect to other ISPs, such as America OnLine (www.aol.com; NYSE: AOL), that are not affiliated with AT&T, one must be an @Home customer to get to AOL. This is like saying that a Bell Atlantic telephone customer can get to a Sprint customer but must be, say, an MCI customer, to get any long-distance service.

America OnLine, Mindspring (www.mindspring.net; Nasdaq: MSPG), and other ISPs want direct access to cable infrastructure on an equal access basis—that is, on an equal footing with @Home. A number of municipalities seeking to have a competitive local data/cable environment have required equal access for cable franchises in their respective localities. Portland, Oregon, was the first city to require equal access in late 1998. AT&T claimed that the city had no jurisdiction to require equal access without a federal mandate. In January 1999, the case was taken to Federal Court, and Portland won. Other cities, such as Los Angeles, are pursuing an open access policy. On another legal front, Internet Ventures, a small ISP in Redondo Beach, California, sought similar access to cable using a different legal argument. In this case, Internet Ventures argued that they must be given carriage on a Must Carry basis. As of this writing, this case is winding its way through the legal system.

For their part, the cable operators argue that allowing competitors to use its cable networks removes the incentive to invest in DOCSIS and the upgrades necessary for high-speed two-way transmission. This is *precisely* the same argument that local telephone companies have used to argue that they should not be required to resell high-speed services that they develop and offer.

The argument for equal access will become more acute when cable operators begin to offer telephone service, as they intend. In that case, AT&T, with its direct access to 25 million subscribers, will offer its long-distance service. No doubt MCI, Sprint, and others will have something to say about that.

Integration of Video and Data Subscriber Units

One of the key differences between video and data is the tradeoff between latency and high-integrity bit rate. In comparison with video, data can withstand a relatively high bit error rate. Data has other error-correction mechanisms, whereas errored bits in MPEG flows quickly degrade picture quality. Therefore, video uses substantially more interleaving, generating more latency. This has led to a difference in FEC and interleaving standardization.

On the other hand, there are many common hardware and software elements between TV and DOCSIS. Some of the commonalties are as follows:

- Use of MPEG framing
- Use of QAM modulation on the forward path
- Use of QPSK modulation on the return path
- Use of concatenated Reed-Solomon forward error correction
- The requirement for a MAC protocol for the return path
- The requirement for local processing to manipulate digital content

The convergence of digital TV set tops with cable modems is encouraged by the fact that set tops are likely to have a built-in IP stack. The first reason is the collection of impulse pay-per-view billing information. Currently, such information is obtained by the carrier by a telephone dial-out from the set-top box during off-hours. With DOCSIS in the set-top box, data collection can happen without a phone call at any time, day or night.

But, additionally, digital video content providers are providing access to Web content to augment their programming. This will require an IP stack and application environments such as Java Virtual Machine (VM) in the set top. IP will also be used to signal video servers and provide the network plumbing for electronic program guides. IP can also be embedded in MPEG frames and can be used by the Java VM in the set top for interactive TV applications, such as electronic commerce. Ethernet controllers are very inexpensive, so the incremental cost of adding an Ethernet port to a digital set top is minimal. Putting IP into a digital set top will reduce the distinction between a cable modem and video decoder.

Without integration, a cable customer who subscribes to both digital video and data services needs two set-top boxes. If the boxes are available at retail, that could get expensive. Also without integration, it would be more difficult to create new forms of broadband interactive applications. Some consideration is being given to integrating the two—that is, having a combined OpenCable and DOCSIS set-top box.

This can be accomplished by modifying the OpenCable schematic shown in Figure 3-4 so that the OOB TX and OOB RX blocks comply with the DOCSIS physical-layer protocol. Also, the MAC block must comply with the DOCSIS standard, as well as comply with ranging and control. Because the DOCSIS and OpenCable elements are separable, this integration is largely a matter of ensuring that the packaging is done in compliance with proper electromagnetic practice and cost.

Another integration approach is a combined OpenCable/DVB set top for use in Europe. DVB is used as the DAVIC data standard in parallel with DOCSIS. In the DVB model, control information is sent to the subscriber in a separate data channel (out-of-band channel) rather than in-band, as is the case with DOCSIS. Therefore, there is reduced overhead in the data channel.

Business Obstacles to Cable

Despite its early and substantial lead in providing RBB services, cable faces business challenges. Many of these challenges emanate from the beginnings of cable when "quick and dirty" solutions were the order of the day. Now it is time to create highly scalable and redundant systems. The potential challengers to cable are deep-pocketed and the stakes are high. Finally, cable has taken on the task of providing full service networking capability, that is, supporting Internet, telephone, and broadcast TV services. This is a big plate to fill.

Upgrade Costs

Cable operators are faced with a large bill for HFC, two-way, and data service upgrades yet to come. The cost components are HFC upgrade, two-way upgrades, head-end data equipment, head-end digital video equipment, and customer premises equipment. An estimate of capital cost per subscriber is as follows:

HFC upgrade ($40,000/mile; 50 homes passed/mile; 62.5 per take rate)	$500
Two-way upgrade	$20
Head-end equipment (CMTS, video and Web servers, and management systems)	$200
Subscriber equipment	$250
Test equipment, tools, training, and initial marketing	$30
Total costs	$1000

The Cost of Digital TV

Despite the fact that analog TV does not afford as many additional channels as digital, MSOs may elect to upgrade to analog instead of digital because of cost. Going digital would add an incremental $200 per set top above the cost of an advanced analog set top and a $3 million to $5 million investment at the head end to capture, convert, edit, and store local content in digital format and to support ad insertion from analog source materials.

Improving analog TV would provide up to 550 MHz of forward bandwidth for up to 80 channels and would add new features such as electronic program guides. MSOs in the United States have ordered more than 4 million new, advanced analog set tops through 1997.

An operator could either deploy the cheaper advanced analog TV service and risk losing a percentage of subscribers to DBS and wireless cable or could spend the millions and retain the same subscribership. Depending on customer erosion, determined by customer satisfaction with advanced analog, the operators might stay with analog. This strategy works if DBS sales level off and MSOs are capable of repairing their balance sheets over the next few years.

Competition

DBS is currently the greatest competitive problem for the cable industry for three reasons. The first is the possibility that cable subscribers will disconnect and subscribe to DBS instead. This occurred after cable rate increases in 1996, and after the Telecom Act of 1996 passed. Interestingly, a majority of DBS subscribers continue to subscribe to cable to retain local programming. But the defections occurring after the 1996 rate increases show that there is limited room for price increases before consumers will choose DBS over cable.

A second competitive problem for cable is that DBS subscribers tend to be high-income households. In a national survey, the *Los Angeles Times* reported in December 1996 that for families with household income of more than $75,000 per year, cable take rates declined in the calendar year 1996 from 75.8 percent to 71.1 percent. High-income households are the ones that tend to opt for more expensive programming packages. When they turn to DBS for premium programming, they either cancel cable altogether or scale back to the basic cable service. Currently, more than 70 percent of cable subscribers accept some form of pay programming. If the percentage drops significantly, this would negatively affect the cash flows of the MSOs. In short, DBS gets the premium service subscribers, who generate better margins. (As a point of comparison, the average DBS subscriber spends about $52 per month, whereas the average cable subscriber spends about $35 per month.)

Finally, with regard to DBS competition, there tends to be less *churn* among DBS subscribers. Churn refers to a customer's changing from one service or service provider to another. In many cases, DBS subscribers have prepaid for a year or more of service. Besides, if you pay a few hundred dollars for a dish, it is unlikely that you will terminate service, even if you do not sign an annual programming agreement. At any rate, recent surveys conducted by Nielsen Media Research and Primestar indicate that DBS subscribers tend to be very satisfied with their service.

In addition to competition from DBS, there is the prospect of digital TV offered by wireless cable operators. They have begun slowly, but have attracted the interest of large telephone companies and are now better capitalized to compete against cable. The technology of wireless cable is largely the same as that for cable and satellite, and significantly less cost is involved in building the infrastructure.

Finally, there is the prospect of digital over-the-air broadcast. This has the potential to provide many more channels of free television. It remains to be seen what would happen to programming and subscription television if there were 30 or more free digital channels per metropolitan area with a healthy measure of HDTV intermingled.

Market Saturation

Even without competition from satellite or telcos, cable take rates have not increased substantially since 1991 when they first topped 60 percent. Subscription has been less than 2 percent annually since then. It seems that every American TV household that wants cable has it. Cable's task is to get more revenue from households that already have it. This is the problem raised by DBS, with its big gains in pay-per-view and premium sports packaging and its superior penetration of high-income households.

Cable MSO management apparently agrees that it is necessary to get more from each subscriber. Since the passage of the Telecom Act of 1996, cable operators have taken the opportunity to raise subscription rates more than twice as fast as the consumer price index, clearly not a strategy for getting new households. Rates were raised an average of 6 to 7 percent in the summer of 1996, with further increases in the first quarter of 1997. It remains to be seen how well the operators can continue to hold share in the face of these rate increases and increased competition.

Operational Issues

HFC brings significant improvements in field operations and network design. Even so, a wide-area HFC plant is difficult to operate. The following are some recurring issues:

- **Amplifier maintenance**—If you adjust one amplifier, others need changing. Maintenance is also temperature-dependent.

- **Power**—Fiber and amplifiers in the field need electrical power. This can be supplied centrally or in a distributed manner. In either case, there are issues of battery maintenance, selecting proper voltage levels, safety, and corrosion.

- **Topological redundancy**—This is expensive in a tree and branch topology. Generally, route diversity is not available between head ends and fiber nodes.

- **Remote network management**—Automated, remote management is generally not available for RF components. Troubleshooting is largely a manual process requiring experienced staff.

- **Staffing**—Upgrades are dependent on a pool of trained operations engineers. Cable wages for field engineers are roughly 10 to 20 percent less than unionized counterparts in the telephone industry.

See Table 3-5 for failure rates of some system components [Large].

Table 3-5   *Failure Rates for Cable System Components*

Component	Annual Failure Rate (%)
Fiber optic cable	0.06%/mile
Coaxial cable	0.12%/mile
Drop cable	1.5%/drop
Power supplies	5%
Amplifiers	3%
Fiber transmitters and nodes	7%

Franchise Fees

Cable franchise fees levied by cities make up about 5 percent of gross revenue. Whether or not this franchise fee would apply to data services is not clear; for the moment, however, data and cable operators seem to be paying it. In addition to franchise fees, some cities levy their charges based on the amount of wiring done in the city. In Troy, Michigan, the home of an early and contentious legal argument over municipal franchise fees, the initial charges are 25 cents per foot per year for overhead wiring and 40 cents for underground. Note that cable operators do not pay municipal franchise fees for telephone service because these franchises are established by agreement with the state public utility commissions. The Telecom Act of 1996 precludes excessive regulation and charging of fees by municipalities, with the view that such impositions would illegally restrict competition. Therefore, the act preempts certain state and municipal rights. Whether the Troy, Michigan, ordinance is unnecessarily restrictive is to be determined in court. Cities argue that they are entitled to compensation for the digging occurring on municipal property. Digging shortens the useful life of streets, and having wiring underground complicates and slows the maintenance process for other city services, such as sewage, which uses conduits close to those used by telecommunications operators.

Must Carry Rules

Must Carry rules are a particular problem for the cable industry. The 1992 Cable Act required cable operators to carry local broadcasts—that is, local over-the-air stations. In part, this Cable Act was enacted to protect the viability of small stations that were threatened by the possible loss of more than half their available audience if they were not on cable. Note that because DBS does not carry local broadcast stations, Must Carry rules do not apply to it.

Because their analog cable networks are strained for channel capacity, cable operators view Must Carry rules as an economic burden. Many want to drop locally produced governmental, public access, educational, and religious programming in favor of, say, more shopping or pay-per-view channels.

The cable industry attacked the provision in federal court, and the case eventually went to the U.S. Supreme Court. The Supreme Court had jurisdiction because the case is framed by the cable operators as a First Amendment, free speech case. The cable operators argued that being forced to carry stations is an unconstitutional abridgment of their free speech rights. In a 5 to 4 decision handed down in April 1997, however, the court ruled against the cable operators, stating that the imposition on local broadcasters, who would be forced out of business, was greater than the imposition on the cable operators.

Closed Captioning and Emergency Broadcasts

Like over-the-air broadcast, cable will be subject to increased responsibilities for closed-captioning and emergency broadcasts. There is a requirement that all content be closed-captioned by the end of 2005. Cable operators estimate that this will cost $500 million or more.

Until now, cable has been exempt from participating in the nation's emergency broadcast system. This changed in July 1997 and will present new operating problems to cable operators. Requirements to participate in local and state emergency notification services are also possible. These services are surprisingly complicated and will require millions of dollars to implement.

Programming Fees

Cable operators are growing weary of rising programming costs in general, but nowhere are they being hit harder than in sports, in which teams are looking to television rights to be their savior from escalating player salaries. Cable operators pay 70 to 75 cents per subscriber per month for ESPN. But ESPN is proposing an increase to $1 to hang onto its half of the National Football League cable package it now shares with TNT. Cable operators pass these fees on to subscribers. When cable rates are raised accordingly, consumer groups protest, which causes political problems for the industry.

Summary

HFC, two-way upgrades and the commitment to digital services (TV and data) solve operational problems of cable operators and expand their product offerings. Consumers get more channels, programmers get more shelf space, Internet service providers get the speed necessary to attract advertising, and cable operators can offer new services. These new services have propelled the stock prices of cable operators and their suppliers to all time highs.

For now, cable is the only game in town for residential broadband. The image of the industry was given a lift by investments made by AT&T, Microsoft, Vulcan Ventures, and other recapitalizations. Nonetheless, cable operators face commercial and technical problems before they can become the full-service networks they aspire to be. Cable is the target for others wanting in on RBB; it must continue to invest or let new and old competitors take marginal revenues. This is painful when cable's base business has a high capital overhead and its financial position is highly leveraged. Table 3-6 summarizes the issues facing those operators who want to make the transition of cable to RBB.

On the horizon are alternative technologies that approach the RBB market differently and that could pose significant competitive pressures to cable. The next chapter covers one such alternative: digital subscriber loop access networks.

Table 3-6   *Challenges and Facilitators for Cable as an RBB Network*

Issue	Challenges	Facilitators
Media	Has a shared media return path that is susceptible to ingress noise, particularly from noise sources inside the home.	Uses hybrid fiber coax, which reduces deep cascades and associated reliability and equalization problems.
		Offers more bandwidth than just coaxial systems.
Noise mitigation	Uses a shared topology, which means that a single noise source can adversely affect a large number of households. Return path is subject to ingress noise.	Uses sophisticated noise mitigation and problem isolation techniques that are under development and that are being investigated in standardization efforts.
Signaling	Requires new methods to remotely control the subscriber unit for return path use.	Uses a scheme in which subscribers are always connected and in which there is no need for a call setup process for data or video, which reduces signaling requirements compared with telephone services.
Data handling capabilities	Requires implementation of two-way HFC or use of telephone return.	Is the natural topology for Internet data. High-speed forward and low-speed return closely maps to Web access.
Standards	Proprietary solutions still popular Standards organizations are trying to balance system optimization with speed to market.	Needed so that cable modems and digital set tops can be made available at retail. Strong support for DOCSIS and widespread effort on OpenCable and DVB

Table 3-6   *Challenges and Facilitators for Cable as an RBB Network (Continued)*

Issue	Challenges	Facilitators
Regulation	Cable is regulated by sometimes aggressive and incompatible municipal franchise agreements. Must Carry, closed-captioning, and emergency broadcast rules incur costs.	Some relief will be supplied by the Telecom Act of 1996, which limits state and local regulatory rights.
Market	Perception of market saturation; cable passes nearly 100 percent of homes in the United States and elsewhere, but has difficulty increasing take rates, especially among high-income viewers.	Is the only game in town as of this date for RBB, multichannel service.
Business/ Financial	Faces potential skilled labor shortages. Faces strong competition from satellite and telephone operators. Cable operators are highly leveraged, and continued development of HFC, digital TV, and data services will require further capital.	Cable operators own many sources of programming. Represents influx of new capital.

References

Books

Adams, Michael. *OpenCable Architecture.* Indianapolis, IN: Cisco Press, forthcoming.

Data-Over-Cable Service Interface Specification (DOCSIS), Radio Frequency Interface Specification, SP-RFIv1.1-I01-990211. Available at www.cablemodem.com.

Farmer, James, Walter Ciciora, and David Large. *Modern Cable Television Technology: Video, Voice and Data Communications.* San Francisco, CA: Morgan Kaufman, 1999.

SCTE Digital Video Subcommittee (DVS). *OpenCable, Copy Protection for POD Module Interface, IS-CP-WD01-990412*: April 1999.

Internet Resources

www.cabledatacomnews.com

Source for cable data statistics

cable.doit.wisc.edu/

David Devereaux-Weber's cable page.

www.cablelabs.com/

CableLabs, the research arm of North American cable operators

www.cablemodem.com/

The Web home of the DOCSIS data specification for cable

www.catv.org/

CATV Cyberlab home page

www.cisco.com

Use the search engine for "DOCSIS"

www.fcc.gov/csb.html

Federal Communications Commission (FCC) cable activities

www.fcc.gov/csb/facts/csgen.html

General Cable Television Industry and Regulation Information fact sheet written by the Cable Services Bureau of the FCC

www.fcc.gov/telecom.html

The Telecom Act of 1996, with proceedings

www.fcc.gov/realaudio/archive

Hearings of the FCC on digital TV transition

www.getspeed.com/

Tells you if there is high-speed service in your area

www.home.net/

@Home is a system integrator for data services over cable networks. Note their SEC filings.

www.multichannel.com/

Cable TV and telecom news

www.ncta.com

National Cable TV Association, the cable industry's lobby

www.opencable.com

Digital TV service over cable networks

www.packetcable.com

Telephone service over cable networks

www.scte.org

The Society of Cable TV Engineers

www.timewarnercable.com/

Time Warner's Cable Service

This chapter covers the following topics:

- Current Telco Services
- Digital Loop Carrier Overview
- xDSL Variations
- Asymmetric DSL
- G.Lite
- Very High Data Rate DSL
- High Data Rate DSL
- ISDN Digital Subscriber Line
- Single-Line Digital Subscriber Line
- Early Provisioning for xDSLs
- Factors in Choosing Which DSL to Offer
- Technical Challenges to xDSL
- Industry Challenges to xDSL
- Success Factors
- Summary

xDSL Access Networks

Cable operators offer their HFC networks for RBB services. How are the telephone companies to counter? Some telcos have toyed with the idea of building HFC networks of their own or buying cable operators. Among these have been PacBell, Telecom Australia, and Ameritech. However, most telcos prefer to capitalize on their existing multibillion-dollar embedded base of subscriber lines by pushing the evolution of a new technology called *digital subscriber line (DSL)*. The subscriber line, often referred to as the *local loop*, is a pair of wires that connects each subscriber to a local telephone building called the *central office (CO)*. DSL uses existing subscriber lines to transmit data at speeds of over 100 or even 1000 times current modem service. Hence, it is the vehicle by which telephone companies can compete against cable for video and high-speed data services.

Before proceeding, we note a semantic distinction between *loop* and *line*. DSL refers to digital subscriber line. For the purposes of this chapter and book, *loop* refers to a physical wire pair between the home and the carrier premises, either a central office or remote terminal. A *line* is a service concept that denotes a capability purchased by a customer. Hence, xDSL refers to *line* because it is a service concept.

DSL is deployed by U.S. telephone operators to modernize their wiring to households. DSL service extends fiber deeper into the neighborhood and closer to the consumer. U.S. phone companies have enormous maintenance requirements for their 171 million wired connections to customers. Regulatory relief and business practice make more than $20 billion per year available for telco maintenance budgets. In the maintenance process, certain upgrades are permissible that have the effect of increasing the bit rate and lowering operating costs.

To make matters complicated, multiple flavors of DSL technologies are emerging. The various DSL technologies discussed in this chapter are high data rate DSL (HDSL), asymmetric DSL (ADSL), single-line DSL (SDSL), ISDN digital subscriber line (IDSL), and very high data rate DSL (VDSL). Collectively, these are referred to as xDSL. Before considering xDSL technologies, a quick look at the history and architecture of the current telco services will be useful.

To date, xDSL services trail cable modem deployment. At the March 1999 meeting of the ADSL Forum, it was reported that, as of December 1998, there were 45,000 domestic U.S. ADSL customers, compared with more than 500,000 cable modem subscribers (330,000 with @Home alone) and 75,000 customers worldwide.

Current Telco Services

Conventional wisdom is that phone wire is too restrictive for high-speed service because customers are accustomed to phone conversations and 56 Kbps modem service. However, the basic characteristics of phone wire have the capacity to carry millions of bits per second. The reason they don't is that present voice service is provided in analog mode and filters are installed on phone interfaces and loops that suppress signals above 3400 Hz. Given these filters, the data-carrying capacity of phone wire is limited to 56 Kbps, using the latest generation of V.90 modems. Other services, operating in a digital mode, occupy bandwidth such as those shown in Table 4-1.

Table 4-1 *Bandwidth Comparisons for Telco Services*

Service	Upper Limit Bandwidth
Voice service	3400 Hz
ISDN (USA)	80,000 Hz
ISDN (Germany)	120,000 Hz
T1 using 2B1Q	400,000 Hz
ADSL	About 1,000,000 Hz

Bandwidth-limiting techniques in the voice network enable economical frequency multiplexing over long-distance lines. If users could have 20,000 Hz per phone line, which is the frequency response of a modern stereo system, bandwidth on the backbone would be reduced by a factor of 6. In addition, as noted in Chapter 2, "Technical Foundations of Residential Broadband," pushing very high frequency through wires creates problems of attenuation and distortion that negatively impact the integrity of the signal.

Today, new modulation, equalization, and error-control techniques make subscriber lines capable of transmission rates greater than 6 Mbps for distances up to 3 miles. How much greater depends on the length of the phone wire between the subscriber and the telephone office, the physical condition of the wires (corrosion, insulation, bridged taps, and crosstalk), and the thickness of the wires (the thicker the wire, the less the resistance and the greater the distance served). Table 4-2 shows the trade-off of distance and speed over 24-gauge phone wire (0.5 mm in diameter).

Table 4-2 *Distance Versus Speed over 24-Gauge Phone Wire*

Phone Wire	Speed	Estimated Distance
DS1 (T1)	1.544 Mbps	18,000 feet
E1	2.048 Mbps	16,000 feet
DS2	6.312 Mbps	12,000 feet
E2	8.448 Mbps	9000 feet

Table 4-2   *Distance Versus Speed over 24-Gauge Phone Wire (Continued)*

Phone Wire	Speed	Estimated Distance
1/4 STS-1	12.960 Mbps	4500 feet
1/2 STS-1	25.920 Mbps	3000 feet
STS-1	51.840 Mbps	1000 feet

Source: Alcatel at frcatel.utc.sk/hwb/ta_AWG.html

Before examining how technology is pushing this envelope, it will be useful to overview two current telephone services—plain old telephone services (POTS) and Integrated Services Digital Networks (ISDN)—as well as the rationale for DSL systems.

Plain Old Telephone Services

Telephone switching equipment, which establishes phone connections, is located in the CO. Customers are connected to the CO over thin-wire pairs, also referred to as local loops. These thin-wire pairs are segmented in lengths of 500 feet. Lengths are spliced together as needed to reach from the CO to the customer's home.

The first 500-foot segment from the CO, 26-gauge wire, is normally 0.41 mm in diameter. This is the thinnest type of phone wire. After the first segment, the phone wire is often a thicker diameter, such as 24-gauge (0.50 mm) or the thickest, which is a 19-gauge (0.82 mm) wire. Because resistance is inversely related to thickness, the thicker-gauge wire is reserved for customers who are farther from the CO. Resistance in the wire is a function of temperature as well as wire thickness. At 70° Fahrenheit, 26-gauge wire has about 40 ohms of resistance per thousand feet; 19-gauge wire induces 10 ohms per thousand feet.

Local loops are bundled in large cables called *binder groups*. The job of the field technician is to cross-connect a drop wire to your home and then to a phone wire in a binder group. Fifty phone wires to a binder group is a typical configuration near the subscriber. Some binder groups contain as few as 20 local loops, and others contain as many as a few hundred. Feeder cables—roughly the first 9000 feet coming out of a central office—can have hundreds or even thousands of pairs bundled together. These are referred to as binder groups as well. Figure 4-1 shows a simplified connection between a CO and customers.

The copper in phone lines, although very thin, adds up when considered network-wide. U.S. telcos are the largest single consumer of copper in the world. The local loop consumes nearly 50 percent of telco capital cost; that is capital cost of a local loop is $1500 to $2000 with about 50 percent being used for materials, including copper. Therefore, a premium is put on having the thinnest possible copper, consistent with transmission fidelity. Thinner wires mean less real estate and fewer material costs. Thinner wires are lighter, also reducing the cost of aerial runs. Generally, minimizing the consumption of copper is a goal in the design of phone systems and is one reason for telcos' interest in fiber technologies.

Figure 4-1   *Wiring Schematic pre-DSL*

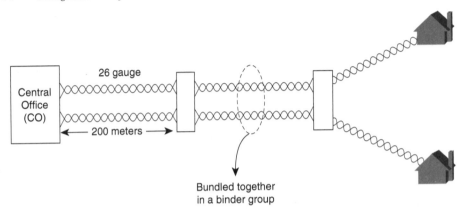

Eventually, a single-wire pair is extracted from feeder cables and distribution cables of fewer wire pairs until the single-wire pair is connected to your house over the drop wire. The drop wire connects to your home in a junction box called the *network interface device (NID)*. The NID is typically a passive device that serves to couple external phone wire to internal phone wire in the home.

Basic Rate ISDN

Basic Rate ISDN (BRI) is a digital service that provides 160 Kbps over phone wire and up to 18,000 feet of 24-gauge wire. Its standard implementation (ANSI T1.601 or ITU I.431) employs echo cancellation to separate the transmit signal from the received signal on a single pair of wires. It uses bandwidth from 0 to about 80 kHz. European systems use 120 kHz of bandwidth. Therefore, provisioning of ISDN and analog POTS on the same local loop is not possible because both services utilize frequencies less than 3400 Hz.

This is not a big deal in the United States because there are less than 1 million ISDN lines provisioned. However, in Europe, ISDN is more widely deployed and therefore there needs to be a coexistence and migration strategy to move ISDN users to xDSL. In Europe, there are more than 6 million ISDN lines, most using a form of ISDN that uses 0 to 120 kHz. The intent is to migrate ISDN users without changing their local loops. The current idea within the European Telecommunications Standards Institute (ETSI; www.etsi.org) is to have ADSL start at 140 kHz and proceed upward and to use an ISDN splitter instead of a POTS splitter. This puts ADSL on a different frequency plan than in the United States.

Limitations of Current Telco Networks

Certainly there is new interest in high-speed services over existing subscriber lines. However, even low-speed data service using telephone modems creates new problems for the phone system. These limitations associated with traditional telco networks are also driving interest in xDSL services.

Space and Distance Constraints

Currently, there are more than 22,000 COs in the United States, serving 171 million lines. Hundreds more offices are served by long-distance carriers (AT&T, MCI, Sprint, and so on), also referred to as *interexchange carriers (IXC)*. The average CO serves 7600 lines; a few serve as many as 100,000 lines. The problem of limited space in conduits in and out of COs is becoming more severe as consumers add second lines for home use. About 20 percent of U.S. homes have added second lines for use in home offices and for talkative teenagers. In Beverly Hills 90210, there is an average of nearly 4 subscriber lines per household (that is, main number, fax, teenager, maid).

Central offices are big, expensive buildings. Reducing real estate needs by using more compact electronics can account for noticeable savings. In places where real estate is at a premium, such as Rome and Tokyo, the sale of telco property can generate enough money to fund digital buildouts of telephone services. In other words, telcos can trade buildings and real estate for new digital infrastructures. Therefore, an incentive exists to move to more compact facilities. One way to facilitate such a move is by installing fiber for new services and distributed switching systems, hence the move to DSLs.

Users obtain services by connecting to the CO. Their distance from the CO dictates the cost of providing the service and, in some cases, the type of service received.

Two standardized range limits exist. Revised resistance design rules (RRD) limit distance to 18,000 feet for 24-gauge and 15,000 feet for 26-gauge wire. RRD rules are used for ISDN. Another range limit, carrier serving area (CSA)—used for HDSL service—limits service to 12,000 feet for 24-gauge and 9000 feet for 26-gauge wire. Half of U.S. lines are within 9000 feet of a CO or remote terminal; 80 percent are within 15,000 feet. (The RRD and CSA distances are estimates because the actual distance is a function of line quality. If a particular local loop has severe impairments, the distances will be shorter than these estimates.)

Internet Problems for POTS and ISDN

Internet service over POTS and ISDN lines is readily offered because of the ubiquity of phone service and the widespread availability of modems and voice switches provisioned for ISDN. The problem for telcos is that both POTS and ISDN use the CO voice switch, and data has a different usage profile from voice.

The major difference is that data sessions are longer than voice calls. A 1996 study conducted by U.S. West showed that voice calls are an average 5.64 minutes in length. Calls to Internet service providers (ISPs) are an average 32.47 minutes—six times the length of a voice call. Longer sessions might mean that the number of ports on the switches is insufficient, causing busy signals. When busy signals become excessive, the telco is obliged to buy more switching equipment. At $500 to $1000 per line, this is an expensive proposition. The economic and practical impacts of these estimates are significant, particularly when extrapolated to reflect the continuing growth of Internet usage.

The difficulties associated with this discrepancy in call length are particularly noticeable in areas of the country that have a lot of Internet dial-up activity, such as California. Because of the inordinate costs to their infrastructure caused by data sessions, Pacific Telesis (now SBC) has asked that ISPs be subject to access fees.

Telcos are searching for ways in which data traffic can be offloaded from voice switches to specialized data communications equipment. xDSL services are a method to do this. This is the basic difference between ISDN and xDSL: ISDN goes through a voice switch; xDSL bypasses it. This makes rollout costs incremental for xDSL, whereas ISDN requires telcos to upgrade their voice switches (at a cost of up to $500,000 a pop) before ISDN can be offered. Therefore, xDSL can be considered a lower-cost platform for data service, even though it offers faster bit rates than ISDN.

Digital Loop Carrier Overview

As urban sprawl continues with new housing developments in suburban and rural areas, distances from homeowners to their COs can exceed RRD and CSA ranges. Building COs to accommodate these distant users is not a good economic option. Therefore, a new class of lower-cost facilities called Digital Loop Carrier (DLC) systems are implemented to multiplex traffic back to the central office.

The motivations for DLC systems are to reduce pressures on existing voice switches, reduce the number of expensive COs, and deploy switching equipment closed to the user. The following section overviews these motivators and the architecture of DLC.

Benefits and Business Rationale of DLC

A more distributed architecture arises from the development of DLC technology. As the number of telephone wires grows, the binder groups become unwieldy. DLC was devised in the 1980s by Bellcore and AT&T to multiplex traffic on the wires in the binder group onto four wires, thereby saving lots of copper; in turn, this means savings in weight and costs. DLC also provides improved operational characteristics due to reduced inventory of discrete lines.

Consider a neighborhood of 24 homes that are served by a common CO. Normally, 24 pairs of wires are connected from the homes to the CO. An alternative approach is to use DLC technology.

Instead of 24 pairs of wires backhauled from the homes to the CO, the 24 pairs are terminated in the neighborhood in a DLC. From the DLC, four wire pairs carry traffic back to the CO using T1 or HDSL, which saves 22 wire pairs. AT&T Bell Labs (now Lucent) improved on this with an SLC-96 product. SLC-96 served 96 homes over five T1s (four active T1s and one spare T1). SLC-96 reduced the need from 96 pairs to 10 pairs. The DLC can be located at pedestals, vaults, telephone poles, or office buildings. Figure 4-2 shows the major components of a DLC connection between a CO and homes.

Figure 4-2   *DLC Schematic*

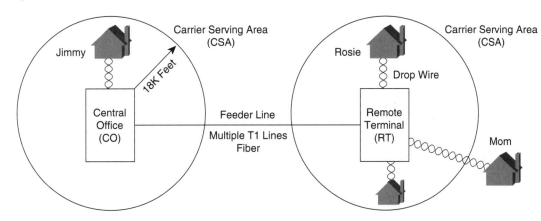

In Figure 4-2, Jimmy lives close to the CO, so his local loop directly connects to the CO. Rosie lives far from the CO, so she cannot be directly connected. Instead, her local loop connects to a DLC that multiplexes her loop back to the CO. Mom lives farther out still. She is connected to the DLC as well, but because she lives outside the range of the CSA, she cannot receive advanced services, such as ISDN, without special equipment such as repeaters.

The connection between the CO and the remote terminal can be a T1 circuit but is more likely to be fiber in modern DLC installations. Examples of such systems are the Lucent SLC-2000 and DSC Litespan 2010. Roughly 20 percent of lines in the United States use T1 or fiber DLC systems. The remote terminals are installed in controlled environmental vaults (CEV), which are underground sites, or street-side pedestals. The CEVs are more compact, less costly facilities than COs. In this architecture, a remote switching terminal can switch calls from Rosie to Mom.

Telcos' investment in existing plants is in the hundreds of billions of dollars, with more than $20 billion spent annually on upgrades. Because they are enhancing their phone wires with new DLC technologies, which introduce fiber into the neighborhood, it makes business sense to investigate using fiber-based transmission coupled with phone wire to offer high-speed services.

xDSL Variations

DLCs represent the most recent innovation in telephone company access networks to consumers. However, DLCs do not provide high-speed services by themselves; they are just vehicles for providing legacy services more cost effectively. To provide high-speed services, whether through a DLC or directly connected to a central offices, new modulation, forward error correction, and loop installation steps are required.

While DLC has more or less been standardized among telephone companies, high-speed DSL services have been graced with a variety of services. In fact, one of the issues with xDSL services is that there are too many of them. This had led to market confusion, controversy, and fragmentation. xDSL has not coalesced around a single data specification in the same way HFC that has. Various xDSLs in alphabetical order are listed here:

- Asymmetric DSL (ADSL), codified as ITU G.992.1, G.DMT, ANSI T1.413
- G.Lite, codified as ITU G.992.2
- High Data Rate DSL (HDSL), commonly used for T1 leased line services in the United States using 4 wires
- High Data Rate DSL-2 (HDSL-2), HDSL using a single wire pair
- ISDN DSL (IDSL)
- Multirate DSL (MDSL)
- Multiple Virtual Line (MVL™) (Paradyne)
- One Megabit Modem™ (Northern Telecom)
- Single-Line DSL (SDSL)
- Very High Data Rate DSL (VDSL)

The variations among these DSLs are distance, speed, symmetry, support for analog telephone, the number of wire pairs required, and factors derived from these, such as location of network termination and cost.

Speed and Distance

Speeds vary from 128 Kbps symmetric (IDSL) to 51 Mbps asymmetric (VDSL). Distances vary from a few hundred meters (VDSL) to a few miles. Distance for a single service varies according to the particular characteristics of a particular local loop. The marketing question is the tradeoff between speed and distance. This tradeoff depends on one's view as to whether customers really need speed greater than T1/E1. Slower-speed xDSLs generally reach greater distances and are more quickly installed because they can cohabitate with other DSLs, analog voice, ISDN, and T1 lines. For most users, T1 speeds or speeds down to 384 Kbps are sufficient for most Internet surfing and e-mail applications. Believers in higher-speed xDSL take the leap that video for various forms will be popular.

Symmetry

The "A" in ADSL means *asymmetric*. This means more speed downstream than upstream, just as in HFC networks. The marketing case for asymmetric service is that it is a better fit for Internet traffic. In actuality, asymmetry became important because telephone companies wanted asymmetric services over legacy phone wire so as not to compete with symmetric service, particularly T1.

With the proliferation of work-at-home applications and personal Web hosting, it is becoming more important to have symmetric service to the home. Homes may generate as many bits as they consume. Cable customers often chafe at being barred from having Web sites at home. Increased demand for symmetric service may pose marketing difficulties for asymmetric network services, but higher-return path speeds pose technical problems, similar to problems posed in cable.

Support for POTS

Some xDSL services provide transparent support for POTS. This means that the low frequency band used by POTS (0 to 3400 Hz) is passed transparently to an analog telephone handset in the home. Therefore, it follows that these frequencies cannot be used for digital modulation. The market requirement for POTS is that legacy phone users can get the new services. Without POTS service, the customer would need to buy a new line to have both xDSL and POTS.

However, frequency-division multiplexing of POTS and xDSL on a single pair raises the risk that the two forms of traffic will interfere with each other. For example, if a user goes off-hook with the telephone handset, there is the risk of interference with data. Alternatively, data traffic can induce a hum into the audio channel.

Services that have no POTS obviously do not have the requirement to separate voice and data because there is no voice. Furthermore, they have use of the longer-reach lower frequencies. To get voice service, it is necessary to have a digital voice capability as part of the digital data stream. An example is Voice over IP (VoIP). Standardization is underway to develop VoIP in the IETF, ITU, ADSL Forum, and other standards bodies.

Location of Equipment

Currently, xDSL carrier equipment is generally designed to run in COs, not remote terminals and certainly not on telephone poles. If xDSL equipment could also be installed in remote terminals or CEVs, the loop to the customer would be shorter, and more speed could be offered.

However, installation in a remote requires compact packaging, low power consumption, and compatibility with existing equipment.

Figure 4-3 depicts several types of DSL, including where fiber is terminated.

Figure 4-3 *DSL Flavors*

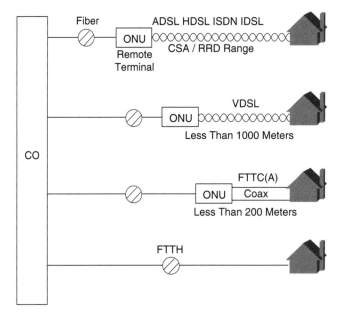

Fiber is terminated in the *Optical Network Unit (ONU)*, which is the equivalent of the fiber node in cable networks. Naturally, the farther you extend the fiber, the shorter the copper local loop can be and the higher the bit rate and the customer penetration rate can be. On the other hand, terminating fiber far into the network creates new problems of remote maintenance, remote powering, availability of remote real estate, up-front cost, and robustness of equipment.

The ONU may be situated as far into the neighborhood as the street pedestal (enabling either VDSL or FTTC), a multiple dwelling unit (enabling either VDSL or FTTB), or the individual residence (enabling FTTH).

The following sections present several DSLs in more detail, beginning with ADSL (details of FTTC and FTTH are covered in Chapter 5, "FTTx Access Networks"). ADSL has received the greatest amount of hype to date. It has also has been standardized by ANSI and the ITU, whereas other DSL options are either proprietary or are not yet completely defined. The vocabulary and speci-fications associated with ADSL provide a good foundation for discussing other DSLs.

Asymmetric DSL

Originally conceived at Bellcore, Asymmetric DSL (ADSL) is a telco-inspired service that offers a high-speed digital service and analog voice service over a local loop.

The original market driver was distribution of video on demand (VoD). When VoD failed to be a hot market opportunity, the supporters of ADSL (like the supporters of HFC) latched onto high-speed Internet access for their business case. With or without video, people believed that more data would come downstream from the CO than upstream to the CO. The business case for ADSL rests strongly on the proposition that data—and data alone, in this asymmetric form—is sufficient to drive infrastructure development. This is yet to be determined in the marketplace, but it is the same business proposition as data over cable.

A key difference between HFC and ADSL is that the users of HFC in a neighborhood share the copper, while ADSL users do not. An ADSL local loop is for the exclusive use of the subscriber, with no contention for bandwidth on that local loop. Therefore, despite the inherently higher bandwidth of cable, a crossover point exists where the ADSL service average bandwidth per user can exceed HFC, given sufficiently high use of HFC.

Another important feature of ADSL is that it provides for passive transmission of analog voice service. This is a surprisingly complicated enhancement that some telephone companies feel obliged to provide, either out of regulatory necessity or out of market necessity to service their legacy customers.

Two industry groups became involved in ADSL specification. ANSI T1.E1 took the responsibility for specifying a standard for modulation technique. This work culminated in document number ANSI T1.413, ratified in 1993. In addition, an industry consortium called the ADSL Forum (www.adsl.com) was created in 1994 to take the modulation techniques specified by ANSI and to discuss how to build end-to-end systems. The ADSL Forum is officially neutral on modulation techniques, although its members have strong opinions on the matter. The ADSL Forum is also specifying systems for other flavors of ADSL, such as VDSL and symmetric DSLs. Important dates in the evolution of ADSL are as follows:

- 1989: Pioneering work is published by Bellcore (Lechleider, et. al).
- 1993: Field trials begin using CAP modulation at British Telecom and Bell Atlantic.
- 1993: ANSI T1E1.4 ratifies DMT as a modulation technique, based on the view that 6 Mb of video would be required for video, specifically to carry four concurrent video streams.
- 1994: ADSL Forum is formed.
- 1996: CAP 1.5 Mbps ADSL gets another shot after ADSL supporters agree that VoD is not the market driver it was expected to be.
- 1997: Trials begin for CAP and DMT.
- 1998: Tariffed service begins in the United States and elsewhere

ADSL Modulation

Although CAP modulation is well-understood and relatively inexpensive, some argue that it is difficult to scale because it is a single-carrier modulation technique and is susceptible to narrowband interference. DMT uses multiple carriers and is standardized by the ANSI committee T1E1.4 (document T1.413) and ITU G.992.1, or G.dmt.

This standard calls for 256 subbands of 4 kHz each, thereby occupying 1.024 GHz. Each subband can be modulated with QAM 64 for clean subbands, down to QPSK. If each of the subbands can support QAM-64 modulation, then the forward channel supports 6.1 Mbps. On the return path are 32 subbands, with a potential for 1.5 Mbps.

CAP and DMT Compared

CAP is a single-carrier technique that uses a wide passband. DMT is a multiple-carrier technique that uses many narrowband passbands as individual carriers. The two have a number of engineering differences, even though they ultimately can offer similar service to the network layers discussed previously.

Adaptive Equalization

Adaptive equalizers are amplifiers that shape frequency response to compensate for attenuation and phase error. Adaptive equalization requires that the modems learn line characteristics—and do so by sending probes and looking at the return signals. The equalizer then knows how it must amplify signals to get a nice flat frequency response. The greater the dynamic range, the more complex the equalization. ADSL requires 50 dB of dynamic range, making adaptive equalization complicated. Only with recent advances in digital signal processing (number crunching) has it become possible to have such equalization in relatively small packaging.

Adaptive equalization is required for CAP because noise characteristics vary significantly across the frequency passband. Adaptive equalization is not needed for DMT because noise characteristics do not vary across any given 4 kHz subband. A major issue in comparing DMT with CAP is determining the point at which the complexity of adaptive equalization surpasses the complexity of DMT's multiple Fourier transform calculations. This is determined by further implementation experience.

Power Consumption

Although DMT clearly scales to RBB and does not need adaptive equalization, other factors must be considered. First, with 256 channels, DMT has a disadvantage regarding power consumption (and, therefore, cost) when compared with CAP. DMT has a high peak to average power ratio because the multiple carriers can constructively interfere to yield a strong signal. DMT has higher computational requirements, resulting in more transistor in the transceiver chips. Numbers are mostly proprietary at this point, but it is estimated that a single transceiver will consume 5 watts of power, even with further advances. Power consumption is important because hundreds or thousands (as carriers dearly hope) of transceivers might be at the CO. This would require much more heat dissipation than CAP requires.

Speed

DMT appears to have the speed advantage over CAP. Because narrow carriers have relatively few equalization problems, more aggressive modulation techniques can be used on each channel. For CAP to achieve comparable bit rates, it might be necessary to use more bandwidth, far above 1 MHz. This creates new problems associated with high frequencies on wires and would reduce CAP's current advantage in power consumption.

Licensing

DMT is a public, open standard. Globespan Technologies (formerly ATT Paradyne) is the licensing agent for CAP. As of this writing, 20 companies have been issued licenses. Among the licensees are Bellcore, Westell, Nokia (Finland), and NEC (Japan). One of the marketing difficulties of CAP is that system providers are reluctant to license the intellectual property from a single source; it makes them feel vulnerable. If there were more licensors of the technology, perhaps CAP would have fared better.

Overview of CAP Versus DMT Summary

This discussion has tried to fairly represent the CAP/DMT debate. Without a doubt, advances will be made in both technologies, which will narrow the various technical gaps. Table 4-3 summarizes the important differences as they exist at the time of this writing.

Table 4-3   *Comparison of CAP and DMT for ADSL*

	CAP	DMT
Power consumption	Lower, fewer gates	Higher peak/average, but will likely narrow gap
Forward carriers	1	256
Return carriers	1	32
Increment	320 Kb	32 Kb
Adaptive equalizers	Needed	None
Licensing	Globespan	Many sources
Standardization	In process	ITU and ANSI
Key competitors	Globespan, Paradyne, Westell	Conexant, Cisco, Alcatel, Amati (now Texas Instruments), Westell, Efficient Networks

---

Convergence of CAP and DMT

In the end, the choice of modulation technique will likely be immaterial. DSP advances will enable these technologies to converge in cost and functionality, and what we are then left with is the question of commercial interest.

The long-term challenges for DMT would appear to be power consumption and latency. In the end, the marketplace needs to speak loudly and clearly as to whether the speed of DMT is truly required by the subscriber.

ADSL Architecture

CAP and DMT advocates certainly differ on the merits of their respective modulation schemes, but they are coming together on further architectural elements of an ADSL system.

The ADSL Forum is, in theory, neutral on modulation technique, leaving this discussion to ANSI. Instead, the ADSL Forum is intended to fill gaps left by ANSI with the objective of creating services from modem standardization.

The ADSL Forum produced a general schematic that is useful for establishing vocabulary. Its version is shown on the ADSL Forum Web site at www.adsl.com/. A version of this schematic—modified slightly to account for DAVIC interfaces—is shown in Figure 4-4.

Content providers transmit information to the CO over the A9 interface (not shown) and the A4 interface that is shown in both Figure 4-4 and Figure 4-5. ADSL advocates anticipate that services will be received from digital broadcast, broadband networks, and narrowband networks, with network management information also terminated in the CO. The DSL Access Multiplexer (DSLAM) will house multiple ATU-Cs (ADSL Transmission Unit-Central Office), as shown in Figure 4-5. The ATU-C is embedded in a line card in the DSLAM; there is one ATU-C per subscriber. The DSLAM aggregates multiple loops—possibly hundreds or thousands of loops—into a few high-speed circuits. The DSLAM multiplexes traffic onto Fast Ethernet or ATM trunks.

At the other end of the phone wire is an ATU-R (ADSL Transmission Unit-Remote) at the subscriber site. The ATU-R can support a multidrop or shared-home topology. This means that only one ATU-R is required even though multiple computers or televisions are connected through it within a home. The ATU-C and ATU-R engage in physical-layer negotiations between the home and the CO. For the purpose of this discussion, they can be considered modems. The ATU-R will connect to terminal equipment in the home using either Ethernet or ATM.

ATU-R should keep management statistics, such as signal to noise ratio, at the physical layer; keep statistics such as packet counts at the network layer; receive software updates; and be remotely manageable by the carrier.

Figure 4-4   *ADSL Reference Model, Adapted from the ADSL Forum Model*
Courtesy ADSL Forum (www.adsl.com/)

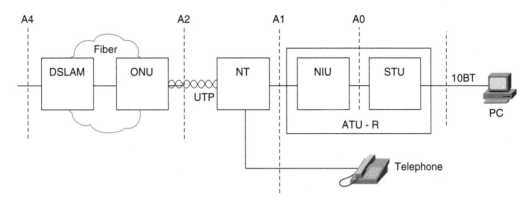

Figure 4-5   *More Detail on an End-to-End Design*
Courtesy ADSL Forum (www.adsl.com/)

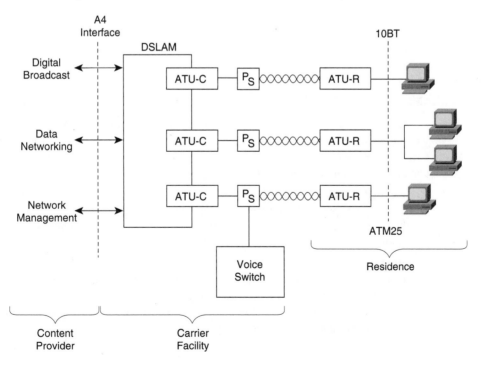

POTS Splitter

The reference model also calls for a POTS splitter (labeled PS in Figure 4-5),which enables the carriage of analog telephone service and digital data/video service on the same loop. A POTS splitter is a low-pass/high-pass filter that separates analog voice from ADSL frequencies and keeps the ADSL signals from creating interference in the telephones. POTS splitting will be discussed in more detail in the section "Principles of Operation of ADSL" later in this chapter.

DSL Access Multiplexer

The access node in the ADSL Forum reference model is referred to as the DSL Access Multiplexer (DSLAM). The primary functions of DSLAM are the following:

- House a set of ATU-C interfaces
- Multiplex traffic from multiple ATU-Cs onto a single, high-speed trunk to the transport network (for example, over an ATM OC-3 circuit)
- Demultiplex traffic from the transport network and assign it to the correct ATU-C
- Negotiate line speed (discussed later in the section "Rate Adaption")
- Serve as a central management platform
- Cause ATM termination in cases where packet mode traffic is delivered to the ATU-R
- Select latency path—that is, the classification of traffic in the forward direction as either high-latency or low-latency traffic (discussed later in the section "Principles of Operation of ADSL")

DSLAMs can be located in a number of locations:

- **Central office**—Incumbent phone companies will put their own DSLAMs into COs or will provide co-location services to competitive local exchange carriers (CLECs). When CLECs locate in COs, they will provide installation and maintenance themselves or will contract out maintenance to the ILECs (virtual co-location).
- **Adjacent site to the central office**—The DSLAM is installed in a CLEC facility near an ILEC CO. The copper loop is extended from the CO to the CLEC DSLAM. This has the problem of lengthening the copper loop, but it removes the need to obtain actual or virtual co-location.
- **Remote terminal**—xDSL services are subject to restrictions on loop length. Remote terminals, or loop carrier systems, are installed farther into the distribution network. DSLAMs can be installed in these remote locations, provided that sufficient space is available and that the DSLAMs do not generate excessive heat. Also, space in remote terminals will not normally be available to CLECs.

- **Customer premises**—For multiple dwelling units (MDU) and commercial parks, there is the possibility that hundreds or thousands of users will be served by a single DSLAM. In this case, a single dedicated DSLAM can be installed on the campus.

One of the main provisions of the Telecom Act of 1996 was to require the ILECs to offer co-location services to competitive carriers. CLECs have often responded that the ILECs have not offered co-location in good faith. They claim that the ILECs overcharge for the space, put operating burdens on the CLECs (such as refusing to permit CLEC personnel into COs for maintenance), or say that space is not available when it is. Of course, the ILECs see things differently. They are clearly in no hurry to let competitive companies onto their premises.

In any case, it seems that all would be better off if there were more cooperation between CLECs and ILECs on the introduction of advanced services. Perhaps, regulation permitting, ILECs can actually invest in CLECs or ISPs rolling out DSL. SBC has an investment in concentric networks. This seems to be a logical business model so that the ILECs and CLECs can jointly confront the cable operators, who have a substantial and lengthening lead in the provision of high-speed data services.

On another note, one estimate (Paradyne; www.paradyne.com/sourcebook_offer) reports that approximately 200 DSL customer lines are necessary on a co-located DSLAM to make co-location profitable. This break-even point can be achieved by the CLEC if it can offer other services, such as T1 leased lines or Frame Relay, from the same facility. Hence, there is innovation in networking equipment that can perform such multiservice functions.

ATU-C and ATU-R Operations

The ATU-C and ATU-R are mostly concerned with the physical layer.

The following issues are involved:

- Frequency allocation
- Echo cancellation and frequency-division multiplexing (FDM)
- Rate adaption

Frequency Allocation

Bandwidth on the phone wire is divided into three parts: legacy analog POTS service, upstream digital service, and downstream digital service.

The POTS bandwidth allocation is well known because it must conform with current use. POTS currently occupies frequencies below 3400 Hz. Therefore, this is not used by the ADSL digital services.

Bandwidth for digital services has two options. One is a frequency-division multiplexing mode, in which upstream and downstream bandwidth are in separate spectra. FDM simply has two half-duplex channels. Return path is transmitted in the range of 25 to 200 kHz. Forward path is transmitted from 250 to 1000 kHz. The top graph of Figure 4-6 illustrates FDM frequency allocation.

Also shown in the top graph of Figure 4-6, the lowest 3.4 kHz is used for POTS voice traffic. At 25 kHz through approximately 200 kHz, upstream bandwidth is provided. Beginning at 250 kHz through 1000 kHz, or even higher, downstream bandwidth is provided.

The issue with FDM mode is that the upstream and downstream channels need to be restricted so that they don't overlap. This reduces the amount of effective bandwidth these channels can use for modulation, thereby reducing speed. Furthermore, while FDM reduces the near-end crosstalk (NEXT) problems, it requires the use of higher frequencies, resulting in shorter reach.

Figure 4-6   *ADSL Frequency Allocation*

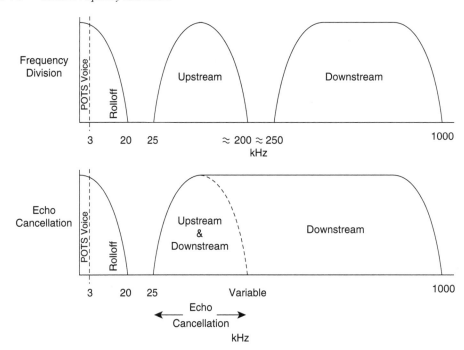

The alternative to frequency-division multiplexing is to extend the frequency range available to the upstream and downstream channels and thereby permit overlap bandwidths as illustrated in the lower graph of Figure 4-6. This case shows that the downstream bandwidth completely overlaps the upstream. In the range of overlap, echo cancellation is required.

Echo cancellation is used to obtain a clean signal in the event that both sides talk at the same time. Echo cancellation is a well-understood technology used in V.32 and V.34 modems and satellite communications. It uses bandwidth more efficiently than FDM, but at the expense of complexity and cost.

In the echo cancellation mode, the sender transmits and remembers its transmitted analog signal. Milliseconds later, it detects a transmission from the other end. That detected transmission is a combination of real data from the other end and an echo of the original transmission. The sender extracts the echo of the original transmission from the combined reception and thereby can recover the intended transmission from the other side. Echo cancellation works well when only one echo exists; if multiple echoes exist, primarily due to bridged taps, cancellation becomes more complicated and less effective.

Echo cancellation was invented for voice transmission over satellites. The long propagation delays (50 ms) annoyed listeners, who could hear themselves talk; echo cancellation was created to alleviate this annoyance. Delays of less than 50 ms need not be cancelled because the human ear does not have that much time-sensitivity.

A downside of echo cancellation is cost. It is more expensive to have an echo canceller in the ATU-R than simply transmitting and receiving on different frequencies. Because of cost, FDM is the preferred mode, although with advances in signal processing, the cost penalty of echo cancellation is becoming less severe.

Rate Adaption

Another function of the ATU-C and ATU-R modems is rate adaption. *Rate adaption* is the process by which the modems determine the bit rate at which they will transmit. This is like the procedures used for data modems over analog lines. A negotiation process exists between the ATU-C and ATU-R to determine line characteristics (mainly impairments) and to agree on the maximum bit rate the local loop can reliably support for the duration of the session.

Because data sessions are long-lived, it is possible that line conditions might change during the session. For this reason, consideration is being given to periodically recalibrating the line to change bit rate on the fly. This yields complications for higher-level protocols such as ATM and MPEG and applications such as RealAudio, but is seen as key to providing maximum bit rate.

End-to-End Architecture

Figure 4-7 depicts a variety of end-to-end architectures for various DSLs.

Figure 4-7 *End-to-End Architecture*
Source: Cisco web site

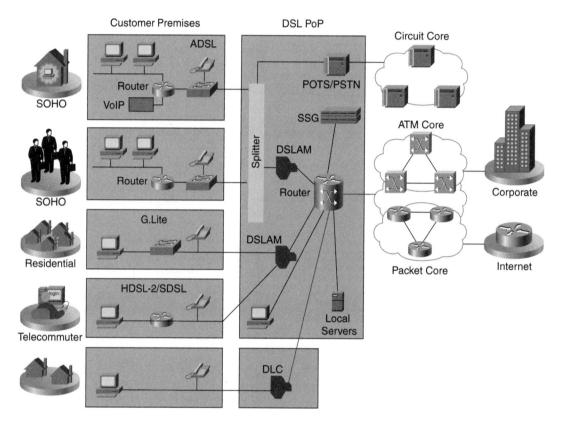

Various customer premises capabilities are outlined in this figure. The most complex customer configuration is denoted as a small office/home office (SOHO) user. This configuration would have multiple PCs and digital voice, VoIP pass through the ATU-C. In addition, there would be POTS service, possibly to support a fax machine. A complex configuration such as this would likely require a full-rate ADSL service, a router on the customer premises, and a splitter.

The second SOHO user would not use VoIP service but would use the digital bandwidth for data only. A residential user who wanted xDSL for educational or entertainment use could have full-rate ADSL or G.Lite (a variant of ADSL, which was introduced later in this chapter) service. Both ADSL and G.Lite users connect to the DSL point of presence (PoP). This is telephone company, either ILEC or CLEC, property. The ADSL or G.Lite user connects to a splitter at the PoP, and the POTS or ISDN service is shunted off to a legacy telephone switch.

The data services from each residential user are connected to the DSLAM. The problem for the carrier at the DSLAM is how to aggregate the potentially thousands of lines coming in from users so as to provide a packet or ATM transport service to the Internet or corporate/government/education networks.

The ADSL Forum selected a technique called PPP over ATM (ADSL Forum document 97-215, "An Interoperable End-to-End Broadband Service Architecture over ADSL Systems, Version 3.0") in December 1997. PPP supports a dial-up model. That is, the service provider configures the service much the same way as it would configure a large-scale telephone dial service. PPP also provides for multiple protocol support and user authentication. PPP encapsulates IP packets with security and other headers, which makes the user packet of variable length. It is codified as Internet RFC 1661, July 1994.

Some carriers would like to have a fixed-length protocol on the local loop to provide a quality of service not thought obtainable with IP on the local loop. Therefore, the local loop is framed using ATM, which makes it necessary to have a *segmentation and reassembly (SAR)* function. This is the process by which Ethernet packets are julienned into fixed-length ATM cells and, conversely, by which ATM cells are reconstituted into Ethernet packets. Ethernet packets are of variable length and can be as large as 1500 bytes; ATM cells are fixed as 48 bytes. Chopping the packets into cells is not a large problem. The bigger problem is how to associate the addresses inside Ethernet packets to ATM cell-addressing information, as well as how to enforce QoS guarantees. The SAR function is in the ATU-R.

The result of PPP/ATM is potentially thousands of ATM virtual circuits entering from the consumers that go to potentially hundreds of Internet sites and corporate sites. An aggregation and routing device is necessary to group ATM virtual circuits so that there is one ATM virtual circuit carrying many user sessions that connects the DSL PoP to an individual Internet site. This is preferable to having one ATM virtual circuit for each connecting customer to that Internet site.

For example, consider the case in which a SOHO user and an SDSL user both want to go to www.cisco.com. They each would have an individual PPP session from their site to the DSL PoP. However, without ATM VC aggregation, both users would also have an ATM VC between the DSL PoP and www.cisco.com. It would be nice if both users could be encapsulated in a common ATM VC because they are both going to the same place from the same DSL PoP. This aggregation makes xDSL systems more scalable.

PPP/ATM provides bandwidth guarantees to the residence. This improves QoS to the terminal equipment because congestion within the home is not a major issue. However, it does put the responsibility for mapping ATM addresses to IP addresses in the ATU-R.

In addition, there is the device called the Service Selection Gateway (SSG). This presents a menu of connectivity options to the end user. xDSL systems in the United States customarily provide open access to any number of customer-selected services. The SSG is a user-friendly way to present those options. Some early discussion revolves around providing SSG capability for cable networks, but their "walled garden" approach makes this less attractive to them.

Also note that HDSL-2 or SDSL customers do not need the services of a POTS splitter either at home or at the DSL PoP. This is because they do not pass POTS service. Thus, these fully digital services have simpler configuration at both ends of the line, at the expense of not supporting analog voice. Otherwise, they have the same architecture as ADSL or G.Lite service.

Finally, the DSL PoP will have local servers, such as Web caches, authentication servers, and network-management platforms. Some of these servers can be farther up from the DSL PoP, but large-scale systems will require distributed services.

Connection Model

Another architectural issue is the connection model for ADSL. The two options are 1. a terminal server model, in which a connection request is made by the end user when data service is requested; or 2. a permanently connected model, in which no connection request is needed.

The terminal server model is well understood by subscribers because it underlies the modem dial-up service used for online services today. A subscriber calls a phone number, an authentication server verifies the user's identity, and a connection is made. Potentially, it is possible for calls to get blocked, but with enough ports, connections are made reliably. The terminal server model offers the advantage of port conservation. It is possible to provision ports for only 2 to 5 percent of potential callers, on the proposition that not everyone calls simultaneously. As long as sessions are relatively short, significant economies of scale are achieved, as telephone companies and information service providers have known for years.

One problem with the terminal server model is that it is not compatible with push mode. When the Internet wants to send you something, you need to be connected with a widely known IP address. It can be argued that push mode is crucial for scalability of RBB, as suggested in Chapter 1, "Market Drivers." Hence, momentum exists for the permanently connected model to be used.

The problem with permanent connections is that the subscriber is consuming network resources (address, port) when not actively using the service.

Principles of Operation of ADSL

Two services are provided by ADSL: transparent access to legacy voice service and high-speed digital service.

Voice Service

Given the frequency allocation of ADSL, the provision of voice service is relatively straightforward. Mindful of the need to provide voice service, ADSL service was designed to use frequencies above the voice band. POTS splitters used in the home shunt the frequencies below 3400 Hz to POTS wiring. Frequencies above the voice band use whatever home wiring is provisioned for high-speed data service to get to the ATU-R. Care should be taken that the splitter will allow frequencies up to 20 kHz to pass to the NID. This enables alarm systems, which use frequencies higher than voice band, to continue functioning. ANSI T1.413 specifies 4 kHz, but most commercial filters will allow higher frequencies to pass. At the CO, a POTS splitter is also used to peel off the voice band and shunt it off to a voice switch.

The POTS splitter shunts the voice traffic back to the NID, where it joins the in-home phone wiring. In the CO, a companion POTS splitter binds the customer phone line to a circuit in the telephone network.

There are three places at which the POTS splitter can be located in the home:

- Low-pass filter at the NID, and the high-pass filter at the ATU-R
- Both filters in the ATU-R
- Both filters at the NID

When considering placement of the POTS filter, the following constraints are considered:

- The ATU-R requires local powering, so it might not be near the NID, which does not require local powering in many countries.
- Voice service should not be subject to impairments of home wiring, so it cannot be far from the NID.
- Low-pass filters are relatively large and will not fit into the NID. These constraints suggest that the POTS splitter and ATU-R should be separated. If the NID, POTS splitter, and ATU-R are each in separate boxes, cost and distance are a concern. In particular, how far can the splitter be from the NID and the ATU-R, and how is a consumer to know where to best locate the splitter? One proposal from British Telecom is shown in Figure 4-8.

Figure 4-8   *In-home Configuration*

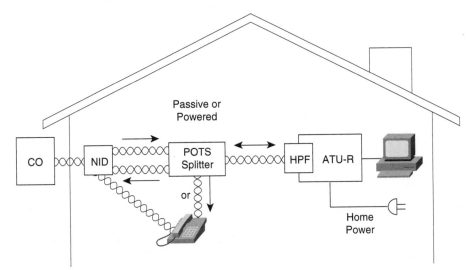

The figure shows the local loop terminating at the NID. Phone wire is used to connect the NID to the POTS splitter. The POTS splitter can either connect back to the NID for phone service, or it can connect directly to a phone. The latter case does not work when multiple phones are in the home. For this reason, wiring to support voice will likely make a U-turn and go back to the NID, at which point it will connect to in-home voice wiring. Wiring for high-speed data service continues to the ATU-R. The ATU-R might or might not have a high-pass filter associated with it. The ATU-R is powered locally and connects to the terminal equipment.

Although the exact location of the POTS splitter is unclear, it is clear that it will be on the customer's property, outside the purview of the phone company. It is the intent of most vendors that the POTS splitter be available at retail, with the telephone company charging an installation fee if required. In Europe, the NID is typically telco owned, which suggest there will be professional installation. Also, if the NID is located inside the home, then protection against lightning is required so that home electronics won't be damaged. For these reasons, professional assistance is likely to be required for splitter installation.

Another issue associated with the POTS splitter is that it is an electromechanical device, so it won't come down in cost significantly.

Finally, the local loop connecting the ATU-C to the POTS splitter must not have any telephones attached to it. Therefore, it is necessary that ADSL have professional installation not only to install the splitter, but possibly to install new inside wiring as well.

The ATU-R will be powered from the home. If power fails and the ADSL modems quit working, the telephone must continue to operate using network powering. A completely passive POTS splitter or an electrical relay in the POTS splitter will preserve telephone service in the event of a power loss.

Digital Service Startup

When the ATU-R is connected to the POTS splitter and local power, it will go through a startup process to get connectivity at the physical and networking layer. Four processes are required:

- Determine latency.
- Determine bit rate.
- Signal higher levels of protocols, such as ATM.
- Perform autoconfiguration.

Latency

Given that ADSL originally was intended for video transmission, the original designers planned for ADSL to be an error-free medium. To accomplish this, the bit stream was heavily interleaved and subjected to forward error correction. ANSI provided for 500 microsecond burst protection against impulse noise, which creates a 20 millisecond latency through the interleaver and modulators.

Data service has no such requirement for burst protection because higher-layer protocols can perform error correction. The option of having no interleaving for data services exists, thereby reducing latency due to interleave delay. This low latency form has a modulator/demodulator delay of 4 milliseconds. Therefore, ADSL provides for two logical data channels: a fast channel and a slow channel.

Video traffic is directed through forward error correction and interleaving; hence, it is on a slow channel. Data traffic bypasses these functions; hence, it is on a fast channel. Bits from the two channels are multiplexed to form a composite stream that is then sent to line coding, or modulation.

How the ATU-C knows to funnel data to the fast or slow channel is negotiated at startup, but the mechanisms are an unanswered question at this time.

Bit Rate Negotiation

A neat twist on ADSL is Rate ADaptive Subscriber Line (RADSL), which enhances CAP and DMT versions of ADSL by allowing the service to adapt to line conditions. The DMT rate can be adapted by using more or less aggressive modulation on each subband. CAP can be adapted by being more or less aggressive in its phase and amplitude modulation. RADSL is a negotiation process between the ATU-C and ATU-R, by which they agree on the maximum bit rate sustainable as a function of the state of the line. Better lines result in more speed.

When the ATU-R is powered on, it probes the line to determine its signal-carrying capacity. Signal-carrying capacity is a function of distance (which means there is a ranging process, very much like that for HFC), noise (owing to bridged taps and crosstalk), and allowable margins. Negotiation can take different forms.

One form, adopted by ANSI, provides for four start-up rate options that are programmable under carrier network management control. Each option is a multiple of 32 Kbps. Thus, there is a large set of possible rates, but only four at a time can be offered by the ATU-C to the ATU-R. The ATU-R selects the highest bit rate possible, consistent with its view of line conditions and allowable margins. It then informs the ATU-C of its choice, and clocks are set. If none of the four rates is acceptable, then the ATU-C can retry with the same set or a different set of four of the proposed rates.

Rate selection is communicated through network management to a management information base (MIB). An ADSL MIB is yet to be defined, but the ADSL Forum has accepted the responsibility for defining it.

By offering a finite number of options, the service provider can offer services at more predictable pricing. Other techniques would be for the ATU-R to offer a bit rate and for the ATU-C to accept. Another approach is the Stalinist approach of not having any negotiation at all. One bit rate is offered, and if line conditions do not permit, then the call is blocked.

The entire process offered by ANSI is expected to take 12 to 20 seconds for the modems to agree on a bit rate. After the bit rate is negotiated, the ATU-R will cache line characteristics. If service is interrupted, then the ATU-R can use the speed previously negotiated to avoid the 20 seconds or so of retraining period. It is expected that in a warm state, the modem can recover from a service interruption in a second or two.

Signaling to ATM

An interesting question of rate adaption is the relationship between the negotiated rate and ATM. ATM relies on knowing the speed to enforce QoS. In particular, it manages two important variables: peak cell rate (the maximum number of ATM cells transmitted per unit time) and average cell rate. These variables are used to determine whether QoS service is available at the time the call request is made.

In an environment in which the line speed is unknown until after session startup, or where the link speed changes during the life of the session, there needs to be a signaling mechanism whereby the conditions negotiated by RADSL can be communicated to ATM so that ATM can enforce its QoS policies.

The signaling mechanisms to determine rate and latency path selection for RADSL and to communicate that information to ATM are ongoing issues. The result might be that RADSL options are few and ATM QoS guarantees are fairly coarse; that is, they are not sensitive to small changes in line state.

Autoconfiguration

Another task at startup is configuring of IP addresses and software filters for the ATU-R. Because each subscriber has a dedicated ATU-C (port), the assignment of IP addressing and packet filters is relatively straightforward. They can be manually configured if the DSLAM is relatively intelligent. If not, some form of software tunnel is required to connect the ATU-C to a device with more intelligence.

During early stages of rollout, while there are a few hundred or perhaps a few thousand subscribers, manual software configuration is a possibility. When things get rolling, however, a new process might be called for, much like the cable industry is obliged to perform, whereby software configuration is done automatically.

The selection of an autoconfiguration technique is in part dependent on whether the ATU-R or the end system is IP-aware. If the ATU-R or the PC is IP-aware, for example, then the autoconfiguration technique can be a DHCP client, which requests an IP address from a DHCP server somewhere in the access network. This, of course, creates cost for the customer equipment. The implications of terminating ATM at various interfaces in the architecture are under investigation by the ADSL forum.

Digital Service Data Transfer

After the startup process is complete, data transfer is relatively straightforward. The ATU-R accepts data from the home network over an Ethernet, ATM25, or another standardized digital protocol. It encapsulates data using techniques mentioned previously in the section "End-to-End Architecture" (refer to Figure 4-7) and then forwards it. Unlike HFC, a MAC protocol is not required because the phone wire is not a shared medium.

Because data sessions can be long in duration—days perhaps—line conditions could change during the life of the session. Increased temperature increases length and resistance of the wire, which are material both for phone wire and coaxial cable. *Dynamic rate adaption* refers to a process by which ATU-C and ATU-R renegotiate maximum bit rate during data transmission in response to changes revealed by periodic testing of line conditions.

Unfortunately, retraining the line during dynamic rate adaption will take as much time as static rate adaption, so a 20-second retraining period might be necessary while the ATU-C and ATU-R do their thing. During renegotiation, data will be lost.

It is undecided as to how frequently dynamic rate adaption should take place, if it is offered at all. Another unresolved question is whether retraining will be required on both the interleaved and the noninterleaved traffic. Having retraining on both is complicated; retraining on data traffic (noninterleaved traffic) does not seem necessary.

Benefits and Challenges of Rate Adaption

Throughout the preceding discussion of digital service startup and data transfer, rate adaption is a recurring topic and is an important technology to ADSL.

Certainly, rate adaption increases bit rate for customers with good phone wire. But the main interest carriers have in rate adaption is to expand their market coverage. Service providers are helped by rate adaption because they can cover greater distances; hence, they can sell to more potential users. Distant users get lower bit-rate service, but without RADSL they wouldn't get service at all. Rate adaption gives telcos comparable market reach to homes passed by cable.

A number of challenges, both technical and marketing, are associated with rate adaption.

When negotiating bit rate at startup, what metrics (characteristics to be measured), algorithms, and measurements will be used by the modems to agree to a bit rate? Possible metrics include distance, which requires a ranging mechanism, frequency response, signal to noise, and phase error. Converging to a set of metrics might be relatively straightforward; agreeing on the algorithms and measurements to derive bit rate is likely to be more contentious. Measurements and algorithms are typically not the sorts of things that can be standardized in public bodies. These are usually the province of competitive advantage and proprietary information.

Different companies will manufacture DSLAMs, ATU-Cs, and ATU-Rs. In particular, the ATU-R will be a retail item, manufactured by consumer electronics vendors who are not involved in making central office equipment. Therefore, agreement on measurements and algorithms is necessary for interoperability. Consumers should not need to concern themselves with purchasing a specific ATU-R that matches the particular ATU-C used in their neighborhood.

Such agreement will be hard to come by and might occur by pairwise collaboration among companies. That is, an ATU-C manufacturer and an ATU-R manufacturer will reach an agreement that will enable the particular combination of modems to be interoperable. Specifically, the metrics, algorithms, and measurements to calculate bit rate must be coordinated. Keep in mind that during renegotiation of bit rate, data will be lost. So, in addition to reaching agreement on how to calculate bit rate, vendors probably will need to agree on rules about when renegotiation is not required.

Another technical problem raised by rate adaption is how to synchronize information about the negotiated speed with information required at higher levels of networking. For example:

- How is a particular ATM VC mapped to a fast or slow channel? Is it by manual configuration?

- When the bit rate changes, should the network and the end system be informed, and if so, how?

- If bit rate increases during a session so that a traffic contract is violated, is it required that the ADSL go into renegotiation?

- If the connection is lost and a reconnection is made at a lower rate, what should the ATU-C or ATU-R tell ATM?

Besides the technical challenges, RADSL creates marketing and administrative problems for setting pricing and bandwidth guarantees. What do you charge the user when the user does not know in advance what speed he will get? Furthermore, the bit rate can change during a session as line conditions change. How this affects pricing is to be determined.

G.Lite (ITU G.992.2)

Due to the problem of POTS splitters, the ITU ratified ITU G.992.2 for splitterless service. This offers the services of ADSL, but at a lower speed. It also is intended to ease installation because a POTS splitter typically requires professional installation.

Even though G.Lite is a splitterless option, it still provides POTS service by reducing the transmission power used to send digital information when the modem detects that the analog telephone handset goes off-hook, either for a voice or fax session. Because there is a new power level used to modulate the line, a *fast-retrain* procedure occurs with the ATU-R to establish proper power levels. This results in a slight cessation of service of about 1 to 2 seconds while the retraining is in process. After retraining, digital service will operate a bit more slowly, but (hopefully) no interference occurs with the analog conversation. How much slower depends on the amount of interference incurred with the analog service. When the analog handset goes back on-hook, the digital service is retrained up to its maximum speed.

In addition to being consumer-installable, G.Lite supposedly has a longer reach than full-rate ADSL and consumes much less power than full-rate ADSL. This reduction in power consumption provides much greater port density at the telco site and makes it possible to put telco equipment into remote terminals and loop carrier systems.

G.Lite also simplifies inside wiring in the home. With ADSL, there should be no analog telephones connected to the wire that connects the POTS splitter to the ATU-C. With G.Lite, phones can be placed anywhere in the home. Therefore, for ADSL, professional installation may be required for both the POTS splitter and the new inside wiring dedicated to data use. G.Lite obviates both reasons for professional installation. However, each telephone in a home with G.Lite may need a small microfilter for some added isolation between the G.Lite service and the telephone service. There is the marketing question of how many of these microfilters need to be sold with the ATU-R for retail distribution.

Table 4-4 compares full-rate ADSL and G.Lite.

Table 4-4   *Comparison of Full-Rate ADSL and G.Lite*

	Full-Rate ADSL	**G.Lite**
ITU Specification	ITU G.992.1	ITU G.992.2
	ANSI T1.413	No ANSI specification
Also known as	G.dmt	Splitterless ADSL
POTS	Yes, using a single splitter in home	Yes, using microfilters at each analog handset
Modulation scheme	DMT	DMT
Dual latency	Yes	No, only an interleaved option is supported
Subbands	256	128
Downstream speed	6 Mbps, maybe more for shorter distances	Up to T1
Upstream speed	Up to T1	Up to 512 Kbps
Professional installation	Yes, for splitter and inside wiring	Hopefully not

Despite its relative ease of installation, a splitterless option may not be popular in countries where the telephone company is still be responsible for internal wiring (which is not the case in the United States). Because those telcos (in France and Germany, for example) are required to make the truck roll in any case, going splitterless offers no installation savings and has the marketing problem of reduced speed. Also, in Europe, local loops tend to be shorter in distance than those in the United States, so their loops tend to be more qualified for higher speeds. This is perhaps why Deutsche Telekom will proceed with full-rate DSL.

Very High Data Rate DSL

Very High Data Rate DSL (VDSL) pushes to the limit what can be transmitted over 24-gauge copper pairs. VDSL's intent is to provide the fastest bit rate regardless of distance, and thereby provide a competitive service to cable by supporting entertainment video. VDSL is enabled due to recent advances in DSP technology, which allow the implementation of sophisticated channel modulation and adaptive equalization schemes. VDSL will modulate single-pair wiring from 300 kHz up to (possibly) 30 MHz over distances from 300 meters to 1000 meters. VDSL starts at 300 kHz to protect the POTS/ISDN service. (Yes, it needs a splitter.) This yields the following service options:

Upstream	Downstream	Distance
12.96 Mbps	12.96 Mbps	1000 meters
2 Mbps	25.92 Mbps	1000 meters
25.84 Mbps	25.92 Mbps	300 meters
2 Mbps	51.84 Mbps or STS-1	300 meters

At a distance of 1000 meters from the ONU, VDSL can support a single channel of HDTV, T1, or E1 data and analog or digital telephony simultaneously.

Some operators, particularly in Europe, believe that it is desirable to have both asymmetric and symmetric systems. Symmetric service, which has higher upstream speeds, would tend to reduce distance but would be more appealing to business-oriented users who would have servers at the client site. This requires agreement on a common spectrum allocation plan and is a prime issue for VDSL. Discussions are in process in ETSI, ADSL Forum, and the ITU (G.vdsl, G.993), with standards to be determined.

The key to providing the fastest bit rate possible is to have the shortest possible length of copper wire and therefore the longest run of fiber possible. To this end, fiber is terminated in an ONU very near the subscriber. Current thought is that the distance from fiber termination to ONU is about 200 meters, with an additional 100 meters on the customer premises, for a total distance of 300 meters from the fiber termination to the terminal equipment.

The ONU can be placed in many locations. If the subscriber resides within 200 meters of a CO or a remote terminal, the ONU can be in the CO or remote terminal, and VDSL service can be provided readily. For subscribers farther out, it will be necessary to locate the ONU in a street pedestal or controlled vault. For residents of a multiple-dwelling unit, where VDSL may have the greatest acceptance, the ONU can be inside the development. But with any of these options, the potential penetration rate is low compared with that of longer-reach services. It is unlikely that VDSL will ever reach a majority of homes in the United States, although it may achieve higher penetration in Asia and Europe because of the higher population densities.

Comparison with ADSL

Because standardization of VDSL is not complete as of this writing, we are limited to comparing the intent of VDSL with ADSL. Certain advantages and characteristics are compared as follows.

	Full-Rate ADSL	VDSL
POTS/ISDN, therefore requiring splitters	Yes	Yes, VDSL subscriber unit will be powered from the home, but will revert to network powering in the event of a power outage.
Modulation technique	DMT, using 256 bands with 4 kHz spacing	DMT, CAP, or QAM DMT modulation would use 256 bands with 40 kHz spacing, or 2048 bands with 4 kHz spacing
Dual latency	Yes	Yes
Spectrum Allocation	Up to 1 MHz	Up to 30 MHz
Downstream bit rate	Various up to 6 Mbps	Various up to 51.84 Mbps
Upstream bit rate	Various up to T1	2 to 3 Mbps
Standardization	ANSI T1.E1 ADSL Forum ITU G.992.1	ANSI T1.E1 ADSL Forum ITU SG 15, G.vdsl, G.993
Distance to ONU	Up to 5000 meters	300 to 1000 meters

High Data Rate DSL

Although ADSL enjoys considerable hype, High Data Rate DSL (HDSL) is the most widely deployed form of DSL, with more than 1 million lines deployed in North America today. The leading vendor of HDSL equipment, in terms of units shipped to date, is Pairgain Technologies (Nasdaq: PAIR; www.pairgain.com). Other vendors are Adtran (Nasdaq: ADTN; www.adtran.com), ADC Telecommunications (Nasdaq: ADCT; www.adc.com), and Orckit (Nasdaq: ORCT; www.orckit.com).

Originally defined by Bellcore, HDSL was created to provide leased-line T1 service to supplant the then-current Alternate Mark Inversion (AMI) modulation scheme. The problem with AMI was that it required frequent repeaters. HDSL was marketed as a repeaterless T1 and saved the telephone companies costs in provisioning a very popular business service. T1 service can be installed in a day for less than $1000 by installing HDSL modems at each end of the line. Installation via AMI costs much more and takes more time because of the requirement to add repeaters between the subscriber and the CO. Depending on the length of the line, the cost to add repeaters for AMI could be thousands of dollars and days to install.

The U.S. standard practice provides two-pair T1 transmission, with a data rate of 784 Kbps on each twisted pair. European standards exist both for a two-pair E1 system, with each pair carrying 1168 Kbps, and a three-pair E1 system, with 784 Kbps on each twisted pair.

In addition, HDSL uses less bandwidth than AMI. By using adaptive line equalization and 2B1Q modulation, HDSL transmits 1.544 Mbps or 2.048 Mbps in bandwidth ranging from 80 to 240 kHz over four wires. This is in contrast to the 1.5 MHz required by AMI. (AMI is still the encoding protocol used for the majority of T1.)

HDSL is heavily used in cellular telephone buildouts. Traffic from the base station is backhauled to the CO using HDSL in more than 50 percent of installations. Currently, the vast majority of new T1 lines are provisioned with HDSL. But because of the embedded base of AMI, less than 50 percent of existing T1 lines are provisioned with HDSL.

HDSL does have drawbacks. First, no provision exists for analog voice because it modulates through the voice band. Second, ADSL achieves better speeds than HDSL because ADSL's asymmetry deliberately keeps the crosstalk at one end of the line or the other. Symmetric systems such as HDSL have crosstalk at both ends.

HDSL-2 is a promising alternative to HDSL. The intention is to offer the same service as HDSL, namely symmetric, fixed-speed T1 service. However, HDSL-2 uses a *single* wire pair, whereas HDSL uses two pairs, or four wires. Because residences have single-pair wiring, they do not have immediate access to HDSL. With HDSL-2, residential users will have immediate access to high-speed, symmetric service. HDSL-2 uses PAM-16 modulation, which is more aggressive modulation than the four levels of 2B1Q and operates over shorter distances (about 10,000 feet).

ISDN Digital Subscriber Line

ISDN Digital Subsriber Line (IDSL) is a cross between ISDN and xDSL. It is like ISDN in that it uses a single wire pair to transmit full-duplex data at 128 Kbps and at distances of up to RRD range (the specified distance for ISDN). Like ISDN, IDSL uses a 2B1Q line code to enable transparent operation through the ISDN "U" interface. Finally, the user continues to use existing CPE (ISDN BRI terminal adapters, bridges, and routers) to make the CO connections.

The user speed of ISDN and IDSL is the same. The big difference is from the carrier's point of view. Unlike ISDN, IDSL does not connect through the voice switch. A new piece of data communications equipment terminates the IDSL connection and shunts it off to a router or data switch. This is a key feature because the overloading of CO voice switches by data users is a growing problem for telcos.

The limitation of IDSL is that the customer no longer has access to ISDN signaling or voice services. But, for ISPs who do not provide a public voice service, IDSL is an interesting way of using POTS dial service to offer higher-speed Internet access, targeting the embedded base of ISDN users as an initial market.

Single-Line Digital Subscriber Line

The term *Single-Line Digital Subscriber Line (SDSL)* has two interpretations. It has been used to describe a proprietary, one-pair, symmetric service using a variety of modulation techniques. It is also the official designation of the ETSI project to develop a standard based on ANSI HDSL-2, but providing variable-rate data, voice, and ISDN without the use of splitters. HDSL-2 is intended to have a single speed in both directions, namely T1. SDSL is expected to be rate adaptable, with a maximum of 2 Mbps.

Early Provisioning for xDSLs

Telephone companies are rolling out ADSL services cautiously. This fact has given pioneering ISPs an opportunity to offer some forms of DSL service in advance of the telcos' proposed ADSL services. Also, some corporations have considered implementing DSL services over private phone wires already installed in their buildings and industrial parks.

A popular underground method of obtaining DSL service is to order dry pair wires from the telephone company and put ATU-C and ATU-R components on it. A *dry pair* is phone wire with no electronics from one end to the other. A dry pair may pass through a telco office, but it doesn't touch telco equipment. It is referred to by a variety of names by different telcos, including the following:

- Burglar alarm wire
- Local Area Data (LAD) circuit
- Modified metallic circuit with no ring-down generators
- Voice-grade 36 circuit

Controversy surrounds recent decisions by some LECs to terminate the availability of dry copper wires, resulting in frustrating attempts by some ISPs to offer early xDSL services. Public hearings in the western United States, for example, are proceeding on petitions by U.S. West to stop offering LAD service.

Factors in Choosing Which DSL to Offer

When selecting which DSL to offer, the technical considerations that a carrier evaluates are length of drop cable, length of fiber, customer bit rate, number of homes supported per ONU, availability of real estate, and cost. They probably also should calculate real user demand for speed.

Why Bother with POTS?

One of the major fault lines separating the various DSLs is whether to have analog POTS service. As the discussions of POTS splitters, inside wiring, and loop qualification have droned on now for years, the case for POTS appears to weaken. The splitter needs professional installation and in Europe is often an active device that requires power. Also, it may be the case that inside wiring is needed. Furthermore, analog voice uses low frequencies, which would shorten the reach of the digital service, thereby reducing its marketability, however small.

Furthermore, voice service is becoming increasingly wireless, and there is rapid development of voice over IP, a purely digital form of voice. Therefore, it seems that any DSL (ADSL, G.Lite, One Megabit Modem, VDSL) supporting POTS is transitional and that eventually is necessary is a fully digital service. Going digital would extend the reach, reduce the installation cost, and likely reduce the amount of time spent in standards meetings.

Table 4-5 compares some of the characteristics that carriers must consider.

Technical Challenges to xDSL

As discussed earlier in the section "Benefits and Business Rationale of DLC," telcos have a number of compelling business reasons to pursue xDSL. The benefit to the customer is faster service than POTS or ISDN. But although the general architecture of DSL service for POTS and ISDN is well known, using the same infrastructure for high-speed services presents new technical problems.

Loop Qualification

The ideal local loop has no loading coils, no changes in wire gauge, and no bridged taps; is well insulated; and is as short as possible. Reality is different. End-to-end performance of the local loop is impacted by loop length, loading coils, quality of end-to-end splicing of wiring segments, multiple changes of wire gauge, home wiring, age, corrosion, hostile binder groups, crosstalk, and bridged taps. Furthermore, most local loops are unnecessarily long as they snake around physical obstructions both indoors and outdoors.

Table 4-5 *DSL Comparison*

	Modulation Scheme	Downstream Bit Rate	Upstream Bit Rate	POTS Support	Comments
ISDN	2B1Q	64 Kbps, 128 Kbps	64 Kbps, 128 Kbps	No	ANSI T1.601 Uses 4B3Q coding in some European countries
IDSL	2B1Q	128 Kbps	128 Kbps	No	Uses ISDN TA
HDSL	2B1Q	Up to 2 Mbps	Up to 2 Mbps	No	Uses four wires; current T1 service
HDSL-2	PAM-16	2 Mbps	2 Mbps	No	Uses two wires; not rate-adaptable
SDSL (ETSI)	2B1Q	2 Mbps	2 Mbps	Yes	Uses two wires; rate adaptable
G.Lite	DMT	2 Mbps	512 Kbps	Yes	ITU G.992.2
ADSL	CAP	1.5 Mbps to 6 Mbps	64 Kbps to 800 Kbps	Yes	Mostly Paradyne
ADSL	DMT	1.5 Mbps to 7 Mbps	64 Kbps to 800 Kbps	Yes	ANSI T1.413
Multiple Virtual Line (MVL)	CAP	768 Kbps	768 Kbps	Yes	Paradyne
One Megabit Modem	QAM	1 Mbps	320 Kbps	Yes	Proprietary to Northern Telecom; resides in Nortel loop carrier system
VDSL	QAM/CAP DMT	12.96 Mbps to 51.84 Mbps	1.5 Mbps to 3 Mbps	Yes	Range of 300 meters for top speeds; ANSI T1.E1.4, ETSI and ITU Study Group 15

Exactly how many of the United States' 167 million lines or the world's 650 million lines are qualified to support ADSL? According to a study by Bell South, only 41 percent of the 12.6 million loops in their region qualify for ADSL. (See www.interconnection.bellsouth.com/products/pdf_coll/adsl_dep.pdf.) CLECs would dispute this figure, arguing it is much higher and claiming that ILECs are low-balling the figure so that they would not be required to unbundle the loops. Telcos today are busy determining the answer using sampling, measurements, and experience gained from the rollout of ISDN and VoD trials.

Crosstalk

Crosstalk, specifically near-end crosstalk (NEXT), is interference that occurs among wires wrapped in a single binder group. Each wire is unshielded; therefore, one wire pair can interfere with another through electromagnetic coupling. In Figure 4-9, Jimmy and Rosie are communicating with Grandma and Einstein, respectively. An example of crosstalk is when Rosie receives transmission from two sources. She hears intended traffic from Einstein and spurious traffic from Jimmy. She will not hear spurious traffic from Grandma because the distance will attenuate Grandma's signal. Hence, the problem is near-end crosstalk rather than far-end crosstalk (FEXT).

Figure 4-9 *Crosstalk Visualized*

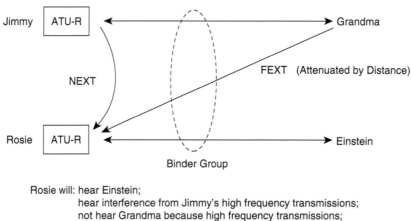

Rosie will: hear Einstein;
hear interference from Jimmy's high frequency transmissions;
not hear Grandma because high frequency transmissions;
be attenuated by distance.

Crosstalk increases rapidly as a function of frequency. Because voice is a relatively low-frequency service, crosstalk is not a problem. But AMI-encoded T1 wires create a special problem because of the high frequencies used by AMI.

AMI requires repeaters 3000 feet from the central office and every 6000 feet thereafter, and consumes more 1.0 MHz of bandwidth. Hundreds of thousands of lines (T1 and E1) exist in the world today. But AMI encoding uses so much bandwidth and creates so much crosstalk that telephone companies cannot put more than one AMI-encoded line in a single 50-pair cable.

Because AMI encoded T1 can use up to 1 MHz of bandwidth, it cannot coexist in the same binder group with ADSL. Identifying which binder groups contain such T1 lines requires accurate record keeping, which has not always been maintained. Some carriers plan to restrict the copper plant that ADSL will use, keeping it separate from transmission technologies that could cause crosstalk.

However, ADSL is intended to coexist with more modern services. In particular, ADSL is specified to operate with multiple ISDN and T1 HDSL services in the same binder over a CSA loop (9000 feet on 26 AWG) at 6 Mbps. It will not interoperate with T1 encoded with AMI—but then, nothing will coexist with AMI.

ADSL uses frequencies up to 1 MHz. VDSL can go up to 10 MHz and can create a massive amount of crosstalk. Because the phone wires and binder groups to be used by VDSL were never specified for such high-frequency operation, crosstalk will be much higher than contemplated for modern cables.

Early deployment will not pose much of a problem because of the few number of users, owing to VDSL's short distance. But, as the network includes more and more VDSL systems, and as crosstalk from other VDSL systems grows, the operator might have to replace some binder groups, resulting in a loss of service to the user as well as incremental installation costs.

One of the criticisms leveled at HFC is that shared media creates a loss of QoS. In a sense, however, the same occurs for point-to-point service such as DSL. A binder group can be considered a shared media because wires in a binder group are not shielded from one another; users can affect other users.

Bridged Taps

Bridged taps are a legacy of phone wiring installation practices, where a pair coming from a CO is branched into a Y form. The idea is to be able to use either branch of the Y to provision new subscribers. This layout has no affect at the low frequencies used by POTS, but it can be a significant impairment for DSL services. That's because the bridged taps are sources of echo. Signals from the CO hit the branching point and go along both branches of the Y. They can then bounce back to the other branch. Sometimes one of the branches is not terminated, which creates signal loss. Echo cancellation works very well when an echo has only one source, but when the original signal bounces off several places, cancellation becomes less effective.

Powering Remote Terminals

DSLAMs and ATU-Cs could possibly be located in controlled vaults and pedestals to increase neighborhood penetration and total available market. For VDSL, it might be necessary to locate equipment on telephone poles to justify a business case. These facilities have limited space; are out in the open; are subject to vandalism, water damage, and other environmental problems; and require powering. One big problem is heat dissipation. xDSL services need to minimize power consumption so that a smaller amount of heat is dissipated. For the moment, CAP has a 3- to 4-watt advantage over DMT in terms of power consumption. Local power will likely be used to power DSL equipment, but battery backup is needed for emergencies. This also puts a premium on low-powered solutions.

Spectral Masking

ADSL is subject to multiple forms of long-term narrowband interference such as crosstalk. AM radio and amateur radio ingress are potential interferors, both of which can operate below 1 MHz. One way to avoid stationary narrowband interference is to mask out the offending frequencies and to avoid using them for ADSL transmission.

Such masking can be accomplished with notch filters, typically passive devices that notch out certain frequencies permanently. If the source of narrowband interference comes and goes, however, then passive filters might be insufficient. Active filters can handle such dynamic interference but are more costly.

The term *spectral masking* refers to the process of notching out specific frequencies. In this environment, DMT operates rather naturally. Those frequencies that are notched out correspond to a certain subband and are not used by DMT. Because CAP modulates the entire spectrum, some adaptive equalization tricks are necessary to make it work with spectral masking.

Impulse Noise

Impulse noise on phone wire has been characterized by Bellcore and, before that, AT&T Bell Labs, so it is fairly well understood. Impulse noise is short-term interference affecting many frequencies, the duration of which is on the order of 100 microseconds, with peak power around 10 millivolts. The solution is to use interleaving and Reed-Solomon forward-error correction. Current thinking is to use RS (200,216) coding for the interleaved (slow) channel.

Impulse noise is the phenomenon that precipitated the discussion on dual latency for ADSL and its complications for networking. One important source of impulse noise is ringer noise from adjacent pairs.

ATU-R Maintenance

The ATU-R is more intelligent than the conventional POTS modem. For example, the ATU-R is capable of making software revisions, such as algorithms, for line calibration changes or if the carrier decides to change encapsulation protocols. Discussions are ongoing as to how software maintenance for the ATU-R is to be accomplished. Resistance is present to the carrier remotely managing it, in part because this is not the model used for current POTS or ISDN service. As in the case of cable modems, ATU-R maintenance raises new problems, such as software updating, and can have serious cost consequences.

Industry Challenges to xDSL

In addition to technical problems, certain industry issues must be addressed before widespread rollout.

Repeating the ISDN Experience

Cable competitors are betting that telcos cannot provide and distribute xDSL services any better than they did ISDN. Given the still lengthy and confusing provisioning process for ISDN, this would seem to be a good bet given the performance of telcos in the United States. Several significant issues must be overcome, such as provisioning, end-to-end protocol architecture, numbering plans, capacity planning, and workforce education.

Regulatory Issues

In the United States, the Telecommunications Act of 1996 required the local telephone companies to unbundle the local loop. This created potentially interesting consequences for xDSL and telephone service.

As of this writing, it is not clear whether telcos are required to unbundle xDSL service. It is possible that only POTS service must be unbundled and that frequencies above it can still be used exclusively by the phone company. Another unclear issue is what cost basis will be used to compensate the telcos for unbundling. The cost basis for POTS service provisioned through DSLs is not the same as that for direct connects: DSLs have lower costs (less trunking copper and smaller CO real estate requirements). States are currently calculating unbundled pricing for local loops, but it is not clear what cost model they will use to determine state-mandated pricing. If states decide on a price based on wiring pairs extending from the home all the way to the CO, then the phone industry catches a break because costs for these are higher than costs for DSLs. On the other hand, if the state uses a cost basis that presumes a high percentage of DSL, then the telcos are not catching a break—they are not being compensated at a rate higher than actual costs. In response, they might extend DSL to reduce costs and meet profit goals implied by state-mandated pricing.

Telcos are upset about unbundling for service reasons as well as financial ones. For example, consider the service issues when a subscriber of one of the new, competing companies uses dry pairs to obtain DSL service. Dry pairs can coexist on binder groups with normal rate-paying customers. It is possible for the user to inadvertently transmit excessively strong signals, thus creating sufficient near-end crosstalk to impair the phone service of everyone else in the binder group. Telcos are worried about getting blamed from the other 49 voice subscribers, so they are voicing such concerns as further arguments against unbundling.

Finally, on the matter of Equal Access, ILECs may have found a curious bedfellow in the cable operators. Cable operators are complaining that regulatory requirements that mandate Equal Access remove the incentive to invest in high-speed networking. ILECs have argued this for years, so it will be interesting to see whether cable operators and phone companies will be subject to the same set of rules.

Broadcast Video

DSL services, even VDSL, have not competed with cable to provide broadcast digital TV. Cable and satellite have early advantages to provide broadcasting. New architectures involving IP multicast and MPEG encapsulation are under consideration to provide a switched digital video capability. This technique will be discussed in the following chapter. For now, however, the primary business case for xDSL primarily rests with data service.

If carriers adopt a terminal server model, they will be restricted to pull mode. If so, then the telcos are vulnerable to ISPs offering lower-speed DSL services over dry pairs and direct satellite providers providing the video.

Home Networking

In addition to problems of external phone wiring, inside wiring can also introduce problems. Some estimate that in older buildings, roughly 10 percent of the home and office wiring and an additional 10 percent of the loop wiring is unusable for xDSL applications. Over time, home repairs, animal damage, corrosion, inside bridged taps, and withered insulation take their toll.

Fixing inside wiring will normally require a technician to come to the site and start over with new equipment. Some telcos are fixing inside wire preemptively for xDSL trials to avoid maintenance calls later. One issue in older homes is asbestos. Rewiring a home that contains hazardous materials is problematic for both the resident and the technician. For this reason, some consider wireless the best answer when asbestos is a known hazard.

Success Factors

Given the number of variables affecting the viability of xDSL, the following questions are among the most important for predicting its future:

- How many systems will be upgraded to DSL for POTS service? Using more DSL systems tends to reduce incremental cost for rolling out service.

- How many loops qualify? The higher the percentage of loops that qualify (including inside wiring), the higher the marketability of the service.

- How well can Web servers deliver significantly faster service to showcase the speed of xDSL networks? If Web servers or the Internet are chronically congested, the value of faster local loops is lost, the same as for cable.

- How popular will competitive technologies become, including ISDN and 56 Kbps modems? These services share cross-elasticity. Users who are content with 56 Kbps or ISDN service might elect to stay with these.

- How will ISPs price high-speed Internet services?

- Does a market exist for access networks that can provide a full range of video and data services over a single network? If so, DSL will not qualify to satisfy it because DSL cannot offer broadcast video. How patient will telephone companies be if their services meet with initial consumer resistance?

Summary

xDSL is the competitive response of telcos and some ISPs to cable operators offering high-speed data service. ADSL will be offered by telephone companies around the world. It leverages their existing wiring, an embedded investment on the order of a trillion dollars. It will also be offered by alternative providers such as ISPs, CAPs, and IXCs over nonservice-carrying wire, known as dry copper or burglar alarm wire. The unbundling of local loops is a requirement of the Telecommunications Act of 1996, which affords alternative carriers access to dry copper. Table 4-6 summarizes the challenges and facilitators to xDSL becoming a successful RBB network.

The next chapter addresses high-speed advancements beyond xDSL, including Fiber to the Curb (FTTC), Fiber to the Building (FTTB), and Fiber to the Home (FTTH).

Table 4-6   *Central Issues for Digital Subscriber Line and RBB*

Issue	Challenges	Facilitators
Media	Number of qualified existing loops is limited.	Huge embedded base worldwide.
	Hostile binder groups, T1 encoded with AMI.	Technical characteristics of the local loop permits higher speeds.
	Existing quality of home phone wiring is problematic in many cases.	DSL enhancements are underway for POTS service, which reduces incremental costs for advanced DSL.
Modulation schemes	Competing standards are CAP and DMT for ADSL.	CAP is relatively mature.
	QAM and DMT for VDSL.	DMT provides superior resistance to narrowband interference and can scale to high speeds.
	2B1Q lowest cost for lower speeds	

continues

Table 4-6 *Central Issues for Digital Subscriber Line and RBB (Continued)*

Issue	Challenges	Facilitators
Noise mitigation	Multiple bridged taps create problems for echo cancellation.	Unlike cable, a point-to-point topology means that a single noise source cannot adversely affect a large number of households.
Signaling	RADSL call setup is a time-consuming process. Mechanism required to signal latency path and RADSL to ATM. Mechanism required to signal dynamic rate adaption to ATM.	xDSL sessions can have a very long duration because they don't connect through a voice switch. This reduces signaling.
Data-handling capabilities	Potentially less speed is offered than cable in the forward path, given lightly loaded cable systems.	Good return path service enables reliable interactive service with known QoS. Multiple ATM and packet mode end-to-end software architectures.
Standards	Too many xDSLs cause market confusion. Differences in modulation scheme, frequency allocation, and carrier provisioning could inhibit interoperability of CO and consumer equipment.	Relatively few bodies are deliberating ADSL and VDSL specifications. Lots of motivation is provided by cable to converge on something.
Business/Financial	Big telephone companies do not have a good track record at rolling out high-speed services, witness ISDN. The question remains of how to transition current ISDN customers to ADSL without rewiring.	Telcos' real estate needs are reduced. Reduces data burden on voice switches and need for new ones. Enormous investment is leveraged in existing infrastructure. A maintenance budget can be used for certain upgrades.
Regulation	The requirement to unbundle local loop inhibits telcos' incentive to invest in local loop technologies. The relationship to universal access is unclear.	Telecommunications Act of 1996 gives CLECs access to ILEC unbundled services Dry copper is available for CLECs to provide service.
Market	Not suited for broadcast video. Not particularly well suited for VoD or nVoD.	Faster Internet service is provided than POTS, 56 Kbps, and ISDN service for consumers. The transition plan from HDSL through ADSL up to VDSL is logical.

References

ADSL Forum document 97-215. "An Interoperable End-to-End Broadband Service Architecture over ADSL Systems, Version 3.0." December 1997.

Allan, Dave (Northern Telecom). "Topics in DSLAM Architecture." *ADSL Forum 96-130:* December 1996.

Dugerdil, Bernard. "ADSL Access Network Reference Model." *ATM Forum 95-0610:* June 1995.

Modlin, C.S. "ATM Over ADSL and VDSL: PMD Specific Attributes That Affect the Network." *ATM Forum 97-0156* February 1997.

Rahmanian, Shahbaz. "Impact of the ADSL Rate Adaptation on QoS." *ATM Forum 96-115:* December 1996.

Articles

Cioffi, John, Vladimir Oksman, Jean-Jacques Werner, Thierry Pollet, Paul Spruyt, Jacky Chow, and Krista Jacobsen. "Very-High-Speed Digital Subscriber Lines." *IEEE Communications Magazine*, Vol 37, No. 4: April 1999.

Goralski, Walter, "xDSL Loop Qualification and Testing," IEEE Communications Magazine, Volume 37, No. 5: May 1999

Issa and Bieda. "The G.DMT and G.Lite Recommendations, Part 1." *Communications Systems Design Magazine*, Vol 5, No. 5: May 1999.

Kwok, Tim. "Residential Broadband Architecture Over ADSL and G.Lite (G.992.2):PPP Over ATM." *IEEE Communications Magazine*, Vol 37, No. 5: May 1999.

Kyees, Phil, Ronald McConnell, and Kamran Sistanizadeh. "ADSL: A New Twisted-Pair Access to the Information Highway." *IEEE Communications*, Vol 33, No. 4: April 1995.

Saltzberg, Burton. "Comparison of Single-Carrier and Multitone Digital Modulation for ADSL Applications", IEEE Communications Magazine, Vol. 36, No. 11: November 1998

Internet Resources

www.adsl.com

The Web home of the ADSL Forum; points to other ADSL sites as well

www.adsl.com/vdsl_tutorial.html

VDSL tutorial from the ADSL Forum

www.analog.com/publications/whitepapers/whitepaper_html/content.html

The DMT versus CAP argument according to Analog Devices

www.cisco.com

Use search engine to find ADSL Technology Glossary and other backgrounders

www.xdsl.com

xDSL news from Telechoice

www.etsi.org

European Telecommunications Standards Institute

www.vdsl.org

Home page of the VDSL Coalition

www.interconnection.bellsouth.com/products/pdf_coll/adsl_dep.pdf

The Bell South loop qualification summary

www.cs.tut.fi/tlt/stuff/adsl/pt_adsl.html

A dated but relevant ADSL tutorial from the Tampere Institute of Technology, Finland

www.fcc.gov/ccb/

FCC Common Carrier Bureau, responsible for regulating telephone company activities

www.fcc.gov/realaudio/archive

Hearings of the FCC, recorded and available via RealAudio, with testimony from telephone company and CLEC executives regarding loop qualification and binder group interference

www.fcc.gov/telecom.html

Telecommunications Act of 1996, with proceedings

frcatel.utc.sk/hwb/ta_AWG.html

Table showing wire gauge versus resistance

ftp.t1.org/pub/t1e1/e1.4/dir98/8e140075.pdf

ADSL standard according to ANSI T1E1

www.getspeed.com/

U.S. high-speed services by area code

www.labs.bt.com/profsoc/access/vdsl.htm

British Telecom and partners on VDSL

www.orckit.com

G.Lite and VDSL white papers

www.paradyne.com/sourcebook_offer

xDSL overview according to Paradyne

www.point-topic.com

UK consulting firm with DSL rollout news

NTT Japan's home page, with information on the company's ADSL trials and plans

www.telcoexchange.com

U.S. availability and pricing of DSL services by area code

www.disisit.com/nettest.html

Cable versus ADSL real time tests

This chapter covers the following topics:

- Fiber to the Curb
- Fiber to the Building
- Fiber to the Home
- Summary

CHAPTER 5

FTTx Access Networks

The deployment of optical fiber from the carrier premises (cable head end or telephone central office) deep into the distribution network enables the implementation of xDSL and HFC innovations.

Because xDSL and HFC bring fiber closer and closer to the home, why not finish the job and connect fiber all the way to the home? Fiber access networks, namely *Fiber to the Building (FTTB)*, *Fiber to the Curb (FTTC)*, and *Fiber to the Home (FTTH)*, are technologies to move fiber closer to the home—and, in the case of FTTH, *into* the home. These are referred to collectively as FTTx.

In particular, fiber to the home (FTTH) is viewed by some carriers and analysts as the Holy Grail of full-service access networks. It promises high bandwidth, immunity to electromagnetic interference, and lower operational costs because it doesn't rust. Why not just remove the metallic elements from the access network entirely? There are good reasons why not, which we explore in due course; first, we look at the promise and the architecture of FTTx networks. That being said, the emphasis of this chapter will be FTTH.

Like cable networks, FTTx networks promise full-service digital networking. Full-service means that a consumer can receive all video, voice, and Internet services from a single carrier, in contrast with today's market, where phone service is delivered by a local phone company, cable TV services from a cable operator, and Internet services from an ISP. Instead, digital telephony, interactive data services, and digital video (digital TV, video on demand, and near video on demand) would come from one service provider.

Much of the impetus behind FTTx among major telco operators is organized by the Full Service Access Network Initiative (FSAN, www.labs.bt.com/profsoc/access). At the time of this writing, the members of FSAN were Bell Canada, Bell South, British Telecom, Deutsche Telekom, Dutch PTT, Telecom Eireann, France Telecom, GTE, Korea Telecom, NTT, SBC, Singapore Telecom, Swisscom, Telefonica (Spain), Telia (Sweden), Telstra (Australia), Telecom Italia, Bezeq (Israel), Chunghwa Telecom, and U.S. West.

FTTx access networks are objects of research, development, and standardization. Current deployments are in the trial and very early rollout stage. However, FTTx offers the promise of speed in abundance, superior security, and network reliability so as to stimulate telcos around the world to support these innovations.

Fiber to the Curb

The term *Fiber to the Curb (FTTC)* has been used to describe a variety of network architectures in which optical fiber is brought close to the residence, where an optical network unit (ONU) couples the fiber to some form of metallic wiring that in turn leads to the residence (see Figure 5-1). Elsewhere you will see references to technologies such as Fiber to the Building (FTTB) and Fiber to the Cabinet (FTTCab). FTTB refers to the placement of the ONU in a multiple-dwelling unit (MDU), such as condominiums, apartments, and office buildings, where the ONU is placed on the MDU premises and where metallic wiring is distributed to the various tenant dwellings.

FTTCab refers to the placement of the ONU in a cabinet in the neighborhood, such as a street pedestal, from which metallic wiring can connect to individual residences. However, FTTB, FTTC, and FTTCab refer to the same basic architecture—that of an ONU within roughly 200 meters of the residence, with metallic wiring going the final leg to the customer application.

Figure 5-1   *FTTC Architecture*

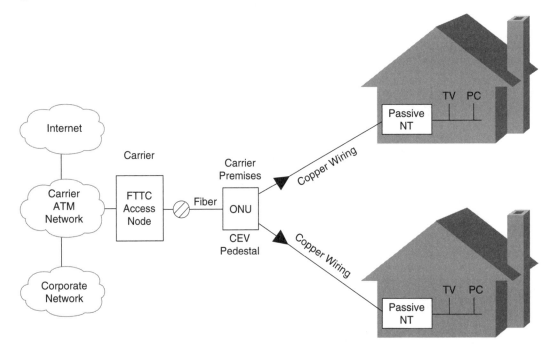

The Digital Audio Visual Council (DAVIC) has specified four variations of FTTC, called, creatively enough, Profiles A, B, C, and D. Profile A specifies the use of coaxial cable as the drop wire to the residence and has the highest speed. Relatively little product development has occurred for this form of FTTC. The companies with the coaxial cable, namely the MSOs, are currently preoccupied with their fiber buildouts, and telephone companies have shown little interest in overbuilding their twisted-pair networks with cable. Competitive carriers are more inclined to use VDSL as well because there is simply more twisted-pair in the world to leverage.

Profiles B, C, and D use twisted-pair copper as the drop wire. When configured with phone wire, Profiles B, C, and D are basically VDSL, with minor variations. Those variations are: 1. the standardization work for VDSL is being carried out in the ADSL Forum, ETSI, and the ITU, (G.993.1), whereas FTTC Profiles B, C, and D have been discussed in DAVIC; and 2. VDSL will have a specification for POTS splitting, which is not specified in FTTC.

The valid bit rates and drop wiring (wire between the ONU and the residence) for the various DAVIC profiles are shown in Table 5-1.

Table 5-1   *Comparison of FTTC Profiles*

DAVIC Profile	Downstream	Upstream	Drop Wire
A	51.84 Mbps	19.44 Mbps	Coaxial cable
B	51.84 Mbps	1.62 Mbps	Coax or phone wire
C	25.92 Mbps	1.62 Mbps	Coax or phone wire
D	12.96 Mbps	1.62 Mbps	Coax or phone wire

Important vendors of FTTC are Next Level Communications, Marconi (formerly Reltec, now a unit of General Electric [UK], www.marconi.com), Broadband Technologies (www.bbt.com, Nasdaq: BBTK), and Alcatel (www.alcatel.com, NYSE: ALA).

While some standardization work in DAVIC has defined physical-layer and MAC-layer specifications over coaxial cable, most of the work of DAVIC has been superceded by DOCSIS, DVB, and OpenCable when specifying higher-level protocols.

Therefore, the term FTTC is largely a generic or marketing term referring to any access network that brings fiber to within a few hundred meters of the residence. The majority of current standardization is happening under the guise of VDSL or HFC.

Fiber to the Building

Due to the short distances separating the residences within a single multiple-dwelling unit, the initial use of FTTC is MDUs, where the cost of a single ONU can be amortized over multiple paying customers. With Fiber to the Building (FTTB or, perhaps as it should be known, Fiber to the MDU), fiber is brought to the premises of the MDU, and metallic wiring is distributed to the tenants using coaxial cable, phone wire, or possibly Category 5 twisted-pair wiring, commonly used for Fast Ethernet. Depending on coaxial cable or phone wire implementation, the ONU is connected to either a CMTS/DVB CMTS or a DSLAM. The property owner will also likely house application servers to deliver video on demand (VoD) or e-mail services to tenants.

From the property owner's point of view, FTTB provides a new role: that of telecommunications operator. It thereby provides a potential new revenue opportunity. Some apartment owners are considering active deployment of FTTB services, requiring all tenants to subscribe to the service. The theory is that tenants would pay a rental premium in an MDU with high-speed network access. The property owner could even be certified as a competitive local exchange carrier, entitling the owner to interconnection with major carriers and collecting settlements. The rental premium could be split between the property owner and the carrier. Because of the high density of MDUs, there is considerable FTTB interest in Asia.

FTTB can be a major transition factor in moving from today's services to FTTH. It is a relatively smooth transition from ADSL to VDSL/FTTC to FTTH. The carrier can start with lower-speed technologies and proceed to higher speeds by pushing the ONU farther into the neighborhood, from the curbside to the MDU to the home. This can be a measured process that can be funded in part by the maintenance budget of the telephone companies, who enjoy regulatory relief for maintenance costs.

Bell South (NYSE: BLS, www.bell-south.com) offers a tariffed service for FTTC called Personal Computer/Data Network Access (PC/DNA). The customer premises connect to the carrier via a pair of twisted-pair phone wires, which in turn attach to an ATM-based fiber optic trunk called Integrated Fiber in the Loop (IFITL).

BellSouth has been testing FTTC since 1995. As of this writing, Bell South has deployed FTTC to more than 100,000 homes and plans to add approximately 80,000 homes annually in areas of new developments.

FTTC Issues

FTTC has many of the costs of FTTH without the benefits. For starters, it is costly to deploy, at least for single-family residences. Furthermore, at least in the United States, MDU tenants may not have the interest or the income to justify high-speed Internet access; they may be served just as well by V.90 modem capability.

Standardization issues also are at work. Competing work is occurring in the ADSL Forum, ETSI, and ATM Forum, and there are proprietary schemes as well. Therefore, it is difficult for manufacturers to get the critical mass of customers needed to drive down costs. Meanwhile, cable and ADSL are revving up quickly, garnering the interest of the popular press and the investment community. As of this date, similar momentum has not been achieved with FTTC.

The result is that specialists in FTTC, such as Broadband Technologies, have fared poorly and need to change their business models.

Fiber to the Home

VDSL and FTTC bring fiber to within 200 meters of the home. These are viewed by some as transition services on the way to bringing fiber from the carrier to inside the customer premises.

Fiber to the Home (FTTH) is fast, is immune to electromagnetic interference, and doesn't rust, so it has lower maintenance costs for the carrier. Bell South is investigating the use of FTTH (in the Integrated Fiber in the Loop [IFITL] project), and similar studies are being conducted by the Canarie Project in Canada, NTT in Japan, France Telecom, and British Telecom.

Until recently, there have been a number of roadblocks to extending fiber all the way to the home, including installation costs, electrical powering, and the precision with which fiber must be handled. Recent technical innovations and application development indicate that each of these hurdles is being confronted, so the prospect of FTTH is not quite as farfetched as once imagined.

FTTH comes in two forms. First is a shared form very much like HFC. It has a shared forward channel and point-to-point reverse channels with a MAC protocol to arbitrate return traffic contention. This form of FTTH is called *passive optical networks (PON)*. The second form is a point-to-point optical service wherein each residence has a dedicated optical channel to the carrier that is shared only by the devices in the home, called dedicated FTTH.

Passive Optical Networks

Passive Optical Networks (PON) is being standardized by ITU SG-15 as Recommendation G.983, "High Speed Optical Access Systems Based on Passive Optical Network (PON) Techniques." The Recommendation describes two service options:

- Symmetric service of 155.520 Mbps (OC-3)
- Asymmetric service of upstream 155.520 Mbps (OC-3) and downstream 622.080 Mbps (OC-12)

The transmission medium consists of one or two single-mode fibers in accordance with ITU-T Recommendation G.652. Bidirectional transmission is accomplished by use of either a wavelength division multiplexing (WDM) technique on a single fiber, or two unidirectional fibers. For cost reasons, the one-fiber system is preferred. In the one-fiber system, the forward path shall be transmitted at 1480 to 1580 nm. The operating wavelength range for the upstream direction shall be 1260 to 1360 nm. The recommended characteristics of the fiber are shown in Table 5-2.

Table 5-2   *Physical Media-Dependent Fiber Characteristics*

Characteristics	Value
Fiber type	1.3 µm zero-dispersion fiber (ITU-T G.652)
Optical path loss	10 to 25 dB (ITU-T G.982 Class B)
	15 to 30 dB (ITU-T G.982 Class C)
Path loss	15 dB
Maximum logical reach	20 km
Minimum supported split ratio	16- to 32-way split

Line coding is On/Off keying. Light ON means a binary 1, and light OFF means a binary 0. This simple form of line coding reduces the cost of the optical components and is highly robust.

FTTH PON looks a lot like hybrid fiber coaxial cable networks (HFC), as opposed to the Very High Bit Rate Digital Subscriber Loop (VDSL) architecture, with which it is often compared. Simply replace the HFC drop wire with single-mode fiber, and reduce the number of homes per cluster from 500 to 1. The nomenclature is different, but the startup functions of FTTH are familiar to observers who know HFC. Some similar functions are ranging, the requirement for a MAC protocol to arbitrate upstream bandwidth utilization, control of transmitted power from the residence to the carrier facility, and a broadcast-based, plug-and-play registration process. In addition, all the Internet startup functions are required, such as the assignment of IP addresses and packet filters.

A schematic of a PON system is shown in Figure 5-2.

Figure 5-2   *PON Architecture*

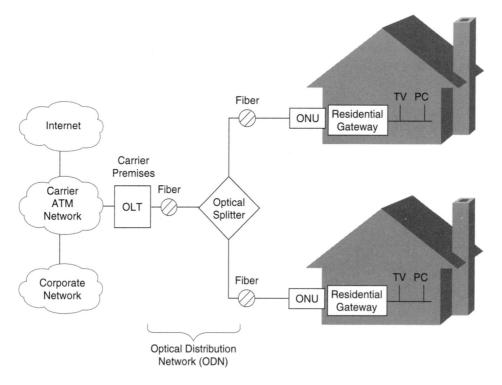

The key elements we discuss are the Optical Line Terminator (OLT), Optical Distribution Network (ODN), and the Optical Network Unit (ONU).

The basic architectural elements are similar to other high-speed access networks. The OLT is the equivalent of the DSL Access Multiplexer (DSLAM) of xDSL networks, or the Cable Modem Terminal Server (CMTS) of HFC data networks. The OLT couples the transport network, usually an ATM backbone, to the local loop network and terminates and provides much of the control for the distribution network. The ODN is the local loop distribution network, and the ONU is the in-home device that connects the home network to the distribution network.

Optical Line Terminator

The OLT would reside in a telco central office or in a loop carrier system. Its functions include these:

- Optical transmission and reception
- Control functions in the distribution network, such as control of transmitted power from the residence to the carrier facility, forward error correction, and interleaving
- Enforcement of the MAC protocol for upstream bandwidth arbitration
- Coupling of the distribution network with the ATM transport network
- (Optional) Enforcement of higher-level protocols, such as address resolution, address assignment, tunneling, and conditional access control
- (Optional) Switching or cross-connection, to relieve the transport network of switching responsibilities

Optical Distribution Network

Within the larger PON architecture, the optical distribution network is comprised of single-mode optical fibers and the passive optical components, primarily optical splitters—hence the word *passive* in Passive Optical Networks. The Optical Distribution Network (ODN) offers one or more optical paths between one OLT and one or more ONUs.

Like electronics, optics suffer from attenuation and are measured in dB. The ITU specifies that the variation in path loss from one home to another be bounded. That is, one home may be closer to the OLT than another home connected to the same OLT; the standard limits the difference in path loss between the two homes to 15 dB.

The distance between the OLT and ONU can be as long as 20 km.

Optical Network Unit/Residential Gateway

The ONU provides the necessary functionality to connect the carrier fiber to the residence. Whereas the ONU for HFC networks serves 500 to 2000 homes, the ONU for FTTH serves one home. It performs functions similar to a digital TV set top box, an HFC cable modem, or an ADSL ATU-R. Its functions include these:

- Optical transmission and reception.

- Cooperation with the OLT to control transmitted power from the residence to the carrier facility.

- Forward error correction and interleaving.

- Enforcement of the MAC protocol for upstream bandwidth arbitration, in cooperation with the OLT.

- Coupling of the distribution network with the in-home network medium, such as plastic optical fiber (PoF), IEEE 1394 Firewire, or some form of metallic wiring. Coupling with an in-home network will involve some form of protocol handling as well, such as speed matching, buffering, and framing

- ATM multiplexing. Multiple devices in the home will be connected to a single ATM port from the home to the carrier. The ONU and residential gateway are responsible for multiplexing the sessions on the fiber link.

Because of the complicated nature of the interface functions, a component called the residential gateway or home network gateway will possibly decouple the purely optical functions of an ONU from high-layer protocol functions.

Some believe that an outdoor ONU would increase location flexibility, facilitate maintenance access, and provide a cleaner demarcation for the network interface. Others believe that the FTTH system will benefit more from the cost reduction of an indoor ONU, thereby making it look more like a piece of consumer electronics. As of this writing, these questions and other specifics of the ONU are reserved for further study and product development.

Proprietary variations of PON exist. For example, Alcatel has developed a product line called SuperPON. It distributes 2.4 Gbps in the forward and shares 311 Mbps on the return from up to 2048 clients. The range is up to 100 km.

Principles of Operation

For downstream data, ATM cells from the Internet, corporate network, or some other source traffic are transmitted through the Carrier ATM Transport Network and received by the OLT. Traffic is forwarded to the ODN, which consists of single-mode fiber that connects to an optical splitter. The job of the splitter is to take the downstream optical wavelength and replicate it optically so that each ONU receives the same transmission. In this way, one laser transmitter at the OLT serves multiple residences. Splitters replicate on the order of 16 to 32 tributaries.

For upstream data, the ONU in the home obtains data from television set tops (for example, channel selection) or from personal computers in the home. The ONU requests permission of the OLT to transmit upstream. The OLT processes requests for bandwidth and grants credits to the ONU for a specific number of ATM cells to be sent by the ONU. The OLT and the ONU must cooperate to arbitrate congestion on the return path. The process of media access control uses a credit-based scheme in which the carrier issues credits for time slots into which the client can send return path data.

The use of time slots means that all home transmitters connected to a common OLT use a common upstream frequency. Therefore, a single-laser receiver at the central office can receive traffic from all residences. This is an important cost-saver and is why shared FTTH is seen as more practical than point-to-point or dedicated FTTH. On the other hand, if the cost of laser components declines, it is possible to consider the case of dedicated fiber connections to the home.

All current PON proposals assume the use of ATM cells to the residence. The application may or may not be an ATM device; if not, the residential gateway would be responsible for the adaptation of the legacy protocol such as IP or MPEG into and out of ATM. This process is called segmentation and reassembly (SAR) and is a common function for ATM devices.

The downstream signal is broadcast to all ONUs on the PON. Each upstream transmission from each ONU is controlled by OLT. A single residence can receive a variety of services, such as data retrieval, television reception, and telephony. Each of these cells is transmitted using TDM techniques. The ONU demultiplexes the optical line format into the various services.

Broadcast television will be supported using switched digital video techniques, just as in the FTTC case. Even though the return path speed of FTTH is faster, the speed at which tuning occurs is still an issue because the critical factor is how fast the access node can create the virtual channel from the content provider to the subscriber.

PON Issues

TDMA upstream optical reception and transmission causes three main difficulties that do not arise in point-to-point transmission:

- A packet arriving from an ONU close to the OLT may have a signal level much higher (due to lower path length-dependent losses) than a following packet arriving from a distant ONU, and the receiver must adapt to the new level within the guard time between packets.

- The timing of the upstream signals is complicated by a path delay that differs from ONU to ONU. In addition, the time-dependent variations in path length—for example, as a result of temperature changes—can also be very different from ONU to ONU. The timing of transmissions from each ONU must be adjusted so that the packets arrive at the OLT separated by the guard time.

- The sum of the spontaneous light from several tens of (nontransmitting) lasers held at threshold is comparable to the signal level from the one transmitting laser, leading to a significant increase in the bit error rate in PONs. This effect is accentuated during the reception of packets from distant ONUs.

In part because of these concerns, future consideration may be given to a dedicated FTTH topology.

Dedicated FTTH

PON is a shared topology; up to 32 residences can share 622 Mbps of bandwidth. If all residences are active, average bandwidth per residence will be less than HFC. This would seem to be disappointing, given the allure and reputation of FTTH.

As more residences subscribe to FTTH, the cluster size will drop from 32 down to as few as 8 because service providers will have proper funding to penetrate the splitters farther into the neighborhood. Ultimately, each home may have a dedicated fiber circuit to the carrier.

New development is studying ways to use *Dense Wavelength Division Multiplexing (DWDM)* to create private virtual paths into the home. DWDM-based systems will enable carriers to allocate wavelengths to customers, providing dedicated bandwidth of up to 155 Mbps in both directions to each home. Figure 5-3 illustrates the use of DWDM in a point-to-point FTTH environment.

Figure 5-3 *Point-to-Point FTTH Architecture*

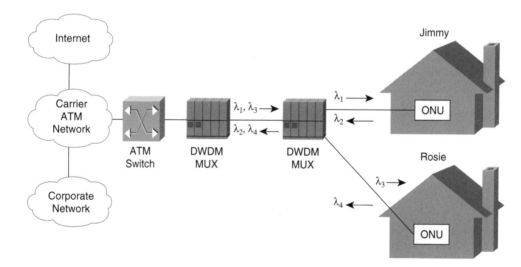

Figure 5-3 depicts content from the Carrier ATM Transport Network that is received at an ATM switching function. In the forward direction, content going to Jimmy is sent on one frequency, and content going to Rosie is sent on another. These frequencies are multiplexed onto a single-fiber loop by a DWDM. At the other end of the loop, the frequencies are demultiplexed and forwarded to the respective households.

A DWDM is basically a frequency division multiplexer for optics. Different frequencies, or colors, travel simultaneously on a single strand of glass fiber. The subscriber will be allocated an upstream and downstream frequency for his exclusive use. In the scenario illustrated in Figure 5-3, Jimmy receives on frequency λ_1 and transmits on frequency λ_2; Rosie receives on frequency λ_3 and transmits on λ_4.

Current versions of DWDMs multiplex 32 or more frequencies per fiber. Certainly, this number will increase with the introduction of lower-cost laser transceivers. For now, however, DWDM is used exclusively in carrier backbones because of cost. Each frequency requires a separate laser. To have a point-to-point FTTH solution, there needs to be further cost reduction with multifrequency lasers.

The advantage of point-to-point over PON is that there is no need for a contention-resolution protocol, and there is a greater degree of privacy. The drawback is cost. With point-to-point, a laser transceiver must be present at the head end for each subscriber. Furthermore, because of possible changes in subscriber usage, it will be necessary to remotely control the transmit and receive frequencies of the laser transmitter in the home.

Secondly, instead of having a passive optical splitter and multiplexer in the distribution network, there is a requirement for an optical switch. An intelligent, active switch is necessary to make sure that a given frequency goes to the correct subscriber.

Therefore, enhancements in lasers and optical switching are required before serious consideration can be given to point-to-point FTTH. But, in the distant future, this will be given further consideration.

Ethernet Local Loop

Other methods of connecting the OLT with the ONU are under consideration. The Palo Alto FiberNet (www.pa-fiber.net) is a group of citizens in Palo Alto, California working with Palo Alto Utilities (www.cpau.com) to introduce FTTH to homes and schools. The group's approach uses gigabit Ethernet switches to move IP packets over 10/100 Ethernet to homes. No ATM, and no telco, yet. Just rights of way, dark fiber, Ethernet switches, and a very technical and well-heeled citizenry.

Another feasibility test is underway in Stockholm, Sweden, conducted by Ericsson, which uses a packet-over-fiber infrastructure. A full-duplex Ethernet local loop is well-developed technology that can support neighborhoods perhaps in the hundreds. After all, switched Ethernet scales reasonably well for business environments. Ethernet can carry MPEG frames for video and is obviously well-matched for data transmission.

The issue with Ethernet is quality of service (QoS). But given the relatively small number of trial participants and the quantity of bandwidth in the core of carrier networks, Ethernet can be a quick and dirty implementation for no other reason than to validate that a consumer market exists for carrier-based Fast Ethernet service.

Benefits of FTTH

FTTH is viewed as the end game for access networks for a variety of reasons. The benefit to the user is greater speed; the benefit to the carrier is lower operational and provisioning costs. By "end game" we mean that the ONU is steadily approaching the home. When it gets there, the greatest possible performance can be achieved.

Return Path Bandwidth

Residences will benefit from more bandwidth—especially in the upstream direction, compared to HFC, xDSL, or FTTC—and thus it is the most appropriate technology for residences to host their own Web sites. Businesses can take advantage of high-speed return for corporate Web hosting.

Remote Provisioning

A key benefit of FTTH for the carrier is its capacity for remote provisioning. Remote provisioning refers to the capability of the carrier to configure customer service from the central office without incurring the cost of a truck roll. Estimates for the operational costs of sending a field engineer to the home vary widely but are bounded by figures of $200 to $500 per incident.

Using remote provisioning, a consumer can elect a service-level agreement on Day 1 that includes 10 Mbps service. Later, the same customer might want 20 Mbps service and, later still, as little as 2 Mbps. Because the bandwidth to the consumer is greater than any of these options, the carrier need only impose some flow-control measures at the central office to restrict consumer bit rate to the requested service level. Eventually, given improved network-management techniques, consumers could be able to conduct provisioning for themselves.

The carrier or the consumer can configure bandwidth for exclusive use for relatively long periods of time (days, or even hours). Remote provisioning would be subject to available link capacity and pricing, but many of the operations and maintenance costs could be reduced.

Remote provisioning of bit rate is enabled by the use of ATM to the home. ATM has the capability to support usage requests expressed in different semantics. Such semantics include peak rate bandwidth, average bandwidth per unit time, and the variability of transmission delay. Of course, monetary costs would be associated with such flexibility, but this would offer greater control for the user and lower provisioning cost to the carrier.

Distribution Network Cost Reductions

In addition to remote provisioning, another cost benefit for the service provider is reduced maintenance costs in the distribution network. These reductions come from reduced powering costs and the reduced costs of outside electronics and cabling. The cost of power to the ONU will be passed to the customer, unlike today's phone service, where the electric power to the telephone is supplied by the phone company. Although this is a small amount of power, the total power consumed by millions of phones adds up.

Greater Reliability

Optical components are immune to RF interference, such as ingress and crosstalk. They don't rust, which extends the usable life of components in the field. Optical signals take longer to attenuate than electrical signals through metal, and there is less corrosion. This all suggests that optical signal quality is superior to that of wired infrastructures and will likely remain so as the infrastructure ages. Fiber also has fewer active repeaters than metallic networks for equivalent distance. This contributes to greater reliability.

Full-Service Networking

FTTH and HFC are alone in their capability to provide full-service networking (FSN). FSN refers to the capability to provide high-bandwidth, multichannel services, such as broadcast television, and narrowband services, such as telephony. Marketers dub this feature *futureproofing,* which implies the capability to accommodate whatever services and content the future holds without changing the infrastructure. Over time, therefore, life-cycle costs are minimized.

Challenges of FTTH

Significant progress has been made in defining requirements and an architecture for PONs. But major problems remain, which promises to delay the availability of standardized FTTH for years to come. Despite the issues, FTTH will continue to be considered an important goal, primarily by the world's telephone operators.

CPE Costs

Lasers are expensive, and the consumer electronics industry has not had the time or the motivation to incorporate lasers into consumer products. Furthermore, there are cost issues of home wiring and residential gateways to support FTTH.

Carrier Capital Costs

Reduced electric bills, reduced provisioning costs, and reduced costs of outside electronics and cabling are long-term benefits for carriers.

But for the short term, major costs are associated with the startup of service. Among the key costs are installing the fiber (which may involve digging); connecting the subscriber equipment in the home (which involves labor and precision equipment); capital costs of the OLT, splitters, and ONU; capital costs of laser transmitters and receivers; new maintenance; and test tools and training.

Central office equipment costs have decreased because reductions in the costs of lasers and wavelength division multiplexers have been considerable in recent years. However, more cost reduction is required to make subscriber equipment FTTH costs competitive with wired infrastructures. For the moment, the startup costs outweigh the operational cost savings and might continue to do so for years to come.

Standardization

While there is basic agreement on ITU SG-15 G.983 standardization, many key elements of an end-to-end architecture have yet to be decided. Among these elements are powering, encryption and conditional access, zapping protocols, startup procedures, and inside wiring. Solutions today are vendor-specific. The lack of standardization means that carriers are reluctant to commit to large-scale commitments.

Power to the ONU

Telephones receive electrical power over the copper loops that carry the voice. Because fiber does not conduct electricity, powering of remote electrical elements in FTTH systems is one of the major issues associated with the deployment of FTTH. A requirement for widespread FTTH is agreement among regulatory agencies, telcos, and consumers regarding power to the ONU. Two powering options exist—namely, network powering and subscriber powering. A mixed architecture, referred to as hybrid powering, is also possible.

Network powering uses an overlay network of metallic wires in which a number of ONUs receive power from the carrier network. It is anticipated that legacy copper wire will be repurposed from carrying voice to carrying power. Even so, network powering for the ONU is costly for the carrier. For FTTH systems to be economically practical, the ONU needs to be powered from the consumer's outlets, with a battery backup provided at either the consumer or carrier's expense in case of emergencies.

With subscriber powering, all subscribers are responsible for the power feeding and therefore pay the electric bill. Some operators expect that the customer may become responsible for the proper operation of the battery backup, as with cellular or cordless telephones today. Subscriber powering is the lowest-cost option for the carrier.

Arguments, primarily from the carriers, will assert that the residential powering problem is diminishing. The use of cellular phones is considerable, and they can be used in an emergency. Other alternatives are batteries, which can operate phones for 8 to 24 hours. Whether this can pass muster with regulatory agencies or the public at large is to be determined.

Switched Digital Video

The PON specification has insufficient bandwidth to offer full-broadcast television. Direct-to-home digital satellites offer up to 144 channels of broadcast television. Upgraded HFC systems will be capable of 700 MHz of analog and digital television. Such systems can provide 50 channels of analog TV and up to 1.5 Gb of digital TV. This is far more channel capacity than an FTTH system with 155 Mbps or even 622 Mbps of shared bandwidth. Therefore, a developing technology called switched digital video (SDV) is indicated to offer a competitive service supporting broadcast TV and VoD. The elements of SDV will be discussed in Chapter 8, "Evolving to RBB: Systems Issues, Approaches, and Prognoses."

Fiber-Handling Problems

Splicing, handling, and bending of fiber are of particular concern. Fiber is a difficult medium to manipulate. When splicing two segments of fiber optic cable end-to-end, the part that actually transmits light is only 50 microns (millionths of a meter) in diameter. If the fiber segments are not perfectly aligned, optical impairment results. Splicing fiber cable requires expensive precision equipment. Technical innovations in development will increase the tolerances with which fiber can be handled, but these need further refinement. Bending is also a consideration—fiber cable cannot be bent excessively without incurring severe attenuation.

Two broad classes of splices exist: fusion and mechanical. Fusion splices operate by melting the adjoining segments together. They provide very low losses at the splice point (0.1dB). Multifiber splicer equipments are available that allow splicing of several fibers in a single operation, thereby saving labor. This is important, because splicing costs in the field are sensitive to labor cost and splice amortization. Costs range from $10 to $40 per splice, depending on these two factors.

Mechanical splicing is based on direct alignment into a simplified connector. Mechanical splices are less expensive than fusion splicing ($10 to $15 per splice), but they create high optical loss and reflectivity. Because of the requirement for cleaner signals, the trend is toward the use of fusion splicing, despite its cost.

In general, electrons traveling through metal wire are much more forgiving than photons traveling through fiber. The increased precision and costs associated with fiber installation as compared to metal wire are ongoing challenges to FTTH.

Connectors

Related to fiber-handling problems is the problem of optical connectors. Optical connectors are used to insert fiber into various active and passive pieces of equipment, such as splitters, OLTs, and ONUs. Connectors are a source of signal loss, but technology has advanced to the point where there is a low insertion loss of around 0.2dB per connection. Techniques have been successfully implemented regarding cutting, polishing, physical contact, and refractive index matching.

Many connectors have ceramic packaging, or *ferrule,* which accounts for a significant fraction of the total cost of the connector parts (30 to 50 percent), so cheaper materials such as glass or plastic are now under development.

Despite advances in splicing and connectorization, field handling of fiber requires well-trained technicians and expensive tools.

Encryption and Wiretapping

Because the cable is shared, data will be encrypted. Encryption, and the fact that fiber is more difficult to wiretap than metallic cables, means that some method of enforcing court-ordered wiretaps must be implemented before widespread use of FTTH will be allowed in the United States and other countries worldwide.

Already, conflict has begun between law enforcement and the telecommunications industry over wiretapping of digital telephony and voice over IP. Techniques used to wiretap analog voice calls do not work when voice becomes a digital application. Law enforcement is asking that modifications be made to digital telephone equipment to facilitate the same level of wiretapping that is possible with the current analog voice network. These modifications involve some costs, resulting in objections from telecommunications carriers and Internet libertarians. This issue is a harbinger of controversies to come, when all transmissions to and from the home will be digital.

Market Acceptance

So far, the interest in FTTH is mainly push from carriers and their equipment suppliers. Very few content providers and consumers are demanding FTTH service. The roster of participants in FSAN are all carriers, mainly European, and their providers. So far, the volume of effort behind FTTH significantly lags behind the standardization and product development work enjoyed by HFC and xDSL. More basically, it is yet to be determined what levels of pricing the public will pay for high-speed services to the home, especially services that do not provide for efficient delivery of broadcast television.

Transition Issues

The success of xDSL and HFC could defer the development of FTTH. Although the prospect of sharing up to 622 Mbps among a handful of homes is enticing, the fact remains that PON offers less bandwidth in the forward direction than HFC. Furthermore, HFC is operational in millions of homes, whereas FTTH is only in the trial stage. Therefore, FTTH service providers will not have the breadth of programming that DBS and HFC have. It is likely that FTTH will have an advantage for pull-mode services, either VoD or pull-mode data, but it remains to be seen if push-mode or pull-mode services will provide the most lucrative funding model for RBB.

Are We There Yet?

Many technical and commercial issues are confronting FTTH. For these reasons, FTTH is hardly heard these days above the marketing din of HFC and xDSL and the hundreds of thousands of their residential subscribers worldwide. As of this writing, very little venture capital is flowing into FTTH, either PON or dedicated. Large telephone companies and their potential suppliers are doing the research and development work. The motivation is largely exploratory. Will FTTH work? Will it be cheap enough for consumers? Will consumers be just as happy with slower access networks? Time will tell.

Summary

As candidates for RBB networks, FTTC and FTTH seem to represent the best of all possible worlds. They hold out the promise of being full-service networks, the elusive single entity that can provide all the high speed and traditional services that consumers are likely to want delivered to their homes. These technologies are also the least established and applied at this point in history, so predicting their future is difficult. Table 5-3 summarizes the challenges and facilitators of FTTH.

FTTx has the potential of the highest bandwidth for two-way traffic, with potentially higher QoS to consumers. The benefits to carriers are reduced operational costs, reduced long-term life cycle costs, and differentiation from cable services.

Fiber is brought closer to the home by HFC, xDSL, and FTTC. FTTH stands to benefit from this progress, but interestingly and ironically, it may be that the last few hundred meters may not be fiber at all. It may not be traversed by coaxial cable or twisted pair either. That last few hundred meters may well be traversed by wireless means, which also benefit greatly from the distribution of fiber farther into the neighborhood. As the distances between the residence and the ONU shrinks, wireless will be capable of offering clear signals at low infrastructure costs. The following chapter discusses the final access network, the wireless local loop.

Table 5-3 *Challenges and Facilitators for FTTx and RBB*

Issue	Challenges	Facilitators
Media	Increased fiber distribution entails digging; requires precision handling, equipment, and training.	Fiber is being installed anyway and will reduce life cycle maintenance costs for carriers.
Modulation schemes	QAM 16 and QPSK need to operate at high speeds.	Digital modulation technique for fiber is simple On/Off keying.
Noise mitigation	Higher speeds create little tolerance for line impairments.	Fiber is more immune to external noise.
Signaling	Switched video signaling must mimic home channel surfing.	FTTx sessions don't connect through a voice switch, thus reducing signaling through the voice switch. PON is passive, not requiring active signaling.
Data-handling capabilities	Speed is less than cable in the forward path for all but dedicated FTTH.	Good return path service enables reliable interactive service with known QoS.
Standards	Standards are lagging behind more established technologies. In particular, standards for end-to-end service architectures are unresolved. VDSL standards are in flux.	Substantial agreement on important PHY-level issues exists. Relatively few bodies are deliberating FTTx specifications, with a relatively little chance of conflict.
Business/ Financial	CPE and infrastructure costs are high. Telcos do not have a good track record at rolling out high-speed services. Questions remain over how to transition customers' home wiring.	Telco costs are reduced for provisioning, powering, and maintenance. The data burden on voice switches is reduced. The maintenance budget can be used for certain upgrades. There is a logical transition plan from ADSL through FTTC to FTTH.
Market	Customers may not want full-service networks. Customers may be satisfied with HFC and xDSL. Support for broadcast video over switched networks has been untested.	The greatest return path bandwidth exists. Enough bandwidth exists to support customers' Web sites.

Table 5-3   *Challenges and Facilitators for FTTx and RBB (Continued)*

Issue	Challenges	Facilitators
Regulation	Mechanisms to support law enforcement wiretapping have not yet been resolved (FTTH). It is uncertain whether regulation will force carriers to provide network powering to the ONU. Unbundling requirements and open access requirements are unclear.	Possible relief from powering requirements will arise if Universal Service can be provided via wireless telephony.

References

Books

Senior, John M. *Optical Fiber Communications,* Second Edition. Upper Saddle River, NJ: Prentice Hall, 1993.

Articles

[DAVIC] Digital Audio Visual Council. "DAVIC 1.0 Specification, Part 8, Lower Layer Protocols and Physical Interfaces." September 1995.

Effenberger, Frank and Kevin Lu. "Overview of FTTH Networks, Past History, Current Status, Future Designs." Proceedings of the International Society for Optical Engineering, Volume 2917: 19-22 November 1996.

ITU SG-15. Recommendation G.983: "High Speed Optical Access Systems Based on Passive Optical Network (PON) Techniques."

Internet Resources

www.canarie.ca

Canada's advanced Internet development organization

www.canet2.net/c3/home.html

Advanced Research & Development Network Operations Centre of Canada; author of a position paper to offer gigabit Internet to all Canadian homes by 2005

www.Bell-South.com

Bell South's Web page

cselt.it/Cselt/euresc/P614/FSAN.html

A quick introduction to Full Service Access Networks, including FTTx, known as Project 614 by CSELT (Italy)

www.labs.bt.com/profsoc/access/

Full Service Access Network Initiative Web site hosted by British Telecom

www.pa-fiber.net and www.cpau.com

Palo Alto, California FiberNet and the City of Palo Alto Utilities discuss FTTx www.rr.cs.cmu.edu/ndg/gndg-ftth.html

FTTx cost estimates from researchers at Carnegie Mellon University

www.americasnetwork.com/issues/99issues/990701/990701light.htm

FTTH views by David Kettler of Bell South

This chapter covers the following topics:

- The Motivation for Wireless
- Reference Architecture for Wireless Networks
- Wireless Characteristics
- Spectrum Management
- Frequency Assignment
- Direct Broadcast Satellite
- Low Earth Orbit Satellite
- Multichannel Multipoint Distribution Service
- Local Multipoint Distribution Service
- Third-Generation Cellular Telephony
- Wireless Issues
- Summary

CHAPTER 6

Wireless Access Networks

The previous chapters pointed to the tremendous strides recently made on wired networks. Copper and fiber networks are becoming more ubiquitous, easier to use, less costly, and, most of all, faster. Furthermore, the transmission capacity of wired networks is considered infinite because carriers can manufacture bandwidth as demand increases.

The Motivation for Wireless Networks

Cables and wires are not without their problems. Digging trenches or climbing poles for installation can involve difficulties, including problems of construction permits and easements, aesthetics of aerial cables, and backhoes that can inadvertently dig up cables— all of this can add up to high installation costs. Furthermore, the cable may be installed in the wrong place, such as an area with a disappointing market for services. In addition, air doesn't rust or fall down in bad weather, as cable and wiring can. To some observers— including the operators themselves—the fixed networks of wired systems look like vulnerable high-capital assets in a world of fast-changing technologies.

Most importantly perhaps is the need for facilities-based bypass by new market entrants who wish to offer competitive voice or Internet service but who don't want to use existing telephone or cable infrastructure. Wireless is the quickest way to start a company, particularly when the distribution of initial customers is sparse.

Each nation's airwaves historically have been a tightly regulated commodity for a variety of reasons. Spectrum allocation is governed not only by commercial interest but also by public interest (public safety, scientific research), technical characteristics, and, of course, a heavy dose of industry input. Spectrum often is underutilized because, unlike today's digital modulation schemes, older modulation techniques used bandwidth inefficiently. In the United States, the FCC granted spectrum licenses for free until 1993, so there was little incentive to develop new modulation technology. Moreover, a good portion of the available spectrum is reserved for either high-priority uses by local agencies such as fire and police departments, or national uses such as Federal Aviation Administration air traffic control, deep satellite telemetry, and military communications. Broadcast TV and radio also consume choice swaths of spectrum. Finally, very high-frequency spectrum (above 20 GHz) was deemed too difficult for commercial use.

Enter technology. With the advent of digital technologies, frequencies above 20 GHz became commercially viable. Secondly, frequencies lower than 20 GHz can support more users at higher speeds, primarily because of digital modulation and compression techniques. Added to these technological advances, policy changes that relocate incumbent license users to less-valued spectrum force both the new bandwidth services and the present license holders to use spectrum more wisely. The recent auctioning of spectrum by the FCC puts a price on bandwidth and thereby creates incentive for efficient use. All these forces conspire to make wireless the technology of choice for new entrants to broadband access. These new entrants include big service providers who want to enter someone else's market.

In the last few years, the U.S. government and world spectrum authorities have authorized many new wireless services. Among these are direct broadcast satellite (DBS), Personal Communications Services (PCS, second-generation digital cellular telephony), Local Multipoint Distribution Service (LMDS), Multichannel Multipoint Distribution Service (MMDS), digital TV spectrum, Low Earth Orbit (LEO), 24 GHz licenses (Teligent), 38 GHz licenses (Winstar, Advanced Radio), Global System for Mobile Communication (GSM) telephony, Wireless Communications Service (WCS), and third-generation cellular telephony (3G).

The sum of these services indicates that over the last few years, the FCC has auctioned, liberalized the use of, or otherwise licensed more than 3 GHz of spectrum for nongovernmental, nondefense, consumer and business services. This compares favorably with the 1 GHz capacity of coaxial cable or the 1 MHz capacity of a twisted-pair copper loop. Furthermore, spectrum holders now enjoy fewer restrictions on what services they can provide. Because voice service requires so little bandwidth, plenty of bandwidth is left over for video and Internet access services. Finally, there will be a tremendous overhang of analog TV spectrum in the low-frequency ranges of 54 MHz up to 700 MHz when TV broadcasters go digital and the government reclaims the analog TV spectrum. This is prime spectrum property.

Finally, the key marketing advantage of wireless is that consumers are willing to pay more for a lower-quality service, if it is wireless. Satellite television services are higher priced than cable and do not have local content programming. Yet, there are more than 9 million subscribers in the United States. Likewise, cellular telephones have poor voice quality, high prices, and low connectivity. Yet, in the fourth quarter of 1998, more than 33 million GSM, cdmaOne, and TDMA handsets were sold worldwide. By the end of 1999, there will be more than 300 million digital telephony users (and this is an *addition* to analog handsets), far exceeding the number of Internet subscribers. Mobile access also is not just for telecommuters. Even soccer moms value their pagers and cell phones as means to keep in touch with kids and provide peace of mind while traveling.

The question of wireless networks is whether or not they work at a reasonable—not necessarily lower—cost. Wireless networks use even higher frequencies than a wired infrastructure, so doubts about its robustness and cost-effectiveness for high-speed data service continue.

However, the convenience of wireless, its proven appeal to consumers, the current plethora of spectrum, the promise of more spectrum, and technical innovations that permit the more aggressive use of spectrum all conspire to position wireless as a key access option.

This chapter discusses the various options for wireless access from the carrier to the home. These technologies include DBS, MMDS, LEO, LMDS, and 3G. Other similar technologies, such as 38 GHz licenses (Winstar [Nasdaq: WCII, www.winstar.com], Advanced Radio Telecommunications [Nasdaq: ARTT, www.artelecom.com]) and a 24 GHz service called Teligent (Nasdaq: TGNT, www.teligent.com), are viewed as extensions of these and will not be covered. Other wireless technologies are used within the home, such as IEEE 802.11, Bluetooth, and HomeRF. These will be discussed in the following chapter on home networking.

Reference Architecture for Wireless Networks

Figure 6.1 shows how wireless networks map to the DAVIC reference model discussed in Chapter 2, "Technical Foundations of Residential Broadband." The return path flows, if any, travel through either wired or wireless networks.

Figure 6-1   *Wireless Reference Architecture*

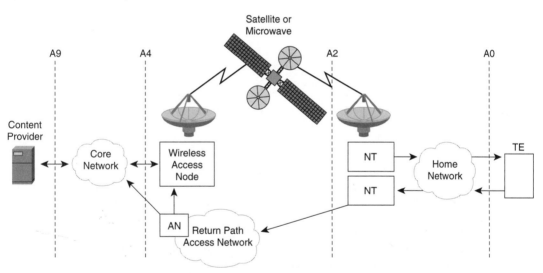

The content provider forwards content through the Core Network and to the wireless access node. This access node reformats data and modulates it for satellite or land-based microwave transmission. A receiving antenna at the home forwards traffic through the Home Network to the terminal equipment, either a TV set-top box or a PC.

In the return path, the consumer uses either the same network used for the forward transmission or another Access Network. Another Access Network is needed when using DBS services, which are one-way services. The return-path network could be telephone return, xDSL, or another wireless service.

Because forward and return-path traffic can use different physical media, traffic sources must be matched so that a single bidirectional session exists between the content provider and the terminal equipment.

This matching can be performed by the wireless access node or another switching or routing device inside the Core Network.

Wireless Characteristics

Wireless Access Networks utilize *radio frequency* (RF) spectrum, which is generally defined as the frequency range of 300 kHz through 300 GHz. This frequency range sits between the electrical equivalent of audible sound and visible light. Audible sound is transmitted as changes in air pressure. Table 6-1 shows the broad classes of frequency definition.

Table 6-1   *Broad Classes of Frequency Definitions*

	From	To
Audible Sound	3 kHz	20 kHz
Radio (RF)	300 kHz	300 GHz
Infrared	300 GHz	10^{14}
Visible Light	$\sim 8 \times 10^{14}$	$\sim 8 \times 10^{14}$
Ultraviolet	10^{15}	10^{17}
X-Rays	10^{15}	10^{22}

The lowest frequencies of the RF spectrum do not propagate readily; the highest frequencies behave more like visible light. Higher frequencies, such as infrared or visible light, can be focused, using reasonably sized antennas. Therefore, a benefit of high frequencies is tighter focusing, which enables sectorized RF transmission, which in turn increases frequency reuse. Lower frequencies also can penetrate household walls, whereas higher RF frequencies are blocked by physical objects, including raindrops, at very high frequencies. Radio frequencies below the AM radio band (500–1600 kHz) cannot be used practically for wireless data. (Note the huge towers required for AM radio transmission). Reasonable frequencies for Access Networks begin at the analog cellular band of approximately 800 MHz and extend upward to 30+ GHz. Otherwise, wireless transmission shares many characteristics of wired transmission, namely attenuation with distance, which ultimately limits range.

The next sections review some basic characteristics useful for comparing wireless Access Networks.

Location

Location refers to where in the RF spectrum the particular service is located. That is, location determines whether the service uses relatively high or low frequency in the RF range.

Amount of Bandwidth

Some Access Networks use as little 10 MHz (for example, block D PCS); others use as much as 1.1 GHz, as for LMDS. Typically, the higher the frequency, the more bandwidth is available. The amount of bandwidth determines the data rate that can be carried.

Modulation

As with wired media, wireless transmitters can permute frequency, amplitude, and phase. Wireless has the added dimension of polarity modulation, which means that waves can be horizontally or vertically polarized to provide an extra degree of freedom. Sectorization adds another degree of freedom: space diversity. These extra two degrees of freedom permit greater frequency reuse.

Footprint

This characteristic refers to the effective radius of service. Some services, such as DBS, have a nationwide footprint or, in the case of Europe, a continental footprint. Broadcast DTV has an effective radius of up to 50 km in relatively flat places. Other services, such as LMDS or PCS, have a relatively small radius, perhaps less than 5 km or so, due to the limited transmitted power available at higher frequencies and the greater attenuation encountered.

The advantage of having a large footprint is that a service can cover many subscribers—even millions—with a single transmitter. For example, a single satellite can beam programming or data to all of the United States or Europe. This reduces cost and has the side benefit of enabling simultaneous reception by every subscriber.

The drawback is that interactive, two-way communications is inhibited as the footprint increases. A larger footprint means that potentially more subscribers would be communicating with the network provider simultaneously. Return-path arbitration becomes increasingly problematic as the footprint increases.

Point-to-Point Versus Point-to-Multipoint

Some wireless communications, such as microwave relay, are point-to-point communications: One transmitter is communicating with exactly one receiver. The alternative is *point-to-multipoint (PMP)* communication: One transmitter communicates with multiple receivers simultaneously, as in satellite and broadcast television.

The advantages of point-to-point communication are privacy, guaranteed bandwidth, and the absence of a bandwidth arbitration mechanism. On the other hand, point-to-point technology also relies on a transmitter and receiver apparatus for each potential session, which increases cost.

For high-frequency communications, the development of point-to-multipoint technology is seen as an important cost-reduction technique because one transmitter can serve many users. For the return path, however, an arbitration mechanism is required. This makes PMP software more complex, but many believe this is well worth the reduced hardware. Point-to-multipoint communication conserves spectrum and reduces capital costs at the central site.

Providing *two-way* PMP capability is the real challenge of wireless access.

Full-Duplex Operation (FDD Versus TDD)

In a point-to-multipoint system, a single transmitter sends bits downstream to multiple receivers. Debate continues to arise between supporters of frequency division duplexing (FDD) or time division duplexing (TDD) to achieve two-way operation.

The established model is frequency division duplexing, which divides the available spectrum into two separate channels: one for upstream and one for downstream. A newer approach called time division duplexing, allows traffic to flow in either direction on the same channel, but in different time slots. TDD is sometimes referred to as ping-pong operation.

FDD has been used for years in cellular telephone. When you talk on a cell phone, you are using frequencies 824 MHz through 849 MHz. When you listen, you are using frequencies 869 MHz through 894 MHz. There is some development of broadband FDD systems by companies such as Netro. Although TDD technology has been used in the Personal Handyphone System (PHS) in Japan and Digital European Cordless Telecommunications (DECT) systems in Europe, it has yet to be commercially deployed in a broadband wireless access system.

At the heart of the debate between FDD and TDD is whether wireless networks will be used for symmetric (voice) and asymmetric (data) applications. The criticism of FDD is inefficient bandwidth utilization, especially for data. With FDD, the upstream and downstream paths are permanently and statically allocated. This means that if traffic is flowing downstream (as in a big Web page download), then the upstream bandwidth is unused. This is not a problem for voice because the amount of bandwidth used (or rather, wasted) is small and because humans tend to talk as much as they listen, so the bandwidth demand is more or less symmetric. For high-speed data and video applications, however, this is not necessarily so. A lot of bandwidth could be flowing downstream, and if half the spectrum is permanently and statically allocated for upstream use, then that upstream bandwidth is underutilized. Because spectrum is so precious, preallocation seems to be an unnecessary waste, at least to TDD supporters.

With TDD, a variable number of time slots flow continuously in both directions. Upstream and downstream users get allocations of time slots into which they can pack data. The number of time slots in both directions can be metered on a fine-grained or coarse-grain granularity. This means that TDD can support bursty transmission in either direction. If a big Web page download is taking place, for example, time slots can be taken from the upstream users and used for downstream traffic.

The issue with TDD systems is that it takes time to turn the line around, and time slot allocation is a tricky software problem. In addition, TDD requires precise timing. All clients in a point-to-multipoint footprint need a common time reference defining time slots. This timing or ranging tends to limit the geographical distance of the point-to-multipoint footprint.

Still, more efficient use of bandwidth for asymmetric and bursty applications has induced new entrants into the broadband TDD space. Broadband TDD systems are under development by WavTrace and Ensemble Communications. The growth of ecommerce and digital entertainment on the Internet may change the traffic patterns of the Internet to benefit either FDD or TDD, but it is too soon to tell how such patterns will evolve.

Licensing

Some spectrum is licensed, and some is not. Licensed spectrum is held by a license holder who is granted exclusive or near-exclusive use of spectrum within a specified geographical area for a specified period of time. Licenses are normally granted by the FCC Mass Media Bureau or the FCC Wireless Transport Bureau, either by auction or by some other waiver.

Unlicensed spectrum can be used by any party that wishes to transmit in the approved passband. Because many transmitters may wish to use some common spectrum, etiquette rules apply, such as limits on transmit power. Such limits reduce the effective radius of the service or otherwise affect the quality of the service.

The obvious advantage of using unlicensed spectrum is the low cost of entry for a service provider, who doesn't pay for bandwidth. The drawback is congestion, even with etiquette rules in place. Moreover, some transmitters may not obey the rules, due primarily to faulty equipment. This is where the government must use its enforcement powers.

This brings us to the broader question of spectrum management.

Spectrum Management

In the United States, the function of spectrum management is shared by the FCC (www.fcc.gov) and the National Telecommunication and Information Administration (NTIA, www.ntia.doc.gov). Other countries have their own national regulatory bodies charged with similar responsibilities, such as the U.K. Office of Telecommunications (Oftel, www.oftel.org) or the Japanese Association of Radio Industries and Businesses (www.arib.or.jp).

The FCC is responsible for managing use of the RF spectrum by the public, including state and local governments. The NTIA, an agency of the U.S. Department of Commerce, is responsible for managing federal government use of spectrum. The functions in the FCC are divided between the FCC Mass Media Bureau (www.fcc.gov/mmb), which regulates activities of TV and radio broadcasters and archives the major decisions concerning digital TV standards; and the Wireless Transport Bureau (www.fcc.gov/wtb), which oversees most other aspects of spectrum management, including allocation, licensing, auctions, cellular telephony, paging, public safety, and other private uses. The joint responsibilities of the FCC and NTIA responsibilities are listed here:

- **Spectrum allocation**—Defining the type of use allowed involves determining such categories as fixed, or mobile, exclusive or shared use, governmental, broadcast, and so on. If spectrum is allocated for shared use, then primary users and secondary users must be designated. Both primary and secondary users can transmit in the assigned band, but secondary users must accept interference from primary users, whereas primary users cannot be adversely affected by secondary users.

- **Assignment rules**—Having defined spectrum allocation rules, assignment rules define who gets to use the spectrum and for what period of time. Frequencies are assigned by auctions and automated licensing procedures.

- **Service rules**—Having defined who gets to use the assigned spectrum, rules are defined for its use. For example, rules might govern the maximum transmit power, point-to-multipoint use, two-way or one-way use, and whether the user is compelled to accept interference from others in the band.

- **Enforcement**—Finally, the appropriate bodies must see to it that license holders abide by the service rules.

Assignment rules, services rules, and enforcement are the more administrative functions of spectrum management. Assignment rules govern the conduct of auctions and other methods to convey allocated spectrum to users. Service rules are largely an engineering function to ensure proper use of the assigned spectrum. Enforcement is a policing function to ensure the assigned entities observe service rules. The most controversial function of spectrum management is spectrum allocation.

Contrary to some conventional wisdom, RF spectrum is not infinite. While it is true that technological advances—primarily digital modulation and compression—make more efficient use of spectrum, those same technical advances induce new service providers and consumers to demand more spectrum. New demand makes spectrum allocation a continuing problem.

New requests for bandwidth occur all the time from new entrants that desire to provide new broadband wireless services. For example, in July 1997, Skybridge (www.skybridgesatellite.com) and Northpoint Technology petitioned the FCC to authorize use of spectrum in the range of 10.7 GHz to 12.7 GHz for new services. The problem was that the frequencies 12.2 GHz to 12.7 GHz were already in use by geostationary satellites, namely direct broadcast satellite. Of course, the direct satellite vendors objected to Skybridge's request.

As a result of the request, a Notice of Proposed Rulemaking (NPRM) was issued in November 1998. In this document, the FCC asked for comments on technical approaches to ensure that the DBS vendors were not impaired and that international agreements would not be violated. Such headaches are the daily fare at the FCC as the organization tries to accommodate new demand from entrepreneurs and established businesses alike.

Spectrum sharing is one technique to accommodate new demand. Spectrum sharing allows two or more license holders to occupy the same frequencies. This is possible if users are geographically dispersed. Therefore, maritime and some land-based transmitters share common spectrum. Otherwise, spectrum use can be coordinated through technical means such as sectorization or antenna discrimination.

Another technique to accommodate new demand is *bandclearing*, which involves the relocation of users from one spectrum location to another. Usually, the vacated spectrum is lightly used or is used by government administrations. The FCC's Emerging Technology Policy 1992 required that the new user pay the incumbent for the costs of relocation (typically new transmitters and receivers) or somehow protect the incumbent from interference. Parties negotiate these costs themselves. Relocation costs were an important consideration when fixed microwave was relocated to make wave for PCS voice. Bandclearing was also used to create spectrum for cellular by reallocating TV channels 70 through 83 in the 1970s. Similarly, new frequency allocation was provided in the 1980s for DTV in 12.2 GHz to 12.7 GHz.

One upcoming example of bandclearing is the clearing of TV channels 60 to 69 (746 MHz to 806 MHz); very few broadcasters use these channels over the air (they are frequently used for cable TV channels). The first step toward this reallocation of analog TV spectrum was undertaken in July 1997 (FCC 97-245, "Reallocation of Television Channels 60–69, the 746–806 MHz Band"). In that NPRM, the FCC proposed that this spectrum be reallocated before the end of the DTV transition period, now scheduled to end in the year 2006. Under the terms of the NPRM, 36 MHz is to be allocated for public safety use, and the remaining 24 MHz is to be allocated for auction.

The big bonanza of bandclearing will come when all analog TV channels can be cleared when over-the-air TV goes digital. However, for now, all nooks and crannies of RF spectrum are heavily used. This means more sharing and less bandclearing.

Unlicensed Usage

The FCC also has allocated spectrum primarily used for applications other than communications, such as microwave ovens, garage door openers, toy walkie-talkies, cordless phones, wireless speakers, home security, and a myriad of other consumer uses. This category includes industrial uses as well, such as of wireless LANs, inventory control, traffic light controls, and backhaul links for licensed services such as cellular and PCS.

Consumer devices using these spectra are dubbed FCC Part 15 unlicensed devices, after the regulation defining the etiquette rules. The main service rule limits transmit power and dictates that such devices accept interference. The basic premise is that low power cannot cause interference. No FCC license is needed to operate a Part 15 device.

NTIA Role

The NTIA manages federal use of spectrum because the federal government is a major user of spectrum. About 20 percent of all RF spectrum is for exclusive government use, and another 40 percent is shared between government and business purposes. Federal spectrum involves defense, Federal Aviation Administration (www.faa.gov), NASA space exploration, maritime navigation, and hundreds of mission-specific and agency uses. One responsibility of NTIA is to define sharing rules among federal users. It goes without saying that Defense Department spectrum is not often shared.

Another role of the NTIA is to manage the interests of the United States in international wireless venues, such as Comsat, Intelsat, Inmarsat, and the World Radio Conference (WRC). The organization does this through its Office of International Affairs, in coordination with the State Department and the FCC.

Spectrum Management Issues

Spectrum management issues arise in part from the unknown factors, such as international relations and technological advancement. The following list reviews some management issues:

- **International spectrum policy versus domestic spectrum policy**—Radio waves cross international boundaries, and satellites, in particular, have large footprints. Therefore, no nation can make decisions on domestic factors alone. For example, the Iridium global telephone services uses frequencies in the range of 1610 MHz to 1660 MHz bands. This conflicts with work of European radio astronomy experiments in the 1610.6 MHz to 1613.8 MHz range. Similarly, the United States has been a major advocate of making additional frequencies available at 1176 MHz for Global Positioning Systems (GPS). However, the Conference of European Postal and Telecommunications Administrations (CEPT) officials point out that this frequency is currently being used by terrestrial aeronautical radio-navigation applications in Europe.

- **International trade**—As an example of this issue, some foreign satellite service providers request access to the U.S. market. How is the United States to grant such requests, given the current tight constraint on allocations and yet preserve its posture of free trade?

- **Government requirements versus business requirements**—National security and safety requirements conflict with business requirements. Public safety generally requires stable allocations, whereas the free market demands maximum flexibility to meet changing market demand.

- **Pace of technology changes**—How should regulators anticipate technology change? For example, can they anticipate aggressive new spectrum-sharing techniques and therefore allocate more shared spectrum? Or should allocations be for exclusive use because no such innovations are expected? New technology may not use frequency in the manner it was originally requested for. Is this a public policy problem?

- **Who should get frequency assignment**—What are the conditions for licensing? Should spectrums be auctioned? Should there be greater protection for existing services? Should there be a secondary market for spectrum? What are the public policy implications of according spectrum the same status as private property?

- **The current regime for allocation**—Rather than the current piecemeal approach to allocating a few megahertz here and there, should allocations be granted on a coarser scale? If so, what are the implications for international coordination of spectrum?

Spectrum management requires a delicate balance among many unrelated factors, such as public policy, foreign policy, technology changes, and business regulation. Therefore, spectrum management—particularly allocation rules—are among the most controversial of the oversight functions of federal regulators in residential broadband.

Frequency Assignment

The result of spectrum management is ultimately frequency assignment. A completely free market approach would auction spectrum and permit a secondary market. However, some interests would find it difficult to participate in auctions. Such interests would include amateur radio, scientific research, and public safety. For example, it would be possible for your local police department to bid for spectrum like everyone else, but the costs would conceivably increase and a certain amount of chaos could ensue in the interim. Hence, the federal government legislatively has set aside frequencies for these public uses.

Other factors impinge upon service rules. For example, radiolocation and radionavigation and shipborne transmissions are high-powered and can interfere with neighboring users.

Therefore, the assignment of frequency demands a balance of many factors. Among these are federal law, the interests of incumbent spectrum holders, the interests of new entrants, technological innovation, public interest requirements, the particular applications of spectrum use, international spectrum coordination and trade, and, finally, lobbying from commercial interests.

One should add that the proceeds from auctions, though interesting, are not a prime motivator for having auctions. Given the size of the federal budget, auction proceeds are modest. However, auctioning does provide an economic incentive to the winner to use the spectrum wisely, so public policy is advanced because more efficient use of spectrum means that more people can benefit from it. In the words of Dale Hatfield, the head of the FCC's Office of Engineering and Technology in 1999, "I always thought the notion was to get the spectrum into the hands of entrepreneurs that are able to use it; that we were not supposed to be managing spectrum to maximize the revenues that were gained through the auction process or gaming it that way. That sounds about as central planning as you can get."

The Future of Auction Proceeds

The U.S. taxpayer has benefited from the auctioning of the nation's airwaves. The aggregate proceedings from 15 FCC auctions account for more than $23 billion for the U.S. Treasury (see www.fcc.gov/wtb/auctions.html for details). Congress, pleasantly surprised by the initial reaction to PCS auctions in the mid-1990s, looked upon the auctions as a relatively painless way of filling federal coffers. That's the good news.

The bad news is that it's possible to have too much of a good thing. The new reality is that spectrum is being used more efficiently, so less of it is needed and auctions stand to generate less income. The market is having trouble digesting the spectrum it has, due partly to technological limitations.

The result is that proceeds from auctions have weakened substantially since the multibillion-dollar proceeds of PCS. In particular, MMDS and LMDS auctions were regarded as less than stellar. Further auctions are planned in the 39 GHz and higher range. Perhaps some time should be given to technology and the markets to digest the spectrum already available.

The result to date is reflected in the current frequency assignment for residential broadband services and certain familiar narrowband services, shown in Table 6-2.

Classes of Wireless Services

To introduce the reader to RBB wireless access networks, this chapter identifies six broad classes of wireless services and shows how RBB wireless are categorized. Similarly, current wireless services are grouped to show similarities between the new and old services. The two columns in Table 6-3 indicate two broad classes of wireless services: narrowband and wideband, or broadband. Narrowband services provide enough bandwidth for voice. Broadband services have more bandwidth, to support video and high-speed commercial uses.

The rows indicate delivery mechanisms. The broad classes are satellite, mobile, and fixed. Satellite services can be distributed from geosynchronous or low Earth orbits. Mobile services are basically the familiar cellular telephone services. Fixed services operate between two stationary endpoints.

The major private commercial use of interest here is broadband wireless access, which are indicated in bold in this table. The next section discusses the first of these services: satellites.

Table 6-2   *Frequency Assignment for Residential Broadband Services and Familiar Narrowband Services*

From (MHz)	To (MHz)	Use
54	72	TV channels 2, 3, and 4
76	88	TV channels 5 and 6
88	108	FM radio
175	216	TV channels 7 to 13
470	746	TV channels 14 to 59 (UHF)
746	806	TV channels 60 to 69, subject to imminent bandclearing
824	849	Cellular telephony (uplink)
869	894	Cellular telephony (downlink)
902	928	Industrial Scientific Medical (ISM) band (unlicensed)
890	915	GSM (uplink)
935	960	GSM (downlink)
1850	1910	Wideband PCS blocks A, B, C (licensed) paired with bands 1930 to 1990
1910	1930	Wideband PCS (unlicensed)
1930	1990	Wideband PCS; Blocks D, E, F (licensed) paired with bands 1850 to 1910
2150	2162	Multipoint Distribution Service (MDS), now combined with Multichannel Multipoint Distribution Service (MMDS)
2305	2320	Wireless Communications Service (WCS)
2345	2360	Wireless Communications Service (WCS)
2400	2483.5	Industrial Scientific Medical (ISM) band (unlicensed)
2500	2596	Instructional Television Fixed Service (ITFS), now combined with MMDS
2596	2644	Multichannel Multipoint Distribution Services (MMDS)
2644	2686	ITFS, now combined with MMDS
5150	5350	Unlicensed National Information Infrastructure (U-NII)
5725	5825	Unlicensed National Information Infrastructure (U-NII)
12,200	12,700	Direct Broadcast Satellite
18,800	19,300	Teledesic downlink
27,500	28,350	Local Multipoint Distribution Services (LMDS), Block A

continues

Table 6-2   *Frequency Assignment for Residential Broadband Services and Familiar Narrowband Services (Continued)*

From (MHz)	To (MHz)	Use
28,600	29,100	Teledesic uplink
29,100	29,250	LMDS Block A
31,000	31,075	LMDS Block B
31,075	31,225	LMDS Block A
31,225	31,300	LMDS Block B

Sources:
www.omega.com;www.ntia.doc.gov/osmhome/allochrt.pdf; www.cabledatacomnews.com/wireless/
www.fcc.gov/oet/info/database/spectrum/spinvtbl.pdf;www.wcai.com; www.fcc.gov/wtb; [McMahan]

Table 6-3   *Classes of Wireless Services*

	Narrowband	Broadband
Satellite	Iridium	DBS
	Globalstar	Teledesic
		Skybridge
		C band
		Ku band
		Ka band
Mobile	Cell phones	3G wireless
	(1G, 2G)	
Fixed	Amateur radio	MMDS
	Public Safety	LMDS
	Government uses	38 GHz
	Research, space	

Direct Broadcast Satellite

While cable operators were talking about digital TV, direct broadcast satellite (DBS) companies were doing it, taking the cable industry by surprise. Early entrants were Primestar, DirecTV, and United States Satellite Broadcasting (USSB), all launched in 1994. Echostar launched in March 1996, and recently Rupert Murdoch's News Corporation launched DBS services BSkyB and JSkyB, for Britain and Japan Sky Broadcasting, respectively.

In the United States, DBS is viewed as a commercial success. Some of the key statistics are listed here:

- DBS has 9 million customers (as of mid-1999). Subscribership is particularly strong considering that customers initially paid up to $800 for a home satellite dish and installation.

- The average DBS subscriber spends about 50 percent more per month than the average cable subscriber (about $52 versus $35 per month). This is due to the upscale sale of DBS and the sales of premium sports and movie packages. In particular, aggressive marketing of sports packages (including college basketball and professional football) has created differentiated content for which DBS has found a ready market.

- Fifty-five percent of DBS subscribers live in areas with cable service, surprising those who thought DBS would serve only areas not served by cable.

DBS Architecture

DBS uses geosynchronous satellites operating in the Ku band (12 GHz downlink/14 GHz uplink). The specific frequencies for DBS are 12.2 GHz to 12.7 GHz.

Table 6-4 shows transponder capacity by orbital slots of DirecTV and Echostar.

Table 6-4   *Transponder Capacity in the United States*

	119° West	110° West	101° West
Echostar	21	29	0
DirecTV	11	3	32

The 101° west longitude measurement lines up over the East Coast of the United States, 119° lines up over the West Coast, and 110° lines up over the Midwest. (Recall from your geography class that 0° lines up over Greenwich in the United Kingdom). From these orbital slots, the satellite can beam programming down to the entire United States. The importance of having many transponders (which are basically microwave repeaters in the sky) is to provide increased channel capacity. The number of programs per transponder depends on the amount of compression used by the operator and is a closely held secret. But with 50 transponders each, Echostar and DirecTV can provide roughly 370 and 500 digital channels, respectively.

Architecturally, DBS is a simple concept, as depicted in Figure 6-2. DBS operators receive analog or digital TV reception from terrestrial sources at a single giant head end. DirecTV's head end, for example, is in Castle Rock, Colorado. The programming is encoded into MPEG for digital retransmission. A control function regulates the amount of bandwidth accorded to each MPEG stream and determines how the MPEG knobs (control parameters), such as group of pictures length, are specified.

Figure 6-2   *DBS Schematic*

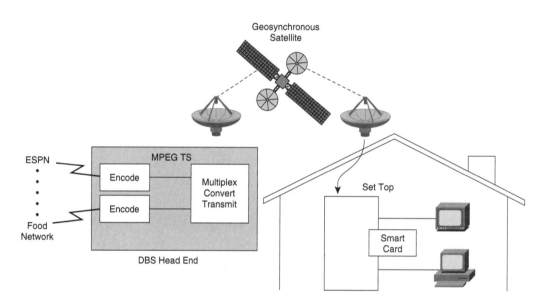

The amount of compression used per program is a closely guarded secret of the DBS operators. For example, ESPN tends to require more bandwidth than the Food Channel. Of course, ESPN has a lot more motion, but more importantly, it has greater viewership and advertising revenue. How much more would ESPN pay for access than the Food Channel? How much extra bandwidth is ESPN getting, and for how much? What MPEG knobs should the carrier use, and what knobs does its competition use? This is not public information. In any event, after compression, ESPN, the Food Channel, and all other channels are encoded into MPEG transport streams, are multiplexed together, and then are converted to the licensed uplink frequency.

The composite stream of 500 or so channels is transmitted up to a geosynchronous satellite. The satellite receives transmission and remodulates to the designated spectrum for DBS. By regulation, DBS satellites are allowed to broadcast at a higher power (120W) than the larger C-band satellite dishes currently used by many households to enable reception on small satellite dishes. This higher-powered transmission and smaller dish distinguish DBS from other forms of satellite reception and have provided DBS with a competitive advantage over the older C-band satellite services.

Although 720 by 480 is the maximum resolution offered today, DBS is capable of higher pixel resolution. In fact, DBS could be an early delivery vehicle for HDTV programming. Some analysts think that DBS will prove to be the most cost-effective means of delivering HDTV to homes in the United States for years to come. This is because most HDTV content is expected to be films, which are easily converted and which the DBS vendors routinely offer. Furthermore, the cost of upgrading to high-definition for DBS is limited to a single head end and the receiving dishes. For over-the-air broadcasters, upgrading to digital means that each individual broadcast affiliate must make an investment.

On some systems, a credit card-sized plug-in board called a *smartcard* is used for key management of conditional access systems. The smartcard plugs into the decoder, and without this card there is no reception. When the conditional access system is compromised by hackers, the carrier can mail replacement smartcards with new encryption keys to subscribers. This costs around $10 per card but is a little more secure than other systems.

Security Using Smartcards

Debate continues about the security and expense of smartcards, but the cards are slowly gaining momentum despite the cost of smartcard readers in set tops. Because carriers are reluctant to replace entire set tops, they typically live with breaches of conditional access. Smartcards give carriers an option, though, and raise the bar slightly against hackers. Of course, hackers are an ingenious lot and no doubt eventually will crack smartcards as well. The question is whether the cost of maintaining conditional access is worth the effort.

European carriers think so. Smartcards will be used in Europe to help DBS service providers overcome a problem not found in the United States. Because of the proximity of national boundaries, and because the issuance of program licenses is sometimes limited by country, it is necessary to provide conditional access by country. For example, a DBS provider might have the right to transmit a certain program in the United Kingdom but not in Spain, where another DBS provider has the program license. In this case, a U.K. resident on vacation in Spain should not be able to use his U.K. smartcard there. Measures are under consideration to provide this extra security, such as by combining information on the smartcard with information about the set top into which it is inserted.

Another use of smartcards is for electronic commerce. Credit information could be infused onto a smartcard so that commercial transactions can be made online without the need to reveal credit card information. If this form of commerce expands, the costs associated with smartcards will fall, making it more attractive for purely conditional access use.

The set-top hardware used by DirecTV is called Digital Satellite System, or DSS. Sony, Thomson Consumer Electronics, Hughes Network Systems, Toshiba, Matsushita (Panasonic), and Uniden all sell the DSS receiving equipment.

Challenges to DBS

DBS sales started out impressively, but some experts believe that DBS penetration will not exceed 15 million to 20 million homes in the United States. DBS faces keen competition from a strengthening cable industry and other wireless technologies, which are discussed later in this chapter. Also on the horizon is digital over-the-air broadcasting. Alphastar, a DBS operator, declared bankruptcy in June 1997. Today the United States has two DBS satellite providers—DirecTV and Echostar—and little prospect for another national provider.

Lack of Interactive Data Service

Although there is a geosynchronous satellite Internet service called DirectPC, it is a relatively small offering of only 12 Mbps of downstream service for the entire footprint of North America; it uses a telephone as a return path.

The lack of a return path for DBS means that it will have only limited interactive capability. What interaction is possible will be only with downloaded Web pages cached in the set-top box.

A possible approach to interactivity would be for DBS vendors to align with xDSL service providers. Modified DBS set-top boxes could embed xDSL modems for return-path and point-to-point full-duplex operation. As of this writing, however, there seems to be little interest on the part of either industry to take this approach.

Local Television Content

Local TV programming is important to viewers. Morning ratings are high because viewers want local weather and traffic to start their day and get to work. Local sports are also important in many communities; high school football is popular in Texas, for instance, while high school basketball is important in Indiana. Another local content issue arises due to time zones. Many people on the West Coast, for instance, are unhappy that some DBS programs are received three hours early because they originate from the East Coast. Finally, local advertisers require stations to broadcast only locally—it does a local restaurant no good to advertise nationally.

The delivery of local content on DBS is hampered by two issues: one technical and one legal. The technical issue is how to reduce the footprint from nationwide to multiple metropolitan areas. This problem is being addressed by the development of a frequency reuse technology, called *spot beaming*. With spot beaming, a single satellite can broadcast to multiple small footprints rather than a single footprint covering the entire country. This is done using sophisticated antenna-shaping techniques originally developed for military satellite applications. But there is not enough transponder capacity for all 1600 broadcast channels in the United States using current technology. If an operator can support "only" 500 channels, it is most likely that it will broadcast only the New York, Los Angeles, and big-city stations.

The Catch-22 for spot beaming is that if the satellite operators have this technology for a specific metropolitan area, then they will likely be subjected to Must Carry requirements just as cable is. As of this writing, mandating legislation is pending. Given sufficient transponder capacity, this should be possible—but it won't be cheap.

Another problem is the payment of royalties by the satellite operators to content producers. The *Satellite Home Viewer Act (SHVA)* provides a compulsory right for satellite providers to retransmit network signals, and the act provides a royalty fee for that right. Satellite providers pay 27 cents per subscriber per month to the programmers and local stations for that right. Naturally, programmers feel that they should receive more, and the DBS providers think that they should pay less. Federal legislation is currently pending to extend the compulsory license and reduce the royalties to 14.85 cents per subscriber per month for networks and slightly more for so-called superstations. Because the right of compulsory retransmission is limited to five years in the newly proposed legislation, the question of access to program content is a continuing problem for satellite operators.

Multiple Home Viewers

Current DBS systems can decode only one channel at a time, so a separate decoder must be purchased for each TV in the home. The requirement to obtain multiple decoders represents a significant cost penalty for most American homes, which have an average of nearly three televisions per home.

Competition

DBS already faces competition from cable operators and soon will compete with over-the-air digital broadcasters. New DBS competition could come online as well. Canada, Mexico, and some South American countries have been granted orbital slots that could beam service into the United States. At least some of them soon will be auctioning off their spectrum; it is expected that some U.S. companies will bid on that spectrum with the intent of servicing the United States.

Both cable and over-the-air broadcasts have the advantage of local content. Cable also intends to offer interactive services, thereby providing a complete package of services.

Finally, competition might come from Multichannel Multipoint Distribution Service (MMDS) and Local Multipoint Distribution Services (LMDS), both of which are discussed later in this chapter.

Standardization

The vast majority of DBS systems worldwide will use the European DVB standard, with the current exception of DirecTV in the United States. When DirecTV begins operation in Japan, it will use DVB. The prospect of the worldwide use of DVB promises some lowered costs as multiple manufacturers make common components. However, interoperability of set tops among different systems is unlikely because too many variables exist in the DVB specification. In addition, differences occur in conditional access and encryption. In some set tops, these security devices are built into the box, making them tamperproof. In others, the security devices are built into smartcards and consequently can be changed. Interchangeable security was a part of the original DVB specification, but it has not been enforced by service providers, who typically have their own ideas about security.

The Role of DBS in Residential Broadband

Because of its one-way capability, DBS is not viewed as an Access Network option for RBB. The role of DBS in this discussion is to further emphasize the importance of television as a market driver and to explore DBS's negative financial impact on other technologies. DBS is instrumental in keeping pricing for cable services low, thereby inhibiting the capability of cable to roll out high-speed services.

Even though it is not a candidate for RBB services, DBS is a spoiler for full-service networks, such as cable, that attempt to provide both data and video services. For the more than 20 percent of homes in the United States that are forecast to receive DBS, the appeal of other technologies such as xDSL rests largely on the strength of their pull-mode data services because DBS already provides high-quality multichannel broadcast service in such homes.

Low Earth Orbit Satellites

Geosynchronous satellites are not the only satellites orbiting the broadband access space. Low Earth Orbit (LEO) satellites have garnered a large amount of interest and press because of their high concept and the participation of heavy-hitters Bill Gates and Craig McCaw. Some conflict has arisen between LMDS and LEO supporters regarding spectrum allocation. Though it is unlikely that the bandwidth of these systems will exceed 1 to 2 Mb, their potential role in RBB is to provide a ubiquitous return path for other one-way technologies. Another possible effect is to siphon off investment and consumer interest from higher-speed services.

Background

Unlike their geosynchronous brethren, which operate at 35,800 km above the equator, LEO satellites orbit the planet at low altitudes. Depending on the system, the altitude of these orbits ranges from 780 to 1400 km, which is above the earth's atmosphere but below the Van Allen radiation belt. At these altitudes, a LEO satellite is in view of 2 to 4 percent of the earth's surface, which means that the footprint of any given LEO satellite is 4000 to 6000 km in diameter.

The low altitude provides two advantages for the consumer. First, latency is short. Phone calls through GEOs incur a 239 millisecond (ms) one-way delay; a round-trip delay is therefore nearly half a second. This causes annoying pauses during voice conversations. One-way latency for LEOs is about 6 ms. The second advantage is lower power consumption. LEOs travel so low that a handset requires very little power to reach it, as compared with a GEO.

Given these advantages and the recent advances in satellite launch technology, a number of companies have initiated development programs. Among these are Globalstar, Motorola, Iridium, Skybridge, and Teledesic. The objective of Globalstar and Iridium is global voice service. The objective of Skybridge (www.skybridgesatellite.com) and Teledesic (www.teledesic.com) is 2 Mbps data service.

Teledesic requested use of paired spectrum in the 28.6 to 29.1 GHz (uplink) and 18.8 to 19.3 GHz (downlink) band segments for its service links, and the use of 27.6 to 28.4 GHz (uplink) and 17.8 to 18.6 GHz (downlink) band segments for its "gigalink" gateway terminals. Teledesic proposes to operate intersatellite links in the 59.5 to 60.5 GHz and 62.5 to 63.5 GHz bands to interconnect each satellite with eight other satellites in the same and adjacent planes (www.fcc.gov/Bureaus/International/Orders/1997/da970527.txt).

SkyBridge, considered by many to be Teledesic's largest competitor, is utilizing the more familiar Ku band (14 GHz up/12 GHz down) for its 80-satellite LEO constellation and expects to be the first broadband system operating when it launches service in 2001.

LEO Architecture

Because LEOs fly at low orbit, they move with respect to the Earth. This means that when as a user on the ground communicates with the LEO satellite, the LEO satellite passes over the horizon whereupon communication stops. To maintain the session, the original LEO must hand off the session to the following satellite. By succeeding handoffs, the session can be maintained. The frequency of handoffs is determined largely by the distance of the LEO from Earth, which determines the footprint size of the LEO. The lower the satellite, the faster it moves with respect to Earth, creating more frequent handoffs. There are possibly hundreds of satellites communicating with each other, handing off user sessions. The original Teledesic system had 840 satellites until a modified design reduced that number to 288. Higher orbits reduce the number of satellites, which is an important component of system cost.

Two different approaches are being taken regarding switching. Globalstar and Skybridge take the "bent pipe" approach, in which traffic is sent from the user up to the LEO. The LEO handles minimal processing of the bits and returns the traffic to the ground as soon as possible. All switching decisions are made on the ground.

Iridium and Teledesic switch traffic in the satellite. Each satellite contains an ATM or packet switch to forward packets to other satellites. When the final satellite is reached, that satellite beams down directly to the end user or the ground station. Switching in the sky minimizes the cost of ground stations and ground switching equipment. It also reduces the requirement to coordinate with local telephone companies for gateway services and settlement payments. However, switching among moving satellite is an enormously complex software problem.

Table 6-5   *Features of LEO Competitors*

	Globalstar	Iridium	SkyBridge	Teledesic
Services	Telephone	Telephone	High-speed data	High-speed data
Downlink bandwidth	2.483 to 2.500 GHz S-band	1.616 to 1625 GHz L-band	Ku (12 GHz)	Ka band 19.3 to 19.6 GHz
Uplink bandwidth	1.610 to 1.626 GHz L-band	1.616 to 1625 GHz L-band	Ku (14 GHz)	Ka band 29.1 to 29.4 GHz
Modulation scheme	QPSK	QPSK/CDMA	N/A	N/A
Switching	On the ground; uses bent pipe approach	In the satellite	On the ground; uses bent pipe approach	In the satellite
Satellites, with spares	56	72	80	288
Maximum bit rate per session	9,600 bps	4,800 bps	TBD	16 Kbps (voice) 2 Mbps (data)
Investors	Publicly traded (Nasdaq: gstrf)	Motorola, Lockheed Martin, Sprint, and carriers worldwide	Alcatel, Loral, Aerospatiale, Toshiba, Mitsubishi, and Sharp	Bill Gates and Craig McCaw

Challenges to LEOs

Not surprisingly, the futuristic and spectacular concepts behind LEOs face some down-to-earth problems. Switching or routing in the sky is rocket science, but there are also more prosaic problems. One of the major initial problems is there is comparatively little military and commercial experience in LEO technology when compared with geosynchronous satellite technology. Therefore, there is a steep learning curve. However, the more prosaic problems are serious as well.

Telephone Interconnection

Voice service will require cooperation with land-based telephone companies. If an LEO customer initiated a phone call to a Pacific Bell user, at some point PacificBell must agree to accept the call. Similarly, LEO operators must sign settlements and interexchange agreements with telephone companies worldwide.

Spectrum Use

Conflict arose between Teledesic and LMDS operators about use of the 29.1 GHz spectrum (Ka band). Eventually, discussions with the FCC resolved the issue. However, LEOs are global systems, so spectrum-utilization problems could recur in other countries that use the same spectrum. Little use of Ka band occurs worldwide, but full global coverage requires spectrum agreements among the S-band, L-band, and Ka band. In addition, radio astronomers are concerned about LEO impacts on their frequency measurements.

Launch Capacity

Finding satellite launch space will be a challenge. More than 1700 satellite launches are planned for the next 10 years for uses other than LEOs. LEOs will require the launch of more than 400 satellites over the next five to seven years. Considering that there were 22 rocket launches worldwide in 1996, which placed 29 satellites in orbit, the launch business needs to add capacity quickly to meet launch demand. To make things worse, about 10 percent of launches fail. Insurance premiums in some cases are nearly 25 percent of payload value. Incidentally, only about 30 percent of satellite launches are handled by the United States. About 60 percent of the world's launches are made by the European space consortium, Ariane. Others in the launch business are China and Russia.

Cost Issues

In general, there is widespread skepticism about lifecycle costs for LEOs. The original estimate provided by Teledesic was $9 billion to launch an 840-satellite constellation. Independent industry observers made much higher estimates. Over the past year, Teledesic reduced the number of satellites to 288 by increasing altitude of the orbits. The following list details some of the cost concerns of particular relevance for LEOs:

- Capital costs for satellite development, construction, and launch. For example, data communications equipment must be modified for operation in space to accommodate environmental factors such as temperature and radiation. This precludes the use of commercial, off-the-shelf data communications equipment. These modification costs are unknown at present.

- Requirement for technical innovations, such as satellite-to-satellite communications at multimegabit rates and satellite-based switching.

- Continuing requirement for ground stations and associated settlement costs.

- Damage due to solar activity and small projectiles.

- Development of new handsets and customer terminals.

- The need to relaunch satellites. The lifetimes of LEOs are shorter than that of GEOs.

The Iridium Experience

Iridium is the first commercial LEO venture, and it provides global telephone service. Unfortunately, the handsets are bulky, the prices are high, and the costs of the satellites are daunting. As of this writing, technical and business problems have forced this highly publicized service into Chapter 11 bankruptcy. The fate of Iridium may have a negative impact on the broadband LEOs.

Nonetheless, the concept of LEOs exhibits a boldness not found except in science fiction. LEOs offer global roaming, a simple worldwide dialing plan, and an instant voice infrastructure for developing countries. In addition, Teledesic and Skybridge are offering megabit service. The impact on RBB is simply that every one-way technology has the possibility of a low-latency return path, which can be used everywhere in the world. More broadly, if successful, LEOs can substantially alter how people think about global communications.

Multichannel Multipoint Distribution Service

The success of DBS convinced telephone companies and other potential cable competitors that delivering digital video to consumers is a viable business. When such competitors analyzed the competitive issues with DBS, they saw that the lack of local content represented the biggest marketing problem.

Thus, some would-be competitors to DBS and cable sought to provide a wireless, multichannel video service with local stations called *Multichannel Multipoint Distribution Service (MMDS)*, referred to by DAVIC as *Multipoint Video Distribution Systems (MVDS)*. MMDS uses 198 MHz of licensed spectrum, which could support 33 analog TV channels, in the range of 2.5 GHz. This is low enough frequency spectrum to support transmission for 50 miles or more. With this range and capability to penetrate rainfall, this spectrum looked ideal for wireless local loop bypass. A number of carriers obtained licenses for spectrum, and a trade association was formed: the Wireless Cable Association (www.wcai.com).

Background

In 1964, the FCC authorized the Instructional TV Fixed Service (ITFS) for educational use. It eventually provided for 23 channels (138 MHz) in the 2.5 GHz range. In 1969, the FCC authorized the Multichannel Distribution Service (MDS) for two channels of pay TV. It used 12 MHz of spectrum at 2.15 GHz.

Later, the MDS operators learned the hard way that they could not make money with two channels. So, they went back to the FCC asking for use of the ITFS spectrum. The FCC agreed, and portions of the ITFS spectrum were used for pay TV. Combined with ITFS, MDS operators would have enough bandwidth to compete with cable, which in the 1970s could provide only 25 to 30 channels themselves.

However, as is often the case, bandwidth was not enough. The problem of MDS was access to program content. MDS operators could not get programs from cable at market rates. This gave rise to arguments about antitrust and unfair competition, but the MDS operators could not really make a go of it.

By 1990, cable had become ubiquitous, but consumers were complaining to the FCC and Congress about rising cable rates and poor service. The result was the Cable Act of 1992, which re-regulated the cable industry and was passed over the veto of then President Bush. As part of that Act, Congress forced cable content providers to sell programming to wireless cable operators at the same prices as they sell to the MSOs. The result was quick and beneficial to the wireless operators. In less than a year, ten wireless cable operators went public. These were companies that included Heartland, CAI Wireless, People's Choice, American Telecasting, and others.

The apparent success of what was then called MMDS attracted the attention of big telephone companies, who saw MMDS as a way to compete against cable for video services. TeleTV was formed as a consortium of Bell Atlantic, Pacific Bell, and NYNEX to offer MMDS video and audio service in Los Angeles and on the East Coast. Pacific Bell began an aggressive rollout in Los Angeles, which was an ideal location for the service: Lots of people living on flat terrain made coverage easy. The incumbent cable operators had no digital plans. Everything looked great for MMDS.

Things began to crumble in 1996. MMDS spectrum was auctioned in 1996, but the income from the spectrum auction was a disappointing $216 million. One can argue that the auction results were hampered because Congress asked that the auction proceed too quickly so that the money would be used in the federal budget for the 1997 fiscal year. Had the auction been postponed until the glut of recent bandwidth auctions was clear and until certain technological improvements were available (as a number of FCC staffers suggested), the results might have been better. But postponement of the auctions would have postponed the availability of service. Again, a conflict arose because of different public policy objectives.

Then the bottom really fell out. In December 1996, Bell Atlantic had second thoughts and wanted to pull out of TeleTV. Then Pacific Bell was acquired by SBC, which showed no interest in MMDS. Digital satellite was selling well, and the phone companies thought xDSL or FTTx service could provide video. Bell South forged on by purchasing MMDS rights to 1.2 million homes in Florida from American Telecasting for $48 million in 1997. This amounts to $40 per home passed, which was really a fire sale.

The small wireless operators were left holding the bag. They thought their relationships with the phone companies were long-term, so they were busy raising debt and capital to roll out service. Their basic technical problem was that their service was still one-way and analog, when two-way digital service was needed. These operators needed to spend money to upgrade—perhaps more money than the telephone companies expected.

The result was a hapless group of wireless service providers who by 1998 were either bankrupt or whose shares were selling for pennies, when they were allowed to be traded.

In September 1998, the FCC passed a single rule that turned things around just as quickly as they had years before. The FCC authorized two-way service, which was previously barred because of potential interference problems from possibly hundreds of new transmitters. MMDS could become a two-way digital service rather than a one-way analog service. The wireless operators quickly jumped at the opportunity, and some began offering service. This is a partial list of initial rollouts of data services over MMDS.

Table 6-6   *MMDS Data Service Providers*

Carrier	City	Equipment
American Telecasting/WantWeb	Colorado Springs, Denver, Portland, Seattle	Hybrid
CAI Wireless	Rochester, Boston	Hybrid, GI
People's Choice	Phoenix, Detroit	Hybrid, GI
Wireless One	Baton Rouge, Jackson, Mississippi	Hybrid

These operators ran out of time and money, and data was unable to save them. However, the cable-based technologies demonstrated by a Hybrid and GI passed a sanity check. Thereafter, Sprint and MCI Worldcom came to view MMDS spectrum as the media they needed to compete against AT&T and its newly acquired cable properties.

In April 1999, Sprint announced the purchase of People's Choice TV (Nasdaq BB: PCTV) for $103 million, lifting its shares from a 52-week low of a mere 16 cents to $8. PCTV service area covers 7.8 million potential customers in 10 cities, including Phoenix and Detroit. Sprint would deliver about 27 Mbps downstream, with a 3.5 Mbps return as part of its developing ION network, under which it intends to bundle local, long-distance, and data service. Sprint also agreed to purchase American Telecasting, Inc.

Also in April 1999, MCI WorldCom announced the purchase of CAI Wireless Corp. (Nasdaq BB: CWSS) for about $408 million. CAI emerged from bankruptcy in October 1998. From bankruptcy to $403 million in eight months—not bad even by Internet standards.

How ironic then, to note that MMDS, previously courted and then jilted by the RBOCs, would become a part of the interexchange carriers plans to bypass the RBOCs.

MMDS Architecture

MMDS occupies 198 MHz of bandwidth in the 2.5 GHz range. This frequency permits long-distance distribution. For example, MMDS services can exceed 50 miles from the transmitter tower. This was the architecture for analog wireless cable initially, with the idea of putting up a single tower and serving millions of homes.

The key technical difference between MMDS and DBS for video service is footprint size. MMDS footprint permits delivery of local content, which MMDS achieves by having local production facilities near each transmitter to insert local over-the-air channels and advertising into the national feeds. The result is a system that is basically identical with HFC. Figure 6-3 shows a schematic of MMDS service.

Figure 6-3   *MMDS Schematic*

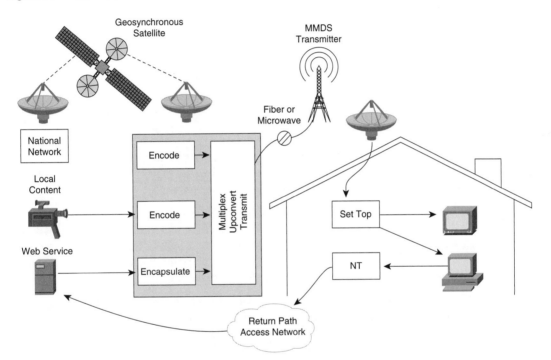

Local content and advertising are acquired over the air, transmitted using MPEG compression and systems specifications and multiplexed with the national programming for local distribution to the viewers. MPEG enables digital multiplexing and thus is a key facilitator of MMDS. Data services also might be received from Web content providers. In this case, the information is in digital format but would require additional processing such as encapsulation into MPEG and address resolution before being transmitted.

After the programming mix is determined, composite programming is delivered by satellite or fiber to the MMDS broadcast tower. Generally, the MMDS head end and the MMDS broadcast tower are not co-located because the tower should be placed at a high elevation.

At the receiving site, a small microwave receiving dish a little larger than a DBS dish is mounted outside the home to receive the signals. A decoder presents the TV images to the TV set. Advanced units will be capable of decoding data for PC users.

The range of MMDS primarily is limited by line-of-sight considerations. In relatively flat areas, if the transmitter can be located high enough, the signal can reach more than 50 miles. Prime One, for example, provides MMDS in Los Angeles and Orange counties in southern California using only two towers. About 75 percent of homes will be capable of receiving MMDS signals reliably; the remaining 25 percent are impeded by line-of-sight problems. Prime One is the successor to Pacific Bell Video Services, which was part of TeleTV before SBC decided to get out of the business. In 1999, Prime One was acquired by MCI Worldcom.

The Prime One service has basic service consisting of digital TV and digital audio. Digital channels are encoded and mixed into MPEG transport streams at a digital video head end. The MPEG transport stream is transmitted over an OC-48 fiber link to the MMDS transmitter atop Mount Wilson. At an elevation of more than a mile, Mount Wilson is also the site of most analog TV transmitters in the Los Angeles basin. The signals are modulated onto the MMDS frequencies and are beamed out using horizontally polarized microwaves. This signal is transmitted over the entire Los Angeles basin and is strong enough to be received on Catalina Island, 40 km from the coastline and 70 km from the transmitter.

The hilly terrain east of Mount Wilson interrupts line of sight for parts of Orange County. To rectify this, the transmission from Mount Wilson is sent to Mount Modjeska in Orange County, which serves as a relay point to viewers unable to receive Mount Wilson signals. The signals from Mount Modjeska are retransmitted as vertically polarized signals, whereas the original signals from Mount Wilson are transmitted with horizontal polarity.

The horizontally and vertically polarized microwaves enable the two transmitters to have overlapping signal coverage. A dish tuned to one polarity will not receive signals of the other polarity. Polarity is a way to achieve frequency reuse and thereby increase the amount of bandwidth and coverage available system-wide. Divicom supplies the MPEG encoder, and Thomson is the systems integrator.

Southern California is particularly well-suited to MMDS. The Los Angeles basin is relatively flat, its tall buildings are spread apart, and it is densely populated so that a single antenna can reach upward of 4 million households. This makes infrastructure investment less than $20 per home passed. MMDS is the least expensive infrastructure built for broadcast video with local content.

However, with the advent of two-way transmission and data services, this model breaks down. Frequency reuse is necessary to have more frequency available, and the footprint size must be reduced so that return-path service won't get too congested. Therefore, as Sprint and MCI Worldcom move into the MMDS space, the architecture of MMDS becomes increasingly cellular and increasingly sectorized.

Another technical hurdle to overcome is the requirement for line of sight. Recent innovations permit the installation of MMDS consumer devices inside the home for single-wall penetration.

Other devices can operate inside the home if facing a window. Indoor installation is a significant improvement over previous MMDS video receivers.

Equipment vendors active in this space are Cisco Systems (through its acquisition of Clarity Communications), Thomcast Communications (comprised of operating units of Thomson-CSF), Newbridge, Spike Technologies, Hybrid Networks, General Instruments, Adaptive Broadband, and others.

Challenges to MMDS

MMDS shares problems common to all wireless Access Networks, as discussed near the end of this chapter. The problems specific to MMDS relate to its recent transition from one-way analog video to two-way digital data. A product transition must occur while continuing to satisfy the embedded base, small as it is. MMDS operators must operate within a cell structure, and customer equipment will be replaced.

Secondly, the amount of spectrum for MMDS may be too small to compete against LMDS and wired infrastructure. Other spectra may become available, such as Wireless Communications Systems (23 GHz) and 38 GHz, which can also compete on a cellular basis.

Finally, MMDS faces competition from cable and satellite for video service.

Local Multipoint Distribution Service

A more aggressive strategy than MMDS is a new delivery service called *Local Multipoint Distribution Services (LMDS)*, also known in Canada as Local Multipoint Communication Service (LMCS). LMDS is a two-way, high bit rate, wireless service under development by a variety of carriers to vastly increase bandwidth. The main differences between LMDS and MMDS are that LMDS occupies much higher frequencies (a disadvantage) but occupies much more spectrum.

Table 6-7   *LMDS and MMDS Compared*

	LMDS	MMDS
Frequency Range	28 GHz	2.5 GHz
Amount of Bandwidth	1150 MHz Block A	198 MHz
	150 MHz Block B	

Using just QPSK modulation, an LMDS Block A service provider can serve more than 2 GBps of traffic per transmitter site. With sectorization and possibly polarity diversity, individual users can get up to 100 Mbps of full-duplex data service, point to point. If an LMDS carrier had 1150 MHz of bandwidth, for example, it would be possible to use 500 MHz for broadcast TV, 50 MHz for local broadcast, 300 MHz for forward data services, and 300 MHz of upstream data. Using only the relatively robust QPSK modulation, this bandwidth can provide the following:

- All the broadcast channels of DBS (500 MHz)
- All local over-the-air channels (50 MHz)
- Up to 1 Gb of full-duplex data service (600 MHz)

In other words, the potential exists to offer more TV than satellite and more data than cable. This frequency plan is just one example of how a carrier could choose to offer service. Other carriers might choose to segment their frequencies differently and would be permitted to do so under FCC rules. If technological hurdles can be overcome and business issues can be addressed, LMDS offers the greatest two-way bit rate of any residential service, wired or wireless, at comparatively low infrastructure costs.

Background

In January 1991, the FCC granted a pioneer's preference license to CellularVision (www.speedus.com, Nasdaq: SPDE), now known as speedus.com, to provide a one-way analog broadcast TV service in Brooklyn, New York. The preference license granted exclusive use of spectrum to more than 3.2 million households. The service used 1 GHz of bandwidth in the 27.5 to 28.5 GHz frequency band. Prior to CellularVision, this spectrum was normally for point-to-point use, but a waiver was granted so that speedus.com could provide a fixed cellular point-to-multipoint operation for video distribution (wireless cable). Cellularvision went public in February 1996 under the ticker symbol CVUS.

The rationale for granting the license was the claim that the company had overcome two problems associated with high-frequency wireless transmission. The first problem was how to get sufficient signal strength from high-frequency transmission. The company addressed this by transmitting in relatively small cells. MMDS can transmit 30 to 70 km in radius. LMDS covers 3 to 6 km, thus accommodating more and smaller cells.

The reliance on multiple small cells gave rise to the second problem. Small cells create problems of signal interference between adjacent cells. CellularVision attacked this problem by using polarity diversity. If adjacent cells use different polarity, then they can use the same frequencies without mutual interference. Armed with these innovations, Cellularvision obtained its Pioneer's license and became the first—and, to date, only—LMDS service provider.

CellularVision offered 49 channels of analog, one-way broadcast service. But analog TV was not a winning business when competing against Time Warner and other cable giants in New York City. So CellularVision, which proved the spectrum is usable but wasn't making any money, began to offer 48 Mbps Internet access instead and changed its name to Speedus.com. With the development of wireless digital technologies, renewed interest has been expressed in

LMDS as a provider of two-way service by other companies in other cities seeking to offer Internet access. Accordingly, the FCC took action to provide more spectrum in the 28 GHz range.

The FCC issued rules governing the auctioning of bandwidth in May 1997. Auctions for U.S. spectrum began in February 1998 with 139 approved bidders. The rules (FCC Notice of Proposed Rulemaking [NPRM] 97-082) mandate the following frequencies to be used for LMDS service in the United States:

- 27.50 to 28.35 (850 MHz)
- 29.10 to 29.25 (150 MHz)
- 31.00 to 31.30 (300 MHz)

These figures represent a total available bandwidth of 1.3 GHz, which is more than twice the bandwidth of AM/FM radio, television, and cellular telephones combined.

The total of 1.3 GHz is offered in two blocks, called Auction Block A and Auction Block B. Auction Block A consists of 1.15 GHz and is located at the following frequencies:

- 27.50 to 28.35 (850 MHz)
- 29.10 to 29.25 (150 MHz)
- 31.075 to 31.225 (150 MHz)

Auction Block B is located at the following frequencies:

- 31.000 to 31.075 (75 MHz)
- 31.225 to 31.300 (75 MHz)

The segmentation of bandwidth creates greater separation between transmitting and receiving frequencies, eliminating the need for filters and ensuring efficient use of LMDS's spectrum.

The NPRM lists the major elements of the LMDS auction rules:

- The LMDS spectrum will be licensed by basic trading areas (BTAs), for a total of 984 authorizations and 1300 MHz of spectrum.
- Two licenses, one for 1150 MHz (Block A) and one for 150 MHz (Block B), will be awarded for each BTA. Note that a Block B spectrum has about the same capability as an MMDS spectrum holder, given that the MMDS spectrum holder uses a cellular infrastructure.
- All licensees will be permitted to disaggregate and partition their licenses.
- The number of licenses a given entity may acquire is not limited. Thus, a single spectrum holder could control Block A spectrum in a majority of U.S. cities. In fact, this occurred when NextLink purchased the spectrum of WNP.
- Incumbent local exchange carriers and cable companies may not obtain in-region 1150 MHz licenses for three years.

- LMDS may be provided on a common carrier or a non-common carrier basis, or both. *Common carrier* status means that the network provider would provide resale rights openly on a nondiscriminatory basis to content providers. *Non-common carrier* status means that the network provider would provide content itself and would not be required to resell the raw transport service.

- Licensees will be required to provide "substantial service" in their service areas within 10 years. This means that licensees cannot hoard the spectrum; the government wants it used.

- Incumbents in the 31 GHz band will be able to continue their operations but will receive protection from LMDS operations only in the outer 75 MHz (31.0 to 31.075 and 31.225 to 31.300) of the band. Incumbents will be given 75 days from the date of the publication of this item in the Federal Register to apply to modify their licenses to operate in the outer 75 MHz of the band, and an additional 18 months to implement those modifications.

- Bidding credits and installment payment plans will be available to small businesses and entities with average annual gross revenues of not more than $75 million.

The provision that prevents telephone companies and cable operators from obtaining in-region licenses for three years is based on the fear that if these groups were to win spectrum, they simply would sit on it for the 10 years allotted before they are required to provide substantial service. Taking the spectrum out of circulation in this way would reduce competition for the existing services. The historic reluctance of local exchange carriers to invade each other's territory, coupled with this provision, will have the effect of keeping them out of the auctions entirely.

The federal auctions began in February 1998 and went through more than 120 rounds of bidding over a period of two months. Eventually 864 licenses were granted, which raised a committed total amount of $578.6 million for the U.S. treasury. The three largest winners were these:

- WNP Communications, a group of venture capital funds (Norwest Capital, Chase Manhattan Venture Fund), which bid $187 million for 40 metropolitan-area licenses

- Nextband Communications, with major backing from Craig McCaw, which bid $135 million for 42 licenses

- Winstar LMDS, a subsidiary of Winstar Communications (www.winstar.com, Nasdaq: WCII), which bid $43 million for 15 licenses

WNP, which paid $187 million for its spectrum, was acquired by Nextlink Communications (www.nextlink.com, Nasdaq: NXLK), the parent of Nextband, for $542 million in January 1999. This transaction makes Nextlink the dominant LMDS spectrum holder, with more than 90 percent of the top 30 markets in the United States.

Unlike the local phone companies, long-distance carriers were not precluded from bidding. They seemed likely bidders because LMDS is a form of local loop bypass. Furthermore, there were no limits on the number of territories owned, so it was possible for a single long-distance carrier to have a seamless national broadband network. Nonetheless, long-distance carriers did not participate—perhaps there was the perception of a wireless bandwidth glut or a lack of confidence in the technology.

Furthermore, many metropolitan areas did not attract any bids at all, and the FCC will attempt to auction these properties at a later time. Other industry observers felt that $578 million was a relatively small amount of money raised in comparison with billions raised in the PCS auctions for narrowband digital telephone services earlier in the 1990s. These observations led some commentators to conclude that the auctions were not successful.

In any case, the relatively low amounts paid meant that the price of spectrum would not be a barrier to service rollout. Time will soon tell whether the auction winners, namely Nextband, got in at the right price.

Spectrum allocation varies in other parts of the world. The Canadian LMCS service is licensed at 27.350 to 28.350 GHz. In Japan, it is 25.25 to 27.50 GHz. In Europe, various bands between 24.5 through 29.5 GHz are planned (CEPT T/R 13-02). This should not present major problems because LMDS is not a mobile service, and hence roaming is not an issue.

LMDS Architecture

LMDS is a small cell technology, with each cell about 3 to 6 km in radius. Figure 6-4 shows a schematic of LMDS service.

Content acquisition at the LMDS head end functions similarly to MMDS, cable, and satellite. National television feeds are delivered by the programmer to a production facility. In many cases, these national feeds come from DBS, but the feeds also can come from other geosynchronous satellite transmission or high-speed wired services such as fiber-optic networks. Local content and advertising are acquired over the air, encoded into MPEG, and multiplexed with the national programming for local distribution. As in the case of MMDS, MPEG is an important facilitator of LMDS because it enables digital multiplexing.

Data services received from Web content providers are already in digital format but would need additional processing, such as encapsulation into MPEG and address resolution, before being transmitted.

The program mix is delivered by fiber to the LMDS broadcast tower. Generally, the LMDS head end and the LMDS broadcast tower are not co-located because the head-end production facilities would be shared among several towers.

An LMDS transmitter tower is erected in the neighborhood, and traffic is broadcast to consumers using QPSK modulation with FEC. It is possible to use QAM modulation, but QPSK was chosen because it is more robust than QAM 16 or QAM 64 and because bandwidth is so plentiful that spectral efficiency is not an issue.

Figure 6-4 *LMDS Schematic*

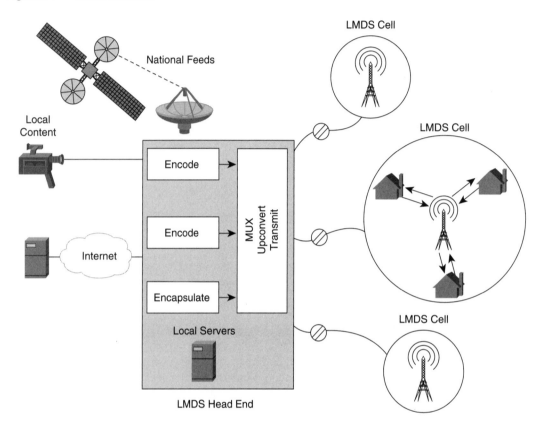

Figure 6-5 depicts consumers receiving the signal on a small dish about the size of a DBS dish or a flat-plate antenna. The dish is mounted outside the home and is connected by cable to a set-top converter, much the same way in which DBS connections are made. The signal is demodulated and fed to a decoder. Unlike DBS, LMDS is capable of two-way service, so both TV sets and PCs must be connected to the satellite dish. Furthermore, a two-way home-networking capability must be supported instead of just the simple broadcast scheme of DBS. This places new requirements on home equipment, which will be explored in the next chapter on home networking.

Figure 6-5   *LMDS in the Home*

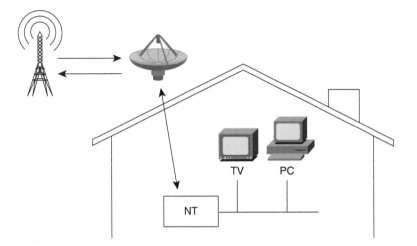

In the return path, the customer transmits to the carrier using the same dish with QPSK modulation. A Media Access Control (MAC) protocol is required because the residences in the coverage area share the return spectrum. In Figure 6-4, for example, all three consumers in the middle LMDS broadcast boundary receive broadcast TV and Internet traffic on the same frequency, say, 27.5 to 28.35 GHz. Likewise, all consumers share the same frequencies for upstream transmission, say, 29.10 to 29.25 GHz. In this case, all three users would contend for upstream bandwidth.

A variety of proprietary approaches for the MAC protocol are under consideration. However, the ITU-T draft new recommendation for LMDS, called J.116 (J.isl), indicates that the MAC should be based on cable modem standards (Annex B of ITU-T Recommendation J.112). This is basically the DOCSIS protocol presented in Chapter 3, "Cable TV Networks." Thus, the cable return-path bandwidth arbitration protocol is broadening its scope to serve other Access Networks. This has the clear benefit of reducing component costs.

One way to increase the amount of frequency available is to use sectorized antennas. These antennas can broadcast to and receive from a pie-shaped segment of the footprint. If frequency hopping is used, it is possible to use different hop sequences with each sector. This technology is illustrated in Figure 6-6.

Jimmy, Rosie, Grandma, and Einstein are all transmitting on the same frequencies back to the head end. If no sectors existed, the four households could contend for common spectrum. However, sectorization enables the same frequencies to be reused in each pie-shaped area. This increases the amount of frequency available by a factor of 4, given 90-degree sectorization. Each sector can have different polarity. If frequency-hopping spread spectrum is used, each sector can have different hop sequences.

Figure 6-6   *LMDS Sectorized*

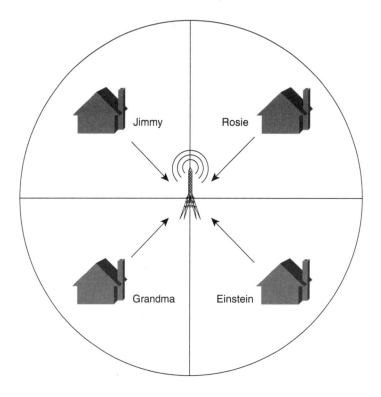

An LMDS tower and transmitter are projected to cost about $500,000 to $1 million each. CellularVision's original layout had 12 transmitters in place in Brooklyn and Queens, New York, providing coverage to 72 square km, which is about 1 transmitter per 6 square km. Assuming that each square kilometer contains 1000 residences, then 6000 homes would be passed per transmitter. This brings capital cost per home passed to $100 to $150. In less dense areas, the cost per home passed increases, but not necessarily linearly with respect to density. This is because it is possible to have fewer transmitters. Local conditions (such as rain and foliage) and the expected customer take rate all have a role in planning cell layout.

Challenges to LMDS

Despite the advantages of LMDS compared to wired networks (including large amounts of bandwidth and relatively low startup costs), the fact remains that only one LMDS provider exists today and that relatively few vendors are developing the product. Texas Instruments, an early LMDS provider with pilots in North and South America, sold its LMDS business to a European company, Bosch Telecom, which was in turn sold to a combination of Cisco Systems and Motorola, to form Spectrapoint. Likewise, Hewlett Packard sold its LMDS operation to Lucent (www.lucent.com, NYSE: LU). These companies would not have sold these businesses had the challenges to LMDS been less daunting.

Competition

The FCC has begun the process of opening additional spectrum bands for fixed wireless applications, including 25 MHz at the 4.6 GHz level and 1.4 GHz at the 40 GHz level. Teligent (Nasdaq: TGNT, www.teligent.com) operates its service at the 24 GHz spectrum tier. WinStar (Nasdaq: WCII, www.winstar.com) and Advanced Radio (Nasdaq: ARTT, www.artelecom.com) operate at 38 GHz. All three have point-to-multipoint services under way in multiple markets.

It is also possible to use newly licensed spectrum in the 2.3 GHz range. This range has the bland name of Wireless Communications Service, or WCS (www.fcc.gov/wtb/wcs/wcsfctsh.html). WCS has an aggregate of 30 MHz available in four blocks. This is very low frequency with excellent propagation characteristics. It would seem that radios in the 2.4 GHz (unlicensed band) or 2.5 GHz (MMDS) ranges could be adapted to WCS. There are no service offerings in this space, but new startup operations are being funded by venture capitalists.

Finally, there is competition from cable, MMDS, and xDSL.

Signal Quality

At 30 GHz, the wavelength of the LMDS signal is about a millimeter in length, whereas MMDS wavelength is 11 times longer and DBS is longer still. With that small wavelength, LMDS signal quality is attenuated by raindrops or a drop of tree sap. LMDS also requires clear line of sight. Because of these problems, LMDS is usable only in relatively flat areas with relatively little foliage. It might be possible to overcome foliage problems with more efficient modulation and antennas, but doing so would incur higher transmitter costs and possible regulatory problems.

The whole issue of getting good signal integrity is still the subject of lively debate. However, field tests in the United States and Brazil (where it rains a lot) have given encouragement that these problems are on their way to being solved. In a Brazilian test run in 1996, Texas Instruments reported that equipment was capable of operating at a radius of 6.5 km. Still, doubts about signal strength persist on Wall Street, where LMDS is viewed primarily as a solution for flat, high-density, low-rainfall, low-foliage areas.

Cell Size

Smaller cell size increases infrastructure cost (necessitating more towers and transmitters) but improves coverage and reliability to consumers. The following list details the main engineering factors that can increase cell size:

- Increased transmission and receiver antenna height
- Increased power
- Overlapping cells versus single transmitter cells

Increasing the height of the transmission and reception antennas greatly improves reception by improving line of sight, mainly by transmitting over trees. The downside is aesthetics and cost. Operators will try to construct towers as high as possible, consistent with local ordinances and tower costs.

In rainy weather, the operator might increase transmission power slightly to get more energy through the network. No adaptive transmit power exists; instead, power levels are set during trials to provide the required coverage. This increases transmitter cost and can cause interference.

Another technique for better reception is to have overlapping cells. In a single transmitter cell, all homes must send and receive to a single tower. Hewlett-Packard found that a single transmitter would reach only slightly more than 60 percent of the homes in a cell due to line-of-sight problems. With overlapping cells, a given household could be within range of two or more towers and could select the tower that provides the best signal strength by measuring power levels. Studies by Hewlett-Packard have shown that overlapping cells can substantially increase penetration rate to nearly 100 percent.

The challenge for LMDS operators will be creating economical deployment strategies. As a point of contrast, the design of cell size and the location for LMDS is unlike that of cellular telephone. Cellular telephone is a wireless system often used by consumers while in transit. For such a system, it is important to start with large cells and gradually split them into smaller cells as usage grows to minimize handoffs. A *handoff* is the process of transferring the responsibility for a cellular voice call from one base station to another as the caller moves out of range of the original cell. During handoffs, voice calls can go silent as the cellular network sorts out which base station is responsible for maintaining the call.

No handoff problem exists in the LMDS case because none of the subscribers are in motion. This means that LMDS operators must start with small cells to maximize coverage and reliability. Such a process is costly and changes deployment strategies from the cellular model. Although broad coverage was the key to success in a cellular network, identifying and serving areas densely populated with potential customers is key to LMDS. Instead of segmenting big cells into small cells (such as with cellular operators), LMDS operators must start with small, well-placed cells and add more small cells as service levels increase.

Carrier Buildout Costs

Due to its small cells, LMDS requires many more transmission towers than MMDS. Because MMDS has about 10 times the transmission radius of LMDS, LMDS requires about 100 times more towers to cover the same area. In addition to construction costs, delays are associated with site selection, easements, permits, and negotiation of rentals. The result is that LMDS is significantly more expensive and time-consuming to roll out than MMDS.

Cost of Consumer Equipment

Unlike DBS antennas, LMDS dishes can transmit as well as receive. This increases cost for consumer equipment compared to DBS. Furthermore, installation costs are associated with LMDS; unlike DBS, for instance, an installer would be needed to align the antenna. Many analysts have concluded that DBS is the upper limit of what consumers will pay for digital TV equipment, and LMDS could push costs beyond that.

Fragmented Area Coverage

Forthcoming LMDS spectrum auctions raise the question of another potential challenge. The current approach to spectrum auctioning in the United States is to conduct separate auctions for different geographical areas, namely the BTAs. This has the tendency to fragment the country into multiple potential providers. Such an approach was taken for cellular telephone and PCS. Benefits of regional auctions include increasing the number of competitors nationwide and increasing auction incomes.

Canada is instituting another approach. There, a nationwide license was issued to MaxLink Communications, Inc., by the Canadian Department of Industry (Industry Canada) for nearly half the population of Canada. This approach offers incentives to the providers because they have a bigger market to exploit with a single license. It remains to be seen if the checkerboard procedure or the national licensing approach serves best to stimulate broadband rollout.

Standardization

LMDS system developers are proceeding on a variety of proprietary schemes. To address this problem, on March 11, 1999, IEEE chartered the 802.16 Working Group on Broadband Wireless Access (BWA, grouper.ieee.org/groups/802/16/). BWA "specifies the physical layer and media access control layer of the air interface of interoperable fixed point-to-multipoint broadband wireless access systems." The project authorization request will be applicable to fixed wireless systems operating between 10 and 66 GHz.

Standardization work has just begun and will need to conclude quickly to keep pace with the progress of competing Access Networks.

Third-Generation Cellular

Third-Generation Cellular (3G) refers to the third generation of Personal Communication Service (PCS) wireless digital voice service. In fact, the frequencies used by 3G overlap PCS frequencies in the United States. To succeed, however, 3G will need to be much more than cellular telephony. It builds on the development of Code Division Multiple Access (CDMA) digital telephony specified as IS-95 and developed largely by Qualcomm (Nasdaq: QCOM, www.qualcomm.com). The IS-95 system uses direct sequence spread spectrum over a 1.25 MHz passband. 3G uses a passband of 5, 10, or 20 MHz, also with CDMA. Hence, the term Wideband CDMA, or W-CDMA, refers to the underlying physical layer.

The concept of 3G is extremely aggressive and has attracted the intense interest of venture capitalists, semiconductor designers, and carriers worldwide. The major features of 3G are listed here:

- 2 Mbps (E1) full-duplex speed for indoor, stationary devices. This would be competitive with a cable or xDSL service.

- 384 Kbps for pedestrian use.

- 144 Kbps for automobiles moving at highway speeds.

- Worldwide roaming.

- Voice and data operation.

- Backward compatibility with existing 2G telephone services supporting IS-95 CDMA, IS-136 TDMA, and GSM.

The interest of 3G in the residential broadband context is that, if a user can obtain 2 Mbps from wireless and get voice service, then who needs a cable modem or xDSL? The presumption is that given the inclination of users to pay for mobility, if 3G works and is cost-effective, it may have an advantage over cable and xDSL.

The first W-CDMA service slated to appear will come from NTT DoCoMo, the world's largest cellular provider, with more than 22 million subscribers, or more than 50 percent of the market share in Japan. The company's service begins early in 2001. The intense interest in 3G was demonstrated by the October 1998 initial public offering of DoCoMo, in which it raised 2.13 trillion yen, equivalent to $18 billion at the exchange rate then. This was and is still the largest IPO ever worldwide, despite a very poor stock market environment in Japan. DoCoMo's first 384 Kbps W-CDMA service will have a return path of 64 Kbps. Car phones are not limited by batteries or size considerations; they are expected to have full 2 Mbps service in 2001.

DoCoMo is not alone in rolling out 3G in Japan. Two competing consortia—one led by Japan Telecom and another by KDD—are expected to announce service in 2001. European launches will follow later that year.

3G Architecture

3G allows for channel bandwidths of 1.25, 5, 10, and 20 MHz of bandwidth, within a band of 120 MHz (FDD). To get 2 Mbps, current thinking is that 20 MHz will be required. For 384 Kbps service for stationary and mobile use, 5 MHz is used. Most early implementations will use the 5 MHz channelization, using direct sequence spread spectrum and QAM16, QPSK, and BPSK modulation. QAM and QPSK will be used on the downlink (from the carrier to the client) and BPSK on the uplink. The spectrum is licensed.

Many ways exist by which to use the allocated spectrum. Within each passband, there can be multicarrier or direct sequence spread spectrum multiplexing. In the United States, spectrum was allocated for FDD and TDD use. A major trick is to design a radio interface that can accommodate any of these combinations. This is required for roaming. However, the ability to quickly discriminate among the TDD/FDD, multicarrier/DSSS, bandwidth options, and so on poses a major problem for semiconductor designers who need to implement these circuits in ASICs for power consumption reasons. It is a complicated problem, but to the winner go tremendous spoils.

Roaming Versus Mandatory Standards

Despite the accord between Ericsson and Qualcomm regarding licensing of certain W-CDMA intellectual property rights, the fact remains that there are engineering differences, notably regarding the air interfaces. Unresolved is the familiar conflict between roaming and standards. Multiple-mode 3G units will be needed for roaming and interoperability; one mode will support the Qualcomm standard, cdma2000; another mode will support TDMA; and the final mode will support the European standard, called Universal Terrestrial Radio Standard (UTRA). Details of 3G based on cdma2000 are found at www.cdg.org, details on 3G TDMA are found at www.uwcc.org, and details on 3G UTRA are found at www.3gpp.org.

European Commission is supporting a proposal to require all European 3G telecom operators to allocate spectrum and license in at least one interoperable standard across all of Europe. This is so that Europeans can roam within Europe using a single air interface, which minimizes cost and thus speeds deployment. The commission doesn't specify which standard would be mandated; that would be up to the operators to agree. However, the standard is likely to be UTRA. Any operator could also offer cdma2000 or TDMA as an option, but UTRA would be required.

At the time of writing, the United States, through the Department of Commerce and the U.S. Trade Representative, is threatening trade sanctions against Europe if this is implemented. The concern is that even though cdma2000 and TDMA would be allowed into Europe, they would be at a cost disadvantage against UTRA. This argument is unfortunate in that the differences to the user of the various interfaces is relatively small.

One can argue that the mandatory use of the GSM standard was instrumental in making GSM cell phones usable in all parts of the world. In the United States, where open competition is the mantra and standardization is viewed with suspicion, it is likely that there will be multiple-mode phones. This is costly and could impede cost reduction and proliferation of service. Therefore, a replay of the GSM experience could arise.

3G Issues

Despite its apparent advantages and strong supporters, 3G is facing serious technical and business problems, particularly for offering 2 Mbps service. Does offering 2 Mbps make sense at all if there is money and demand for simple voice service? The current generation of mobile, digital voice telephony has many improvements to make in global roaming and voice quality. There will also be innovations, such as the integration of mobile, digital telephony with personal digital assistants (PDAs), such as the PalmPilot. But the possibility of competing for xDSL and cable data subscribers makes 3G attractive. Yet here again is another example of a high-concept service that must overcome some prosaic technical and commercial issues.

Marketing Questions

The long-standing arguments on TDMA, CDMA, and GSM overlook the problem that 3G can offer more services than voice. The question is, which services? Should 3G offer high-fidelity voice to consumers? Will it really compete with cable modems and xDSL for data service? Will it cannibalize 2G PCS voice? Should it support utility metering and home security, which are low-speed services? Should it be an always-connected, low-signaling service, or should it be used as a dial-up model? How much will consumers and businesses pay for the convenience and speed? Will a flat rate or a metered rate be required at initial product rollout?

Furthermore, should 3G services be targeted to consumers at all? Traditionally, new high-tech products and services were targeted at business users first, often starting with vertical markets. But the Internet and particularly the cable modem home market may be a better early target.

Carriers don't really know the answer to these questions, mainly because the consumers don't either. Therefore, initial services will wisely use flexible technology platforms that support a range of services and pricing models; changes will be made later.

Globally Consistent Spectrum Allocation

For global roaming and a standardized, mass-produced air interface to exist, consistent spectrum allocation is necessary worldwide. This is not the case at present.

Different regions have different amounts of spectrum allotted for 3G: 395 MHz to Europe; 230 MHz to the Americas; and 320 MHz to Asia. What's more, there is consensus that this is not enough; more must be allocated.

Business Case for High Speed

Given the relatively small spectrum allocation for 3G, should any speeds higher than 384 Kbps be offered by carriers? Multiplying user speeds by a factor of 5 would correspondingly reduce the number of concurrent users on the system and hence possibly reduce revenue potential. It may be that the sweet spot of the service will be about 144 Kbps to 384 Kbps to maximize the number of users and differentiate itself from second-generation telephone services.

3G Transition Issues

For many carriers, an important transition issue is finding a flexible radio that can handle 3G and existing digital cellular technologies, TDMA (IS-136), CDMA (IS-95), or GSM technology. TDMA advocates want to be sure that 3G is backward-compatible with TDMA; the same is true for CDMA and GSM. That basically is what the UWCC, cdma2000 Consortium, and UTRA are all about. UWCC is lobbying to be sure that 3G is backward-compatible with IS-136—likewise with cdma2000 for IS-95, and UTRA for GSM. No one wants the installed base of digital cellular telephony obsoleted by 3G.

The European Technology Standards Institute (ETSI) decision to adopt DoCoMo's technology as a major part of its third-generation standard gives DoCoMo suppliers, Lucent, and Japanese manufacturers a major opportunity in shaping 3G for both Europe and Japan. Because GSM is available in 118 countries with 324 separate networks serving more than 150 million subscribers, it is likely that DoCoMo's early entry forces carriers who now offer GSM services to adopt DoCoMo's W-CDMA standard.

Wireless Issues

High-speed wireless access has been a long time coming. It has been discussed for years, only to disappoint. It has been disappointing because the possibilities are so clear. These are instant infrastructure (no digging), facilities-based bypass of local telephone networks, and mobility. However, all wireless services are confronted by a common set of problems that have hampered the introduction of various wireless services, including cellular telephone.

Real Estate and Transmission Towers

Despite the technology required to make wireless work, wireless is in large part a real estate problem. LMDS and 3G have relatively small footprints, about a few kilometers in diameter. This means that tower and transmitters must be located in thousands of locations in the country—about 10,000 locations are necessary to provide coverage comparable to cellular telephone. Bell Atlantic Mobile, for example, operated from 1400 towers prior to its acquisition of NYNEX.

The first problem wireless service providers have is simply to find the space. Not any location will do; site selection is a complicated engineering problem. The second problem is to pay for the space. Frequently, property owners, aware they are suddenly sitting on a potential windfall, will exact what is called "greenmail" from the prospective service provider when selling.

Following prodding from wireless providers, the FCC issued a Notice of Proposed Rule Making in June 1999 that builds a public record to determine the regulatory latitude the FCC possesses to assist wireless carriers' access to roof space of buildings.

In particular, the question raised under the 1996 Telecom Act is: Does the FCC have the authority to impose nondiscrimination orders on real estate owners who have already allowed telephone or utility companies access to their buildings? That is, if a building owner allows a telephone company access to their building, must it accord the same access to a CLEC? In addition, the FCC seeks to develop a record on whether state and local rights-of-way and tax policies are having an impact on facilities-based competition. For example, local governments often impose rights-of-way taxes as part of telco licensing to help defer the costs of road construction. Fixed wireless carriers say that because they do not dig up streets, they should not have to pay these taxes. Do either state or federal authorities have preemptive rights or responsibilities?

In addition to property owners, municipalities also have obstructed the construction of new towers based on aesthetics. Another legal question is to what extent the state PUC or FCC have to preempt municipalities.

Wireless can also be deployed from free-standing towers. Such towers are owned by utility companies and even companies specialized in building and operating towers primarily for communications services. Such companies are now publicly traded. Among these are Pinnacle Holdings (Nasdaq: BIGT), WesTower Communications (Amex: WTW), American Tower (NYSE: AMT), and Crown Castle (Nasdaq: TWRS).

If transmitter space cannot be obtained in quantity, then deployment of high-frequency wireless technologies becomes more costly. As of this writing, all these issues are unresolved; when decided by the FCC, they will no doubt be litigated.

International Spectrum Coordination

Spectrum is allocated differently in different parts of the world. This particularly affects satellite systems but can impact terrestrial services as well. In the satellite arena, for example, Iridium uses frequencies in the range of 1610 MHz to 1660 MHz. However, these frequencies are protected by the European Union for use by radio astronomers conducting experiments in the 1610.6 MHz to 1613.8 MHz range.

Similarly, the United States has been a keen proponent of making additional frequencies available at 1176 MHz for Global Positioning Systems (GPS). However, the Conference of European Postal and Telecommunications Administrations (CEPT) points out that this frequency is currently being used by terrestrial aeronautical radio-navigation applications in Europe, and it could cost several million dollars to relocate the users.

In terrestrial services, there has been widespread agreement that 3G is a good idea, but North America, Europe, and Asia have each allocated a different amount of frequency. This can negatively impact the interoperability of 3G devices for roaming travelers. Furthermore, there is worldwide agreement that more spectrum should be allocated for 3G than what was previously allocated in each continent, but the amount of increase is contentious because domestic constraints govern how much can be added.

Competition from Cable and xDSL

Wireless will always be at a bandwidth disadvantage when compared to cable and xDSL services. This is because wired bandwidth can be manufactured; more fiber simply can be laid as demand requires. Furthermore, cable and xDSL are deploying ahead of LMDS, MMDS, and 3G. If bandwidth or time to market are more important marketing requirements than ubiquity or mobility, then wireless is a tougher sell.

Deregulation and Standardization

On balance, deregulation will let businesses operate more efficiently and will fairly price spectrum. On the other hand, by letting market forces dominate, a bit of uncertainly is created as standards are fragmented. This already is the case in the U.S. digital cellular market. The United States has CDMA and TDMA solutions, and roaming is more restrictive than in Europe, which has settled on GSM. The effect of openness and deregulation when competing against more controlled models from Europe remains to be seen.

The Ideal Spectrum

Despite the available of lots of wireless access services, it seems that the ideal spectrum is elusive. Wouldn't it be nice if a band existed which had the quantity of bandwidth of LMDS with the placement of bandwidth of MMDS? It would be even nicer if such bands existed for licensed and unlicensed use. Similar bands could be used for FDD or TDD use, and others for point-to-point or multipoint use.

Spectrum allocation is in large part captive to the legacy of decades of prior allocations. Existing users can't be moved. There are too many taxi cabs, police cars, and microwave ovens in place.

Perhaps with the freeing of analog TV spectrum, some relocation would be possible so that optimized broadband Access Networks could be built. Public policy should see to it that the transition of analog TV to digital stays on schedule.

Summary

Multiple wireless options exist that potentially can support RBB services. The services discussed in this chapter—DBS, LEO, MMDS, LMDS, and 3G—overlap but have enough differences to attract their particular segment of users. Table 6-8 compares features among these options.

Table 6-8   *Feature Comparison of Wireless Access Networks*

Feature	DBS	MMDS	LMDS	LEO	3G
Bandwidth	500 MHz	198 MHz	1150 MHz (A-band) 150 MHz (B-band)	Depends on license Teledesic has 300 MHz	Multiple bands in increments of 1.25 MHz, 5 MHz, 10 MHz, 20 MHz
Spectrum range	12.2 to 12.7 GHz	2.150 to 2.162 GHz 2.500 to 2.686 GHz	27.50 to 31.30 GHz	19 GHz (downlink)	1.9 GHz
Downstream bit rate capacity	Roughly 1 Gb	Roughly 1 Gb	Roughly 2.0 Gb	2 Mbps	144 Kbps, automotive 384 Kbps, pedestrian 2 Mbps, indoor fixed
Return path	Telco return, digital cellular, or xDSL	MMDS return, telco return, digital cellular, or xDSL	LMDS return	29 GHz (uplink)	1.9 GHz range, FDD
Footprint	Nationwide	50 miles radius possible, but will likely be cellular	2 to 4 mile radius	Roughly 300 mile diameter, in constant motion	Cellular telephony spacing
Homes passed per cell	Nationwide	Greater than 1 million, but will likely be cellular to reach a few hundred	A few thousand	Thousands	Few hundred
U.S. service providers	DirecTV, Echostar	MCI Worldcom, Sprint	Nextlink, Winstar	Teledesic, Skybridge	Nearly every PCS service provider, eventually
Rainfall attenuation	Negligible	Negligible	Problematic	Potential problem	Negligible

Table 6-8   *Feature Comparison of Wireless Access Networks*

Feature	DBS	MMDS	LMDS	LEO	3G
Challenges	Lack of local content for TV Lack of a return path	Must build cellular infrastructure DBS and cable competition for video Historically poorly capitalized service providers	Most costly wireless rollout; many towers Rain, foliage Requires dense residential use; urban areas only	Cost Iridium legacy Will it work? Cooperation of national carriers	Requires backward-compatibility with 2G and 1G cellular telephony. Standards squabbles International spectrum coordination Will the market be satisfied with 2G? Will carriers offer more than 384 Kbps, preferring to have more customers?
Facilitators	Successful broadcast TV story with good content	Lowest-cost infrastructure Data services and equipment already developed based on cable modem technology Accommodates local content TV Can use indoor receivers Influx of new capital from Sprint and MCI Worldcom	Most bandwidth in both directions Accommodates local content TV	Instant infrastructure worldwide, including on the high seas. Can bypass national carriers.	Excellent spectrum location. Carriers such as NTT DoCoMo are running out of 1G and 2G spectrum. Consumers like mobility. Extensive venture capital and product innovation. Major thrust in Europe, which sees a market niche begun with GSM.

Table 6-9 summarizes the ways in which various features of wireless services act to challenge or facilitate their prospects for succeeding as an RBB network.

Table 6-9   *Challenges and Facilitators for Wireless as an RBB Network*

Issue	Challenge	Facilitator
Media	Difficult transmission characteristics exist. Line of sight is usually required. Multipath and interference present continuing problems.	Minimal installation and maintenance concerns exist. Fast service rollout will be available after the target market area is decided.
Spectrum	Different spectrum allocations in different countries require coordination for global service and equipment development. The perfect spectrum allocation for broadband is missing.	Spectrum is plentiful due to recent modulation and compression techniques and newly usable high frequencies. Lots more is bandwidth available when analog TV frequencies are freed.
Local content service	Service is not available for DBS until spot beaming and copyright issues are resolved.	Services provide market advantages to LMDS and MMDS for TV service.
Data-handling capabilities	Implementation of a return path for DBS and MMDS is feasible but expensive. MMDS, DBS, 3G, and LEOs may not have enough bandwidth.	Technology maps well to Internet data; high-speed forward and low-speed return paths closely map to Web access and push-mode data. LMDS will offer the highest two-way bit rate of any residential service if technological challenges are solved.
Market	Technology has been late to market compared with wired infrastructures. Wired infrastructures can manufacture bandwidth as the market requires. Customer demand is unclear for high-speed mobile services.	Consumers like mobility and will pay a premium for it. Technology builds on the cellular telephone infrastructure and marketing experience.
Business/ financial aspect	Expenses incurred during auctions could deplete capital required for service rollout. Real estate problems, roof rights, and tower costs are disadvantages. Preemption of property owners and local municipalities may be required.	Fast infrastructure rollout is possible. Cost per home passed is lower than with a wired infrastructure. U.S. interexchange carriers appear willing to invest, in part because it provides a bypass of LECs. This offers an option for facilities-based bypass of telco and cable access.

This chapter completes the survey begun in Chapter 3 of specific networks that could provide RBB service. The next chapter turns to the home networking, the point at which the carrier network's responsibility ends and the resident's begins.

References

Articles

Adachi, Fumiyuki, Mamoru Sawahashi, and Hirohito Suda. "Wideband DS-CDMA for Next Generation Mobile Communications Systems." *IEEE Communications* Vol. 36, No. 9: September 1998.

Correia, Luis, and Ramjee Prasad. "An Overview of Wireless Broadband Communications." *IEEE Communications* Vol 35, No. 1: January 1997.

Dahlmann, Erik, Bjorn Gudmundsun, Mats Nilsson, andJohan Skold. "UMTS/IMT02000 Based on Wideband CDMA." *IEEE Communications* Vol. 36, No. 9: September 1998.

Honcharenko, Walter, Jan Kruys, Daniel Lee, and Nitin Shah. "Broadband Wireless Access., *IEEE Communications* Vol. 35, No. 1: January 1997.

Kniseley, Donald, Sarath Kumar, Subhasis Laha, and Sanjiv Nanda. "Evolution of Wireless Data Services, IS-95 to cdma2000." *IEEE Communications* Vol. 36, No. 10: October 1998.

Larson, Doug. "DBS vs. Cable." *Communications Technology Magazine* Vol. 16, No. 5: April 1999.

Morinaga, Norihiko, Masao Nakagawa, and Ryuji Kohmo. "New Concepts and Technologies for Achieving Highly Reliable and High-Capacity Multimedia Wireless Communications Systems." *IEEE Communications* Vol 35, No. 1: January 1997.

Internet Resources

www.fcc.gov/oet/info/database/spectrum/spinvtbl.pdf

U.S. Spectrum Inventory Table

nwest.nist.gov

Broadband Fixed Wireless site hosted by NIST

grouper.ieee.org/groups/802/16/

IEEE 802.16 Broadband Fixed Wireless

literature.omega.com/posters.html

Spectrum allocation chart

www.3gpp.org

Third Generation Partner Project, supporting 3G based on UTRA, the European approach to W-CDMA

www.arib.or.jp

Association of Radio Industries and Businesses, Japan. Spectrum managers for Japan. This site is in Japanese only

www.cdg.org

CDMA Development Group, supporting 3G based on IS-95, the Qualcomm approach to W-CDMA

www.cmcnyls.edu

NYU Law School Communications Media Center

www.dbsdish.com/dbs/a0.html

A consumer's guide to DBS from the DBS Connection

www.directv.com

The home page for DirecTV, with mostly programming choices

www.fcc.gov/mmb

FCC Mass Media Bureau, for television and radio information

www.fcc.gov/oet/

FCC Office of Engineering and Technology

www.fcc.gov/telecom.html

Telecom Act of 1996

www.fcc.gov/wtb

FCC Wireless Telecommunications Bureau; PCS, xMDS, WCS

www.itu.int/imt/

IMT-2000 Web site, hosted by the ITU

www.law.cornell.edu/uscode/17/119.html

Satellite Home Viewing Act, paragraph 119, which discusses royalties and broadcast restrictions on DBS www.ntia.doc.gov

National Telecommunications and Information Agency, U.S. Department of Commerce

www.ntia.doc.gov/osmhome/osmhome.html

Spectrum allocation information from the U.S. Department of Commerce/NTIA/Office of Spectrum Management

www.oftel.org

U.K. Office of Telecommunications. Spectrum managers for the United Kingdom

www.skybridgesatellite.com

Skybridge, a LEO

www.spectrapoint.com/

Web site for SpectraPoint, an LMDS equipment vendor

www.speedus.com/

Provides wireless service to a tough audience: Brooklyn

www.teledesic.com

Web site for Teledesic, a LEO

www.uwcc.org

Universal Wireless Communications, supporting 3G based on the TDMA

www.wcai.com

Wireless Cable Association; MMDS information

www.wirelessweek.com

A wireless weekly

This chapter covers the following topics:

- Home Network Requirements
- Home Network Architecture
- Topology Alternatives
- Home Media Alternatives
- Residential Gateway
- Summary

CHAPTER 7

Home Networks

The function of Access Networks is to transfer bits to and from the home. The Home Network distributes the bits among devices in the home (TVs, PCs, DVD players, game stations, stereos, alarms, and so on) and between the home devices and the Access Network. The Home Network is a local-area network (LAN), not unlike LANs operating in businesses today. However, Home Networks and business LANs differ somewhat. Home networks have more stringent requirements to support entertainment video, to simplify ease of use, and to reduce cost. One cost-reduction technique would be to use existing home wiring, if possible, or to use a wireless solution. The home-networking market continues to gain importance as Access Networks increase in speed, but this market is taking on a fragmented appearance in doing so. Standards include Bluetooth, IEEE 802.11, HomePNA, HomeAPI, UPnP, HomeRF, Jini, HIPERLAN, Firewire, and VESA.

The objective of this chapter is to describe requirements, issues, and alternatives for home networking and thereby frame the discussion for readers wanting to pursue this complex topic. The remainder of this chapter is organized as follows:

- Home Network requirements
- Home Network architecture
- Topology Alternatives
- Home media alternatives
- Residential Gateway
- Summary

Home Network Requirements

Home Networks are not new. For years, telephone companies, cable companies, and electric utilities have installed wiring in homes for the transmission of voice, analog television service, and electric power. In addition, many newer homes have networks for environmental control systems to regulate air conditioning and heating. Some Home Networks exist for intercoms, entertainment systems, and home security systems.

Identifying Home Network requirements is difficult given the lack of consensus about what services, media, and administrative responsibilities define a Home Network. Thus, the network requirements mentioned in this chapter are not necessarily universal but should constitute a superset of requirements. This section begins with connectivity options: different services and levels of interconnectivity among them that can constitute the Home

Network. We then examine specific technical requirements associated with some or all of the options.

Connectivity Requirements

Figure 7-1 depicts the various connectivity options for in-home traffic.

Figure 7-1   *Home Network Connectivity Options*

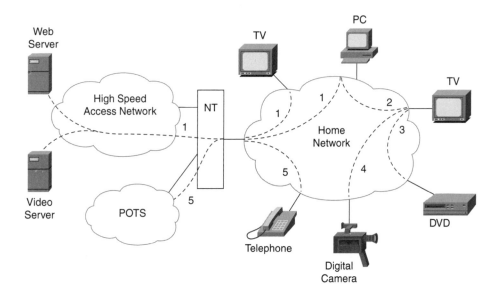

Case 1 shows the required traffic from the network termination (NT) to various devices within the home. Multiple devices on the same Home Network create a challenge when they access the same or different carriers simultaneously. The TV viewer, for example, might be viewing interactive TV, while the PC user might be active in a Web-browsing session. The resulting challenges include address resolution, bandwidth allocation inside the home, and signaling.

In Case 2, traffic is moved from the PC for display on the television set. Currently, a TV set costs much less than a PC monitor of comparable screen size (a Sony 17-inch TV costs a lot less than a Sony 17-inch monitor). Thus, using a TV monitor instead of a PC monitor can reduce the total cost of home computing, but doing so requires a high-speed interface between the PC and the monitor.

In Case 3, a viewer wants to watch a movie that is stored on a high-capacity storage device, such as the new digital video disc (DVD) currently being promoted by CE vendors. DVDs have enough storage capacity for an entire movie in high definition with five-channel surround sound on a single disc. DVDs also store computer data. Initial versions hold 4.7 GB, far exceeding today's CD-ROM. A DVD can even read today's 600 MB CD-ROMs and is expected to be the dominant form of mass storage for the home as well as the business. Access to these devices most likely will be a requirement of Home Networks.

A variation on Case 3 is multiple viewers watching the same show in different rooms, suggesting some form of broadcast or multicast within the home.

In Case 4, the TV displays output from a digital camera in real time. A challenge here is that the camera is unlikely to have built-in memory and processing capability. Therefore, another home device, such as a set-top box, is required to provide signaling support on behalf of the camera so that the camera can direct its output to the correct display device.

In Case 5, narrowband devices such as telephones, meters, and home automation controls could require access to an external carrier network. Though these devices require little bandwidth, they do have high requirements for availability—more so than video or computing. In addition, narrowband devices present new problems of address resolution and network management.

A number of technical requirements emerge for consideration given these five connectivity options, and these requirements are discussed next. In addition, connectivity raises issues of network topology and wiring options, both of which are discussed later in this chapter.

Upstream Multiplexing and Bandwidth Arbitration

In the upstream path, packets from multiple users might need to be forwarded to the Access Network simultaneously. In this case, multiplexing and bandwidth arbitration are required. The multiplexing can be as simple as time-division or frequency-division multiplexing. If the offered bandwidth exceeds the return-path bandwidth, some form of contention resolution is required. This gives rise to the requirement for a Media Access Control (MAC) protocol in the home.

Connection to Multiple Access Networks

Furthermore, multiple users may need to switch traffic to different destination Access Networks. Cable modems, for example, don't provide access to xDSL networks, and vice versa. Access to multiple video feeds might exist, such as video on demand (VoD) from different content providers going to different viewers in the home. Jimmy's TVs, for example, might connect to a cable provider, while Rosie's might connect to DBS. Today, each TV has its own set-top box and is bound to that particular network. It is at least preferable that each TV be given the choice of the Access Network to which it connects.

Also, it is very likely that different family members will be connecting to different Internet service providers simultaneously. The Home Network must be capable of directing output from the home to the proper content provider.

Connection to multiple Access Networks would require an intelligent packet-forwarding capability, as is found in routers and bridges.

Connection to Multiple Home Networks

Just as it is possible that there will be multiple Access Networks, it is also possible—and even likely—that there will be multiple Home Networks. There may be a coaxial cable network in the home to deliver video and a wireless network for the cordless phone. Both networks may be required to communicate with a home control network, to monitor air conditioning or a security system. In the case of multiple networks, the need again exists for intelligent packet forwarding so that traffic entering the home gets to the right Home Network.

Intrahome Networking

If there is substantial intrahome networking that requires quality of service guarantees (for example, DVD to TV), that traffic will likely compete with traffic entering the home from the Access Network. If the Access Network contributes relatively little bandwidth to the Home Network, bandwidth guarantees for in-home traffic are not adversely affected. But if the Access Network floods the Home Network, there is the likelihood of contention for Home Network bandwidth.

Another issue is to provide signaling for intrahome calls. For example, how is a piece of consumer electronics equipment addressed? What are the semantics of a TV requesting a specific program from the DVD? How does a digital camera route real-time output to a specific PC or TV? How does a Palm Pilot route traffic to a printer? Some form of signaling for home use is required.

Traffic generated within the home will need to have a device that can connect disparate home networks for seamless interoperability.

Distance Requirements

The Home Network should cover all parts of the home. Of course, some homes are bigger than others, and greater distances pose problems of power, attenuation, and installation cost. The magic number seems to be 100 meters as a reasonable diameter for a Home Network, to accommodate indoor and outdoor use. Of course, most homes are not that big. But neither is wiring done in a straight line. Greater distance is required to accommodate the twists and turns of house wiring. Of course, wireless solutions are line-of-sight and may not require that much reach, but their distance may be limited by interior walls and fixtures.

Electromagnetic Compliance

Regulations for safety and interference exist in every country in the world, some more stringent than others. In the United States, consumer electronics equipment must comply with FCC Part B and Underwriters Laboratory (UL) safety and emissions regulation. This has been a problem for some technologies, such as the use of electric powerlines for data service.

Ease of Installation

Because consumers have problems with programming VCRs, they could be in for even more interesting challenges installing RBB equipment. Of course, the easiest solution for consumers would be to avoid installation altogether by using existing wiring. Whether or not existing wiring is up to the job depends on what the job is—that is, how much bandwidth is required over what distance. Some technologies explored in this chapter require rewiring, while others don't. Assuming that rewiring is required, ease of consumer installation means limiting or avoiding the use of specialized tools or skills. This could preclude certain forms of cabling, such as fiber optics.

Network configuration for home computers poses difficulties for consumers because it requires network addresses, network management capability, filters, network address translation, and other software functions. More of these functions are discussed along with Residential Gateways, in due course. Suffice it to say here that technical support of customers is a large factor in why residential-based Internet service has not been a profitable business to date. Many companies have abandoned the residential side in favor of providing Internet services to corporate users. These companies generally have their own in-house network administrators to address users' questions and problems. Autoconfiguration will be key in making RBB services profitable enough to be an attractive business proposition.

Speed

Our view is that RBB requires support for entertainment video. This means that at least 2 Mbps is needed for a single DTV stream of moderate quality. Higher-quality SDTV, HDTV, and multiple video streams will impose a need for higher speeds. In many cases, the speed requirement for a Home Network could be even higher than for many business LANs.

Remote Management

Remote network management enables the service provider to monitor, diagnose, and possibly fix network service problems in the home without making a house call. Some functions of remote management are listed here:

- Address assignment
- Diagnostics

- Software update
- Network statistics gathering
- Performance monitoring

Therefore, it can be argued that the Home Network requires more speed, more management, equivalent network software functionality, and less cost than many equivalent business LANs.

Home Network Architecture

The general case of the Home Network is shown in Figure 7-2. It consists of one or more Access Networks that attach to the home at the NT.

The Home Network can be viewed as a federation of subnetworks that must be connected to each other, each of which must be connected to one or more Access Networks. These subnetworks are linked together throughout the home to form an integrated Home Network. Such subnetworks can be classified by application. There may be a Powerline subnet, a Phoneline subnet, a TV subnet, and so on. Accordingly, if a device in any particular segment wants to communicate with a device on another segment, a local packet-forwarding function is indicated.

Figure 7-2   *Home Network Schematic Network Termination (NT)*

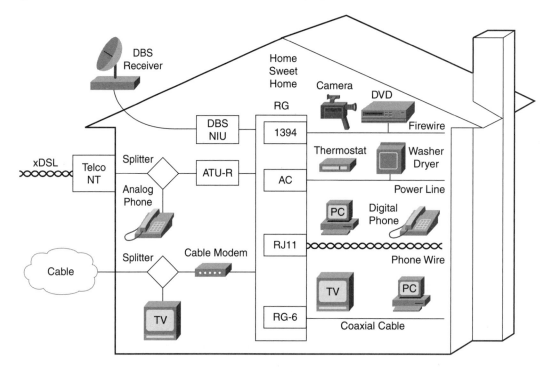

The network termination (NT) is the legal and commercial demarcation point between the carrier and the consumer. This means that if something goes wrong on the carrier side of the NT, the carrier is obligated to fix it. If something goes wrong on the other side, the consumer fixes it, usually by calling the carrier, but occasionally by doing it herself. The NT is generally a passive device that performs no changes to the bits or analog signals on the line but that can provide some minimal physical-layer functions. In some cases, the NT might not exist as a discrete piece of equipment but is a virtual point at which carrier responsibility ends by agreement.

An example of the NT is the Network Interface Device (NID) used by telephone companies. The telco NID is the box on the side of the house to which the telco technician attaches phone wire from the neighborhood telephone pole.

In addition to providing a demarcation point, the NT can perform one or more of the functions detailed in the following list:

- **Coupling of home wiring to carrier wiring**—Access wiring terminates here, and Home Network wiring begins.

- **Grounding**—This provides an electrical ground for devices attached to the Home Network.

- **Lightning protection**—This prevents devices on the Home Network from being damaged in the event that lightning hits the Access Network.

- **RF filtering**—In the upstream path, low-pass filters can be installed to prevent unwanted signals generated inside the house from polluting the upstream data path.

- **Splitting**—In the forward path, a single signal can be replicated so that multiple devices in the home can receive the same feed.

- **Interdiction**—As an authentication measure, forward-path signals can be intercepted selectively, such as for premium television channels. When a subscriber pays for a new service, interdiction of a particular program can be lifted.

- **Loopback testing**—To test the integrity of the Access Network (including the drop wire), the NT can provide a test mechanism whereby the carrier injects a signal into the network and receives an echo back from the customer NT. If the echo is successfully received by the carrier, the Access Network is assumed to be functioning properly.

- **Provisioning**—For FTTH systems, the NT might be the device whereby services can be remotely provisioned by the carrier.

Splitter

A second piece of passive equipment in some architectures is the splitter. This is a prominent component of ADSL and HFC, and it performs frequency demultiplexing and replication. This device also separates the Home Network into distinct pieces, allowing each to use wiring and signaling optimized for a particular function.

In the ADSL case, the POTS splitter peels off the low-speed voice frequencies from the high-speed ADSL frequencies. Its operation is discussed in Chapter 4, "xDSL Access Networks." The result is two sets of internal wiring: one for voice and one for high-speed data. The HFC splitter creates two identical networks; all frequencies are present on both output links. Splitters introduce some frequency attenuation and distortion and are also the source of ingress noise on the upstream. However, splitters perform a useful function to reduce the cost and complexity of distributing signals throughout the home in an inexpensive manner.

Network Interface Unit

The Network Interface Unit (NIU) is the home device that encodes and decodes bits to and from the Access Network. For HFC networks, the NIU is the cable modem. For ADSL networks, the NIU is the ATU-R.

The following list details the basic functions of the NIU:

- Modulation and demodulation of signals to the Access Network
- Forward error correction
- Enforcement of the MAC protocol
- Regulation of physical-layer-dependent control functions, such as power management in the case of HFC, or rate adaption in the case of ADSL

The NIU pairs with the access node (AN), such as the CMTS (in the case of HFC) or the DSLAM (in the case of ADSL), to enforce the MAC protocol and other control functions. For HFC, for example, the CMTS cooperates with the consumer cable modem to participate in ranging and frequency relocation.

In some cases, it is possible to package the NIU with the NT or with a more intelligent device called the Residential Gateway.

Residential Gateway

When different networks are joined—in this case, the Home Network and the Access Network—a gateway must perform the basic functions of media translation and address translation. One of the architectural options under consideration to perform these functions in the home is called the Residential Gateway (RG). Media and address translation can also be performed by the NIU, but the RG is designed for further software functions. The following list details other potential networking functions of the RG:

- Packet forwarding
- Media translation
- Speed matching
- IP address acquisition
- Network address translation

- MPEG and IP coexistence
- Packet filtering
- Authentication and encryption
- System management

Some application functions of the RG are listed here:

- MPEG decoder
- Personal video recorder
- Web browser/e-mail client

Details of RG functions listed here are discussed later in this chapter.

Set-Top Unit

After data passes through the NIU or RG, it passes to the set-top unit (STU). The STU is a device that interfaces legacy audiovisual (A/V) equipment to the broadband network. A common STU is the digital TV set-top decoder, in which the STU accepts MPEG packets from the Home Network and translates the packets for presentation on an analog TV set. If a digital TV exists, then the STU can perform other functions, such as connecting a digital camera to the Home Network or controlling an infrared remote control.

A key architectural goal is for the interface between the Home Network and the STU to be standardized to achieve cost reductions. DAVIC specifies this as the A0 interface. With a standardized A0, multiple STUs are possible in the home, each of which can service a different piece of terminal equipment.

Terminal Equipment

Terminal equipment (TE) is the generic term used to refer to televisions, personal computers, digital cameras, audio systems, and storage systems. A single Home Network has multiple pieces of TE connected to the Home Network infrastructure, which in turn suggests multiple STUs, one for each TE.

Having multiple TEs and STUs necessitates an addressing scheme within the home, as well as methods to multiplex and demultiplex traffic. TEs might be legacy devices, such as analog TV sets, or new devices specifically designed for digital home use with embedded STUs. The interface between the STU and the TE is dependent on the TE, so there is little standardization work for this interface.

Topology Alternatives

Finally, the Home Network architecture should consider topology alternatives. Some of the proposed Home Networks operate as a bus, some in a star configuration, and some daisy-chained. These configurations are depicted in Figure 7-3.

Figure 7-3   *Home Wiring Topologies*

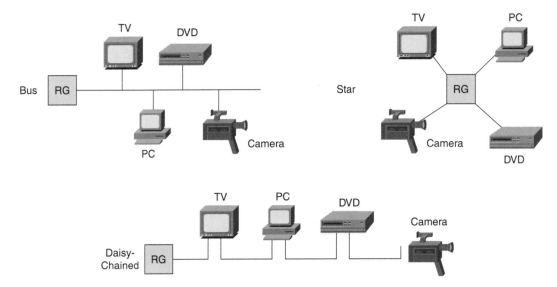

The bus configuration provides economic use of wiring, requires only a single network connection per device, and is well-suited to the broadcasting case. On the other hand, this configuration requires bandwidth arbitration, and demultiplexing is advised. Furthermore, because the bus is a shared infrastructure, it is susceptible to impairments caused by malfunctioning equipment. For example, if the PC begins to spew extraneous signals, the TV could be adversely affected.

The star configuration isolates traffic per device and therefore can guarantee bit rate per device. This is good for video and for problem isolation. Furthermore, a malfunctioning device would not adversely affect other terminal equipment. In some situations, however, such as broadcast video, broadcast is useful. In this case, packets must be replicated, which creates a processing burden and necessitates the greatest amount of wiring. Finally, a star configuration requires the use of a switch so that packets can exit onto the correct interface. This increases total system cost and introduces an active single point of failure.

Unlike the bus and star configurations, daisy chaining is not common in the commercial LAN world except as a means to connect peripherals to a single computer. This configuration involves the minimum amount of wiring but requires two ports per device. Daisy chaining is similar to the bus but does not require preprovisioning.

Home Media Alternatives

In many types of media, bits flow among terminal devices in the home. Due to the interest in residential broadband, new companies and technologies are emerging constantly. Among the more promising approaches are these:

- Phone wire, standardized as HomePNA
- Coaxial cable, now used to distribute cable TV in the home
- Home electrical circuits or powerline
- Firewire, or IEEE 1394b
- Category 5 wiring, used for Fast Ethernet in business locations
- Wireless, standardized as IEEE 802.11a, 802.11b, HomeRF, and Bluetooth

Phone Wire

Telephone wire is used today to distribute voice service from the NID to the individual telephone handsets in the home in a bus topology. A study by [Kerpez] characterized the performance of home phone wire for data purposes and concluded that, given proper precautions, telephone wire could be used for high-speed data even though it wasn't engineered for that purpose. Recent innovations have enabled the use of this legacy wiring for high-speed service. One standard for developing phone wire is promoted by the Home Phone Networking Alliance, or HomePNA (www.homepna.org).

The current version of HomePNA is 1.0, which is based on technology from Tut Systems. Because it passes analog voice, it must modulate above the analog telephone frequencies. Accordingly, it is very much like xDSL, but the modulation scheme is different. Version 1 provides only 1 Mbps. However, in July 1999, the HomePNA announced that technology from a startup company called Epigram was chosen as the basis for a Version 2 standard for 10 Mbps. Seeing a good thing in process, Broadcom acquired Epigram in April 1999.

The ITU is getting in on the act by chartering a committee, called G.pnt., to study phone wire networking. The scope of the committee is to develop interoperable home-networked transceivers for point-to-point and multipoint data communications using existing home wiring. Its goal is to extend xDSL access technologies. This effort is being strongly driven by telephone operators, and currently the goal is to achieve a recommendation by October 2000.

HPNA has already begun discussions of the next generation of the specification and has targeted 30 to 33 Mbps as the logical next step. Broadcom, among others, believes that phone line networking is capable of 100 Mbps.

HomePNA has the support of more than 90 companies, including Advanced Micro Devices, Broadcom, Conexant, Intel, Lucent, and National Semiconductors.

Phone Wire Issues

Phone wire has the advantage of being in place today in virtually all homes. Incremental costs, therefore, are minimal. However, some problems persist.

- **VDSL spectral compatibility**—HomePNA and VDSL are feared to have spectral incompatibility problems. Therefore, care must be taken to be sure that modulation schemes or other techniques are used to prevent interference.

- **Connectivity**—All the networked PCs must be plugged into jacks on the same phone line. If you have multiple lines in the home, the devices cannot broadcast to each other because they are on a different bus. A bridge (or router) connects the extensions.

- **Japan**—As of this writing, home phone line networking is not legal in Japan. This is an oddity, a remnant of when regulators worried about telephone crosstalk. However, not having Japan's consumer electronics companies involved slows the pace of cost reduction.

- **Home noise sources**— Proximity to refrigerator or air conditioning motors (or other high-power wideband sources) can cause excessive interference.

Coaxial Cable

Coaxial cable is a high-speed bus normally installed by the cable operator but owned by the homeowner. The physical problems of coaxial cables are similar to those of twisted-pair wires, but home cable is generally newer and often can be used for high-speed networking without upgrading. However, if the consumer has installed a splitter or an unauthorized set-top box, the chance exists that the wiring is sufficiently disturbed to render it unusable for data.

A final problem with both twisted-pair wiring obtained from the phone company and coaxial cable obtained from the cable operator is that they don't go to all rooms in the house. For example, if you want to leverage your in-home coax for telephone use, you might need to string extra cabling to the kitchen, where you have a telephone handset on twisted-pair wires but no cable TV. In this case, you would need to rewire your kitchen.

Powerline

For ubiquitous service in the home, nothing surpasses electrical circuits, also called powerline service. All devices need electricity. If you can use the same plug for electricity and connectivity, you have cost savings and convenience. Because of the advantages of ubiquity, powerline has been pursued as a home networking solution for years. Many systems in deployment are using low bit rate modulation for everything from baby monitors to electric meter reading and power management. Most are below 10 Kbps.

However, technical advances have accomplished trial versions of multimegabit powerline. Work is organized by a trade association called International Powerline Forum (IPF, London). Companies working on a solution include Enikia, Intellon (partly owned by Microsoft), Interlogis (an offshoot of Novell), and Northern Telecom.

IEEE 1394b (Firewire)

Because of our view that digital TV is a significant market driver for RBB, and because IEEE 1394 is not widely available, this section discusses IEEE 1394b, or Firewire, in a little more detail.

IEEE 1394 is a new form of cabling and software architecture for consumer electronics and personal computing. It originally was developed by Apple under the name Firewire as an interface for multimedia peripherals to Apple PowerPCs. After its submission to IEEE for standardization, the product was given the designation of IEEE 1394, but it is often still referred to as Firewire. Apple and Thomson continue to hold the intellectual property rights, which apply primarily to firms devising integrated circuits to implement the protocol, not to downstream manufacturers of adapter cards and end users. The original 1394 specification had a limit of only 5 meters in distance. A successor, IEEE 1394b, extends the range to 50 meters.

Firewire has garnered the support of CE manufacturers as a high-speed, daisy-chained network for the attachment of consumer entertainment equipment such as stereo sound equipment, digital cameras, digital video discs (DVD), and digital television sets. Firewire supports the speeds necessary to accommodate multiple streams of digital video and is the medium of choice for CE vendors. Additionally, PC NICs will be available. Apple is the holder of the original intellectual property and intends to ship Firewire on Powerbook and desktop computers in 1999. Sony currently is shipping a digital camera with a Firewire port. Japanese manufacturers such as Sony and Toshiba are shipping DVDs and digital decoders with Firewire. There is considerable momentum from the CE industry behind Firewire, if not the computer and telecommunications industries.

The following list details the attributes of Firewire:

- Speeds of 98.304 Mbps, 196.608 Mbps, and 393.216 Mbps, commonly referred to as 100 Mbps, 200 Mbps, and 400 Mbps. Work is under way to define an 800 Mbps capability.

- Single-wire cabling for all devices, such as no more separate video cables for audio and video.

- Combined isochronous and asynchronous modes.

- Hot-pluggable devices, which are devices that can be added to or removed from the network without interfering with working devices.

- Optional power-passing capability from an IEEE 1394 hub to various pieces of terminal equipment.

- Plug-and-play capability for PC and TV connections.

- Strong support among consumer equipment manufacturers.

- Support for digital TV and IP protocols.

Firewire Architecture

Figure 7-4 shows the elements of Firewire's RG. The home-use IP router function defines the address translation of IP to and from Firewire, which has its own numbering plan. The MPEG-2 stream-handling function is concerned with MPEG interaction with Firewire. In particular, this function maps MPEG programs to Firewire channels.

Figure 7-4 *Firewire Schematic*
Courtesy of Mitsubishi Electric (www.mitsubishi.com)

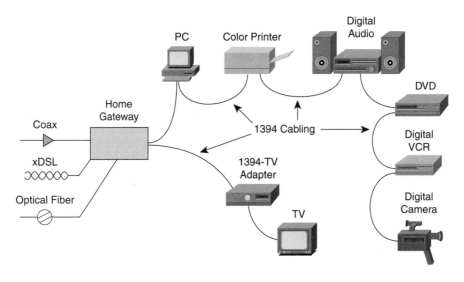

Firewire Principles of Operation

A Firewire network supports daisy-chained and star topologies. Each Home Network consists of a root node, which contains a global view of all devices attached in the home and discerns the topology from control traffic crossing the network. The root node can be any Firewire device, but an RG is a logical place for this function.

The software standard specifies a protocol stack encompassing addressing, timing, bandwidth reservation, and Media Access Control.

Each Firewire-compliant device contains a configuration read-only memory (ROM) that is embedded in digital set-top units, NICs, and consumer electronic devices. This ROM contains the equivalent of an Ethernet MAC address, the speed requirement of the device, and information on whether it operates in asynchronous or synchronous mode. The configuration ROM provides the plug-and-play capability of Firewire. Enough intelligence exists in this ROM to enable it to participate in the configuration process. The result is that the consumer plugs in the Firewire connector, and the device is fully capable of participating in the local network.

When devices power on to the network, an event called the bus reset occurs. In the bus reset, each device broadcasts the contents of its configuration ROM. The root node listens to all the traffic, distills it, and develops a topology. After the bus reset, the root has a global picture of who is attached to the network, their speed requirements, their requirements for isochronous support, and their identifier.

This protocol has both asynchronous and synchronous support. This is achieved by using a slotted protocol reminiscent of some HFC media-control protocols.

An important function of the RG in the Firewire model is to bind the 1394 channel identifier to an MPEG PID or IP address.

Firewire Issues

Firewire represents a very high-end Home Network architecture that is particularly well-suited for video transmission, including broadcast TV. Nonetheless, despite the plug-and-play feature, simplified cabling, speed, and support of the CE industry, Firewire faces hurdles.

The following list details some of the challenges for Firewire:

- Rewiring in the home is required. Firewire does not run over legacy wiring.
- Firewire requires some form of RG. The root device is an inherent part of the architecture.
- The cost is significant compared to that of legacy systems. The Firewire cables are new, the interfaces are new, and there is a requirement for new devices such as set-top units, the root processor, and home rewiring.
- Little support exists for Firewire apart from the consumer electronics industry and Apple. Further information can be obtained from the 1394 Trade Association Web page at www.firewire.org.

Category 5 Wiring

Those familiar with internetworking recognize that home networking presents roughly the same problem as local-area networking for business use. A natural consideration would be to install some form of commercially implemented local-area network (LAN) technology, particularly Fast Ethernet (100 Mbps), which is enough to support multiple TV streams and even HDTV. It would be possible to have three or four concurrent HDTV NTSC programs, with multimegabit data service and telephony over a broadcast Fast Ethernet in the home. Given the familiarity of FE at work, this seems to be a logical home medium. Business Ethernets are configured as a star or bus topology, and either can be used in the home. However, to combat congestion problems, Ethernets are increasingly configured in star topologies.

Home networking differs in several ways from the LAN model. First is the requirement to accommodate broadcast digital TV. No LAN protocol is designed specifically for this role. It is widely believed that video services require isochronous networking. Isochronous networking provides bits at a fixed rate over time. Ethernet and its higher-speed brethren do not explicitly provide for isochronous service. ATM is being considered for point-to-point video, but no economic architecture exists for the broadcast case.

Second, the Home Network must be easier to use than a business LAN because there won't be a system administrator to help you configure your IP address or program your access list. Plug-and-play is a requirement.

Third is cost. The Home Network probably won't be paid for by the boss. Consumer electronics is highly cost-sensitive, and vendors are accustomed to small margins, which is a bit of a rude awakening for networking companies accustomed to 50-percent-plus margins.

New Wiring for New Residential Developments

The problem with Category 5 wiring and Firewire is that they require new wiring. This negatively impacts their appeal, but both provide better service. Mindful of the demand among homeowners to be wired, forward-thinking homebuilders are preinstalling Category 5 twisted-pair and RG-6 coaxial cable in new-home construction in addition to normal phone wire. An example is Pardee Homes, which builds in Los Angeles, San Diego, and Las Vegas (www.pardeehomes.com). In the Huntington Heights development, every family room and bedroom is equipped with two sets of Category 5 wiring and a pair of RG-6 coaxial cables. Two sets of Category 5 wiring means that each room can have separate telephone and data services.

Furthermore, standard home phone wiring is a daisy-topology. In Pardee's case, wiring is installed in a star configuration. This configuration provides more robustness and stability because a malfunctioning computer or phone will not affect other devices. Furthermore, the star terminates in an indoor passive hub, located in either a coat closet (near the burglar alarm wiring) or a laundry room (close to the NID). The hub can be located with a home router or gateway so that the homeowner can install his modems and Web servers in a mini telecom facility. The incremental cost to the builder for the hub and the high performance is less than $1,000 per new home.

Even for their lower-priced homes, which would not have the Category 5 and coaxial cable to every room, Pardee installs Category 5 in lieu of cheap phone wiring in every room. Given the millions of new housing starts in the United States per year and the millions more homes undergoing remodeling, there is the likelihood that millions of homes can be capable of high-speed networking every year, in the normal course of construction and remodeling.

We therefore view the problem of home wiring as diminishing.

Wireless

The regulatory and technical changes facilitating the development of wireless access networks are having a beneficial effect on the introduction of wireless home networks. New frequencies are being considered, and technology is addressing previous issues of robustness and cost.

Several new standards are emerging with different design assumptions and supporters. The ones discussed herein are IEEE 802.11b, HomeRF, Bluetooth, and HIPERLAN (for High Performance Radio LAN) because of our view that these have lead positions as of this writing. Other standards exist, and others will no doubt emerge. But these illustrate technical and commercial issues and solutions that can be applied to contemplate other wireless technologies as they emerge.

IEEE 802.11a and IEEE 802.11b

In July 1997, the IEEE adopted the 802.11 standard supporting 1 and 2 Mbps data rates in the 2.4 GHz band with frequency-hopping spread-spectrum (FHSS), direct-sequence spread-spectrum (DSSS), and infrared physical layers (grouper.ieee.org/groups/802/11/main.html).

However, the 2.4 GHz ISM band is getting crowded, and there is not a lot of spectrum anyway. Also, because 2 Mbps is insufficient to handle large amounts of video, the 802.11 committee created two extensions, called Task Group A (TgA) and Task Group B (TgB), to work in a different frequency location and to offer more bit rate. TgA is creating 802.11a, which requires mandatory support of 6, 12, and 24 Mbps data rate service in the U-NII band (5 GHz). TgB is creating 802.11b, which provides 11 Mbps service in the 2.4 GHz band. Additionally, Task Group A has set a goal of making the physical layer the same as the European Standards Telecommunications Institute broadband radio-access network, to allow both standards to use the same radio and to drive down costs.

802.11a and 802.11b will use the same MAC layer as the original 802.11 but will use different modulation. 802.11a uses orthogonal frequency-division multiplexing (OFDM, similar to the modulation used by European digital TV transmission). 802.11b uses a complementary code-keying waveform (CCK), using technology from Harris and Lucent. 802.11b specifies a negotiable bit rate from 1 or 2 Mbps at 400 feet up to 11 Mbps at 150 feet (see Table 7-1).

Major challenges for designs operating at 11 Mbps include modularizing and shrinking the radio. However, Apple Computers made a surprising announcement with its introduction of the Airport module for its new iBook series of laptop personal computers (www.apple.com/airport/faq2.html). It announced an 802.11b implementation using Lucent technology that allowed an iBook to connect at 11 Mbps to a central home wireless hub. The initial list price was $99 per iBook and $299 for the hub. This was an aggressive move and one that surprised many because it established 802.11 as a contending home network solution.

302 Chapter 7: Home Networks

Table 7-1 *A Comparison of the 802.11 Standards*

	802.11	802.11a	802.11b
Frequency range	2.4 GHz ISM	5.3 GHz U-NII	2.4 GHz ISM
Bit rate	1 to 2 Mbps	6, 12, and 24 Mbps	11 Mbps
Modulation scheme	Phase shift keying (PSK) in ISM band; baseband coding for infrared	OFDM	CCK
Vendors	Proxim, Harris	NTT, Breezecom, NEC, Lucent, Aironet, Symbol	Apple, Alantro, Symbol, Harris, Lucent, Aironet

HomeRF

HomeRF supporters view the 802.11 family of standards as too expensive for consumer use. In particular, there seemed to be no need to support direct sequence or infrared for high-speed home use. So a consortium of companies sought to modify 802.11 by mandating only frequency hopping to accommodate a consumer market.

Version 1.0 specifies a protocol called Shared Wireless Access Protocol (SWAP). SWAP specifies the carriage of voice and data over the 2.4 GHz ISM band. It also specifies voice support for six telephone conversations using the European Digital Enhanced Cordless Telephone (DECT) protocol. DECT provides a 32 Kbps voice service using ADPCM coding. Thus, it attempts to be a more integrated solution than 802.11 or Bluetooth (discussed later), which are focussed on data. It remains to be seen whether an integrated cordless phone and data solution can meet the cost requirements needed for home use and for which HomeRF has criticized 802.11. The 802.11 and Bluetooth camps assert that DECT is not an economic way to handle voice. Their approach is to use a packet voice approach, such as Voice Over IP.

SWAP specifies frequency-hopping spread spectrum transceiver in the 2.4 GHz ISM band. It achieves 2 Mbps service using frequency shift keying (FSK) modulation, a well-known (some would say ancient) line-coding scheme that also is very low in cost. Because it handles voice, SWAP supports both isochronous service (for voice) and asynchronous service (for data). It does so by mixing both voice and data packets into a common frame. Each frame is stuffed with voice and data bits, and then the transmitter hops to another frequency. Each frame is 20 milliseconds, so SWAP hops at 50 hops per second. It hops in the same manner as 802.11, but with what is claimed to be a lower-cost radio.

FHSS has issues with respect to speed in that it takes time to settle on a new frequency. Therefore, it remains to be seen whether it can be made to exceed 1 to 3 Mbps to be competitive with 802.11b. On the other hand, FHSS technology is well known, and it may be that HomeRF and Bluetooth can keep a niche in the low-end, low-cost segment of the wireless LAN market. On the other hand, HomeRF is specifying a second version to operate at 10 Mbps.

Further information can be found at www.homerf.org.

Bluetooth

Bluetooth is another attempt at using 2.4 GHz ISM spectrum for home use. Like HomeRF, it is based on the FHSS specification for 802.11, but it does not require the DSSS—nor does it provide telephone support. As a result, Bluetooth is positioned as a very low-end, low-cost wireless home solution.

Bluetooth was originally developed in Scandinavia by Ericsson (Nasdaq: ERICY, www.ericsson.se) and Nokia (NYSE: NOK, www.nokia.com; www.nokia.fi) to provide a low-cost point-to-point peripheral attachment solution for computers, telemetry, and metering. However, as the interest in high-speed networking grew, Bluetooth and its adherents positioned themselves as home media protocols as well. Bluetooth specifies a single-chip solution for a frequency-hopping spread spectrum transceiver. It hops over 100 channels and thereby provides a secure medium. Further information can be found at www.bluetooth.com.

HIPERLAN

Bluetooth was developed in Europe primarily for low cost. HIPERLAN (High Performance Radio LAN) was developed in Europe for speed. Version 1.0 was specified in 1996, but not much happened in the market after the initial introduction. However, the move to home LANs has stimulated this technology, as it has other technologies. As of this writing, HIPERLAN has the high ground among wireless LANs in terms of speed. HIPERLAN uses 100 MHz of bandwidth in the low end of the U-NII band, between 5.15 and 5.25 GHz, with a maximum transmission power of 1 watt to achieve 23.5294 Mbps of service. Although the usable bandwidth to the user is more like 18 Mbps, HIPERLAN alone among the wireless LAN protocols has the reach (35 to 50 meters indoors) and speed to handle multichannel television.

As with 802.11a, the use of the U-NII band by HIPERLAN makes sense because of the cacophony of wireless devices already in the home at 2.4 GHz ISM. Those devices include toys, garage door openers, cordless phones, microwave ovens, and other consumer devices not intended for communications use.

Version 1 supports Ethernet, and Version 2 supports ATM. The specification work is the responsibility of the Broadband Radio Access Network (BRAN) group of ETSI (www.etsi.org/bran/bran.htm). As a cost-reduction measure, HIPERLAN uses the same modulation scheme as GSM telephones, called for Gaussian minimum shift keying (GMSK).

Further information can be found at www.hiperlan.com.

For a comparison of the wireless LAN technologies, see Table 7-2.

Table 7-2   *A Comparison of Wireless LAN Technologies*

	802.11b	**HomeRF**	**Bluetooth**	**HIPERLAN**
Frequency range	2.4 GHz ISM	2.4 GHz ISM	2.4 GHz ISM	5.15 to 5.25 GHz U-NII
Bit rate	11 Mbps	2 Mbps, version 1.0; 10 Mbps, version 2.0	2 Mbps; 20 Mbps demonstrated	23.5294 Mbps
Modulation scheme	CCK	FSK	—	GMSK
Vendor Sampling	Apple Airport, Lucent, Harris	Intel, Motorola, Proxim, Sharewave, Compaq	Nokia, Ericsson, Intel, IBM, Toshiba	Thomson, ST Microelectronics, Nokia, Harris
Web site	grouper.ieee.org/ groups/802/11/	www.homerf.org	www.bluetooth.com	www.hiperlan.com, www.etsi.org/bran/ bran.htm

Residential Gateway

Having discussed Access Networks and home media, now comes the problem of how to connect the Access Network to the Home Network to provide an end-to-end solution. This is essentially the same problem businesses have in connecting LANs to wide-area networks: Doing so involves having an intelligent device that copes with networking problems. In the case of residential service, there are additional problems in handling video and supporting a consumer market.

Several home media standards will survive for long transition periods, creating interoperability challenges. For example, how will a TV monitor connected to Firewire obtain images from a PC connected to phone wire? Or how will a wireless Personal Digital Assistant direct printer output to a Category 5 connected printer? Important questions arise regarding addressing, signaling, system management, and the like.

Residential Gateway Functions

Figure 7-5 illustrates the functions and interfaces of a Residential Gateway (RG).

Figure 7-5   *Residential Gateway Interfaces*

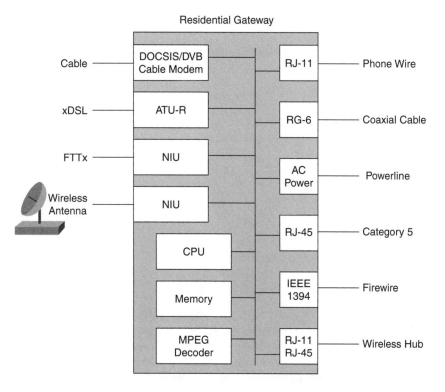

Keep in mind that these represent a superset of potential RG functions. In different network configurations, some of these tasks could be unnecessary or performed by other components. First we discuss network problems:

- Packet forwarding
- Media translation
- Speed matching
- IP address acquisition
- Network address translation
- MPEG and IP coexistence
- Packet filtering
- Authentication and encryption
- System management

Packet Forwarding

To address the previous problem in which a TV monitor connected to Firewire obtains images from a PC connected to phone wire, or in which a wireless Personal Digital Assistant directs printer output to a Category 5-connected printer, some form of intelligent packet forwarding, or routing, is indicated. It is possible that traffic from all devices can be broadcast on the internal LAN, but this has scaling and congestion problems because there is expected to be video on the home LAN.

Likewise, there are the cases shown back in Figure 7-1. A TV and PC can be connected to the same or different access networks. At the same time, there is traffic within the home. An RG is the device that arbitrates various types of traffic to ensure fairness and quality of service. As the number of potential Access Networks and Home Networks proliferates, connecting them all with common addressing and service characteristics becomes an issue for a rather intelligent Home Networking device.

Media Translation

In some cases, the physical wiring of the Access Network is identical to that of the internal network. Cable TV networks, for example, use coaxial cable on the drop wire and inside the home. Media translation is not needed in such cases.

However, in most cases the Access Network physical medium differs from the Home Network medium. The Access Network might be wireless, for example, as with LMDS or DBS, but internal distribution might be handled over a wired infrastructure. Similarly, new forms of inside wiring, such as a home's AC power circuits, might be used. Whenever the inside and outside wiring differ, they likely could use different frequencies, have different modulation schemes, and require retransmission. The dissimilarity of the networks forces the need for media translation at the RG, where the networks couple.

Speed Matching

In addition to the problem of media translation, the various media operate at different speeds. The Home Network might be faster than the Access Network, or vice versa. Whenever speed mismatches occur, buffering is required so that the higher-speed network does not overwhelm the lower-speed network. The RG performs the buffering.

IP Address Acquisition

Terminal equipment accessing the Internet requires IP addresses so that packets originating on the Internet or corporate networks can unambiguously address the home TE. Readers familiar with the IP protocol suite will recognize that several options exist. Among these are DHCP

Server and DHCP Relay. Manual, static IP addressing is another option. It remains to be seen which of these functions will be performed by the RG.

For readers less familiar with these protocols, the rest of this section provides a brief overview. Packets from the Access Network do not say "Jimmy's TV" or "Rosie's PC" in the packet header. Some form of globally significant addressing is required, such as an IP address or an ATM address. A mechanism is required to associate the IP address in the packet header with the home device. What IP address is to be used by the consumer, and by what mechanism is it to be applied to the PC and advertised to the rest of the world? The consumer can manually configure his own IP address, but this is error-prone and highly consumer-unfriendly.

A more user-friendly way to enable address acquisition for the home TE is to have the RG operate the Dynamic Host Configuration Protocol (DHCP) server function. With the RG acting as a DHCP Server, it can supply IP addresses to multiple home computers from a pool of addresses provided to it by the carrier. These addresses can be advertised by the gateway throughout the Access Network and to the Internet at large.

However, having the RG perform DHCP Server functions imposes some processing and storage requirements that might not be desirable. Another possibility is to perform DHCP Relay. In this technique, the TE broadcasts a request for an IP address. The RG recognizes DHCP requests and relays them to a server in the Access Network or content provider network specifically addressed in the RG to provide IP addresses. The DHCP Server returns the address to the RG, which in turn relays it to the TE. This centralizes the role of dynamic address assignment in the network.

Network Address Translation

The IP address provided by the Internet service provider may or may not be globally unique. An example of a globally unique identifier is a telephone number. If your phone number were not globally unique, someone else could be getting your phone calls. So, within the global telephone system there is a hierarchical format that begins at the top with the country code, then the area code, then the serving office number, and finally a suffix identifying your telephone number. It is possible—even likely—that someone else in the country has the same serving office number and suffix as you, but the two numbers are differentiated by the area code. Likewise, internationally, two phone numbers are differentiated by the country code.

The Internet does not have this luxury because there are not enough IP addresses. The current IP version 4 (IPv4) standard, used around the world today, has only 32 bits. While it is possible to sequentially number all the computers in the world (perhaps 32 bits implies about 4 billion), doing so would preclude a numbering hierarchy such as we have with telephone numbers. So, IP service providers typically allocate private addresses, out of their own imagination.

The problem of global address ambiguity is solved by a function called network address translation (NAT). The function of NAT is to convert the private address used locally by a consumer Home Network to a public, globally unique IPv4 address. This seems to be a rather straightforward table lookup that matches private to public addresses. However, because of some functions of certain IP protocols, such as the File Transfer Protocol (FTP), some care must be taken to determine which are protocol-specific. FTP, for example, does some tricks with the IP address before a file transfer is enabled.

NAT also creates problems of network security. Some security protocols depend on having a static IP address. Some firewalls are keyed according to a specific IP address. If a user's IP address changes because the NAT translates to a different IP address at a later date, penetration though a firewall is blocked. This is the equivalent of having your area code change, which happens from time to time in the telephone world. Here, when your IP address changes, there may be some firewall somewhere that is dependent on having your previous address.

Finally, it may be necessary to translate the port address (which identifies a particular IP application). This function is called port address translation (PAT), or port following.

If NAT/PAT translation is required, a logical place for it will be in the RG.

Residential Networking and IPv6

Because of the problems created by address depletion and NAT, some Internet experts, including the late Jon Postel, Research Director of the University of Southern California Information Sciences Institute and author of the seminal specifications of the Internet, believe the migration to a new IP protocol is needed. The successor to IPv4 is IPv6, which provides for a 128-bit address space. This is enough addressing to individually address every molecule on Earth, and some not on Earth as well. Certainly, as IP devices become smaller, more numerous, and embedded in our environment, the proliferation of addressing becomes a more difficult problem. It is simply not cost-effective to have a NAT/PAT translator on my wristwatch, with the attendant service provider protocol handling.

Today Internet service providers are reluctant to implement IPv6. It involves work, and their networks must cope with IPv4-to-IPv6 translation during a transition period. There is also no global czar of IPv6 addressing, a global agency that doles out codes and enforces etiquette.

However, for the Internet to scale to billions of low-cost devices, as it must for the consumer and embedded environment, that transition must be made. Waiting until later would only make the transition more painful.

MPEG and IP Protocol Coexistence

The emergence of digital TV raises the likelihood that both MPEG and IP traffic will be networked to the home. MPEG will convey digital TV, and IP will convey Web pages. Datacasting moves IP packets inside MPEG frames. Internet providers want to encapsulate MPEG inside IP. Another way to convey both protocols is to use some form of time-division or frequency-division multiplexing.

Whether encapsulation or multiplexing is performed, the multiprotocol case raises the possibility that the RG will be responsible for protocol handling. In the case that one protocol is encapsulated inside the other, for example, a device that de-encapsulates the inside protocol is required. If the protocols are multiplexed, demultiplexing is required.

Packet Filtering

The gateway can perform a firewall function to prevent unauthorized packets from entering the home. The packet filters might be controlled by the consumer or the carrier. The consumer, for example, might want to restrict the flow of adult material into the home. Similarly, the carrier might want to prevent the flow of premium programming to customers who don't pay for it.

It is also possible to perform filtering in the access node (such as DSLAM or CMTS). By filtering packets in the network rather than in the RG, costs associated with filtering (such as memory and processing) are reduced, which is an important consideration for consumer-purchased equipment. However, distributing functions such as filtering into the RGs generally makes the functions more scalable.

Authentication and Encryption

Carriers might require customers to authenticate themselves to receive service. Encryption would be required for carriers and consumers who want to keep their transmissions private. Both authentication and encryption require some form of intelligent device that can apply relevant protocols, such as Radius or TACACS, and that can manage passwords and keys. The RG is a logical place for these processes.

One open issue is whether to authenticate the residence or the device. Authentication to the residence would require only one password for the entire home, whereas device authentication requires a password for each device. It is unclear whether the additional complexity is worth the additional security.

System Management

The RG is a relatively complex piece of consumer equipment, more complex in terms of software than any device currently in the home. For this reason, it is unreasonable to ask the consumer to assume the role of administrator for the gateway. This role is likely to be assumed by the service provider or content provider. The following list details some system-management functions:

- Automatic configuration
- Installation and management of applications
- Alarm monitoring and surveillance
- Fault management and recovery

- Software updates and fixes
- Performance management
- Accounting

Apart from networking functions, other candidate functions specific to applications can reside in the RG. Some examples include these:

- MPEG decoder
- Personal video recorder
- Web browser/e-mail client

MPEG Decoding

Normally, MPEG decoding is performed in a digital STB. However, because the gateway must provide for IP coexistence, it is also possible—and sometimes logical—to co-locate the decoder with the IP stack in the same box. Because many CE vendors do not want to put the decoder into the TV monitor, for modularity and cost reasons, a separate decoder is needed anyway. Integrating a decoder with the IP stack saves some shelf space in the home.

Personal Video Recorder

Taking video one step further, it is possible to integrate a hard disk drive with the MPEG decoder to store video programming, just as one would record onto videotape. TiVo (www.tivo.com) and ReplayTV (www.replaytv.com) are competing in this new consumer electronics space. The personal video recorder (PVR) also has a program guide and a feature to bypass commercials. When coupled with a CD-ROM burner attached to Firewire, interesting networking problems arise. (Also, scary piracy scenarios arise for content developers.)

It is also likely that Web caches will proliferate at home. This is to enable consumers to be content providers, allowing the world to see such personal things as their baby pictures. This, too, would require a hard disk connected to a network.

Web Browser/E-mail Client

If an IP stack is required in the set-top box, why not include the Web browser and e-mail client? Portal service providers would like this because it can create a hermetically sealed environment to completely surround the viewers' Internet/TV experience. This environment is sometimes called a Walled Garden. Service providers that provide an RG will likely provide the user interface as well.

RG Attributes

Based on its likely functions, some of the RG's necessary characteristics begin to emerge. Let's take a look at some of these.

Operating Systems

The RG is certainly a computer, and thus it requires an operating system (OS) to regulate resource allocation such as memory and processor utilization. Because computer memory is responsible for a large part of the cost of a computer, and because the market for consumer electronics is highly cost-sensitive, the OS is required to have a small footprint. That is, the OS should occupy the smallest amount of memory practical. The OS also should accommodate real-time operation and multitasking.

Challenge to Microsoft?

Because Microsoft's Windows 95 requires a considerable amount of memory and does not support multitasking, it is not viewed as appropriate for RG use. This has given rise to new developments in the OS and middleware product development space. Many vendors see the RG as an opportunity to compete against Microsoft's Windows in an emerging OS space. Among the more prominent of these is Sun, with the Java/Jini environment.

Other OS and middleware offerings targeted at digital set tops and consumer electronics include OpenTV, by OpenTV (www.opentv.com); David, by Microware (www.microware.com); and PowerTV, by PowerTV (www.powertv.com). Basic OS kernels are offered, such as VxWorks, by Wind River (www.wrs.com); pSOS, by ISI; and QNX.

Of course, Microsoft has not sat idly by. It has responded with a small footprint offering of its own, called Windows CE (some would say Wince). But Microsoft has made important agreements and acquisitions with digital set-top providers and consumer electronics vendors. The company will continue to be a force in this emerging market.

It remains to be seen how the developments of new OSs that provide real-time operations and multitasking on a small footprint will evolve. Specifically, it will be interesting to watch the impact, if any, this market will have on the pervasiveness of the Windows/Intel (Wintel) architecture.

Carrier Management

It is likely that the RG will be under some form of carrier management, at least during early product introduction. This means that the Access Network provider will remotely control the RG. Carriers would be responsible for handling software downloads, extracting invoicing information, and providing customer configuration. Carrier management is motivated by the complexity of the device and the desire for user-friendliness. The RG thereby would fall under the model the cable operators use for the set-top box: The box is owned and maintained by the carrier and is rented to the subscriber. This is different from the consumer electronics model, in which the item is owned and maintained by the consumer.

Standardization

For the RG to be as low-cost as possible, many parts of it require standardization. This particularly applies to the Access Network and Home Network interfaces. Standardization includes modulation components, forward error correction, and MAC protocols. However, it also includes standardization of the software environment. A number of industrial consortia are emerging to address the software environment. Among the prominent of these are the following:

- Open Service Gateway Initiative (www.osgi.org), which is pushing the Java/Jini/HAVi story; no sign of Microsoft here. OSGI necessitates the existence of at least one Java Virtual Machine (JVM) in the home network. This JVM can be in the home PC, a set-top box, a TV, or a VCR. Other home devices that cannot run Java will use the central JVM processor as a proxy to obtain services, such as name service, application installation, and application management.

- Universal Plug and Play Forum (www.upnp.org), which is promoting the Windows CE story; no sign of Sun here. This is basically the same story as OSGI, but it requires Windows in the home.

- Home API Working Group (www.homeapi.org), which is developing a software developer's kit (SDK) running on Microsoft Windows that will let software developers write programs that can connect to home appliances as well as entertainment devices. Largely, more push comes from Microsoft and Intel.

- Video Electronics Standards Association (VESA, www.vesa.org), which is specifying the use of IEEE 1394b as the home backbone protocol and is capable of connecting to other networks, such as Ethernet, HomePNA, CEBus, and X-10. The push largely comes from consumer electronics vendors emphasizing systems aspects of the delivery of home video. However, Intel has provided important contributions, specifically managing the specification of IP over 1394 in the IETF. IP is specified as the network layer, and Web servers and browsers are used to access devices over the network with an XML interface for device-to-device control. The VESA Home Network Committee is coordinating its work with EIA/TIA TR 41.5, EIA/TIA 42.2, IEEE 1394b, the DAVIC physical layer technical committee, the 1394 Trade Association, the Consumer Electronics Manufacturers Association (CEMA, part of EIA), UPnP Forum, and CableLabs.

Cisco IOS Involvement

Whatever the outcome of the OS and API wars, it is likely that the Cisco Internetworking Operating System (IOS) will be the networking software component of many RGs. Cisco provides the majority of the routing equipment used in the public Internet and supplies private networking equipment as well. Given Cisco's presence in cable, xDSL, wireless, and routing, it makes sense that Cisco would extend its influence into the home.

RGs will have IP stacks, packet filters, network translation software, and other pieces of networking software. To capture this market, Cisco has established its Consumer Line of Business.

An important question on the evolution of Residential Gateways is how the internetworking operating system will interact with the computing operating system. This remains to be seen.

Examples/Possibilities

The variety of Access Networks, in-home networks, and user functions gives rise to many possible RG configurations. A few alternatives are presented here, with the caveat that other configurations will be marketed and that, on the flip side, none of these may happen.

The Telecommunications Industry Association (TIA) TR41.5 committee has been working on a Residential Gateway project for some time. The organization completed work on a proposed Technical Systems Bulletin (TSB) providing "Recommended minimum application, feature and operational requirements" of an RG at a meeting in November 1998. (Details can be found at the Web site www.tiaonline.org.)

A home networking control platform is under development between Matsushita Electric and Nintendo using Nintendo's next-generation Dolphin video game console. The combined development is called the Home Information Infrastructure (HII) system, a networking architecture for connecting and controlling domestic audio and video equipment. Rival architectures include Sony Corp's HAVi specification.

The cable industry is well under way with the standardization of DOCSIS and DVB for data and OpenCable and DVB for digital TV over cable. A device is in development that takes in digital TV and DOCSIS data and emits digital TV over an RGB cable or IEEE 1394 and emits data over an Ethernet cable. In theory, the box will use the DOCSIS channel for TV conditional access as those conditional access systems become ready. The box has a built-in Web browser that uses TCP/IP over the DOCSIS data channel and an Ethernet port on the back for use by the consumer. It is also possible to add voice ports to this gateway. The voice ports connect to voice encoders in the gateway so that the DOCSIS channels can be used for digital telephony. The consumer only needs to plug in his RJ-11 cable from the phone into the gateway. Some other kind of home networking will be needed to send data around the house.

Residential Gateway Issues

Before home networking becomes commonplace, issues apart from technology must be addressed by vendors and carriers.

Copy Protection

The new generation of audiovisual digital terminal equipment (such as digital video cassette recorders and DVDs) will provide high-quality displays of sight and sound. Furthermore, with digital technology, it is possible to make copies of content indefinitely without loss of quality. That is, one can make copies of copies, and the last copy will look and sound as good as the original.

This concerns content developers—namely, film studios and the music recording industry. An informal, broad-based group called the Copy Protection Working Group (CPTWG) is addressing the issue of copy protection. The group is comprised of the major motion picture studios, CE firms, computer companies, and the music recording industry. CPTWG is investigating the following three aspects of copy protection:

- Device authentication, by which physical devices such as DVDs, digital TV sets, and VCRs are certified as compliant with copy protection. A compliant device will send content only to another compliant device.

- Content encryption, which provides for the encryption of content on the digital medium using techniques that are permitted for export by the United States and other governments. Most governments, including the United States, have rules forbidding the export of high-grade encryption technology. CPTWG encryption must be exportable because of the worldwide trade in consumer electronics (mostly from Asia) and content (mostly from the United States and Europe).

- Copy control information (CCI), which includes rules that control the number of copies of a particular piece of content that can be made by a specific device. The content, for example, would specify that zero, one, or an indefinite number of copies can be made by a particular device.

Without stringent copy protection, content providers believe that they cannot enforce their copyrights and will be reluctant to provide their best content in digital form.

Partnering

The Home Network is the turf on which many industries will converge. Individually, none of them so far seems to have all the requisites to succeed. Table 7-3 indicates some industries and their strengths and weaknesses with respect to home networking.

Table 7-3   *Candidate Home Networking Industries*

Industry	Companies	Strengths	Weaknesses
Consumer electronics	Japan, Korea, Philips Game and TV manufacturers	Consumer channels Branding Capability to leverage content sales Very powerful CPUs, more powerful than desktop PC processors	Lack of Internet expertise Lack of carrier experience
Digital TV set-top manufacturers	Thomson, General Instruments, and Scientific Atlanta	Strong MPEG background Alliances with cable carriers	Lack of Internet expertise
Internet vendors	Cisco, Nortel, Lucent, 3Com	Internet expertise Alliances with telco and cable carriers for data Systems experience	Lack of consumer channels and branding Not accustomed to low margins Lack of broadcast video experience
Telephone companies	Local exchange carriers Long-distance carriers	Branding Retail sales Systems experience	Lack of a multichannel infrastructure; digital TV will be tricky Historically lethargic product introduction
Cable operators	AT&T, Time Warner, Cox, Comcast, Adelphia, Cablevision, Paul Allen	Consumer marketing entertainment Broadband infrastructure; can do digital TV Successful introduction of high-speed data service	Return-path problems Scaling problems Competitive problems from satellite for their bread-and-butter revenue

continues

Table 7-3   *Candidate Home Networking Industries (Continued)*

Industry	Companies	Strengths	Weaknesses
Wireless operators	DBS companies LMDS license holders Sprint, MCI Worldcom	Low rollout costs MPEG digital channel capacity Local content, except DBS Branding, for telcos and DBS	Lack of branding and capital (except for telephone companies) Late to the market Real estate and pole rights
Broadcasters	NBC, ABC, CBS, PBS, Fox, BBC (U.K.), and NHK (Japan)	Low rollout costs; owners of free spectrum Branding Local content	Lack of Internet experience Return-path problems

The CE industry, for example, has strong consumer channels, understands consumer-support issues (such as how to deal with returns), and implements excellent branding. This industry also has strong computer processing experience with recent success in games. The problem is networking. Products of the CE industry do not require addressing, software management, filtering, and other functions familiar to networking vendors and carriers.

Networking vendors face marketing challenges when dealing with the consumer market. They are accustomed to higher margins on hardware products because they do not sell disposables to subsidize equipment sales. As a contrasting example, video game vendors recover the cost of the game players by selling game cartridges. Networking vendors have few consumer channels, no infrastructure for customer support, and therefore little consumer branding.

Given their complementary weaknesses and strengths, as well as the scale of investment in product development and risk, different industries are likely to form new alliances to address the Home Network problem. The key to winning in the home market is the development of strong partnerships. Exactly which partnerships will be formed and for which markets remains to be seen.

Fixed RG Versus Modular RG

For homes attaching to multiple Access Networks, each Access Network will require a network-specific NT and NIU. A cable modem, for example, cannot be used for xDSL systems. This raises an important packaging question for the RG: How will it accommodate multiple Access Networks? In a related question, if a consumer changes Access Networks, is he required to change the RG, or will the RG have a modular design that can accommodate multiple Access Networks with the addition of a PC card or a similar attachment?

The flexibility of a modular design will increase the cost of the RG. Additionally, a modular RG will do little to reduce churn. Carriers must consider, for strictly commercial reasons, whether they need to retain the account control that a carrier-specific NIU will provide.

Rewiring the Home

Notwithstanding the improvement in the home rewiring situation noted previously under Category 5 wiring, rewiring a home is nonetheless a big problem for most homeowners. Renters could be precluded entirely. Old homes could have asbestos problems. High-quality homes have lath and plaster and real wood, which are difficult to penetrate. Proponents of Category 5 wiring and Firewire must confront arguments against rewiring when constructing their business case. Most leading-edge users of Home Networks simply leave their cables dangling.

The marketing imperative is to get to market fast, so there is much interest in reusing legacy wiring (phone wire, powerline) or using wireless solutions. In any case, the carrier installing the Access Network probably will be responsible for the Home Network. As such, the carrier likely will perform some form of installation for a fee. Whether or not the carrier's responsibility for installation makes rewiring scenarios untenable from a business perspective remains to be seen.

Installation Services

Because Access Network operators are frequently responsible for inside wiring, some have decided to outsource the installation. An interesting development is the role IBM Corp. (www.ibm.com, NYSE: IBM) has decided to play. IBM has rarely been considered as a residential service or equipment provider, but a new service called IBM Home Director (www.ibm.com/homedirector) establishes IBM in the residential broadband service arena.

IBM Home Director has teamed with Bell Atlantic and Ameritech to provide installation of coaxial cable and various telephone wires, depending on their needs. IBM is also developing a series of computer applications that will run on the new infrastructure, including a home management application.

The foundation for the Home Director system is the Home Network Connection Center, the in-home hub for a complete structured wiring solution. The Connection Center brings together various types of wire in the home, including coaxial, Category 5, and telephone, into a central location so that video, data, and telephony can be distributed throughout the home.

Without such installation services, the installation of high-speed home networking is largely a do-it-yourself effort.

Full-Service Home Networking

Because separate networks exist for phone, cable, power, and home automation, the question arises whether there is a strong market need to integrate services on a single Home Network architecture—that is, a full-service home network.

The perceived advantages of full-service home networking to the customer are simplified ordering, wiring, and maintenance. The disadvantage to the consumer is that a single network makes the consumer vulnerable to a single-network outage and possibly could make the customer captive to a single Access Network provider.

The candidates for full-service Home Networks are coaxial cable and Firewire. Only cable would not require home rewiring, but use of it requires subscription to cable or FTTC Access Networks.

The advocates of full-service networking include the ATM Forum, the cable industry, and supporters of Fiber to the Home. The ATM Forum sees ATM as the best way to offer latency control to applications. The cable industry's interest is motivated by the fact that it has the most widespread physical infrastructure to offer both digital TV and data services to the home.

ADSL and various wireless local loop technologies do not offer the prospect of full-service home networking for both broadcast video and data. This might not be a disadvantage to these industries, because the economic case for a full-service network in the home is not yet established.

Summary

The Home Network is where computing, networking, broadcasting, and consumer electronics converge (or collide). Because it is situated on the customer's premises, the Home Network has the special challenge of being user-friendly, low-cost, and supportive of entertainment. The key elements of a Home Network are home media and a Residential Gateway. The options for home media are listed here:

- Phone wire
- Coaxial cable
- Home electrical circuits or powerline
- Firewire, or IEEE 1394b
- Category 5 wiring
- Wireless, standardized as IEEE 802.11a, 802.11b, HomeRF, and Bluetooth

ilitators are summarized in Table 7-4.

The next chapter examines some end-to-end software issues required to combine Access Networks and Home Networks into a coherent economic system.

Table 7-4 *Central Issues for Home Networking and RBB*

Issue	Challenges	Facilitators
Home Network equipment	Integration of NT, NIU, and RG functions is needed for cost reduction. Modularity is needed to support multiple Access Networks and Home Network topologies and technologies.	Collaboration and competition exists between multiple vendors, including game players, TV decoders, and internetworking vendors.
Use of existing home wiring	Impairments might be excessive. Cost of upgrading and repair is high.	A minimum cost scenario exists. Wiring is owned by homeowner, who is responsible for maintenance and upgrades. New home construction often includes home media. Wireless is making good progress.

continues

Table 7-4   *Central Issues for Home Networking and RBB (Continued)*

Issue	Challenges	Facilitators
Intelligent Residential Gateway	Costs, choice of operating systems, programming complexity, and standardization are troublesome.	RG facilitates connectivity, scaling, a wider variety of services, ease of use, and carrier maintenance.
Standards	A consensus is needed on a multitude of functions. Coordination is required among numerous standards bodies and geographical areas. New standards and industry consortia are proliferating.	Basic standards are established for Service Consumer System (DAVIC), use of ATM (ATM Forum RBB Working Group), ADSL reference model (ADSL Forum), and Firewire (IEEE). There will likely be networking standardization.
Support for video	Support requires high-speed networking, quality of service controls, and signaling. (How does TE inform network of speed requirements?)	Video enables funding via the familiar advertising model.
Full-service networking	This approach makes it difficult to put all services on legacy networks. The consumer loses all services when the one big network goes down. This option also doesn't exist now; do we need it? Many consumers like a modular approach—witness home stereo systems.	Full-service networking provides account control for the carrier. This option makes life simple for the consumer. The lowest-cost option is available to the consumer.
Market	How much responsibility will the carrier accept for inside wiring, and what will be the costs to the consumer?	Faster home wiring will improve services, especially for video. This is necessary to support faster Access Networks.
Industry structure	Multiple industries are involved, each with differing requirements.	Partnerships and alliances are forming.
Business/Financial	Cost of and responsibility for rewiring are troublesome. Cost of new adapters and RG is high.	Maybe rewiring isn't such a problem, given recent trends in new home construction and home remodeling.

References

Articles

ADSL Forum Working Text 011-R2. "Interfaces and System Configuration for ADSL: Customer Premises." *ADSL Forum*: December 1996.

Fujimori, Taku H., and Richard K. Scheel. (Sony Corporation) "An Introduction to an IEEE1394-Based Home Network." *ATM Forum, 95-1378*: October 1995.

Kerpez, Kenneth. "10Base-T Transmission Over Existing Telephone Wire Within Homes." *IEEE Transactions on Consumer Electronics* Volume 44, Number 4: November 1998.

Kurioka, Tatsuya, Junji Numazawa, Hiroki Minami, and Haruo Okuda. "Television Home Server for Integrated Services." *IEEE Transactions on Consumer Electronics* Volume 44, Number 4: November 1998.

Quayle, Alan, and Steve Hughes. (BT Labs) "The Nature of the Home ATM Network." *ATM Forum, 97-0163*: 10–14 February 1997.

Winkelgren, Ingrid. "The Facts About Firewire." IEEE Spectrum, Volume 34, Number 4: April 1997.

Internet References

grouper.ieee.org/groups/802/11/

IEEE 802.11 Wireless Local Area Networks

grouper.ieee.org/groups/802/15/

IEEE 802.15 Wireless Personal Area Networks

www.1394ta.org

IEEE 1394 Trade Association home page

www.apple.com/airport/faq2.html

Apple computer's 802.11b product, the Airport

www.bluetooth.com

The home of the Bluetooth Consortium

www.davic.org

Part 5 gives the DAVIC view of the Home Network, which the organization calls the Service Consumer System www.etsi.org/bran/bran.htm

ETSI broadband radio access network (BRAN) home page

www.hiperlan.com

Hiperlan hype, with white papers

www.homeapi.org

Home API, supporting application interfaces for home appliances

www.homepna.org

The home of the Home Phone Networking Alliance

www.homerf.org

The home of the Home RF consortium

www.ibm.com/homedirector

IBM's residential installation service

www.osgi.org

The home of the Open Services Gateway consortium

www.upng.org

The home of the Universal Plug and Play Group

www.vesa.org

The home of the Video Electronics Standards Association, supporters of IEEE 394

This chapter covers the following topics:

- Server Congestion
- Cache Selection
- Addressing Issues
- Connection Model
- Equal Access of Multiple Networks
- Transmission Protocol
- Television over the Internet
- The Systems Problem
- Full-service Networking
- Prognoses
- The Key Predictor of RBB Success

CHAPTER 8

Evolving to RBB: Systems Issues, Approaches, and Prognoses

Access Networks and Home Networks have made tremendous strides over the past few years. The research and development work of companies, standards bodies, and academics worldwide has resulted in technologies that move megabits over thin wires and thin air. There has been a flood of venture capital, startup companies, multimillion-dollar mergers, and initial public offerings (IPOs) of publicly traded stock. Product introduction moves at a rate faster than anticipated.

But Access Networks and Home Networks are still only parts of the larger puzzle to provide large-scale, end-to-end systems for Internet and entertainment services to the home. Important systems problems beyond the scope of any single network must be overcome, as well as problems beyond the scope of business networks. These are some systems issues addressed here:

- Server congestion
- Cache selection
- Addressing
- Equal access
- Transmission protocol selection
- How to limit the scope of Internet broadcasts to conform with licensing restrictions
- How to provide broadcast video services over the Internet
- Advantages and issues of full-service networking

This is meant to be only a subset of systems issues confronting service providers. Trials of RBB networks to date are concerned with resolving primarily physical-layer challenges, such as modulation and forward error correction. However, to service millions of users cheaply with good monitoring by the carrier, a systems approach is required. This chapter reviews some systems challenges and some approaches to provide RBB service. At the end of the chapter, the text presents social issues and makes some remarks about prognoses.

Server Congestion

An important scaling problem for the Internet is server congestion. The antidote is a technique referred to as server caching, which is the replication of content at geographically dispersed places. Instead of millions of users converging on a single server, content of a popular server is replicated and accessed by users elsewhere. Figure 8-1 illustrates the concept of server caching, with the original cache being replicated via the Internet and the Access Network. The user accesses the server cache through the Access Network.

The following list details the basic requirements of server caching:

- The original server and the caching server have the same content.

- The process of synchronizing the databases doesn't generate excessive traffic.

- The consumer reaches the nearest server without having to explicitly identify the server.

- Cache hits are counted reliably, just as if the hit had occurred at the original server,

Figure 8-1   *Server Caching*

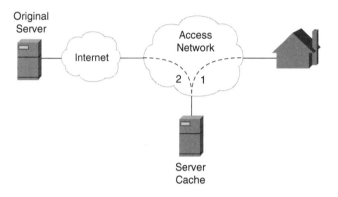

A number of approaches can be used with server caching. The first is to have the original source periodically multicast updates to the replicating servers. This requires IP multicast in the network and creates the potential problem of updating servers unnecessarily. Even servers that service relatively few requesters would receive the periodic updates.

A second approach is to have the local router forward requests to the nearest server cache, as illustrated by Path 1 in Figure 8-1. If an updated record exists, it is returned to the user. If no match exists, the request for information is forwarded to the original server via Path 2 in Figure 8-1, which answers the request. In so doing, the replicating server notices the response and caches it. The cached entry is aged in a time appropriate for the nature of the content, the request rate for the page, and the cache server resources. All requests in the interim are answered by the replicating server until the record is removed. The entry then is refreshed, possibly with a modified record after the next cache miss. This technique enables the replicating server to keep a minimum amount of information, which minimizes backbone congestion.

One problem with either approach is that the hit to the cache may not be counted as if the hit were made directly to the original server. If the transaction occurs at the cache, the originating server may be unaware of the transaction. This is important to advertisers who want to be sure they have the highest count of viewers.

An approach to solving this has been devised by Akamai Networks (www.akamai.com). (*Akamai* means *cool* in Hawaiian.) Akamai caches the highest bit rate content, normally video streams and complex still images. The textual, low-bit-rate parts of a Web page are retrieved from the original server. This technique permits an accurate count of page hits, while at the same time the high-bit-rate images are offloaded to the caches.

Caching high-bit-rate content separately from low-bit-rate content represents the type of subtle challenge to system integrators in scaling the Internet.

Cache Selection

A single cache, of course, won't do. There must be multiple caches of the same original content, possibly located around the world for popular Web and video streaming sites. An interesting technical problem is how to determine the optimum cache from which content should be retrieved.

Consider the case of a master Web site located in Silicon Valley. Caches are installed on the East Coast, Europe, and Japan. Now consider the case of a user in Australia. Which cache should provide the information?

Intuitively, the nearest cache as measured in geographical terms is preferred. In this case, the nearest cache geographically would be Japan. But there may be instances when that cache is down, or when the link between Australia and Japan is heavily used, or when the link speeds between Australia and Europe are faster than to the other caches, or when the number of administrative domains (BGP hops) is greater between Japan and Australia.

The general approach to the logistics of cache selection is to modify the root server of the Domain Name System (DNS) of the domain being interrogated. The modification is to give the DNS the responsibility of maintaining the IP address of each cache. When the user requests the site, a real-time calculation occurs of the distance between the end user and each cache. This distance refers to a metric that enables the DNS to return the best cache.

The selection of metrics, however, is more art than science. It could include link utilization, the number of router hops, the number of administrative domains, link speeds, or other measures. So, innovation is under way to develop new algorithms and modifications to DNS. Among the current products are Cisco's Distributed Director and Akamai Networks, mentioned previously.

Addressing Issues

The scale of RBB creates a major problem with address proliferation. In fact, each residence—and each device in the residence—must be identified uniquely. This requires the management of large address spaces. How are customers to be addressed in a systematic manner, and how are addresses to be supplied to the residence and made known to the rest of the world?

In the case of the telephone network and postal services, addresses are supplied by the carrier. You get your phone number from the phone company and your zip code from the U.S. Postal Service. The addressing plans provided by these service providers assist them in routing traffic to the residence. The address is more than just an identifier; it is also an aid to networking.

The problem in the case of RBB is that situations exist in which addressing is supplied by the content provider, not the Access Network provider. A telecommuter, for example, must be a part of the addressing domain of the corporate network, even though he is connected to a telephone company or cable network. In the case of MPEG-based video services (broadcast TV, video on demand), the PIDs are under the control of the content provider. If the Access Network provides access to multiple video content providers, there is the potential problem of ambiguous PIDs, because two or more video providers might use the same PID for different programs. The result of both cases is the need for a mapping of network provider addresses to content provider addresses.

Similarly, devices on the internal Home Network, mainly personal computers, require IP addressing. The Home Network IP addresses can be globally significant addresses or private addresses. If private addresses are provided, a network translation function in the home is required to translate private addresses to globally significant addresses.

Consumers are familiar with address management problems that occur when telephone area codes are reassigned or when names of streets are changed. Similar problems occur in data networking. Address assignment, acquisition, and network address translation are important elements of the general systems problem of address management.

Connection Model

Today's dial modem users connect to the Internet through a remote access server (RAS). A RAS answers the telephone call from the modem, authenticates the call, and facilitates a connection.

The terminal server model has served consumers well for online services and the Internet. For many RBB applications, however, another model is preferable in which the consumer is always connected to the network, such as in a business local-area network (LAN). The following list details some of these applications:

- **Personal Web servers in the home**—This trend is encouraged by faster speeds, large PC disks, authoring freeware, and second phone lines.

- **Push-mode data**—To receive data unattended, the network connection must be on.

- **Internet telephony**—The consumer must be connected to the Internet before receiving an Internet phone call.

- **Business applications**—Examples of these, such as software updates and push-mode data, are always connected to a local-area network (LAN).

When permanently connected to the Access Network, the consumer is relieved of the dialing process, making the system easier and faster to use. Another advantage of always being connected is that the carrier can perform certain functions, such as software modification, without involving the consumer. This facilitates ease of use.

The drawback of always being connected, however, is that an idle consumer device consumes some network resources, a little bit of bandwidth, and a little bit of memory. More importantly, always being connected means consuming an address even when the address is not in use. On the whole, though, RBB networks will gravitate toward the always-connected model because of ease of use and new applications.

Equal Access to Multiple Networks

RBB will afford consumers access to multiple content providers through a common Access Network. As an example, your local phone network offers free and equal access to multiple long-distance providers and Internet service providers.

The same term and concept can be applied to data service. For example, a parent might want to be connected to work, while his daughter might want to surf the Internet for recreational or educational use. The father could use an Access Network that provides transit to his corporate network. The corporate network should appear to him just as if he were connected to a LAN at work. This network always would be connected, fast, secure, and accessible to all corporate applications. The daughter, who simply needs Internet access, has no particular service requirements other than connectivity.

The work-at-home requirement involves a number of complications. First, the connection must be authenticated by the corporate network. Second, the work-at-home user should be a part of the corporate IP numbering plan rather than the Access Network numbering plan. Both these requirements exist for security reasons and do not apply to the casual Internet user. How can a single Access Network interface accommodate both users?

The approach for this is called tunneling. Tunneling is the encapsulation of a user's data packet within another packet, which is referred to as the tunnel. The inner packet is the user's real data. The outer packet refers to the carrier network providing the equal access. An illustrative tunneling technique is called the *Layer 2 Tunneling Protocol (L2TP)*. Its role is illustrated in Figure 8-2. The user establishes a PPP connection to an authentication server on the Access Network. The L2TP provides open connectivity to multiple content providers, which the user specifies in the PPP packet. In the voice case, the user specifies the destination by dialing a phone number. In the IP case, the user specifies a destination domain, such as cisco.com.

Figure 8-2   *Layer 2 Tunneling Protocol (L2TP)*

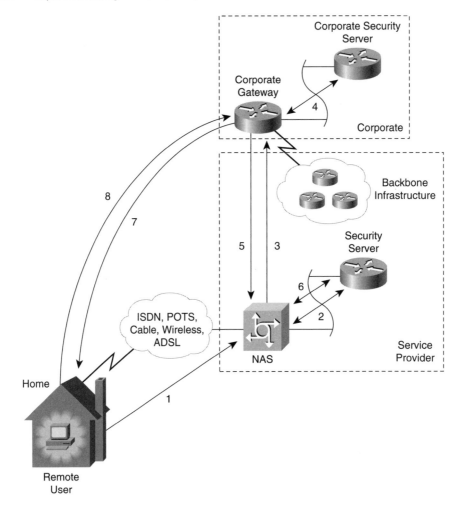

The L2TP process, described in Figure 8-2, follows these steps:

   1 The remote user initiates PPP, and the Network Access Server (NAS) accepts the call.

   2 The NAS authenticates the remote user (by verifying username, password, and destination domain) using a security server.

   3 The NAS initiates an L2TP tunnel to the desired corporate network. A tunnel is an encapsulation of each packet within another IP packet.

4 The corporate gateway confirms acceptance of the call and the L2TP tunnel.

5 The NAS logs acceptance.

6 The security server authenticates the remote user and accepts or rejects the tunnel.

7 The corporate gateway exchanges PPP information with the remote user. An IP address is assigned by the corporate gateway to the remote user.

8 End-to-end data is tunneled between the remote user and the corporate gateway. The remote user is logically connected to the corporate internal network.

The daughter's connection can be made directly to the public Internet without an L2TP tunnel. The NAS forwards her packets to the Internet without intervention of the security server. For further details on L2TP, see the Cisco home page at www.cisco.com and search for L2TP.

Transmission Protocol

When a data or video packet is sent to or from a residence, it is encapsulated in a transmission protocol. The selection of transmission protocol represents a networking challenge because competing approaches are available, each of which has advantages and disadvantages. Systems using different transmission protocols cannot interoperate directly. The current candidates are IP, MPEG, and ATM. With IP encapsulation, all packets are sent over the Access Network to the Home Network in IP packets. MPEG packets are encapsulated inside IP. The Home Network obtains the IP packets, determines that the contents are really MPEG, de-encapsulates the packets, and forwards the MPEG packets inside to the set-top decoder function.

With MPEG encapsulation, the reverse process is used. MPEG is sent to the home and is decoded by the digital set-top box. IP packets are indicated by a PID number. MPEG demultiplexing then forwards the data PIDs. This approach is used by DOCSIS, which has specified that IP data packets sent to the residence will be transmitted in MPEG frames.

With ATM encapsulation, both IP and MPEG packets are transported in ATM cells using AAL5 adaptation. MPEG streams are differentiated from IP packet flows based on virtual channel (VC) numbers. Multiple VCs would exist between the carrier and the residence and would possibly be bundled together in a virtual path (VP).

Microsoft has ATM support in WinSock (its communications interface for Windows) and therefore can perform the de-encapsulation function inside the PC.

The advantages and disadvantages of each encapsulation method are summarized in Table 8-1.

Table 8-1   *Comparison of Encapsulation Methods*

Protocol	Advantages	Disadvantages
IP	Enables native transport over the Internet. Would permit content providers to bypass broadcast TV or cable by distributing content directly over the Internet.	If more video bits than data bits are present, this option involves the greatest amount of de-encapsulation among the three alternatives. Has possible issues with IP addressing, which could require upgrading to the next generation of IP (an expensive process). Without the use of advanced queuing techniques, packet latency is not guaranteed, which places extra buffering and time-synchronization complexity on the MPEG decoder.
MPEG	Nearly all compressed digital video content, satellite, and DVD is already in MPEG TS format. Well-suited to point-to-multipoint access networks. One-way; good for video.	This option is not amenable to a point-to-point environment and has no addressing that identifies a specific user. Communication is one-way; bad for transactional or interactive communications.
ATM	Permits transparency of multiple protocols. Allows for ATM quality of service. Gives carriers the flexibility to establish pricing based on quality of service.	Few ATM terminal equipment models exist for consumers today, especially for video. This option involves costly signaling and addressing methods. This option is not well-suited to point-to-multipoint access networks.

Television over the Internet

TV broadcasters today do not deliver programming over the Internet. A few radio stations broadcast live on www.broadcast.com, but you don't see Disney or CBS/Viacom do the same. The reasons for this are part technical and part commercial. The commercial issues are discussed first. Key issues are listed here:

- **One-time content creation**—How does the broadcaster create content once and have it rendered over the air and on a broadband Internet connection?

- **Scope**—The Internet cannot limit the broadcast to specific users only. Its delivery will almost always conflict with existing agreements.

- **Repurposed content**—How can content be repurposed so it can be offered under different licensing terms, and how will MPEG4 interactivity help?

- **Switched Digital Video (SDV)**—What technology can be used to offer 100 or more channels of TV over a point-to-point network?

One-Time Content Creation

Broadcasters transmit the same content to everyone, whether or not the receivers have broadband connections. This is not a problem for over-the-air broadcasts because all TVs have more or less the same display characteristics. One problem with putting TV on the Internet is that receivers have substantially different network connections. Some have 28 Kbps modem connections, and others can have 6 Mbps, such as over ADSL.

Therefore, does it make sense to make two different versions of *The Simpsons* or to broadcast two different feeds of *Monday Night Football,* one for low-speed Internet users and another for broadband users? And, if so, how are the broadband users to be targeted? So far, there is limited appeal for broadcasters to go through the exercise of multiple versions of the same content. The result is that there is no special content on the Internet from broadcasters for broadband users.

One approach alluded to in Chapter 2, "Technical Foundations of Residential Broadband," is layered multicast. Different receivers join different multicast groups. Content from multiple multicast groups is aggregated in the receiver to produce an additive, higher-quality presentation. Layered multicast is a work in process.

Scope

TV stations in the United States are granted exclusive franchises for specific geographical areas by the major networks. A local broadcaster has a monopoly on, say, ABC in a single metropolitan area. Internationally, when a content provider such as CNN or MTV offers programming in other countries, typically that content will be offered through a cable operator or a satellite operator that pays for the privilege.

With the Internet, these license arrangements are bypassed. The Internet is always connected everywhere. If MTV were to be put onto the Internet, a viewer could watch it without obtaining cable or satellite service. Of course, one can blithely say that such license agreements should be allowed to terminate. But we are talking real money. Therefore, in the short term, one of the obstacles to having TV broadcasts on the Internet is how to distribute them in a manner that preserves existing contracts.

One approach to be considered is virtual private networks (VPN), which create closed user groups within a common IP infrastructure. Members of a VPN can send and receive IP packets among each other through a common IP infrastructure, as if they had their own private network. IP receivers that are not members of the VPN cannot get the packets.

Repurposed Content

One way out of both the one-time content creation problem and the licensing problem is to repurpose the content for other uses. For example, a broadcaster has a football game that is provided to affiliates and independent stations for one-way broadcast. The broadcaster could create an interactive version of the same event for Internet use. Or the broadcaster could transmit an MPEG-4 version of the event, with localized objects or objects specifically designed for Internet use or interactivity.

MPEG-4 encoding of events and programs gives broadcasters flexibility in altering content and making it available for a wide variety of receivers.

Switched Digital Video

The technical problem is how to deliver 30 frames per second to the home over the Internet to mass audiences. The short answer is switched digital video (SDV). SDV is a solution only for xDSL and FTTx networks. Broadcast media—namely, cable and satellite—have multichannel capability. There is enough bandwidth to simultaneously transmit possibly hundreds of channels. Point-to-point networks don't have that bandwidth luxury.

To offer multichannel TV services, switching is required. Switching involves the selection and forwarding of a video stream over the local loop. Current thought on how SDV works is shown in Figure 8-3. The design uses IP multicast in lieu of a broadcast physical medium. Routers R1 through R5 support one or more multicast groups. Two program sources are shown, one for the BBC and one for MTV. Each is connected over a 10 Mbps or 100 Mbps Ethernet connection, denoted as 10/100. The encapsulation is MPEG over IP. The Ethernet switch can groom the multiple program streams into a single-gigabit Ethernet interface to a router, R1.

R1 is the first router that receives the video streams from the BBC and MTV channels. It replicates packets for the BBC multicast group and the MTV multicast group to routers R2 and R3. R2 and R3 in turn replicate packets. Eventually, one tributary of both multicast trees is reached at router R5. R5 can connect to one or more DSLAMs, which in turn connect to ATU-Rs.

The user changes channels using an infrared controller to select, say, the BBC. An STB, which has been modified to support IP multicast, issues a multicast join request to join the BBC multicast. Because the join request is serviced at R5, which is the router closest to the home, the transaction time to honor the request is brief, perhaps as little as 1 second. This is roughly the same amount of delay that a viewer of broadcast satellite experiences. When the user changes channels, the set-top box issues a multicast leave (that is, to leave the BBC multicast group) and joins another multicast group, such as the multicast group for MTV.

R5 is statically connected to both the BBC and the MTV multicast trees. This means that BBC MPEG packets are flowing to R5 even if no one connected to the R5 DSLAM is watching the BBC. This is a change from normal multicast. In normal multicast, when all local members of a multicast group leave that group, the multicast tree is pruned. For example, in the normal case here, no one is watching the BBC at the R5 DSLAM, so the BBC multicast tree would terminate at R2. This is to conserve bandwidth on the link between R2 and R5. However, because of the need for rapid response time, the trade-off is made to keep the multicast intact all the way to R5. Otherwise, R5 would need to reattach itself to the multicast tree at R2 in real time while the user is sitting at home with his channel-changer in hand.

Figure 8-3   *Switched Digital Video*

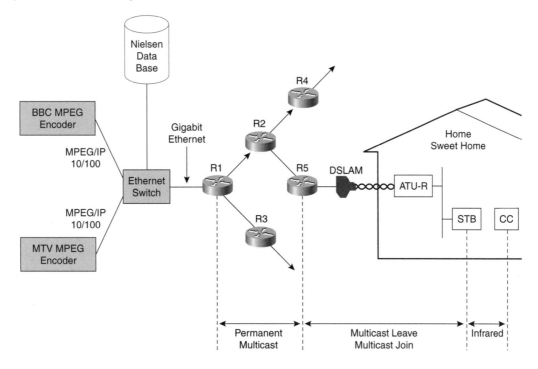

SDV has two advantages over broadcast: greater program selection and more accurate program ratings.

Greater Program Selection

On broadcast media, the number of programs to be offered is constrained by the amount of bandwidth the operator has. For example, direct broadcast satellite is limited to 500 MHz. To offer more channels than cable, the satellite industry had to develop digital and compressed program feeds. Even with advanced compression techniques, satellite would be limited to perhaps 150 to 200 channels, and cable would be limited to perhaps 500 channels.

With SDV, R5 need not terminate only two multicasts; it can terminate hundreds—and potentially thousands—of multicasts. Very little router resources are required to maintain these static multicast trees. The number of channels is limited by the number of multicast groups, which can flow through the IP infrastructure. There is, of course, a bandwidth constraint. The link between R2 and R5 would need to be an OC-48 link to carry 800 channels, but such speeds are well within the fiber and router capacity with current equipment. And why would an operator need more than 500 channels? The answer is for pay-per-view, video on demand, near video on demand, business broadcasts, or who-knows-what new programming.

More Accurate Ratings

Currently, program popularity is measured by Nielsen ratings, which require a sample of viewer households to fill out diaries. Naturally, many viewers will say they are watching *Masterpiece Theatre* when they are really watching *Jerry Springer*. So advertisers are interested in getting a more accurate count.

By having a switched infrastructure, it is possible to note each channel change issued by the viewer: Simply count the multicast joins and leaves. This presents a privacy problem, but the technical capability can be assembled to get a complete picture of viewer behavior.

The Systems Problem

The systems problem suggests that there is a lot more to building RBB networks than simply connecting an Access Network to a Home Network. Lots of other pieces must be integrated. Among these are the following:

- Web caches, to distribute Web pages
- Video server caches, to provide streaming video services
- Changes to DNS to identify the optical cache to access
- Multicast-enabled routers, to provide broadcast services on point-to-point networks
- Authentication servers, such as TACACS, to verify users
- DHCP servers, to supply IP addresses
- Tunneling servers, to provide equal access
- Firewalls, to filter packets from consumer systems
- Network address translators, to support private address spaces
- Network management systems, to diagnose and repair end-to-end systems

Full-Service Networking

A major issue is whether the Access Network provider will offer full-service networking. Full-service networks (FSN) are Access Networks that are intended to provide everything, including broadcast TV, Internet access, video on demand (VoD), and even voice telephony. FTTx and cable are considered to be the likely alternatives for FSNs. However, xDSL networks could also participate. An important alternative carrier offering full service is RCN (Nasdaq: RCNC, www.rcn.com). RCN is building on its relationships with Boston Electric Power and Potomac Electric Power, two large utility companies, to offer full service over fiber built along utility rights of way.

Proponents argue that FSNs offer the lowest-cost alternative for subscribers to receive all services—certainly lower than subscribing independently to multiple Access Networks. They also argue that it would be easy for the subscriber to use, because she would have a single interface to a variety of services. Finally, for the carrier, offering an FSN would tend to reduce customer churn because a consumer would be more reluctant to part with a single service if that service came in a bundle. The control of customer churn is an important marketing requirement of any monthly service.

Case Study: Time Warner Pegasus

A leading example of a system offering video services and interactivity is the Time Warner Pegasus system. This is not strictly an FSN, because it does attempt to offer telephone service. Furthermore, high-speed data services are offered by another Time Warner company called Roadrunner, which shares a common ATM backbone but uses the Access Network differently. Nonetheless, Pegasus is an interesting case because of its plans to carry broadcast video, video on demand, and IP connectivity on a single network. A closer look at this particular network reveals some of the general questions and problems facing network implementers who are contemplating this most complete and integrated option of RBB methods.

After some experience with a preliminary FSN trial in Orlando, Florida, Time Warner will implement a new end-to-end, full-service network called Pegasus (see www.timewarner.com/ rfp). Whereas the original Orlando trial used ATM end to end, Pegasus uses ATM in the Core Network, and MPEG and IP in the distribution network. At the set top, video is separated from data using frequency-division multiplexing or MPEG demultiplexing for in-band data.

The Orlando FSN proved the technical capability of HFC as a full-service network. Its costs were high because it was an innovative experiment. Pegasus is billed as a deployable form of the Orlando FSN.

The Pegasus system is mainly designed to provide services for analog TV, digital TV, VoD, and two-way data service for control purposes, but it also provides services for minor data applications through a single set-top box.

These services are provided through three types of channels. The Forward Application Transport (FAT) channel is a 6 MHz channel encoded using QAM 64 or QAM 256. VoD and broadcast TV are distributed on the FAT channels. The Forward Data Channel (FDC) is a 1 MHz channel encoded using QPSK to yield a T1 data channel in the forward direction. The Reverse Data Channel (RDC) is a QPSK-modulated 1 MHz T1 data channel in the reverse direction and is compatible with the DAVIC signaling specification. The FDC/RDC provides the following:

- Two-way real-time signaling for VoD
- Delivery of set-top authorization messages
- Network management of the set-top box
- IP connectivity for set-top applications, such as Web browsing (in conjunction with the FAT channel for high-bandwidth services)

Figure 8-4 illustrates the major components of the Pegasus network. Analog broadcast is received at the head end and is retransmitted on a FAT channel. Digital broadcast is received at the head end in MPEG packets with QPSK modulation. Satellite delivery generally is encoded in QPSK. Cable delivery is encoded using QAM 64. In addition, the encryption techniques used by satellite differ from those used by cable. The Broadcast Cable Gateway (BCG) remodulates and re-encrypts the satellite digital video into a form standardized on cable networks.

Figure 8-4   *Pegasus Full-Service Network*

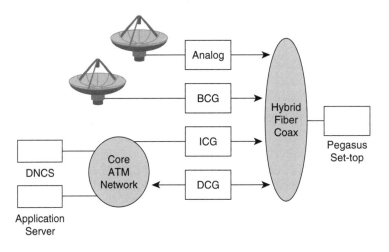

The Interactive Cable Gateway (ICG) is used in the early phase of Pegasus to enable the integration of video with data into the FAT channels. This is required, for example, to embed Web content into a program or to enable electronic commerce if it needs video. Video and data are received from the Core Network over ATM at links of 155 Mbps. ICG is required to match the speeds of 155 Mbps to the FAT channel, which runs at 27 Mbps. Newer versions of Pegasus will require that media servers perform the integration of video and data onto a FAT channel by using specifications standardized by the DVB.

A Data Channel Gateway (DCG) provides a two-way real-time data communication path between the Pegasus set top and both the application servers (which perform such tasks as program selection) and the Digital Network Control System (DNCS), which performs set-top authorization, set-top management, and purchase information collection. The DCG is essentially an IP router with QPSK interfaces.

A schematic of the Pegasus set top is shown in Figure 8-5. Beginning on the left side of the schematic, cable input is received from the drop cable through the QPSK receiver (FDC channel) and the RF tuner (FAT channel). An integrated MPEG and IP transport processor performs PID selection and forwards MPEG packets to the MPEG decoder and graphics processor; IP packets are forwarded to the CPU bus.

Figure 8-5   *Pegasus Set Top*
Courtesy of Time Warner Cable (www.timewarner.com/)

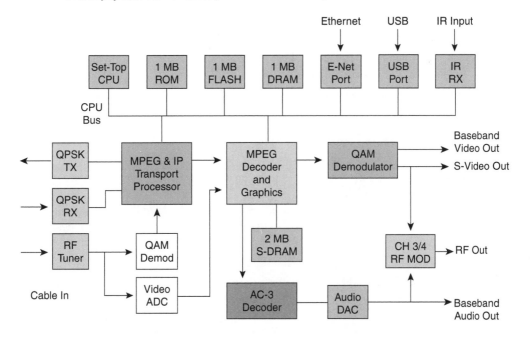

For MPEG processing, a digital TV channel is demodulated in the QAM demodulator and is forwarded to the MPEG and IP transport processor. Audio PIDs are directed to the AC-3 decoder and then to an audio out socket. Video PIDs are decoded in the MPEG decoder and the graphics processor, then are fed to an NTSC encoder, and finally are sent to video out (either S-Video, baseband, or RF).

Analog video is received on a FAT channel and forwarded to the Video ADC, the analog-to-digital converter. The digital feed goes to the MPEG decoder, where it is processed as digital video.

IP packets are forwarded to the CPU bus and then to a set-top CPU. Outputs are available for Ethernet and Universal Serial Bus (USB). USB is a new peripheral attachment standard that provides for 12 Mbps. A USB socket on Pegasus will enable standard peripherals, such as keyboards, joysticks, and printers, to be connected to the Pegasus set top. (Further information on USB is available at www.usb.org.) Infrared input (IR input) is received by the set-top box for television controls. Controls are sent in IP packets upstream through the QPSK transmitter (RDC channel). Finally, an Ethernet connector is used to connect Pegasus to a PC or a game console.

Note that in this architecture, no requirement exists for routing a Residential Gateway (RG). A network with this amount of bandwidth might not require downstream demultiplexing because each piece of terminal equipment (TE) can be granted a forward data stream from the carrier premises. Consider the case of 500 residences sharing 2.7 GB, each residence with 2.7 active users watching TV or browsing the Web. In this case, each active user in the neighborhood can be granted exclusive use of 2.0 Mb with the downstream demultiplexing performed at the head end rather than in the residence. This moves intelligence out of the home and into the carrier premises, thereby reducing total system cost.

With the introduction of digital broadcast, more channels will originate in digital form, and the amount of analog bandwidth will drop over time. In this environment, cable networks can achieve their FSN promise.

Benefits of Full-Service Networking

FSNs tend to reduce complexity to the consumer (because there is only one network to deal with) and reduce overall costs to consumers who want a wide variety of services. A single NIU, RG, and STU is amortized over a variety of services. There is also a single billing system and customer service infrastructure. All-in-one service motivates long-distance carriers to offer combined television, video on demand, voice, and Internet services. Instead of dealing with a number of providers, the consumer pays one bill and possibly achieves certain discounts accordingly.

For the carrier, FSNs tend to create better account control and reduce customer churn. A customer cannot simply drop one service; he must drop a bundle of services if he wants to change carriers. FSNs also provide a better marketing information database. By offering more services to the subscriber, more is known about the consumer, so it is possible to target the market more aggressively.

Challenges of Full-Service Networking

For many consumer products and services, there is always competition between a full-service model and an appliance model. For example, many consumers prefer stereo sound equipment in components rather than in a single, integrated boom box. The appliance model permits piecemeal optimization of each component as technology advances. This is also a lower-cost entry for consumers who want to try only one or two services. It has been argued that in the consumer space, very few products have been integrated successfully, except for the integrated VCR/TV and perhaps the boom box. Full-service networking faces similar technical and commercial challenges.

FSN Versus Cell Phones

A large part of the value proposition of FSN is voice service. For cable, CLEC, and wireless operators, it is better to have a small percentage of the voice business than a large percentage of the Internet and TV businesses, both of which are dwarfed by the telephone business. Cable, for example, has revenues on the order of $40 billion, whereas telephone companies have revenues in excess of $200 billion. However, widespread voice on an FSN must overcome the success of cellular phones. Cell phones may very well limit the appeal of voice on FSNs, especially among higher-income households.

Place Your Bets Up Front

Many carriers fear that moving to a full-service network is an all-or-nothing proposition—place your billion-dollar bets up front. It will take two to three years to see what competition emerges, and five to ten years to get an accurate picture of financial results.

It would be financially less risky if the carrier could add services and bandwidth capacity incrementally. But FSNs must develop capabilities for multiple services simultaneously rather than developing a single capability, such as voice only or data only. In addition, those combined services depend on having all the required bandwidth at the outset. For both services and bandwidth, a significant up-front investment is required.

Incomplete information on customer preferences, pricing sensitivity, competitive landscape, scaling properties of the technology, and the regulatory environment make FSN seem like a long-odds gamble to many companies. As an indicator of what other potential carriers can expect, the Time Warner FSN in Orlando was not an entirely reassuring experiment. Only familiar services such as VoD proved popular. Unfamiliar services such as interactive shopping and news-on-demand did not fare well. It is unclear whether the market drivers mentioned in Chapter 1, "Market Drivers," will in fact be popular enough in the early years of RBB rollout to keep the carriers' interest.

Biting Off Too Much

Telephony, video, and data delivery systems individually are large systems that have been subject to optimization for years by lots of talented people. When optimizing large systems, it is not necessarily true that one obtains a globally optimal result by optimizing everything at once. Sometimes better results are achieved by segmenting the problem, optimizing each subproblem independently, and then adding the results together. This is especially true when each subsystem is substantially different. Instead of trying to optimize voice, video, and data simultaneously in a single system, it might be more cost-effective to optimize each system independently and simply provide three networks.

Billing Complexity

Finally, this chapter ends on a light note. The diversity of user services available on a single full-service network invoice can lead to complicated billing problems. A customer could end up with an invoice such as the one shown in Table 8-2.

Table 8-2 *Full-Service Network Conglomerated Invoice*

Connection Charges	
Basic Fee	$1.00
Multimegabit surcharge	$19.95
Basic telephone charge	$4.95
Caller ID	$0.50
Caller ID blocker	$3.00
Basic television service	$9.95
Internet service provider	$2.95
Equipment Charges	
Residential Gateway service fee	$1.00
Memory upgrade	$5.00
Firewire adapter	$1.00
OpenCable PoD Module Replacement	$7.00
Wireless LAN Interface	$0.50
Software Services	
IP addresses (four IP addresses, $3.00 each)	$12.00
Voice-to-email conversion service	$1.00
Email-to-voice conversion service	$3.00
Web hosting service	$1.00
Storage charges (1 GB)	$4.00
Software filters to screen out:	
Political campaign commercials	$10.00
Sex scenes rated R	$0.50
Software agents to select:	
Sex scenes rated X	$10.00
Independent films released within the past year	$1.00
E-Commerce Charges	
Invoice service fee	$1.00
Online stock trading commissions (20 trades at $1.00)	$20.00
Home Shopping Network purchases (See Attachment A)	$25.00

Table 8-2   *Full-Service Network Conglomerated Invoice (Continued)*

Premium Channels and Pay Per View	
The Nintendo Channel (Mario Party Surcharge)	$10.00
"Interactive Jeopardy" play for pay fee	$5.00
NCAA basketball access charge	$1.00
NCAA basketball chat room fee	$5.00
Credits	
Six-month commitment discount	($10.00)
Winnings from "Interactive Jeopardy"	($2.00)
Home Shopping Network returns (See Attachment B)	($20.00)
Total Charges	**$134.30**

Please Note: We have deducted this amount from your e-banking account.

There is a degree of user-friendliness as well as an unbundled costing that will take some thought to present to the consumer.

Prognoses

As they evolve into integrated RBB networks, existing access and content providers are trying to gauge their own chances of success against the competition. In nearly every major urban area of the world, there will be several providers of high-speed residential services. The possible franchise holders include service providers of DBS, MMDS, LMDS, cable, and xDSL services from the incumbent and competitive telephone companies. Later, FTTx services from the ILECs and some alternative carriers will be introduced. In addition, narrowband service will be available from the electric utility and several telephone companies. Finally, telephone service will come from telephone carriers, cellular carriers, and digital PCS.

This adds up to a dozen competitors for the combined residential voice, video, and data market in a specific area. Table 8-3 shows standards activity that demonstrates the competitive nature of access markets.

Table 8-3   *Service Delivery Standards by Access Network*

Access Network	**Voice**	**Data**	**Video**
Broadcast TV	—	Datacasting	ATSC, DVB, ATVEF
Cable	PacketCable	DOCSIS	OpenCable
			DVB
ADSL G.Lite	Analog voice, legacy service	PPP/ATM	Switched digital video

continues

Table 8-3   *Service Delivery Standards by Access Network (Continued)*

Access Network	Voice	Data	Video
Other DSLs	Voice over IP	PPP/Ethernet	Switched digital video
	Voice over ATM	PPP/ATM	
xMDS	Voice over IP	TBD	Multichannel digital TV
	Voice over ATM		
Fiber to the Home	FSAN	FSAN	Switched digital video
3G Wireless	Digital voice	TBD	—

No Shortage of Competition

This book now offers its first bold prediction: There will be neither shortage of Access Networks nor standardization of applications. Fresh investment will continue to come from the following:

- Internet service providers and their equipment suppliers
- The telephone industry
- The cable industry
- TV broadcasters
- Wireless local loop providers
- Electric utilities
- Hollywood studios
- Consumer electronics vendors

Supporting and joining them will be an army of start-ups well-funded by venture capital that, in turn, have billions at their disposal with the mandate to change the world.

Beyond that, predictions get harder. Experience teaches that predicting the past is difficult, but predicting the future is *really hard.* Nonetheless, it's tough to resist the urge.

We Can't Determine Winners Solely from the Technologies

It's often asked, which access network will win? Will cable or xDSL or broadband wireless dominate the residential market?

The view of this book is that a variety of Access Networks will persist for the reasons mentioned in this chapter and in Chapter 1, which discussed the locations of these many Access Networks. However, it can be said that success for any single company or technology will not be determined by technology characteristics. Business considerations will dominate—considerations such as staying power, flexibility and incrementalism, and how well-matched the content is to the technology. The capital outlays are too big, and there are always difficulties in calibrating consumer demand and pricing, even for well-established businesses. Persistence and deep pockets are more important in discerning winners than mere technology.

Fiber and Wireless Will Play Bigger Roles

Over time, fiber will extend farther into the neighborhoods and closer to the end user. A fiber node close to an end user benefits cable, twisted-pair, and wireless. But it benefits wireless particularly because wireless has the shortest reach at multimegabit speeds and therefore benefits most from shorter distances. Also, consumers and businesses have reacted well to wireless technologies in the past. Finally, regulators have a major incentive to encourage facilities-based bypass of the telephone company local loop. Therefore, it's possible to conclude that success in wireless telephony, broadcast TV, and satellite TV will be repeated for Access Networks and Home Networks.

There Will Be an Impact on Mass Culture

High-speed Internet access will likely have a major cultural impact. How will it play out is not clear at this early point. In one direction, residential broadband will enable wider selection of content. This has the effect of enabling the process of cocooning, by which individuals become immersed in a narrow set of interests, thereby retreating from a common mass cultural experience. Society in this case becomes narrowly segmented among groups of people who increasingly have less and less to do with each other. Whatever its flaws, mass culture does have the effect of bringing lots of people together to share an experience, even if it is just a *Seinfeld* episode or a Superbowl game. With thousands of TV channels, VoD, and interactive chats with video, there is the possibility that fewer people will participate in common, national experiences, a phenomenon reflected in declining network TV ratings.

On the other hand, the cultural impact may go the direction of cultural blurring. People from different cultural or national backgrounds can share their interests and uniqueness. The result is a convergence of taste, particularly among the young, to a common mass culture—one could say an Internet mass culture. The world has already experienced how the globalization of television via satellite has made American pop culture familiar around the world. This is seen as a problem to some national authorities who view American pop culture—and, therefore, the Internet—as a threat. Even some Americans think American pop culture is a bad idea.

But the point here is that residential broadband, on either a national or an international scale, can either fragment or blur cultures.

Social Issues Will Become More Contentious

Apart from its impact on mass culture, residential broadband raises other social issues:

- **The conflict between law enforcement and privacy**—There is already controversy about whether to extend federal wiretap capabilities to digital telephony and Internet access, under the same terms that are required for analog telephony. Some Internet advocates assert that the Internet is somehow different and should be exempt from police snooping.

- **The conflict between public safety and freedom of expression**—When Web sites provide detailed instructions on how to create bombs and spew hate messages, the public becomes concerned with whether Internet censorship takes precedence over freedom of expression. Some technical innovation can provide some protection. However, over time, those innovations, based largely on packet filtering, will spring leaks. Some nontechnical approaches may ultimately be considered by a population victimized by some excesses.

- **Universal service for broadband**—On the other hand, the Internet has clear benefits, and those who can afford it are buying it. What about those who can't afford it? Should public policy encourage broadband access, as it has narrowband telephone access? Some laissez-faire economists say "no" to cross-subsidies as the way to achieve it—and think that if universal service for broadband is not achieved through market means, it wasn't meant to be. A digital divide is emerging worldwide and is further fragmenting society, as mentioned previously.

- **The scope of law enforcement**—The Internet respects no national boundaries, so the scope of national laws can be violated. For example, gambling is illegal in many cities and states, but the Internet makes gambling readily available in those places. Other questions exist as to tax authority, preemption of local laws by national law, and the comparable treatment of e-commerce businesses with brick-and-mortar businesses. Jurisprudence has a long tradition of geographically-based authority that is undermined by the Internet. A new take on law and regulation is needed when the Internet becomes ubiquitous.

The Key Predictor of RBB Success

Ultimately, when dealing with consumer markets, winning comes by matching content to the appropriate distribution method.

Broadcast TV was the technological fit for a passive mass audience because of its one-way distribution of video and sound. From its earliest days to the present, from *I Love Lucy* to *The Simpsons,* from the first televised Olympics to the most recent NBA finals, television's programmers have sought to tap into broad, shared entertainment preferences. Broadcast TV was and still is an ideal advertising delivery mechanism as well, a fact that has subsidized it and ensured its continued existence.

The Internet is the technological fit for the active, two-way, point-to-point dissemination of information. That information is useful for research and business. The Internet could be a platform for entertainment as well, especially entertainment tailored to individual tastes and interactive participation. It, too, is an example of a technology that has evolved as an optimal combination of content and distribution.

RBB will take whatever form is needed to deliver the critical market drivers, the new content, and applications. For example, high-definition content would tend to favor higher-bandwidth networks, particularly cable and LMDS. Chat-room activity combined with broadcast TV favors networks that can provide integrated voice services. If program selection is a dominant driver, xDSL could be a cost-effective method of delivering this application. If Internet access alone is preferred and viewers obtain their TV over the air, networks with a strong return-path story have an advantage.

It is not clear at this point what the dominant market drivers will be. For that matter, new applications and content are certain to emerge. The point is that there is no one best Access Network for all services. Some technologies fit certain content better than others.

The success of RBB depends on finding the market drivers. The technology will follow.

RBB-Related Companies and Organizations

When looking at the list of important players in the first edition of this book only two years ago, the changes are remarkable. Many players—important players—from two years ago have gone by way of acquisition. Chief among these are TCI and MediaOne, now parts of AT&T. However, new companies have come into play, thereby showing the robust activity in RBB. This is a list of the players mentioned in this book, as well as a few others. We apologize for any omissions.

Table A-1 *Equipment Providers*

Company	Products	URLs	Stock Ticker
3Com	Cable modems and ATM switches	www.3com.com	COMS
Adaptec	Firewire components	www.adaptec.com	ADPT
Adaptive Broadband	MMDS and other 2 GHz wireless equipment	www.adaptivebroadband.com	ADAP
Alcatel	Systems for xDSL, FTTC, FTTH, and ATM switches	www.alcatel.com	ALA
Amati Communications Corporation	xDSL systems	www.amati.com	AMTX
Analog Devices	xDSL systems	www.analog.com	
Apple	Firewire components	www.apple.com	AAPL
Aware, Inc.	xDSL systems	www.aware.com	AWRE
Blonder Tongue	Cable systems components	www.blondertongue.com	
Broadcom	QAM modulators and demodulators, silicon for digital set-top boxes, and single-chip cable modem solutions	www.broadcom.com	BRCM

continues

Table A-1   *Equipment Providers (Continued)*

Company	Products	URLs	Stock Ticker
Cisco Systems	Cable modem systems, xDSL systems, LMDS systems, MMDS systems, residential gateways, home networks, ATM switches, IP routers, internetworking software (IOS)	www.cisco.com	CSCO
Com21	Cable modems systems	www.com21.com	CMTO
Conexant	xDSL component supplier, mainly HDSL-2 and SDSL (formerly Rockwell)	www.conexant.com	CNXT
Copper Mountain	xDSL equipment	www.coppermountain.com	CMTN
DiviCom	MPEG encoders and decoders	www.divi.com	CUBE
Efficient Networks	xDSL equipment	www.efficient.com	EFNT
Epigram	Home network components using phone wire; and HomePNA version 2, owned by Broadcom	www.epigram.com	
Ericsson	3G wireless systems	www.ericsson.se	ERICY
Flowpoint	xDSL equipment	www.flowpoint.com	
Gemstar	Electronic program guides	www.gemstar.com	GMST
General Instrument	Cable modems, cable system components, MMDS components and systems, and digital set tops	www.gi.com	GIC
Intellon	Home network components using powerline	www.intellon.com	

Table A-1 *Equipment Providers (Continued)*

Company	Products	URLs	Stock Ticker
Lucent Technologies	DLC systems, ATM switches, IP routers, and wireless systems	www.lucent.com	LU
Marconi	FTTC systems	www.marconi.com	GEC (London)
Matsushita	Holding company for Panasonic	www.mei.co.jp	MC
Microsoft	OS for digital set tops, owner of WebTV, investor in cable MSOs	www.microsoft.com	MSFT
Microware	OS for digital set tops, called David	www.microware.com	
Mitsubishi Electric	Digital TV components, Firewire components, and residential gateways	www.melco.co.jp	
Motorola	Cable modems, LEO systems, 3G wireless systems, LMDS systems with Cisco; xDSL; equity owner in Iridium	www.motorola.com	MOT
Netopia	xDSL equipment	www.netopia	NTPA
Nokia	3G wireless systems and xDSL equipment	www.nokia.fi www.nokia.com	NOK
Nortel (Northern Telecom)	Cable modems systems, DLC systems, ATM switches, IP routers, 3G wireless, and LMDS systems	www.nortel.com	NT
OpenTV	Software development environment and OS for digital set tops	www.opentv.com	
Orckit Communications Ltd.	xDSL systems and VDSL components	www.orckit.com	ORCT

continues

Table A-1   *Equipment Providers (Continued)*

Company	Products	URLs	Stock Ticker
PairGain	xDSL systems, mainly HDSL for T1 lines	www.pairgain.com	PAIR
Panasonic	Consumer electronics	www.panasonic.com	
Paradyne	xDSL systems; leaders in CAP	www.paradyne.com	
PowerTV	OS for digital set tops	www.powertv.com	
Proxim	802.11 equipment provider	www.proxim.com	PROX
Qualcomm	WCDMA/3G wireless systems	www.qualcomm.com	QCOM
ReplayTV	Personal Video Recorder	www.replayTV.com	
Samsung	Consumer electronics and cable modems	www.samsung.com	
Scientific Atlanta	Cable modems, cable system components, and digital set tops	www.scientific-atlanta.com	SFA
SGS-Thomson Microelectronics	Microelectronics and Firewire components; holding company for TCE and TSI	www.st.com	STM
Sony	Consumer electronics and cable modems	www.sony.com	SNE
Spectrapoint	LMDS equipment provider, jointly owned by Cisco and Motorola	www.spectrapoint.com	
Switchcore AB	Full Custom ASICs for networking	www.switchcore.com	SCOR (Swedish Stock Exchange)
Terayon Corporation	Cable modems	www.terayon.com	TERN
Texas Instruments	xDSL, DSPs, and Firewire components	www.ti.com	TXN

Table A-1   *Equipment Providers (Continued)*

Company	Products	URLs	Stock Ticker
TiVo	Personal Video Recorder	www.tivo.com	
Tut Systems	Home networking over phone wire	www.tutsys.com	TUTS
Westell	xDSL systems	www.westell.com	WSTL

APPENDIX B

Professional Organizations and Regulatory Agencies

Table B-1 *Professional Organizations and Regulatory Agencies*

Organization/Agency	Description	URLs
ADSL Forum	Standards development for ADSL	www.adsl.com
Advanced Television Systems Committee	Standards development for over-the-air digital TV broadcasting	www.atsc.org
	Software development environment for datacasting	
Advanced TV Enhancement Forum	Software development environment for datacasting	www.atvef.com
ATM Forum	Standards development for residential networking based on ATM	www.atmforum.com
Bluetooth Coalition	Standards development for short-distance wireless	www.bluetooth.com
Cablelabs	Research and development for North American cable MSOs	www.cablelabs.com
cdmaOne	3G based on CDMA	www.cdg.org
Communications Research Centre of Canada	Canadian Department of Industry researching broadband	www.crc.ca
Digital Audio Visual Council (DAVIC)	Standards development for Access Networks and Home Networks	www.davic.org
Digital Video Broadcasting Project (DVB)	European organizations specifying the future of television	www.dvb.org
European Telecommunications Standards Institute (ETSI)	Telecommunications standardization body	www.etsi.org
Federal Communications Commission	Federal rules of the road for telephony, wireless, and cable in the United States	www.fcc.gov

continues

Table B-1 *Professional Organizations and Regulatory Agencies (Continued)*

Organization/Agency	Description	URLs
Home Phoneline Networking Alliance (HomePNA)	Association for home networking using phone wires	www.homepna.org
HomeRF	Association for home networking using spread-spectrum wireless	www.homerf.org
IEEE 802.11	Wireless local-area networks	grouper.ieee.org/groups/802/11/
IEEE 802.14	Development for a standard for cable data modems	www.walkingdog.com
IEEE 802.15	Wireless personal-area networks	grouper.ieee.org/groups/802/15/
IEEE 802.16	Broadband fixed wireless	grouper.ieee.org/groups/802/16/
International Electrotechnical Commission (IEC)	Electronics standardization in Europe	www.iec.ch
MCNS Partners Ltd.	Authoring the DOCSIS standards for cable data modems	www.cablemodem.com
National Association of Broadcasters (NAB)	Trade association and lobbying arm for U.S. radio and television broadcasters	www.nab.org
National Cable TV Association	Trade association and lobbying arm for U.S. cable interests	www.ncta.com
National Institute of Standards and Technology, U.S. Department of Commerce	Broadband wireless testing	www.nwest.nist.gov
National Telecommunications and Information Administration (NTIA)	Part of the U.S. Department of Commerce; spectrum information, federal use of spectrum, Internet naming, and other networking odds and ends	www.ntia.doc.gov
Office of Telecommunications, UK	The watchdog of UK telecommunications	www.oftel.org
OpenCable™ Initiative	DTV standardization for cable	www.opencable.com
Packet Cable	Telephony standardization for cable	www.packetcable.com

Table B-1   *Professional Organizations and Regulatory Agencies (Continued)*

Organization/Agency	Description	URLs
Society of Cable Television Engineers (SCTE)	Digital TV over cable	www.scte.org
Society of Motion Picture and Television Engineers (SMPTE)	Video standards development for film and TV	www.smpte.org
Universal Terrestrial Radio Standard	3G based on WCDMA	www.3gpp.org
Universal Wireless Communications Consortium	3G based on TDMA	www.uwcc.org
VDSL Alliance	Promoting VDSL over DMT	www.vdslalliance.com
Video Electronics Standards Association	Specifying standards for digital set tops	www.vesa.org
Wireless Communications Association	Trade association for the wireless broadband industry	www.wcai.com

Service Providers

Table C-1   *Service Providers*

Company	Service	URLs	Stock Ticker
@Home	Systems integrator to provide data services over HFC networks	www.home.net	ATHM
Adelphia	Cable MSO	www.adelphia.com	ADLAC
Advanced Radio	38 GHz service provider	www.artelecom.com/	ARTT
Ameritech	Local exchange carrier, cable operator	www.ameritech.com	AIT
AT&T	Largest interexchange carrier in the United States, and largest cable operator in the United States	www.att.com	T
Bell Atlantic	Local exchange carrier	www.bellatlantic.com	BEL
Bell South	Local exchange carrier	www.bellsouth.com	BLS
British Telecom	Dominant service provider in the United Kingdom; equity interests in DBS, FTTx trials	www.bt.net	BTY
Canal Plus	Cable system in France	www.cplus.fr	
Ciena	Fiber optic transport systems	www.ciena.com	CIEN
Comcast	Cable MSO, partly owned by Microsoft	www.comcast.com	CMCSA
Covad	xDSL service provider	www.covad.com	COVD
Cox Communications	Cable MSO	www.cox.com	COX

continues

Table C-1 *Service Providers (Continued)*

Company	Service	URLs	Stock Ticker
Deutsche Telekom	Dominant telephony provider in Germany and the largest cable MSO in the world	www.dtag.de	DT
DF1	DBS service provider in Germany	www.dfl.de	
DirecTV	DBS service provider	www.directv.com	GMH
Echostar Communications Corporation	DBS service provider	www.echostar.com	DISH
Globalstar	Low earth orbit service provider	www.globalstar.com	GSTRF
GTE	Local exchange carrier	www.gte.com	GTE
Knology Holdings	Full-service access network provider	www.knology.com	
News Corporation	Rupert Murdoch's vertically integrated, global satellite, broadcasting, publishing empire; includes Fox network, *New York Post*, and British tabloids	www.newscorp.com	NWS
Nextlink	Largest holder of LMDS spectrum in the United States	www.nextlink.com	NXLK
Northpoint	xDSL service provider	www.northpointcom.com	NPNT
NTT (Nippon Telegraph and Telephone Corporation)	Dominant service provider in Japan; ADSL provider, FTTx trials	www.ntt.co.jp	
RCN Corporation	FTTx services	www.rcn.com	RCNC
Rhythms	xDSL service provider	www.rhythms.com	RTHM

Table C-1 *Service Providers (Continued)*

Company	Service	URLs	Stock Ticker
Rogers, Shaw, Cogeco, and other Canadian data/cable services	Cable data services in Canada	www.wave.ca	
SBC Communications Inc.	Local exchange carrier.	www.sbc.com	SBC
Speedus	LMDS service provider, formerly CellularVision	www.speedus.com	SPDE
Sprint	Interexchange carrier, MMDS spectrum holder	www.sprint.com	FON
Teledesic Corporation	Low earth orbit service provider	www.teledesic.com	
Time Warner	Second-largest cable MSO in the United States; content owned includes Warner Brothers, Castle Rock, Turner, TNT Broadcasting, Hanna Barbera, *Time*, *Life*, *Fortune*, *People*, *Sports Illustrated*, and others.	www.pathfinder.com www.timewarner.com www.timewarnercable.com	TWX
US West	Local exchange carrier.	www.uswest.com	USW
Videotron	Cable system in Canada; owner of Wavepath	www.videotron.ca	
Wavepath	Internet service provider using MMDS	www.wavepath.com	
Winstar	38 GHz service provider	www.winstar.com	WCII
Worldcom/MCI/ Uunet	Interexchange carrier, MMDS spectrum holder	www.wcom.com	WCOM

INDEX

Symbols

@Home Web site, 359
2B1Q (2 binary, 1 quaternary), 65–66
3Com Web site, 349
3D animation, tearing, 7
3G (third-generation cellular), 272
    architecture, 273–274
    problems with, 274–277
    spectrum, 276–277
    wireless, 60
5C copyright protection, 138
24 GHz services (Teligent), 235
1394 Trade Association (firewire.org) Web site, 299
1996 Telecom Act, 3G (third-generation cellular), 276

A

ABC television network, 8
absorption (wireless transmissions), 88
ACATS (Advisory Committee on Advanced Television Systems), 11
access networks, 58–61, 63
    AN (Access Node), 61–62
    competition, 343–345
    FTTx, 211
        FTTB (Fiber to the Building), 213–214
        FTTC (Fiber to the Curb), 212–214
        FTTH (Fiber to the Home), 214–227
    home networks, 285
        architecture, 290–293
        bandwidth, 287
        Category 5 wiring, 299–300
        coaxial cables, 296
        connectivity, 287–288
        distance, 288
        firewire, 297–299
        HomePNA (Home Phone Networking Alliance), 295
        installing, 289
        management, 289–290
        NIU (Network Interface Unit), 292
        powerlines, 296
        regulations, 289
        requirements, 285–287
        RG (Residential Gateway), 292–293, 304–317
        set-top boxes, 293
        speed, 289
        splitters, 291–292
        TE (terminal equipment), 293
        upstream transmissions, 287
        wireless, 300–304
        wiring topologies, 294
    multiple networks, 63, 329–331
    NT (Network Termination), 62–63
    ONU (Optical Network Unit), 62
    permanent connections, 328–329
    wireless, 233–235
    xDSLs (digital subscriber lines), 165, 172
        ADSL (asymmetric DSL), 175–192
        ATU-R maintenance, 202–203
        bridged taps, 201
        crosstalk, 200–201
        digital television, 204
        distance, 172–173
        dry-pair wires, 197
        equipment, 173–174
        G.Lite, 192–193
        HDSL (high data rate DSL), 195–196
        home wiring, 204–205
        IDSL (ISDN DSL), 196
        impulse noise, 202
        local loops, 198, 200
        POTS support, 173
        regulations, 203–204
        SDSL (single-line DSL), 197
        selecting, 197–198
        spectral masking, 202
        speeds, 172–173
        symmetry, 173
        VDSL (very high data rate DSL), 194–195
Access Node (AN), 61–62, 235- 236
Adaptec Web site, 349
Adaptive Broadband Web site, 349
adaptive equalizers (ADSL), 176
ADC Telecommunications Web site, 195
addresses
    cable TV data services, 145
    IPv6, 308
    problems with, 327–328
    RG (Residential Gateway), 306–310
Adelphia Web site, 359
ADSL (asymmetric DSL), 165, 172, 175
    architecture, 178–186
    CAP/DMT comparisons, 176–178
    digital services, 188–190
    G.Lite, 60, 172, 192–193, 209
    modulation, 176

E

echo cancellation
  ADSL (asymmetric DSL), 183
  wiring problems, 81
Echostar, 138, 247, 360
e-commerce, 30
  ITV (interactive television), 24
  transaction fees, 45
economy (analog television), 10
Efficient Networks Web site, 350
electronic program guide (EPG), 106–107
e-mail, RG (Residential Gateway), 310
emergency broadcasts (cable TV), 159
encapsulation
  MMDS (Multichannel Multipoint Distribution Service), 259
  protocols, 331–332
encoders
  digital television, 17
  MPEG-2 temporal compression, 101
encryption
  cable TV data services, 145–146
  digital television, 17
  FTTH (Fiber to the Home), 226
  IP Multicast, 95
  RG (Residential Gateway), 309, 314
end-to-end architectures (xDSLs), 183–186
end-to-end system latency, 33
enhanced pay-per-view, 28–29
EPG (electronic program guide), 106–107, 132
Epigram Web site, 350
equalizers (ADSL), 176
equipment
  LMDS (Local Multipoint Distribution Service), 266–271
  RG (Residential Gateway), 309
  xDSLs (digital subscriber lines), 173–174
e-rebates, ITV (interactive television), 24
Ericsson Web site, 303, 350
errors, FEC (forward error correction), 71–73
Ethernet
  ADSL (asymmetric DSL), 185
  Category 5 wiring, 299–300
  FTTH (Fiber to the Home), 221
ETSI Web site, 303, 322
European analog television, 5
European DTV and datacasting specifications Web site, 51

European Telecommunications Standards Institute (ETSI) Web site, 168, 208, 355
external impairments, wiring, 79

F

Fabry-Perot lasers, 129
Fairchild Electronics, 140
far-end crosstalk (FEXT), 200–201
fast channel ADSL (asymmetric DSL), 189
Fast Ethernet, 299–300
FAT (Forward Application Transport) channel, 337
FCC (Federal Communications Commission)
  ACATS (Advisory Committee on Advanced Television Systems), 11
  analog television, 9
  datacasting, 40
  digital television regulations, 12–15
  HDTV issue, 11–15
  home network regulations, 289
  wireless networks, 234
FCC Common Carrier Bureau Web site, 208
FCC DTV channel allotments Web site, 51
FCC Mass Media Bureau Web site, 240
FCC on digital TV transition Web site, 163
FCC Web site, 208, 355
FCC Wireless Transport Bureau Web site, 240
F-connectors (cable TV), 123
FDD (frequency division duplexing), 238–239, 273
FEC (forward error correction), 71–73
feeder cables
  cable TV, 122
  POTS (plain old telephone services), 168
FEXT (far-end crosstalk), 200–201
FHSS (frequency hopping spread spectrum), 73–75
fiber nodes (cable TV), 126
fiber optics, 81–86
  attenuation, 84
  bandwidth, 83
  costs, 85
  damage, 84–85
  dispersion, 84
  FTTx networks, 211
    FTTB (Fiber to the Building), 213–214
    FTTC (Fiber to the Curb), 212–214
    FTTH (Fiber to the Home), 214–227
  future of, 345
  HFC (Hybrid Fiber Coaxial)
    cable TV, 124–128
    costs, 157–158

H

O

O&Os (network owned and operated) television stations, 8
ODN (optical distribution network), 217
OFDM (orthogonal frequency-division multiplexing), 68, 301
Office of Spectrum Management (OSM), 120
Office of Telecommunications, UK Web site, 356
OLT (optical line terminators), 217
One Megabit Modem, 172
one-way television transmission, 117
ONU (Optical Network Unit), 62, 212, 217–218
    FTTC (Fiber to the Curb), 212
    FTTH (Fiber to the Home), 224
    VDSL (very high data rate DSL), 194
OOK (On/Off keying), 65
    fiber optics, 82–83
    FTTH (Fiber to the Home), 216
Open Service Gateway Initiative Web site, 312, 322
OpenCable Initiative, 134–137, 356
OpenCable Web site, 134, 163
OpenTV Web site, 23, 311, 351
operating systems, RG (Residential Gateway), 311
optical line terminators (OLT), 217
optoelectronics (cable TV), 128
orbits, LEO (Low Earth Orbit) satellites, 252–253
Orckit Communications Ltd Web site, 195, 351
organizations, 349–357
original images, 101
OSM (Office of Spectrum Management), 120
outages (fiber optics), 85

P

Packet Cable Web site, 356
packets
    cable TV data services, 144
    datacasting, 39
    Ethernet, ADSL (asymmetric DSL), 185
    filtering RG (Residential Gateway), 309
    forwarding RG (Residential Gateway), 306
    IP Multicast replication, 92–94
    MPEG-2 Transport Stream, 102–103
    prioritization, 96–97
pads (cable TV), 124
Pairgain Technologies Web site, 195
PairGain Web site, 352

PAL (Phase Alternation Line), 4
Palo Alto FiberNet Web site, 221
Palo Alto Utilities Web site, 221
Panasonic Web site, 352
Paradyne, MVL (Multiple Virtual Line), 172
Paradyne Web site, 181, 352
partnerships, RG (Residential Gateway), 314–316
passive optical networks (PON), 215–217, 219
PAT (port address translation), 308
PAT (Program Association Table), 104–105
pay per view, ITV (interactive television), 22
PC/DNA (Personal Computer/Data Network Access), 214
PCR (Program Clock Reference), 105
PCS, 3G (third-generation cellular), 272
    architecture, 273–274
    problems with, 274–277
    spectrum, 276–277
PCTV (People's Choice TV), 258
PEG (public, educational, and government) cable TV, 119
Pegasus system (Time Warner), 337–340
Pennsylvania Cable TV association Web site, 118
People's Choice TV, 258
perception limitations, 96
performance
    Moore's law, 89
    networks, 89–90
permanent access network connections, 328–329
Personal Communication Service, see PCS, 272
Personal Computer/Data Network Access (PC/DNA), 214
personal video recorders (PVRs), 310
personal Web servers, 328
P-frames (MPEG-2 temporal compression), 99–101
Phase Alternation Line (PAL), 4
phase errors, wiring, 79
phase shift keying, see PSK
phones
    QAM (Quadrature Amplitude Modulation, 67
    see also telcos (telephone companies)
photons, fiber optics, 82–84
physical layer
    ADSL (asymmetric DSL), 181-183
    cable TV data services, 143, 145–147
picture quality
    digital television, 17
    MPEG-2 compression, 108

R

radio bandwidth, 5
radio frequency (RF) components
  digital televisions, 14
  wireless networks, 236–237
RADSL (Rate ADaptive Subscriber Line), 189–190
ranging cable TV data services, 144–145
RAS (remote access server), 328
rate adaption, ADSL (asymmetric DSL), 183, 189–192
Rate ADaptive Subscriber Line (RADSL), 189–190
ratings (television), SDV (switched digital video), 336
RBB (residential broadband), 3
  competition, 343–345
  funding, 43
    advertising, 45–46
    e-commerce transaction fees, 45
    subscriptions, 44
    work-at-home subsidies, 44
  see also market drivers
RCN Corporation Web site, 336, 360
RDC (Reverse Data Channel), 337
real-time
  datacasting, 41
  digital cameras, 287
  ITV (interactive television), 22–23
rebates, ITV (interactive television), 24
receivers, WWW and digital television convergence, 33
reception, digital television with antennas, 22
red-green-blue (RGB) monitors, 7
redundancy, cable TV costs, 158
Reed Solomon calculations
  FEC (forward error correction), 71–73
  interleaving, 72
reference models, 55–56
  access networks, 58–61, 63
    AN (Access Node), 61–62
    multiple networks, 63
    NT (Network Termination), 62–63
    ONU (Optical Network Unit), 62
  ADSL (asymmetric DSLs), 179–180
  core networks, 56–58
  home networks, 64
  wireless networks, 235–236
regulations
  3G (third-generation cellular), 277
  analog television, 9
  digital television, 12–15

home networks, 289
  xDSLs (digital subscriber lines), 203-204
regulatory agencies, 355–357
remote access server (RAS), 328
rendering images (digital television), 16–17
ReplayTV Web site, 23, 310, 352
replicating packets (IP Multicast), 92–94
repurposed content (Internet television broadcasts), 333–334
requirements (home networks), 285–286
  bandwidth, 287
  connectivity, 286–288
  distance, 288
  installing, 289
  regulations, 289
  upstream transmissions, 287
Residential Gateway, see RG
resistance (wiring), 78–79
return path transmissions, see upstream transmissions
Reverse Data Channel (RDC), 337
reverse transmissions, see upstream transmissions
revised resistance design rules (RRD), 169
RF (radio frequency)
  cable TV, 123
  digital televisions, 14
  filters, 291
  wireless networks, 236–237
RG (Residential Gateway)
  firewire, 298–299
  home networks, 292–293, 304–305
    carriers, 311–312
    configurations, 313
    copy protection, 314
    e-mail, 310
    fixed/modular RG comparisons, 316–317
    installation services, 317
    IP addresses, 306–310
    media translation, 306
    MPEGs, 310
    operating systems, 311
    packet forwarding, 306
    partnerships, 314–316
    personal video recorders (PVRs), 310
    rewiring for, 317
    speed matching, 306
    standards, 312–313
    Web browsers, 310
  Time Warner Pegasus, 339
RGB (red, green, blue) monitors, 7
Rhythms Web site, 360
roaming, 3G (third-generation cellular), 273–274
routers, signaling, 90–91
RRD (revised resistance design rules), 169

S

CCIE Professional Development

Cisco LAN Switching

Kennedy Clark, CCIE; Kevin Hamilton, CCIE

1-57870-094-9 • AVAILABLE NOW

This volume provides an in-depth analysis of Cisco LAN switching technologies, architectures, and deployments, including unique coverage of Catalyst network design essentials. Network designs and configuration examples are incorporated throughout to demonstrate the principles and enable easy translation of the material into practice in production networks.

Advanced IP Network Design

Alvaro Retana, CCIE; Don Slice, CCIE; and Russ White, CCIE

1-57870-097-3 • AVAILABLE NOW

Network engineers and managers can use these case studies, which highlight various network design goals, to explore issues including protocol choice, network stability, and growth. This book also includes theoretical discussion on advanced design topics.

Large-Scale IP Network Solutions

Khalid Raza, CCIE; and Mark Turner

1-57870-084-1 • AVAILABLE NOW

Network engineers can find solutions as their IP networks grow in size and complexity. Examine all the major IP protocols in-depth and learn about scalability, migration planning, network management, and security for large-scale networks.

Routing TCP/IP, Volume I

Jeff Doyle, CCIE

1-57870-041-8 • AVAILABLE NOW

This book takes the reader from a basic understanding of routers and routing protocols through a detailed examination of each of the IP interior routing protocols. Learn techniques for designing networks that maximize the efficiency of the protocol being used. Exercises and review questions provide core study for the CCIE Routing and Switching exam.

CISCO SYSTEMS

CISCO PRESS

www.ciscopress.com

Cisco Career Certifications

CCNA Exam Certification Guide

Wendell Odom, CCIE

0-7357-0073-7 • AVAILABLE NOW

This book is a comprehensive study tool for CCNA Exam #640-407 and part of a recommended study program from Cisco Systems. *CCNA Exam Certification Guide* helps you understand and master the exam objectives. Instructor-developed elements and techniques maximize your retention and recall of exam topics, and scenario-based exercises help validate your mastery of the exam objectives.

Advanced Cisco Router Configuration

Cisco Systems, Inc., edited by Laura Chappell

1-57870-074-4 • AVAILABLE NOW

Based on the actual Cisco ACRC course, this book provides a thorough treatment of advanced network deployment issues. Learn to apply effective configuration techniques for solid network implementation and management as you prepare for CCNP and CCDP certifications. This book also includes chapter-ending tests for self-assessment.

Introduction to Cisco Router Configuration

Cisco Systems, Inc., edited by Laura Chappell

1-57870-076-0 • AVAILABLE NOW

Based on the actual Cisco ICRC course, this book presents the foundation knowledge necessary to define Cisco router configurations in multiprotocol environments. Examples and chapter-ending tests build a solid framework for understanding internetworking concepts. Prepare for the ICRC course and CCNA certification while mastering the protocols and technologies for router configuration.

Cisco CCNA Preparation Library

Cisco Systems, Inc., Laura Chappell, and Kevin Downes, CCIE

1-57870-125-2 • AVAILABLE NOW • CD-ROM

This boxed set contains two Cisco Press books—*Introduction to Cisco Router Configuration* and *Internetworking Technologies Handbook,* Second Edition— and the *High-Performance Solutions for Desktop Connectivity* CD.

www.ciscopress.com

Cisco Press Solutions

Enhanced IP Services for Cisco Networks

Donald C. Lee, CCIE

1-57870-106-6 • AVAILABLE NOW

This is a guide to improving your network's capabilities by understanding the new enabling and advanced Cisco IOS services that build more scalable, intelligent, and secure networks. Learn the technical details necessary to deploy Quality of Service, VPN technologies, IPsec, the IOS firewall and IOS Intrusion Detection. These services will allow you to extend the network to new frontiers securely, protect your network from attacks, and increase the sophistication of network services.

Developing IP Multicast Networks, Volume I

Beau Williamson, CCIE

1-57870-077-9 • AVAILABLE NOW

This book provides a solid foundation of IP multicast concepts and explains how to design and deploy the networks that will support appplications such as audio and video conferencing, distance-learning, and data replication. Includes an in-depth discussion of the PIM protocol used in Cisco routers and detailed coverage of the rules that control the creation and maintenance of Cisco mroute state entries.

OpenCable Architecture

Michael Adams

1-57870-135-X • AVAILABLE NOW

Whether you're a television, data communications, or telecommunications professional, or simply an interested business person, this book will help you understand the technical and business issues surrounding interactive television services. It will also provide you with an inside look at the combined efforts of the cable, data, and consumer electronics industries' efforts to develop those new services.

Designing Network Security

Merike Kaeo

1-57870-043-4 • AVAILABLE NOW

Designing Network Security is a practical guide designed to help you understand the fundamentals of securing your corporate infrastructure. This book takes a comprehensive look at underlying security technologies, the process of creating a security policy, and the practical requirements necessary to implement a corporate security policy.

CISCO SYSTEMS
CISCO PRESS

www.ciscopress.com

Cisco Press Solutions

OSPF Network Design Solutions

Thomas M. Thomas II

1-57870-046-9 • AVAILABLE NOW

This comprehensive guide presents a detailed, applied look into the workings of the popular Open Shortest Path First protocol, demonstrating how to dramatically increase network performance and security, and how to most easily maintain large-scale networks. OSPF is thoroughly explained through exhaustive coverage of network design, deployment, management, and troubleshooting.

Top-Down Network Design

Priscilla Oppenheimer

1-57870-069-8 • AVAILABLE NOW

Building reliable, secure, and manageable networks is every network professional's goal. This practical guide teaches you a systematic method for network design that can be applied to campus LANs, remote-access networks, WAN links, and large-scale internetworks. Learn how to analyze business and technical requirements, examine traffic flow and Quality of Service requirements, and select protocols and technologies based on performance goals.

Internetworking SNA with Cisco Solutions

George Sackett and Nancy Sackett

1-57870-083-3 • AVAILABLE NOW

This comprehensive guide presents a practical approach to integrating SNA and TCP/IP networks. It provides readers with an understanding of internetworking terms, networking architectures, protocols, and implementations for internetworking SNA with Cisco routers.

For the latest on Cisco Press resources and Certification and Training guides, or for information on publishing opportunities, visit **www.ciscopress.com**.

Cisco Press

Committed to being your long-term resource as you grow as a Cisco Networking professional

Help Cisco Press **stay connected** to the issues and challenges you face on a daily basis by registering your product and filling out our brief survey. Complete and mail this form, or better yet ...

CISCO SYSTEMS

CISCO PRESS

Register online and enter to win a FREE book!

Jump to **www.ciscopress.com/register** and register your product online. Each complete entry will be eligible for our monthly drawing to win a FREE book of the winner's choice from the Cisco Press library.

May we contact you via e-mail with information about **new releases, special promotions** and customer benefits?

❒ Yes   ❒ No

E-mail address _____

Name _____

Address _____

City _____ State/Province _____

Country _____ Zip/Post code _____

Where did you buy this product?

❒ Bookstore   ❒ Computer store/electronics store
❒ Online retailer   ❒ Direct from Cisco Press
❒ Mail order   ❒ Class/Seminar
❒ Other_____

When did you buy this product? _____ Month _____ Year

What price did you pay for this product?

❒ Full retail price   ❒ Discounted price   ❒ Gift

How did you learn about this product?

❒ Friend   ❒ Store personnel   ❒ In-store ad
❒ Cisco Press Catalog   ❒ Postcard in the mail   ❒ Saw it on the shelf
❒ Other Catalog   ❒ Magazine ad   ❒ Article or review
❒ School   ❒ Professional Organization ❒ Used other products
❒ Other_____

What will this product be used for?

❒ Business use   ❒ School/Education
❒ Other_____

Cisco Press

ciscopress.com

How many years have you been employed in a computer-related industry?

❒ 2 years or less ❒ 3-5 years ❒ 5+ years

Which best describes your job function?

❒ Corporate Management ❒ Systems Engineering ❒ IS Management
❒ Network Design ❒ Network Support ❒ Webmaster
❒ Marketing/Sales ❒ Consultant ❒ Student
❒ Professor/Teacher ❒ Other _____

What is your formal education background?

❒ High school ❒ Vocational/Technical degree ❒ Some college
❒ College degree ❒ Masters degree ❒ Professional or Doctoral degree

Have you purchased a Cisco Press product before?

❒ Yes ❒ No

On what topics would you like to see more coverage?

_____

_____

Do you have any additional comments or suggestions?

_____

_____

Thank you for completing this survey and registration. Please fold here, seal, and mail to Cisco Press.
Residential Broadband, Second Edition (1-57870-177-5)

Indianapolis, IN 46278-8046
P.O. Box #781046
Customer Registration—CP0500227
Cisco Press

Place
Stamp
Here

Cisco Press
201 West 103rd Street
Indianapolis, IN 46290
ciscopress.com

PACKET

Packet magazine serves as the premier publication linking customers to Cisco Systems, Inc. Delivering complete coverage of cutting-edge networking trends and innovations, *Packet* is a magazine for technical, hands-on users. It delivers industry-specific information for enterprise, service provider, and small and midsized business market segments. A toolchest for planners and decision makers, *Packet* contains a vast array of practical information, boasting sample configurations, real-life customer examples, and tips on getting the most from your Cisco Systems' investments. Simply put, *Packet* magazine is straight talk straight from the worldwide leader in networking for the Internet, Cisco Systems, Inc.

We hope you'll take advantage of this useful resource. I look forward to hearing from you!

Jennifer Biondi
Packet Circulation Manager
packet@cisco.com
www.cisco.com/go/packet

☐ **YES!** I'm requesting a **free** subscription to *Packet*™ magazine.

☐ No. I'm not interested at this time.

☐ Mr.
☐ Ms.

First Name (Please Print)   Last Name

Title/Position (Required)

Company (Required)

Address

City   State/Province

Zip/Postal Code   Country

Telephone (Include country and area codes)   Fax

E-mail

Signature (Required)   Date

☐ I would like to receive additional information on Cisco's services and products by e-mail.

1.0 Do you or your company:
- A ☐ Use Cisco products
- B ☐ Resell Cisco products
- C ☐ Both
- D ☐ Neither

1. Your organization's relationship to Cisco Systems:
- A ☐ Customer/End User
- B ☐ Prospective Customer
- C ☐ Cisco Reseller
- D ☐ Cisco Distributor
- DI ☐ Non-Authorized Reseller
- E ☐ Integrator
- G ☐ Cisco Training Partner
- I ☐ Cisco OEM
- J ☐ Consultant
- K ☐ Other (specify):

2. How would you classify your business?
- A ☐ Small/Medium-Sized
- B ☐ Enterprise
- C ☐ Service Provider

3. Your involvement in network equipment purchases:
- A ☐ Recommend
- B ☐ Approve
- C ☐ Neither

4. Your personal involvement in networking:
- A ☐ Entire enterprise at all sites
- B ☐ Departments or network segments at more than one site
- C ☐ Single department or network segment
- F ☐ Public network
- D ☐ No involvement
- E ☐ Other (specify):

5. Your Industry:
- A ☐ Aerospace
- B ☐ Agriculture/Mining/Construction
- C ☐ Banking/Finance
- D ☐ Chemical/Pharmaceutical
- E ☐ Consultant
- F ☐ Computer/Systems/Electronics
- G ☐ a. Education (K–12)
- ☐ b. Education (College/Univ.)
- H ☐ Government—Federal
- I ☐ Government—State
- J ☐ Government—Local
- K ☐ Health Care
- L ☐ Telecommunications
- M ☐ Utilities/Transportation
- N ☐ Other (specify):

PACKET